ADMINISTRATIVE PROCEDURES FOR THE ELECTRONIC OFFICE

ADMINISTRATIVE PROCEDURES FOR THE ELECTRONIC OFFICE

ARNOLD ROSEN
Professor, Secretarial Science
Nassau Community College and
Former President
International Information/Word Processing Association, 1979-1980

EILEEN FERETIC TUNISON
Editorial Director, Office Group
Hearst Business Communications, Inc., UTP Division

MARGARET HILTON BAHNIUK, Ed.D.
Associate Professor, Business Education
Cleveland State University

175 YEARS OF PUBLISHING
1807 1982

JOHN WILEY & SONS
New York   Chichester   Brisbane   Toronto   Singapore

Cover and text design: Suzanne Bennett
Editor: Dr. Leonard B. Kruk
Supervising copyeditor: Ellen MacElree
Production supervisor: Sherry Berg

Library of Congress Cataloging in Publication Data:

Rosen, Arnold, 1932-
Administrative procedures for the electronic office.

  Includes index.
  1. Office practice. 2. Office practice—Automa-
tion. 3. Secretaries. I. Tunison, Eileen Feretic.
II. Bahniuk, Margaret Hilton. III. Title.
HF5547.5.R67   651'.068   81-11431
ISBN 0-471-08700-9   AACR2

Printed in the United States of America

10 9 8 7 6 5 4

To my wife, Estherfay, and my son, Paul
To my parents, Eileen and Joseph Feretic
To my husband, Eugene Bahniuk, and my parents,
Audrey and Joe Hilton

ABOUT THE AUTHORS

ARNOLD ROSEN

Arnold Rosen is Professor of Secretarial Science at Nassau Community College in Garden City, New York.

He has taught at New York City Community College and Hunter College, and in the New York City school system. Professor Rosen is the author of several journal articles on aspects of word processing and has written several books on word processing and machine transcription.

Professor Rosen is affiliated with several education and professional organizations. He organized and served as chairperson for the International Information/Word Processing Association Educator's Advisory Council and served as International President of IWP from 1979 to 1980.

Professor Rosen received his B.S. degree in Business Administration from the Ohio State University and his M.S. degree from Hunter College.

EILEEN FERETIC TUNISON

Eileen Feretic Tunison is the editorial director of the Office Group of Hearst Business Communications, Inc., UTP Division. She has been an editor writing about the office products industry since 1972. In addition to her duties at UTP, Ms. Tunison has written a number of freelance articles on the office products industry, including an article on word processing for the *New York Times*.

She received her B.A. degree in Journalism/Communications, from Fordham University, and is listed in *Who's Who in America*.

Ms. Tunison has given seminars on the technology and people aspects of the office, has taught a secretarial procedures course, and served as a consultant on various office systems projects.

MARGARET HILTON BAHNIUK

Margaret Hilton Bahniuk is Associate Professor of Business Education at the Cleveland State University in Cleveland, Ohio.

Professor Bahniuk received her B.S. degree from East Tennessee State University, her M.A. degree from Bob Jones University, and her Ed.D. degree from the University of Tennessee.

Dr. Bahniuk has written several journal articles in the Business Education and Office Administration area and is a coauthor of a book on writing business letters and reports. She has been a speaker at numerous seminars and professional conferences. She was recently elected secretary/historian of the Office Systems Research Association (OSRA), a new association of people from four-year colleges and universities as well as business and industry who are concerned about office administration practices.

Dr. Bahniuk is listed in *Outstanding Young Women of America* and in *Who's Who of American Women.*

PREFACE

Over the past decade the office—which serves as the brain, nervous system, and communications center of an organization—has experienced drastic changes. As a result, the operating formulas that prevailed for so long are giving way to more efficient and productive procedures to obtain, process, distribute, and store information.

The office environment, long considered a stepchild in the structure of most organizations, is enjoying increased prominence and attention as the impact of the information revolution is increasingly felt.

In a little more than a decade, microelectronic technology has blossomed from an expensive space-age curiosity into an irresistible force that is rapidly shaping today's office. Thanks to the development of the microprocessor, a computer on a chip, we are able to produce and process information with ever increasing swiftness and accuracy. However, this development has also created a greater need for professionally trained managers, secretaries, clerks, operators, and specialists capable of analyzing, designing, and implementing the systems needed to process this information.

The evolution that has characterized secretarial procedures in the business world has necessitated a corresponding change in the structure of curriculum, course content, and teaching materials in the schools. Traditional curriculum and textbooks that were once adequate for the training of secretarial and business education students no longer meet the needs of today.

Administrative Procedures for the Electronic Office explores office operations and procedures in a unique way. It traces the evolution of office information systems and presents a balance between conventional and advanced electronic systems and procedures.

In 27 chapters, which are organized into seven major sections, *Administrative Procedures for the Electronic Office* illustrates and interprets these new systems, and compares and contrasts them with yesterday's methods.

The text is comprehensive in scope, but, as is necessarily true of all such efforts, selective in detail. The chapters are organized into major segments that present the student with a logical sequence of equipment technology, followed by procedures and techniques. All of the advanced technologies used in the office are described in this book.

The text will examine changes in terminology, business forms, equipment, and supplies. The term "secretary" will be replaced by the title "executive assistant" and the role of manager will be nonsexist to reflect an increased awareness of the changing role of women in the office.

These changes characterize the thrust of this textbook, which is designed for teachers and students who are excited and challenged by the future of office technology. It is written for those who are willing to question traditional organizational patterns and arrangements and for those who have the ingenuity and resourcefulness to accept, embrace, and devise better ways of providing information services when they enter the business world.

Included in this text are the latest developments in office information technologies and equipment; however, in such a rapidly changing field, it is impossible to present material that completely reflects the current state of the art. Therefore, the authors have tried to present, as clearly as possible, principles of lasting value and to augment these values with examples of present "proven" administrative procedures so the text material will remain useful for a long time. Photographs, charts, and line drawings are used extensively to illustrate the concepts presented.

No text of this size can be attributed to individual authors, although we must bear responsibility for its content. We were particularly fortunate to have a wealth of feedback through the publisher in the form of many rounds of reviews. Special thanks are extended to Ms. Mimi Will, Foothill College; Ms. Ann Linkenheimer, Mentor, Ohio; Ms. Alice Petkus, Indian Hills High School; Mr. Ron Kapper, College of DuPage; Ms. Mary Sumner, New York University; and Ms. Dorothy Sutton, Harrisburg Area Community College, for their help and intelligent criticism. We also want to thank Dr. Leonard Kruk, our editor, as well as the editorial and production staff at Wiley for their support and professional guidance.

Acknowledgement and appreciation is also extended to Lorraine Lear, Executive Director, and the staff of the International Information/Word Processing Association for contributing material and resources.

We acknowledge and thank all the office systems manufacturers and business and professional organizations which supplied many photographs.

Arnold Rosen
Eileen Feretic Tunison
Margaret Hilton Bahniuk

CONTENTS

SECTION I.
THE EXECUTIVE ASSISTANT CAREER

CHAPTER 1. THE ROLE OF THE SECRETARY   3
Definition of a Secretary / 4
Functions of an Executive Assistant / 5
Description of Traditional Approach / 7
Description of the Electronic Office / 9
Summary / 14

CHAPTER 2. CHARACTERISTICS NEEDED BY THE
EXECUTIVE ASSISTANT   18
Human Relations Skills / 19
Technical Skills / 20
Personal Skills / 22
Summary / 29

CHAPTER 3. ORGANIZING AND PLANNING WORK FLOW   33
Organization of Work Area / 34
Organization of Desk / 35
Keeping a Calendar / 38
Time Management Planning / 40
Summary / 43

SECTION II.
INFORMATION PROCESSING

CHAPTER 4. THE TYPEWRITER: MANUAL, ELECTRIC, ELECTRONIC,
AND TEXT EDITING   53
History of the Typewriter / 54
Electric Typewriters / 55
Electronic Typewriters / 58
Text-Editing Typewriters / 59
Supplies / 72
Maintenance / 74
Training / 75
Summary / 75

CHAPTER 5. WORD PROCESSING   79
Definition of Word Processing / 80
Components of Word Processing / 81
Word Processing in the Electronic Office / 90
Summary / 91

CHAPTER 6. TYPING TECHNIQUES

96

Techniques for Professional Typing / 97
Making Carbon Copies / 98
Making Corrections / 99
Error Correction and Editing in Automated Typing / 106
Specialized Typing Techniques / 109
Summary / 109

CHAPTER 7. WRITTEN BUSINESS COMMUNICATIONS

116

Principles of Writing / 117
Writing Letters / 119
Writing Memorandums / 133
Writing Reports / 136
Summary / 136

CHAPTER 8. METHODS AND PROCEDURES OF INPUT

143

Methods of Input / 144
Summary / 151

CHAPTER 9. DICTATION/TRANSCRIPTION EQUIPMENT AND PROCEDURES

158

Types of Equipment / 159
Measuring Productivity of Dictation / 166
Administrative Dictation / 169
Techniques of Good Dictation / 170
Summary / 174

CHAPTER 10. COMPUTERS

179

Types of Computers / 180
Processes of Computers / 182
Computer Software / 189
Modes of Operation / 190
Distributed Data Processing / 191
Summary / 192

SECTION III.
COMMUNICATION TRANSMITTAL SYSTEMS

CHAPTER 11. MAIL HANDLING EQUIPMENT

200

Incoming Mail / 201
Outgoing Mail / 203
Summary / 207

CHAPTER 12. TECHNIQUES FOR PROCESSING MAIL

209

Procedures for Handling Incoming Mail / 210
Procedures for Handling Outgoing Mail / 213
Summary / 220

CHAPTER 13. THE U.S. POSTAL SERVICE 224

Classes of Mail / 225
Special Services / 226
Postage Meters / 230
Area Mail Processing / 231
Mail Problems / 231
Vertical Improved Mail (VIM) / 232
Forwarding Mail / 233
Mail Service and the Future / 233
Electronic Mail / 234
Summary / 236

CHAPTER 14. TELECOMMUNICATIONS 240

Telephone Systems / 241
Features of Telephone Systems / 243
Telephone Accessories / 247
Future Developments for the Telephone / 249
Electronic Mail / 250
Summary / 258

CHAPTER 15. TELEPHONE TECHNIQUES 262

Techniques for Incoming Calls / 263
Techniques for Making Outgoing Calls / 267
Emergency Calls / 269
Annoyance Calls / 269
Changing Telephone Procedures / 269
Summary / 270

SECTION IV.
DUPLICATION AND PHOTOTYPESETTING EQUIPMENT

CHAPTER 16. PHOTOTYPESETTING EQUIPMENT 279

Description of Phototypesetting Equipment / 280
Type Styles and Sizes / 280
Strike-On Typesetters / 282
Phototypesetters / 284
Photocomposers / 288
Partnership of Phototypesetting and Word Processing / 288
Summary / 289

CHAPTER 17. COPYING AND DUPLICATING EQUIPMENT 292

Types of Reproduction Equipment / 293
Use of the Print Shop / 307
Collating / 307
Binding / 309
Summary / 310

SECTION V.
RECORDS MANAGEMENT

CHAPTER 18. FILING EQUIPMENT 317
Definition of a Filing System / 318
Types of Filing Equipment / 318
Automated Filing Systems / 327
Computerized Filing / 328
Word/Data Processing Filing and Microform Filing / 330
Summary / 333

CHAPTER 19. FILING PROCEDURES 338
Guidelines for Retention of Files / 339
Procedures for Filing / 340
Desk Drawer Files / 352
Portable Files / 354
Guidelines for Manual Filing Systems / 355
Automated Filing Systems / 357
Techniques of Magnetic Media Filing / 357
Filing in an Open Plan Office Environment / 361
Future of Records Management / 361
Summary / 363

CHAPTER 20. MICROGRAPHICS EQUIPMENT 367
Advantages of Microforms / 368
Types of Microforms / 369
Microform Process / 370
Microform Readers / 372
Summary / 377

SECTION VI.
EXECUTIVE ASSISTANT SKILLS AND RESPONSIBILITIES

CHAPTER 21. LOCATING AND USING REFERENCE TOOLS 383
The Information Cycle / 384
Methods of Locating Information / 386
Reference Tools for Executive Assistants / 390
Summary / 392

CHAPTER 22. MAKING TRAVEL ARRANGEMENTS 396
Methods of Handling Travel Arrangements / 397
Travel Funds / 400
Travel Insurance / 401
Modes of Travel / 401
Room Arrangements / 404
Preparation of the Itinerary / 405
Organizing for Travel / 406
Overseas Travel / 406

Follow-up on Travel / 408
Summary / 409

CHAPTER 23. SETTING UP MEETINGS 413
Informal Meetings / 414
Conventions / 417
The Agenda / 422
Minutes / 423
Summary / 426

CHAPTER 24. USING THE CALCULATOR 430
Applications for the Calculator / 431
Selection of a Calculator / 434
Summary / 437

SECTION VII.
THE BUSINESS WORLD

CHAPTER 25. THE OFFICE ENVIRONMENT 447
Types of Office Environments / 448
The Human Element in the Office Environment / 452
Systems Furniture / 454
Office Lighting / 454
Summary / 456

CHAPTER 26. JOB HUNTING, RÉSUMÉS, AND INTERVIEWS 460
Job-Hunting Strategy / 461
Sources of Employment / 462
Résumé Writing / 466
Letter of Application / 468
The Job Interview / 468
Summary / 471

CHAPTER 27. CAREER OPTIONS 476
Alternative Job Choices / 477
Summary / 483

APPENDIX
REFERENCE GUIDES

Abbreviations / 489
Additional Sources of Information / 490
Addressing Envelopes / 492
Capitalization Rules / 492
Compound Words / 494
Easily Confused Words / 495
Footnotes and Bibliographies / 498
Forms of Address / 499

Manufacturers of Text-Editing and Word Processing Systems   /   500
Metric Equivalents   /   503
Number Rules   /   503
Proofreader's Marks   /   504
Punctuation Rules   /   505
Punctuation Styles for Letters   /   508
Spelling Rules   /   509
Word Division Rules   /   511

SUBJECT INDEX / 513

ADMINISTRATIVE PROCEDURES FOR THE ELECTRONIC OFFICE

THE EXECUTIVE ASSISTANT CAREER

Today's executive assistants not only need to be proficient in the traditional areas in which they have always worked, but they also need to be aware of developments in word processing, data processing, records management, and electronic mail.

People today can choose to work as generalists in traditional areas, or they can choose jobs in one of the more recent types of executive assistant careers that have opened up as a result of new office technology.

The executive assistant performs tasks that enable the executive to work more efficiently and effectively. To be successful at performing these tasks, executive assistants need to possess certain human relations, technical, and personal skills. ■ Chapter 1   The Role of the Secretary
☐ Chapter 2   Characteristics Needed by the Executive Assistant
☐ Chapter 3   Organizing and Planning Work Flow

SECTION
I

THE ROLE OF THE SECRETARY

A secretary can be described in many ways. The description is usually dependent upon such things as the type of company, the size of the company, the philosophy of the company, and the type of office equipment used in the company. This chapter defines and describes the role of a secretary; it introduces you to the many career opportunities available in the changing office environment.

Today's secretary needs to be cognizant not only of the traditional secretarial areas—typing, filing, and other clerical work—but also of such areas as word processing, data processing, records management, and electronic mail. Each of these areas is introduced in this chapter.

At the end of this chapter, you should be able to:

1. Formulate a working definition of a secretary. ☐ 2. List the major responsibilities of secretaries. ☐ 3. Define the traditional and automated approaches to office work. ☐ 4. List the advantages of the traditional and automated approaches to office work. ☐ 5. List the disadvantages of traditional and automated approaches to office work. ☐ 6. List career opportunities available for the traditional secretary and for the secretary who works in the automated office.

CHAPTER
1

DEFINITION OF A SECRETARY

According to the *American Heritage Dictionary*, a secretary is "a person employed to handle correspondence, keep files and do clerical work for an individual or company." This is hardly an adequate definition of what a secretary is and does. The Professional Secretaries International (formerly National Secretaries Association) defines a secretary as:

> . . . *an executive assistant who possesses a mastery of office skills, who demonstrates the ability to assume responsibility without direct supervision, who exercises initiative and judgment, and who makes decisions within the scope of assigned authority.*

Secretaries have been labeled office assistants, administrative assistants, office technicians, support technicians, and administrative specialists. For this book, though, we will use the term used by the Professional Secretaries International which refers to secretaries as executive assistants.

The executive assistant performs literally hundreds of tasks, both small and large, that enable the executive to work more efficiently and effectively. The stereotype of the boss who is helpless without an executive assistant is not too far from the truth. The executive often does not know where certain files are, how to reach a particular person, or the best way to get a letter through the mailroom quickly. In fact, it is not necessary for the executive to know this information because that is part of the executive assistant's job.

EXAMPLE OF THE IDEAL SECRETARY

A very appropriate, if unusual, example of the ideal executive assistant is Radar, the corporal on the television show M*A*S*H*. Radar has all the necessary forms typed and ready for the colonel's signature—sometimes before the colonel is even aware that they are needed. He anticipates the colonel's needs, tries to shield him from unnecessary aggravation, and acts as a go-between in many situations. He knows how to get things done, either by going through channels or by circumventing them when necessary. He is aware of the dynamics of the army camp and knows when to bring potentially harmful situations to his boss's attention. In short, Radar is a near-perfect executive assistant.

SHORTAGE OF EXECUTIVE ASSISTANTS

In recent years, the executive assistant's image has suffered. Too often, the executive assistant has been portrayed in print and on film as little better than a "go-fer," a person who goes for coffee, lunch, and the boss's laundry. The scandals in Washington, D.C., about highly paid executive assistants who could not type, file, or write adequate letters have harmed their image.

To a certain extent, the Women's Liberation Movement may also have inadvertently turned women away from careers as executive assistants. In this case, the intent was not to downgrade the executive assistant but to upgrade the kinds of work the executive assistant performs. Women's Liberation sought to gain more recognition for the importance of the executive assistant's role, to ensure that the job is not a dead-end position, and to provide additional career options for those women who want them.

All of these factors have resulted in a growing shortage of executive assistants since fewer people are choosing these careers. This is an unfortunate situation because the changing business world now needs executive assistants more than ever before. Changes in the way business is conducted have created new types of executive assistant jobs and have opened up new career paths.

A person who chooses an executive assistant career today can work in a traditional job or can choose one of the newer types of jobs that have been created as a result of the new sophisticated equipment and operating procedures now utilized by many companies. In any event, today's executive assistant is a professional.

FUNCTIONS OF AN EXECUTIVE ASSISTANT

All executive assistants, regardless of the type or size of the company, are information expediters and public relations representatives for their companies.

INFORMATION EXPEDITER

Today's business world revolves on information—information on the buying and selling of materials; information on contracts, mergers, and business deals; information on world currency and competitive pricing; information on who is selling what to whom; and information on everything going on in the business world.

Research studies have shown that the largest portion of an executive's time is spent receiving, sending, and acting on information. To perform effectively, executives must have timely, accurate, and complete information on which to base their decisions. For this to happen, there must be people to expedite the flow of information into and out of the executive suite. This is the primary function of today's executive assistant—to expedite information.

This may not seem important until you realize that the economic health of any organization is directly related to the accuracy, completeness, and timeliness of its information. A firm cannot compete effectively in today's business world unless it has all the information it needs when it needs it.

The executive assistant is a vital link in the information chain, the go-between or messenger between the executive and the outside world. This outside world may include clients, competitors, or other people in the same company. As an information expediter, the executive assistant's basic duties include receiving incoming information; evaluating, organizing, and storing information; and preparing outgoing information.

Receiving incoming information involves such traditional tasks as answering the telephone, opening the mail, and receiving interoffice memorandums and telex messages.

Evaluating, organizing, and storing information requires the executive assistant to make value judgments. For instance, the executive assistant may have to decide which messages are important enough to call the executive at home or in the field and which ones can wait until the executive returns to the office. The executive assistant has to sort through the mail to find priority items that must be answered immediately and evaluate incoming messages to find which ones can be handled without disturbing the executive. The executive assistant has to determine which items to retain for future reference and which to "file" in the wastebasket. In short, the executive assistant evaluates every piece of incoming information to determine its priority level, its need for a response, and its reference value.

Preparing outgoing information is a large part of almost every executive assistant's job. This involves making telephone calls; typing documents from longhand, shorthand, or machine dictation; revising previously typed information; making photocopies of documents; preparing documents for mailing; and delivering them to the mailroom or mail carrier. The good executive assistant must not only be a skilled transcriptionist and typist but must also be able to compose accurate, well-written business letters and reports.

PUBLIC RELATIONS REPRESENTATIVE

Interacting with people comprises a large portion of the time of executive assistants. They are representatives of their companies, their bosses, and themselves. The executive assistant's world is a large one, encompassing all the people working in the company, as well as suppliers, clients, and competitors.

To be a good PR (public relations) person, the executive assistant must follow a few basic rules. First, you must be courteous to all the people you meet, regardless of their titles or their behavior. This means that you must be polite to the mail clerk as well as the company president, even if they are not courteous to you.

The executive assistant should not get involved in office politics. It is a dangerous game, and very few people win at it. The same holds true for office gossip and back-biting. Eventually, these people are recognized for their disruptions and are avoided or dismissed.

A good executive assistant cooperates with other people in the firm and tries to be helpful to others even when technically it is not part of the job. Executive assistants who constantly say, "That's not my job!" will not impress others with their willingness to cooperate.

Figure 1.1
Interaction with people (Courtesy of Westinghouse Electric Company).

Professional behavior and dress are two hallmarks of the PR-conscious executive assistant. Dress and behavior reflect not only on the professionalism of the company and the boss but also on you. Therefore, it is essential that you

☐ Act in a professional manner (by showing a courteous and cooperative attitude to all).
☐ Turn out professional quality work (carefully typed and proofread correspondence).
☐ Look the part of a professional (businesslike dress and carefully groomed appearance).

DESCRIPTION OF TRADITIONAL APPROACH

Executive assistants are alike in that they all expedite information and interact with other people, but they differ in the methods used to perform these two functions. Some firms prefer for their executive assistants to use traditional approaches to information processing, while other firms favor the use of automated systems.

One of the primary distinguishing characteristics of traditional executive assistants is that they are generalists; that is, they perform all the support functions needed by the people for whom they work. There is no division of their functions into typing and nontyping jobs. Traditional executive assistants do everything from taking shorthand dictation or transcribing machine dictation, to typing and revising documents, to processing incoming and outgoing mail, to answering and placing telephone calls, to filing, to setting up meetings and making travel arrangements.

Another major characteristic of traditional executive assistants is that, for the most part, they use standard office equipment. This equipment might include electric typewriters, dictation/transcription equipment, telephones, copying machines, and some type of mail handling equipment. Traditional executive assistants perform most of the routine office work; automated systems are used infrequently, if at all.

Career paths for traditional executive assistants vary according to the size and attitude of particular firms. In some cases, executive assistants begin in typing pools or as assistants to one or more junior executives. As their skills increase, traditional executive assistants may be given jobs working for middle or upper management, or they may be promoted as their bosses are promoted. In fact, it is very common in traditional arrangements for the careers of executive assistants to be tied to the success of their bosses. Most traditional executive assistants report directly to the people for whom they work, rather than to a supervisor.

Eventually, traditional executive assistants may work for only one person, and that person is usually a top-level executive. In this position, they may do higher level work and may have another executive assistant to perform routine office tasks. Since only top managers have this type of assistant, these jobs are necessarily limited.

The traditional approach to executive assistant support has a number of advantages. First, they can work in almost any size company and in any industry. Second, traditional executive assistants perform such a wide variety of jobs that they learn a number of skills. Third, these skills are easily transferred from one company to another. Fourth, traditional executive assistants can rise in the organization to work for a top-level executive.

On the other hand, there are some disadvantages for executive assistants in the traditional approach. First, they must spend a considerable amount of time performing routine office tasks that could be handled by automated systems, thereby freeing them for more productive and interesting work. A good example of this is the time spent retyping documents that have been revised.

Second, executive assistants will find it hard to become specialists in a particular area since they will have to perform so many diverse tasks. Another disadvantage is that traditional executive assistants are often promoted along with their bosses, rather than on their own merits. Finally, it is often difficult for traditional executive assistants to move into supervisory and nonsecretarial positions.

DESCRIPTION OF THE ELECTRONIC OFFICE

An increasing number of firms are taking an automated or electronic approach to executive assistant support and other office functions. The reason for this approach is mainly economic. Today's office is the most labor intensive section of American society. In the industrial or factory environment, the use of machinery has eased the physical labor of factory workers, while increasing productivity by up to 90 percent. Research and engineering departments have been similarly improved through the use of new technology.

The office has been the last holdout. While the factory was increasing productivity by about 90 percent, the productivity of the office worker increased only 5 percent. Yet, the salaries of office workers are rising at a rate of 6 percent to 8 percent a year. Since the cost of equipment for the office is dropping, it is inevitable that more companies will begin to automate a number of office functions. For many firms, it will become an economic necessity.

According to Booz, Allen & Hamilton, a management, technology, and market research consulting firm, three to four million organizations will be using electronic office systems by 1990. This is quite a change for the office, which remained virtually unchanged for 50 years. This change is particularly important to executive assistants since their jobs will be one of the first to be affected by any changes in the way the office operates.

Many executive assistants fear that the electronic office will be an office without people. They visualize a room full of machines, perhaps with a token human to oversee the operation. The reality of the situation provides a much more pleasant picture, an office where machines do the simple, routine chores, leaving the people free to pursue creative, thinking work. In the electronic office, machines will not replace people. Rather, the electronic office will provide all white-collar workers—executives as well as assistants—with the tools (machines) they need to do their jobs better.

From management's point of view, the motivation behind the electronic office movement is an economic one. By putting each employee's talents to the best possible use, a firm will be able to increase productivity, which in the long run will save money and enable the company to improve its operating efficiency.

From the employee's point of view, the major advantage of the electronic office is the promised relief from some of the routine work. If you think about how appliances such as washing machines, vacuum cleaners, and dishwashers have improved the working conditions of the homemaker, you may begin to realize the possible advantages automation can bring to the

Figure 1.2
Electronic office environment (Courtesy of Digital Equipment Corporation).

office. Present technological advances, and the new ones that will be introduced in future years, should make the jobs of the white-collar workers,
especially the executive assistant, more creative and more interesting.

Right now no one knows what the office of the future will be since the
technology involved is constantly changing; however, there are some areas
that experts agree will be vital components of the electronic office, such as
word processing, data processing, electronic mail and communications, and
records management. All of these areas will be discussed in detail in the
following chapters, but this chapter will center on how each of these areas
will affect the executive assistant function.

WORD PROCESSING

Firms that are beginning to incorporate technological changes into their
operations usually start with word processing, an area that has the most
direct impact on the executive assistant. Word processing is a natural first
step toward the electronic office since the other areas can be built upon it.
And, from management's point of view, word processing can produce quick
results since the executive assistant's function involves a number of routine
tasks that can be automated fairly easily.

Many people are scared off by the name word processing. They wonder
if it is anything like data processing, that mysterious field that deals with
computers. They visualize a room filled with robot-like executive assistants
working at strange looking machines. Other people say word processing is
just another typing pool.

Figure 1.3
Robot-like executive assistants (a common misconception).

Word processing is neither of these things. Actually, it is a very simple concept. The goal of word processing is to help a business run more efficiently and economically by automating part of the process involved in getting ideas on paper in an acceptable format.

Many firms have opted for a less rigid division of labor. For instance, a company may decide to give all its executive assistants word processing typewriters so that typing and revisions can be handled more rapidly. This gives the executive assistants more time to handle administrative functions as well.

Other organizations may initiate work groups, where several executive assistants share the administrative and typing work by dividing the tasks on a daily or weekly basis. In such a situation, Executive Assistant A might work on the text-editing typewriter every Monday and Wednesday and do nontyping jobs the remaining three days. Executive Assistant B might work on the text-editing typewriter on Tuesday and Thursday, and Executive Assistant C would work on the machine on Friday. The arrangements are as varied as the number of firms.

The main importance of this arrangement to the executive assistant is that it affords options from which to choose. The executive assistant can decide to be an administrative support assistant, a correspondence assistant, or both. And, no matter what choice is made, the executive assistant can later decide to change that decision because word processing works best when

Figure 1.4
Word processing environment (Courtesy of AM International).

it is a flexible arrangement, one that provides for the growth of the executive assistant as well as the employer.

Another advantage of word processing is that it gives executive assistants a chance to advance into other types of jobs, if they desire. It opens up career paths that had been previously blocked.

Executive assistants who are involved with word processing can learn some valuable skills that may help to further their careers. Of course, executive assistants have always developed many of these skills, but the chance to put them to good use was not often available.

DATA PROCESSING

While word processing is the area of office technology that is having the greatest impact on the role of the executive assistant, other areas are also having an effect. Increasingly, business executives need to rely on some form of computerization to handle their jobs more effectively. Many of these executives have computer terminals or stations in their offices. These terminals, sometimes called managerial work stations, resemble word processing typewriters and operate in much the same fashion.

An executive who has a computer terminal (or even a mini- or micro-computer) in his or her office can use the terminal to get information from the main computer (called a mainframe) over telephone lines. The information will either appear on the terminal's display screen or will print out on the terminal's printer.

The terminal can also store information electronically. Think of the way a song is "stored" on a record, cassette, or cartridge. In a similar manner, data (information) can be stored on computer tapes or diskettes. When the tape or diskette is put into the terminal or minicomputer, the information can be displayed on the screen or played out on the printer.

The computer can also perform arithmetic functions. For instance, suppose the executive stores each month's sales reports in the computer. As these figures come in, the executive assistant enters them into the computer terminal. If the executive needs an updated quarterly report comparing the reports for the current quarter with reports for the two preceding quarters, the computer can provide this information.

Many word processing typewriters also have some of these computing capabilities. In such a case, these functions are performed by the executive assistant. The executive assistant may enter information into the system, update data, and print out reports. Increasingly, companies are advertising for cathode ray tube (CRT) or terminal operators, and a working knowledge of these pieces of equipment presents another job opportunity for the executive assistant who has the appropriate background.

A major New York City bank is experimenting with a management work station. This work station consists of two terminals, one for the executive and one for the executive assistant, that share a common processor or "brain" and a printer. These work stations perform word processing and data processing functions, as well as electronic mail and electronic filing. This idea of a work station combining several capabilities and linking the executive and executive assistant into one system could be a major component of the electronic office.

ELECTRONIC MAIL AND COMMUNICATIONS

Postal rates keep going up and the delivery of mail keeps slowing down; however, the mail system is the major avenue of written business communications and will be for some time to come. Concern over the costs and delays of the mail system has led many companies to look for alternate ways of sending and receiving mail. One of the most viable alternatives is electronic mail.

Electronic mail refers to a way of sending documents over telephone wires from one location to another. This can be done in different ways. For example, a facsimile machine scans a written document, drawing, or photograph and converts the lines into electronic impulses which are sent over the telephone to another facsimile machine, which converts the electronic impulses back into the written document, drawing, or photograph.

Word processing typewriters with communications capabilities can also send documents over phone lines, but these documents must be composed of alphanumeric data. Communicating word processors cannot send drawings or photographs over phone lines.

Most electronic mail systems are within a company and are used only to send intracompany mail. In such a setup or network, each office of the company would have one or more facsimile machines or communicating editing typewriters. (Facsimile machines cannot at this time communicate with editing typewriters.) Messages would be sent from one office to another electronically.

Other electronic mail systems involve computers and terminals. At certain periods during the day, the mail computer polls (or calls) each terminal to see if it has any mail to go out to another terminal. At the same time, the computer gives the terminal mail from other terminals.

With many electronic mail systems, the executive assistant is the person who is responsible for sending and receiving the mail. This is especially true when the system involves the use of communicating word processors. It is another area of responsibility that is being given to the executive assistant, thus expanding the role of the executive assistant still further.

RECORDS MANAGEMENT

Records management is another component of the electronic office. In the office of the past, and sometimes in the office of the present, records management meant simply filing documents in a standard file cabinet and, with fingers crossed, trying to dig out the documents again at some future date.

That situation is changing rapidly. Today, we have rotary files, automated files, mobile files, micrographics files, and computerized files. The variety of filing systems on the market today seems limitless. As new office systems, such as word processing, are introduced, new types of filing systems are created to accommodate them. Thus, we have files for cassettes, magnetic belts, microforms, cartridges, and diskettes.

Today, records management means more than just filing. It involves everything from the storage of paper, microforms, and magnetic media to electronic storage of data. Here again, the executive assistant plays a vital role. The executive assistant traditionally has been in charge of records management, but there has never before been such a variety of materials to be filed or such a selection of files in which these materials can be stored. Filing procedures also are being developed to keep pace with the new equipment and materials.

SUMMARY

People choosing a career today are in an enviable position—they have more career choices than ever before. They can choose jobs as traditional executive assistants (those who perform the whole range of executive assistant duties, including typing and nontyping administrative work), or they can choose one of the more recent types of executive assistant careers that have opened up as a result of new office technology. These alternatives allow prospective executive assistants to choose jobs that suit both their talents and their personal likes and dislikes.

Some of the major executive assistant duties include:

1. Receiving incoming information.
2. Evaluating, organizing, and storing information.
3. Preparing outgoing information.
4. Interacting with outside agents (the executive assistant's public relations role).

There are different kinds of executive assistants.

1. The traditional executive assistant is a generalist who performs all support functions needed by the executive, including typing and administrative duties.
   a. The traditional executive assistant generally uses standard office equipment.
   b. There are both advantages and disadvantages in starting a career as a traditional executive assistant.
2. The increasing use of automated office equipment has created a number of other career options for executive assistants.
   a. The executive assistant can be a correspondence assistant.
   b. The executive assistant can be an administrative assistant.
   c. Other options available for the executive assistant are working with computers, electronic mail networks, and records management.

CHAPTER RECALL EXERCISES

1. What are the major duties of today's executive assistant?
2. Explain the executive assistant's role as information expediter.
3. Why is the executive assistant's public relations role so important?
4. Describe the traditional executive assistant.
5. What are the advantages of becoming a traditional executive assistant?
6. Why are more companies installing electronic or automated office equipment?
7. What impact does automated equipment have on the executive assistant's role?
8. What is a management work station?
9. Briefly describe the executive assistant's responsibility in working with electronic mail.
10. How is the executive assistant's records management function changing?

PROBLEMS AND APPLICATIONS

1. Based on the information in this chapter, develop your own definition of an executive assistant.

2. List all the similarities between the roles of the traditional executive assistant and the word processing assistant. Then list the differences between the two roles.

3. Interview two executive assistants to determine their three major responsibilities.

    a. Ask them for descriptions of their jobs (if they are available).

    b. List their three major responsibilities in order of priority and the approximate amount of time they spend each day on these responsibilities.

4. Go to your library and consult the *Dictionary of Occupational Titles* for a definition of an executive assistant.

5. In the library consult the *Occupational Outlook Handbook* for a prediction of the number of jobs available for executive assistants this year.

6. The Women's Liberation Movement has made executive assistants conscious of many of the "duties" (making coffee, running personal errands for supervisors, and doing other tasks that are not job related) they perform on their jobs. Is this consciousness raising good or bad? Write a paragraph expressing your opinion.

7. Use the *Business Periodicals Index* to find an article on the changing role of executive assistants or on the growing shortage of executive assistants. Summarize this article.

8. Review the classified advertisements in your Sunday newspaper and cut out all the executive assistant (secretarial) job requests. Separate the jobs into traditional and nontraditional jobs and then compare the job requirements (education, skills, and experience) for the two job classifications. Note the types of companies that are advertising for executive assistants to fill jobs using the automated approach.

LANGUAGE SKILLS DEVELOPMENT

1. Learn to spell the following words:

feasible	procedure
oriented	satellite
permissible	

    a. Have someone dictate the words to you; note the ones you missed and study them until you can spell each one correctly.

    b. Correctly use each word in a sentence.

    c. Using the word division rules, determine the best place to divide each word.

2. Proofread and edit the following paragraph. Type a correct copy of the paragraph.

Over-flowing oil stocks and reduced gas use can cause oil companys to cut gas prices at the wholsale level. Gas now cost from one to three cents less a gallon. However some stations are paing from 1 to 2¢ more for a galon of gas at wholesale. Dealers in most cases can chose wether or not to pass the price breaks on to customers.

3. Rewrite the following sentences for correctness, clarity, and conciseness:
   a. At this point in time I am reluctant to give advice.
   b. A subject and its verb has to agree.
   c. Its my understanding that a squirrel will sometimes bury it's food.
   d. Just between you and I, making beds is a waste of time.
   e. The data is presented in the second chapter of the report.

HUMAN RELATIONS INCIDENTS

1. After much persuasion, your employer purchased a new electronic typewriter for your desk. This is the first electronic typewriter in your department. Almost every day someone asks to use your typewriter for a special job during one of your slack intervals. In order for other people to use the electronic typewriter, it would require a limited amount of training on your part; but you do not want others to use your typewriter. You detect that some of the people in the department are starting to resent you because of this situation. Should you let other people use the typewriter when you aren't using it? How should you handle this situation?

2. You have just been hired as executive assistant to Mr. Connor, Ms. Moore, and Mr. Deal in the Engineering Department. On the first day at your new job you learn from Mr. Connor that part of your job is to make coffee each morning for the department. You do not drink coffee and do not want to make coffee for the other members of the department. Is this part of your job responsibilities? Should you make coffee for the department? How should this situation be handled?

CHARACTERISTICS NEEDED BY THE EXECUTIVE ASSISTANT

As indicated in Chapter 1, the executive assistant's job is thriving, and predictions are that the employment outlook will continue to be favorable. The impact of office technology will certainly change the role and specific tasks of office jobs, but what about the general characteristics needed by executive assistants? Will electronic computers and other automated office equipment drastically change the human relations, technical skills, and personal qualities needed by executive assistants? Obviously, jobs involving a high degree of specialization and machine-centered tasks will attract a different type of person than more traditional jobs.

Successful executive assistants possess certain skills and attitudes that provide them with attractive rewards not only of compensation but of satisfaction in doing a job well. These executive assistants rise to the top of their career ladders. A better understanding of the complexity and wide range of characteristics needed will help you make a career commitment.

At the end of this chapter you should be able to:

1. Discuss the human relations skills needed by the successful executive assistant. ☐ 2. List the technical skills needed by executive assistants. ☐ 3. Discuss the personal skills needed by successful executive assistants.

CHAPTER 2

HUMAN RELATIONS SKILLS

There is a mistaken notion that executive assistants who work in a highly specialized environment where division of work is well-defined do not readily interact with people. Most executive assistant jobs involve human relations; the ability to get along with others is necessary whether the executive assistant is working in a centralized word processing center of a giant corporation or as a private executive assistant to an insurance agent in a traditional environment.

When you analyze the job description of an executive assistant working in a word processing center (an area where automated equipment and specialized personnel are concentrated to systematically process information), you form varied impressions. There are those who visualize a highly automated, introverted person sitting behind the console of a text-editing typewriter (electronic equipment that can record keystrokes on a magnetic media, revise or change text, and replay it, error-free at high speed) in a modular work station with little or no human contact, working on repetitive tasks and lacking any semblance of creativity. Obviously, this is a limited perception which a surprisingly large percentage of business people have.

The fact is, however, that there is human interaction. Executive assistants are part of a team and must confer with their coworkers, supervisors, and a variety of word originators (individuals who create ideas); in fact, there may be more interaction required for this type of executive assistant than for one working in a traditional environment. Instead of dealing with one

Figure 2.1

An example of teamwork (Courtesy of IBM).

boss, the executive assistant will more than likely work with several bosses, as work comes into the center from a variety of sources.

What are these extraordinary human relations qualifications that characterize the successful executive assistant? Business people, consultants, and professional associations have participated in surveys and evaluations in order to determine which traits make a composite of a superior executive assistant. The results are surprisingly reliable because most of the survey results zero in on a cluster of attributes. The list of desirable traits includes perception, thoughtfulness, insight, awareness, sensitivity, and concern for others. These human relation traits are the basis for the highest levels of boss/executive assistant teamwork.

TECHNICAL SKILLS

In addition to human relations skills, an executive assistant needs some technical skills, too. An executive assistant is a professional. Like an automobile mechanic, cosmetologist, or brain surgeon, the executive assistant must possess a predetermined group of high-level technical skills. These skills include typewriting, shorthand, and machine transcription.

TYPEWRITING

Typewriting is the basic skill for executive assistant occupations, and knowledge of the standard typing keyboard is a springboard for moving into the highly automated world of electronic keyboards and computers.

SHORTHAND

Knowledge of shorthand enhances an executive assistant's list of desirable traits. Shorthand may make the difference between initial hiring and/or advancement on the job if competitive peers are equal in other traits because it gives the executive assistant an invaluable skill to use on the job, whether as confidential notetaker or as a research assistant jotting down summaries of information read.

Shorthand skills are very useful for personal use in the business office, for taking telephone messages, and for taking instructions.

MACHINE TRANSCRIPTION

The growing use of dictating equipment makes knowledge of machine transcription a vital executive assistant skill. Machine transcription involves transcribing from a recorded voice. It is a distinct and different skill than shorthand, but it also requires training in English usage and meticulous attention to spelling and correct word usage, just as shorthand does.

THE ART OF DICTATION

A well-trained executive assistant skilled in the art of dictation can relieve a busy executive of much routine correspondence. Willingness and skill in composing and dictating original correspondence in addition to answering routine correspondence will demonstrate your potential for promotion to an administrative position.

ENGLISH USAGE

Of all the traits included at the top of the list of the qualifications that executives request of executive assistants, language arts remains their first choice. There is a growing reliance on executive assistants who not only can transcribe dictation accurately from someone else but who perform creative writing on their own. To do this successfully, a knowledge of correct English, word choice, and other elements of correct communications is essential.

PROOFREADING SKILLS

Closely allied to English usage is the necessity to produce a correct final document that not only lacks errors but is attractively placed on the page. Proofreading requires high personal standards for executive assistants. Before a document is sent out, it should be perfect in every detail. An executive assistant should not settle for sloppy, inaccurate, or misspelled work, even if the boss might let it slip by. After proofreading each document, an executive assistant should ask, "Am I proud of it?" "Am I certain my employer will sign it?" "Will this reflect favorably upon my company?"

PUBLIC RELATIONS SKILLS

An executive assistant has the unique position of enhancing the company's public relations. First impressions are important and lasting. The executive assistant may be the first person an outside visitor of the company meets. Creating and maintaining a positive company image requires courtesy, patience, sensitivity, and good human relations. Every time you pick up the phone or greet a visitor, you meet the public.

Greeting Visitors. A stranger's attitude toward your company will definitely be affected by the way the stranger reacts toward you. You should deal with everyone—visitor, custodian, chief accountant, company president—with equal kindness. From the time you greet visitors until the time they leave the office, you are the official representative for your organization—usually the first and last person that visitors see. The following suggestions may be helpful in greeting visitors:

1. *Make the visitor feel at ease.* When visitors come to your office, especially for the first time, they may feel a bit nervous or ill at ease. Your job should be to make visitors relax and to make them as comfortable as possible.
2. *Take the initiative in being helpful.* If you see a stranger who appears lost or neglected in the reception area, take the initiative with a friendly offer of help. The best way to handle visitors is to treat them the way you would like to be treated if you were in their position; remember that they are guests visiting the company.

3. *Make visitors feel important.* By greeting visitors with courtesy and respect, you make them feel welcome and important.
    a. Address visitors by their names. (Ask them to spell their names, if there is any doubt.)
    b. Extend your arm for a handshake and a smile; positive eye contact will indicate your sincerity and willingness to assist.
    c. Be helpful by offering to hang up their coats and get them something to drink or read.
    d. Respond to their questions and show an interest in them.

Telephone Courtesy.   Although telephone techniques are presented in detail in a later chapter, it is appropriate to mention telephoning here as an integral part of public relations. Telephone communication with the public is another way to broadcast the company's positive image. Even if you are answering a phone at someone else's desk, be courteous and be sure to let the caller know your name. Volunteer to take a message. Don't treat the call casually just because it is not your phone.

   All of these public relations activities may result in thousands of dollars' worth of business for your company, not to mention the intangible good will that results from such interaction. Kindness and consideration should be used when dealing with the public, in person or by phone. The executive assistant should be an ambassador of good will.

PERSONAL SKILLS

Certain personal skills are needed for an executive assistant to be successful. As we examine the general personal characteristics of an executive assistant, certain common denominators emerge that are applicable to all executive assistants regardless of their job descriptions or particular companies.

CREATIVITY

Most of us think of creativity as the domain of an artist who paints a beautiful picture by meticulously mixing the correct amounts of oil paints to create the brilliant colors of a sunset or the cool waters of an ocean. As an executive assistant, you must use your creative talents to transcribe a flawless document from a myriad of input—handwriting, shorthand symbols, human voice—in various stages of disarray. You must use your creativity and ingenuity to handle any deadline crises for projects or for dealing with sensitive people problems.

RESPONSIBILITY AND DEPENDABILITY

This means that once an executive assistant is given a job to do, the boss can consider it done and done well and forget about it. The employer does not have to worry about checking and rechecking the work because the

THE FINAL DOCUMENT

HANDWRITING
SHORTHAND NOTES
COMPUTER PRINT-OUTS
TAPES

Figure 2.2

Creativity is a part of an executive assistant's job.

executive assistant is able to complete each assigned task accurately, completely, and within a specific time frame.

ORGANIZATION

From the moment the executive assistant walks into the office in the morning until the end of the day, work is planned and priorities of tasks are scheduled. The executive assistant disposes of work in an orderly fashion; although a schedule is planned, the schedule is not rigid. You are flexible and creative enough to rearrange work tasks if unexpected rush jobs occur.

MOTIVATION

The executive assistant is a self-starter. You should have the knowledge and good judgment to grasp an idea or suggestion and react positively for the company without elaborate instructions and details. If, for instance, the boss needs routine reports prepared, you should know exactly what to do (type, duplicate, and distribute), in what format, with what duplicating process, and to whom to distribute the reports. Self-motivation presents an image to others working with you, who will pick up on your positive attitude and productive energy.

LOYALTY

An executive assistant should possess an inner loyalty to the boss and to the company. It does not mean that you are in love with every minute of every day on the job. Rather, it means that you enjoy your work, have faith in the company's products or services, and have established a mutual respect for your coworkers. You become the best advertisement for the organization, and these expressions of loyalty go a long way toward creating a positive image—not only to the outside world but also to coworkers, which creates a cohesive team spirit of cooperation within the company.

KNOWLEDGE OF THE COMPANY

The executive assistant knows how to react to telephone inquiries and can solve routine customer problems because he or she usually knows and understands company policies. A thorough knowledge of the company's products or services and markets can be a tremendous asset for a top-level executive assistant. Whether your company is a small domestic manufacturing firm or a large multinational corporation, you should be sufficiently familiar with pertinent laws and regulations which may affect company policies. You will be able to assist your boss more advantageously if you understand the internal workings of your company.

ETHICS

The definition of an executive assistant (secretary) has its origin from the Latin word secretum (secret) and means "one entrusted with secrets." By the very nature of executive assistant work, matters of great importance cross your desk, are transmitted by telephone, or communicated face to face. Corporate matters having far-reaching effects are shared with the executive assistant before they become public knowledge. To expose such developments can seriously jeopardize the company's position in terms of its relations with the public or competitive firms. You must be totally trustworthy to merit your employer's confidence and to be entrusted with the handling of highly confidential and personal materials.

Personal ethics involve being fair in using company time and materials. An executive assistant is expected to arrive punctually in the morning, take a reasonable lunch break, and avoid being abusive when it comes to coffee breaks. These breaks are usually on your own without anyone keeping tabs on you. The executive assistant gives a fair day's work for a fair day's pay regardless of who is watching. Personal ethics also involve not abusing the company's materials by using time and materials for personal tasks such as typing personal letters or using the copying machine for personal records.

A professional executive assistant maintains professional and personal ethics "to the last." When a position is terminated, you should give the company the appropriate (usually two weeks) notice. And after leaving the company, you should not burn your bridges behind you by spreading unfavorable and idle gossip. If you have nothing nice to say about the company, say nothing.

GOOD LISTENER

The ability to follow oral instructions is a trait that is often overlooked and most demanded by business. Yet, listening is part of every communication, and communication is really the heart of office work. Being a good listener implies absorbing all the details and making clear in your mind that you understand all the objectives and directions necessary to complete a given task. Poor listening usually stems from early childhood when parents and teachers were habitually repeating instructions to children. They assumed that children or students would not understand the first time around. As a result, this repetition of instructions fostered complacency and little motivation for the listener to listen vigorously and to try to get to the heart of the subject.

The ability to listen, think clearly, and follow instructions the first time they are uttered makes for a responsive and productive person. It does not mean that you should hesitate to ask questions any time instructions are not clear. There is nothing wrong with repetition, if it is the exception and not the rule.

FLEXIBILITY

All of these personal characteristics, traits, and attitudes add up to a person who will predictably function in an office with a high degree of success. But will these same traits and qualities help you when you are confronted with change, specifically office automation?

Since the turn of the century, the office has been undergoing some change, but the acceleration of this change has been phenomenal during the past decade. This acceleration is the result of a great need for change. The pace of today has brought on a parade of new office products and systems such as the widespread use of text-editing devices, time-shared systems, communicating terminals, high-speed copiers, facsimile machines, advanced dictating systems, minicomputers, electronic mail, optical character recognition technology, fiber optic technology, and micrographics equipment. These new products and systems emerge on the market constantly, enticing more and more companies to adopt these new technologies in an attempt to meet the problems of rising workloads and steadily increasing executive assistant salaries.

In every organization there are people (executive assistants included) who are afraid of change; they are used to operating in the same pattern and work environment. The companies that are concerned with survival have embraced office automation as something not evil or morally dehumanizing; they have accepted change for the better, for the improvement of current

Figure 2.3
The winds of change.

office operations, and as a means for more productive work and a happier work force.

The executive assistant must place the company's welfare above his or her own immediate comfort and must be flexible and willing to move with the waves of change. Flexibility is the willingness and ability to change; it goes hand-in-hand with professional growth, responsibility, and greater rewards. It may mean giving up some obsolete skills, skills that you have worked hard to acquire but skills that may not be compatible with the new technology planned for the office.

For the executive assistant, change involves more than just a willingness to relearn or restructure work habits. It involves a new dimension, a change in the inner psyche and a change of attitude. Survival means looking at the bright side of any situation and embarking on a new career path; it involves the challenge of learning new equipment or attaining new horizons and being totally immersed and committed to new growth and vitality.

If you are satisfied with the status quo of your job, it may be an obstacle to getting ahead. It keeps you from going out and seeking the new, the different, the challenging. Make the most of a new project and a new assignment. There might be an opportunity waiting for you to move up to a job with more responsibility.

MATURITY

The ability to weather the storms of office crises with poise and grace is a prized executive assistant trait. Emotional maturity, or lack of it, manifests itself in many ways. There may be deep-seated emotional problems, un-related to the job, that cause a person to "blow up" or avoid handling situations because of personal hang-ups.

PROFESSIONALISM

Although the technical skills and human relations characteristics that we discussed earlier are in no sense all-inclusive, they do present a fairly good compilation of traits most frequently desired by business people for success in a professional executive assistant career.

For those who aspire to move up the career ladder as a professional executive assistant, there is a set of strategies to undertake to launch an intelligent plan for self-improvement. The best way to begin a self-improvement program is to take stock of your own assets and liabilities and then simply work on improving those assets that you have and eliminating any liabilities.

How do you become a successful executive assistant? How do you attain the human relations characteristics that make for a successful executive assistant? You can develop many of these characteristics by listening, watching, and learning, not only what other people say and do but also what they do not do. Don't overlook little things; observe first-rate executive assistants on the job. Listen to the tone of their voices as they speak on the phone. Watch their motions. Are they hurried and flustered or calm and controlled? Are their work stations cluttered or orderly? Look beyond expensive ward-robes and observe a sense of well-groomed appearance, excellent posture, and a snappy gait.

Professional growth and self-improvement are positive ways to upgrade your status and performance. Here are some ways you can enhance your performance and professional career:

Education. There are times when executive assistant students question the value of a college education when their counterparts in high school can readily attain entry-level employment. The value of a college education will bear fruit when the well-educated executive assistant can face unique prob-lems with a broader outlook and an acute awareness of national and inter-national problems. The combination of a strong liberal arts background and good technical skills is the requisite that more and more employers are looking for in hiring executive assistants.

Upgrading Technical Skills. Although typing on the job will help you maintain a marketable skill level, special typing applications and study can be used for self-improvement. Shorthand skills can be polished by reviewing outlines, brief forms, and theory. Faster speeds can be acquired by obtaining and using recordings of various speeds dictated in a variety of accents and applications. There are always classes available in your community for review and skillbuilding as well.

Improvements in language arts and basic mathematics skills can be easily achieved in many ways. The acquisition of good textbooks, the conscientious relearning of theory and rules, and the completion of exercises will go a long way toward improving these important office skills. Programmed learning packages or multimedia learning kits can be an enjoyable way of learning.

Learning New Skills. As more companies acquire new and sophisticated equipment, executive assistants should be prepared to learn the new electronic devices. Experience in operating text-editing typewriters, visual display terminals, OCR (optical character recognition, a form of data input employing optical scanning equipment), and other sophisticated equipment will add to your value as a well-rounded executive assistant. Usually, equipment manufacturers will train employees in-house (at the equipment manufacturer's branch office). In addition to company-sponsored software packages, several commercial publishing companies are offering learning packages using multimedia and individualized instruction approaches.

Being Professionally Certified. Executive assistants aspiring for professional recognition should plan to become a Certified Professional Secretary (CPS). A CPS is one who has successfully completed an examination developed and administered by the Institute for Certifying Secretaries, a department of Professional Secretaries International, and who has met the secretarial experience requirements.

The purposes of the CPS program are:

1. To improve secretarial personnel by giving specific direction to an educational program and by providing a means of measuring the extent of professional development.
2. To provide secretaries with the assurance which comes from having attained a professional educational standard.
3. To promote the professional identity of the exceptional secretary.
4. To assist management in selecting qualified secretaries.
5. To plan and sponsor additional programs of continuing professional development for the Certified Professional Secretary.

The examination is based upon an analysis of secretarial work, with emphasis on judgment, understanding, and administrative ability gained through education and work experience. It includes skills, techniques, and knowledge in the following six areas: behavioral science in business, business law, economics and management, accounting, secretarial skills and decision making, and office procedures and administration.[1]

SUMMARY

Office personnel have weathered many a storm in the constantly changing sea of office technology, equipment, and procedures. The professional characteristics and the intangible assets that the executive assistant brings to the job remain constant. The technical office skills and human relations characteristics are just as necessary in the traditional office as they are in the electronic office.

1. Positive human relations and sensitivity with working with others are essential characteristics of the executive assistant working in a traditional or highly automated environment.
2. There is executive assistant creativity in producing correct and attractive documents.
3. Executive assistant technical skills are a necessary part of the characteristics of an executive assistant. These skills are typewriting, shorthand, machine transcription, dictation, English usage, proofreading, and public relations skills.
4. Special personal characteristics are necessary to be a successful executive assistant. They include such traits as being creative, well-organized, motivated, loyal, knowledgeable, ethical, flexible, mature, and professional.
5. Professional growth and self-improvement can enhance the executive assistant's performance and professional career through education, upgrading technical skills, learning new skills, and being professionally certified.

CHAPTER RECALL EXERCISES

1. What are three human relations skills needed by a successful executive assistant?
2. Will the automated office environment necessarily change the general personal characteristics required of the executive assistant? Explain.
3. What does executive assistant creativity mean?
4. Why is it important for the executive assistant to understand company policy?

[1]A description of these six parts and an example of a CPS examination can be found in the *Secretary*, a journal published by the PSI. Further information on the CPS rating may be obtained by writing to Professional Secretaries International, 2440 Pershing Road, Suite G10, Crown Center, Kansas City, Missouri 64108.

5. Briefly explain the difference between professional (company) ethics and personal ethics.
6. List some of the new technologies that will effect changes in office operations.
7. Explain why most people resist change.
8. Is there a correlation between age and emotional maturity? Explain.
9. Why do employers seek college-educated executive assistants?
10. List some of the ways an executive assistant may upgrade technical skills.

PROBLEMS AND APPLICATIONS

1. You are employed as an administrative executive assistant to the president of a large pharmaceutical company. The Office Services Department of the community college from which you recently graduated has asked you to participate in a freshman student forum. You are asked to make a ten-minute presentation about your job, how college helped you advance on the job, and some of the skills and characteristics needed by an executive assistant on the job. On a sheet of paper, outline your presentation.

2. Many articles have been written about how shorthand is becoming archaic. These articles relate how shorthand is not needed in the electronic office and maybe not even in the traditional office today. Do you agree or disagree with these statements? Write a defense for your opinion, giving the reasons why or why not. Type a copy of this defense.

3. Write a letter to the Professional Secretaries International and ask for information on the CPS examination. Display on a bulletin board the information you obtain.

4. Do a telephone survey of five companies in your area and ask the following questions:

   a. What technical skills are needed for a job as executive assistant in your company?

   b. What are the speeds needed for typewriting and shorthand?

   c. What percentage of accuracy is needed for typewriting and shorthand?

   d. Do you administer other types of employment tests, such as business math, business English, proofreading, and filing?

5. Contact your local Professional Secretaries International Chapter to determine what programs and study courses they offer for those people interested in taking the CPS examination.

6. Look at the classified ads in your local paper to determine what skills are needed for executive assistant (secretary) jobs. Classify the skills as technical, human relations, and personal. List the skills requested in these advertisements.

LANGUAGE SKILLS DEVELOPMENT

1. The following memo has been typed for a company president to send out to all employees. You are to check it for accuracy before it is duplicated and distributed. Identify and correct all errors. Retype the memo.

> To the Members of the Staff;
>
> The company uses Petti cash funds to expidite reimbursement of necessary emergency expenditures.
>
> Purcharers must not acceed $24 from any 1 vendee on the same day. These expenditures are eventually deducted from the using department buget and maynot normally acceed two hudnred dollars per month per department.
> Sincerly,
>
>
> Alex Smith

2. Mr. Moore hands you a letter which he has written in longhand. He requests that you type it, proofread it, and submit it directly to the corporate vice-president. He indicates that he has to leave the office immediately. "Type the letter word for word and sign my name," he instructs you.

    While typing it you notice the expression, "use your digression about hiring a temporary executive assistant if the work piles up." It looks incorrect and you check to make sure. You remember his instructions; his handwriting, however, is clear and unmistakable. What course of action would you take?

3. Rewrite the following sentences for correctness, clarity, and conciseness:
   a. Barking furiously, I finally feed the dog.
   b. Falling from the sky, Jim saw the meteor.
   c. Let me say how much I appreciate you coming to the grand opening.
   d. The company always sends their statements on time.
   e. Waiting patiently in the car, the gas tank was finally filled by the attendant.

4. Learn to spell the following words:

compatible	significant
ingredient	symmetrical
response	

5. Using the correct word division rules, divide the words in question 4.

HUMAN RELATIONS INCIDENTS

1. Mark recently took a job to work in a local word processing center near campus. Having performed with honors in a classroom setting and having a background as a marine, the job seemed like an excellent arrangement for both parties. The first few weeks involved training on new equipment taught by one of the senior executive assistants. During one of the training sessions, Marie, the senior assistant, corrected some of his procedural operations, and apparently she must have hit a raw nerve. Mark stormed out of the building in disgust. In spite of Mark's experience and excellent grasp of equipment technology, he lacked some vital skills. Why do you think Mark reacted the way he did? Could Marie have prevented this incident? What can Mark do now to make amends?

2. Eve was the executive assistant to Ms. Barnes in the Graphics Department. Eve just hired a cooperative education student from the local college. During the interview, the college student was dressed appropriately, but on the first day of work, the student showed up in jeans and a printed tee-shirt. Since the company frowns on such informal dress for employees, Eve thinks she should talk to the college student. What should she say? Should Eve not talk to the student? Should companies enforce a dress code for their employees? What is acceptable office dress for women? What is acceptable office dress for men?

ORGANIZING AND PLANNING WORKFLOW

Have you ever observed the desks or work stations of office workers? Some desks are neat and orderly, with everything in its proper place. Others are a shambles. A messy work station looks like someone has ransacked it with in-basket items piled high, file folders stacked on the desk, and unemptied ashtrays, crumbled coffee cups, and assorted bits and pieces of paper cluttering the desk.

This can be a source of embarrassment for the executive assistant as well as the company. Imagine a visitor coming in to see you. It can be awkward when you would have to clear off a chair in order for the person to sit down; and if the visitor asked for a particular report, you might have to rummage through unruly piles of assorted papers before you finally found the report.

Many people complain that they do not have enough hours in every day to accomplish the duties and responsibilities they have. In some cases this lack of accomplishment is due to a lack of organization, not only of the work area but also of the hours and minutes that fill each day.

At the end of this chapter you should be able to:

1. List the principles for organizing a work area. ☐ 2. Know how to keep a calendar. ☐ 3. Set up a time schedule for your day. ☐ 4. List the principles of time management.

CHAPTER 3

ORGANIZATION OF
WORK AREA

The need for a clean-up day can be inspired by a variety of sudden revelations. You are running out of available space on your desk or in your files. You are embarrassed by your work area when the president of the company or an important visitor comes into your work area. Or, your need for a clean-up might manifest itself more gradually. It seems reasonable that time could be saved and frustrations avoided if you did not have to search for papers and working tools but could locate them immediately when they are needed.

Cleaning your work station and putting things away in an arbitrary fashion can be very unproductive unless you have a plan of action to get to the bottom of those paper piles. Here are some specific suggestions:

1. *Plan a time schedule for your cleaning up.* The materials on your desk may have been accumulating over a period of weeks, months, or even years. You need to tackle this task without interruption, which may necessitate some early arrivals or late departures from work. Once you start the job, stay with it until it is completed.

Figure 3.1
Disorganized work area (Courtesy of Herman Miller).

2. *Develop your strategy.* Study your work area and determine in advance the best approach. If the work area is a complete disaster, you might need to start working inside out. Get everything out in the open by emptying out the insides of the desk drawers and cabinets. If your problem is less scattered, determine which file folders should be put away first and which desk drawers need immediate attention.

3. *Set priorities and standards.* If you look at your work surface too long, you may feel frustrated and overwhelmed. The biggest stumbling block is deciding which items to keep and which items to throw away. This may be determined in advance by deciding by category or by age of the material what items you really should keep. A knowledge of the laws of retention of records would be helpful.

4. *Set high standards for yourself.* Standards and self-discipline should motivate you to action. If you are a compulsive collector of objects and find it difficult to part with your objects, ask yourself some tough questions:
   a. Do I really need this?
   b. Is a duplicate of this stored in a central file so that I really don't need to keep this copy?
   c. Does this have anything to do with the work we are currently doing or will it ever be of use in the future?

5. *Be creative in redesigning your office work area.* If an organized look means new methods of organizing materials or files, be inventive if it works better than the traditional way. Think of new, more useful categories in which to divide materials as they come into your office.

ORGANIZATION OF DESK

The desk and work area often say a lot about your personality. A cluttered desk may reflect a sense of disorientation and lackadaisical attitude toward your job. A super-neat desk with a daily application of high-gloss furniture polish and each item meticulously placed on the desk may also be extreme and more of a compulsion than a requirement of the actual executive assistant work. A desk should be neat yet functional. The tools and resources needed to do a good job should be placed in appropriate positions within easy reach. Here are some helpful suggestions for organizing your desk.[1]

TOP OF THE DESK

As a general rule, it is a good idea to keep off the desk all objects that are not in constant use. Don't let papers, coffee cups, or books accumulate on your desk. When you finish using a stapler or scissors, put them away. You

[1]These prototypes of desk arrangements apply to the traditional single-pedestal desk; however, more and more offices are using an open landscape environment with modernistic work stations. The partitions include hanging components where shelving and cabinets are suspended above the work surface.

should organize your desk to suit your personality and work requirements. Some of the items the top of the desk might contain are (Figure 3.2):

1. Telephone.
2. Calendar.
3. Reference books (dictionary, word-division manual, handbook, company manual, company telephone directory).
4. In/out trays.
5. Small rotary file (for names and addresses and telephone numbers of clients, customers, or sales people).
6. Tickler file (or other memory devices).

WIDE CENTER DRAWER

This drawer is usually reserved for frequently used office supplies. A compartment tray in the front of the drawer might contain such small items as paper clips, rubber bands, scotch tape, ruler, pens, and erasing supplies.

TOP SIDE DRAWER

This drawer is used for stationery. If there is a front partition, you may wish to stack envelopes or index cards. The rear section should come equipped

Figure 3.2
Reference books (Courtesy of Wilson Jones Company).

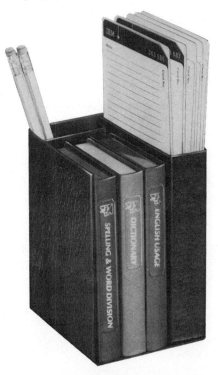

Figure 3.3
Top side drawer with supplies (Courtesy of Herman Miller).

with a sloping division with dividers for letterhead stationery, plain bond paper, carbon sets, memorandum paper, company office forms, and mailing labels. (Figure 3.3)

MIDDLE SIDE DRAWER

The middle drawer can be used for surplus supplies such as pencils, pens, marking felt-tip pens, extra notebooks, glue, typewriter ribbons, and cleaning fluid.

BOTTOM SIDE DRAWER

This drawer is usually designed to accommodate personal belongings, such as facial tissues and coffee cups.

ADDITIONAL STORAGE FACILITIES

Your desk may contain a file drawer. This may be in addition to the regular file cabinets located near your work station. The desk file should contain documents and correspondence that are used frequently in the daily course of business. As the frequency of their use diminishes, they should be transferred to another file cabinet.

Your work area may contain a supply cabinet, and you may be responsible for arranging and checking its contents. The most frequently used supplies should be placed on the most accessible shelves. Like items should be

Figure 3.4
Top side drawer with supplies (Courtesy of Herman Miller).

Figure 3.5
File drawer (Courtesy of Herman Miller).

grouped together—boxes of envelopes in one section, paper in another, and cleaning fluids in another. Identify the packages on the outer wrapping paper and take inventory at least once a week. When a new item arrives, place it on the proper shelf in back of or under the older supplies.

Once the physical surroundings of the executive assistant's work station are in order, a better atmosphere is created, one that is more conducive to the executive assistant work function. (Figure 3.6)

KEEPING A CALENDAR

The executive assistant is responsible for maintaining the office calendar. Usually, you will have a calendar in your work area and a duplicate calendar for the boss's office. The calendar is used to record such items as appointments, conferences, reminders, and holidays. It is important that both calendars are maintained and consistent; do not trust your memory to keep track of office business.

The calendar needs to be accessible to your boss, to you, and in some cases to other people who might need to know the boss's schedule. Because the calendar on your desk might be public, don't put items on it that might be personal or confidential unless the items are coded.

Some bosses prefer to carry a pocket calendar and make their own appointments when they are out of the office. If that is the case, you need to work out an arrangement so you can keep an up-to-date copy of the appointments made so you can schedule other appointments accordingly.

You need to determine from your boss if there are certain times he or she would like to keep free. It may be that your boss likes to keep the mornings free to do desk work and would like to schedule appointments for the afternoon only. Or, your boss might not like to have appointments scheduled

Figure 3.6
Organized work area (Courtesy of Digital Equipment Corporation).

for the day after a trip out of town. Whatever the boss's preferences, keep them in mind when scheduling meetings and appointments.

The calendar should have all the pertinent information about an appointment: the person's name (first and last name spelled correctly), the place (address and room number), the time, the item of business, and a telephone number to reach the other party if the appointment needs to be delayed or canceled. Toward the end of a year, you will probably be maintaining two calendars—one for the current year and one for next year.

A calendar can also be used to warn of approaching deadlines so you can take care of needed business. You might have to remind your boss of these deadlines far enough in advance for him or her to finish some item of business. You might also need to notify or remind other people of scheduled meetings or appointments. Make it a point to look ahead in a calendar on a regular basis so you can be prepared to meet deadlines.

You will find it helpful to put on your calendar company holidays and vacations to remind you not to schedule meetings during these times. You might wish to put on your calendar some personal reminders for your supervisor, such as birthdays and anniversaries. The calendar is a type of tickler file.

Calendars come in a variety of sizes and styles. One of the most popular calendars has each day divided into half hour segments to help you in scheduling appointments.

TIME MANAGEMENT PLANNING

Time wasted is time lost. It occurs when you try to do too much or spend time on unimportant tasks. One of the key reasons why many office workers do not have enough time is that they lack the ability to predict with any reasonable accuracy just how long a particular task will take.

PRELIMINARY STEPS

The intelligent managing of time is planning tasks and assignments and starting them at the right time—when your work will not be interrupted, when time estimates are reasonably accurate, and when work schedules permit you to accomplish more in a given period of time. The following guides are useful in managing your time more efficiently:

1. *List your activities.* In order to effectively plan an intelligent work schedule, a list of activities or tasks is needed.

2. *Break activities into component parts.* From a broad-based list of executive assistant activities, the next step would be to break each activity into its component parts; and then estimate how much time it would take you to complete each unit. For instance, how long would it take you to develop a product research report for your employer? How long would it take for collecting data, writing the first draft, getting the draft approved, typing the final document, and duplicating and distributing the copies? Do not assume that you can remember each item. It is best that you write each step involved on a piece of paper.

a. Estimate the time for each task. As you work on the assignment, keep track of the time it takes you to complete each job. You might devise a form that looks like Figure 3.7.

b. Compare your estimated time with your actual time. This will be helpful in gauging the actual time if these tasks occur again. Unexpected interruptions should be taken into account when calculating estimated time.

Continue to break activities into component parts until you do it almost without thinking. Keep a record of actual versus estimated time until it is clear to you that you have become skilled in estimating time values. As you develop skill in estimating, you can probably eliminate the need for writing each part down. However, make sure you resume this practice whenever you undertake a new and challenging task that will become part of your regular executive assistant routine.

3. *Assign priorities.* You need to make certain that what has to be done by a specified time is accomplished. Other tasks that are necessary but of lesser importance should be scheduled and worked on if time permits. If an

THINGS TO DO TODAY

	Project	Est. Time	Actual Time
1			
2			
3			
4			
5			
6			
7			
8			
9			
10			
11			
12			
13			
14			
15			
16			
17			
18			
19			
20			

Figure 3.7
Things-to-do list.

emergency arises, the schedule must be flexible enough to accommodate it. Priorities can be classified into the following categories:

a. *Daily tasks.* Daily tasks become routinized and experienced executive assistants perform these jobs without direct supervision. It is important not to delay doing these tasks or they can pile up and disrupt the best-planned schedule. Daily tasks might include telephone work, correspondence, filing, mail, and daily meetings.

b. *Special tasks.* These special tasks include one-shot projects that are not usually recurring and may be as varied as researching a special report or replying to a special campaign or program. Since these projects occur infrequently, the executive assistant should adjust the established work plan to fit in these special tasks.

c. *Long-range projects.* Time should be set aside each day to plan for long-range projects. It is wise not to wait for the last few days to begin work on such projects. Examples of long-range projects that may be due several months ahead are redesigning the file system, updating mailing lists, revising correspondence manuals, streamlining business forms, revising price sheets, or planning an itinerary for a trip.

d. *Emergency peak load.* If you know ahead of time that a special project will swamp you with paperwork, you might suggest contacting an outside temporary agency for assistance; or, you might be able to distribute the workload to the correspondence or word processing center.

METHODS OF TIME MANAGEMENT

After establishing the preliminary steps of listing your activities, breaking them into component parts, and estimating the time for each task, the next step in an executive assistant's work plan is to make a time schedule. You can design a special form by preparing a master stencil on which the time and type of activities are indicated. Once the form is designed and copies are duplicated, you should keep a supply in your desk.

The first entry in the time schedule will be the date, and then the activities will be listed in appropriate time segments. The time column may be pre-printed into 15- or 30-minute segments or it can be left blank to be filled in on a daily basis. This form can be a great boon to the company. If the executive assistant is out for the day, the replacement can easily follow the tasks.

An additional aid would be to purchase a desk calendar with space for entries in the time slots.

The best designed form in the world is meaningless if it is not followed. The purpose of assigning work priorities is to analyze working habits for the time and motions spent on routine tasks so that the executive assistant can plan time for high-priority work. This is a personal barometer of your work habits.

Some people work best in the morning and should assign the most creative work to that time. By midafternoon they may taper off, and routine work, which does not require high levels of concentration, should be scheduled. Other people are slow starters who find it difficult to wake up and get organized. Their creative work should be done in the afternoon when they are at their peak of efficiency. Of course, all schedules must revolve around the boss's needs, and the executive assistant must be flexible.

Try to avoid distractions when you start a job. Stick to it until it is completed. Good planning helps if you have a tendency to be easily distracted, to scatter your time over a number of projects and wind up with little to show for it. Devise an intelligent plan to decide the three or four most important jobs that face you each day. Then undertake them one at a time. Try not to let yourself be interrupted by anything or anybody. If an occasional interruption is unavoidable, get back to the unfinished job just as soon as you can. Don't leave it partially complete and start something else.

Those people who get things done rarely let themselves fall into the trap of being diverted or interrupted. Wise time managers decide what comes first and stick with it until that particular job is complete. Then they proceed to tackle the next job assignment.

After you have been working with a time schedule for some time, you will be in a better position to analyze and refine the schedule for improvement. Change may mean rescheduling morning work for the afternoon, including new tasks in the schedule, or dropping other tasks that have been delegated to other staff members. Daily schedules may be changed to weekly schedules which may be designed and filled out on Fridays for the following week.

Organizing and planning workflow can be the executive assistant's best device for an efficient and productive day's work. A sense of teamwork and spirit of cooperation is needed between the executive and coworkers to discover the jobs to be done, their priorities, and an intelligent order in which to do them. The plan, once established, should be followed with a degree of reasonable flexibility to accommodate unexpected events. At such times you must know how to revise your work schedule to take into account the changing situation.

SUMMARY

An organized desk and work area can help you be more productive. The executive assistant needs to have proper tools and supplies handy to use instantly.

In order to be more efficient, the executive assistant needs to keep an accurate and up-to-date calendar of appointments, schedules, and reminders. Another way to be more efficient and productive is to develop a time management plan to help you effectively schedule your activities.

1. A clean-up day is one solution for a disorganized work station.
2. Guidelines to clean your work station are: (1) plan a time schedule, (2) develop your strategy, (3) set priorities and standards, (4) set high personal standards, and (5) be creative.
3. The executive assistant's tools (resource materials) must be within easy reach and readily accessible.
4. The top of the desk might contain a telephone, calendar, reference books, in/out tray, and small file.
5. The executive assistant's desk file should contain documents that are used frequently in the daily conduct of business.
6. One of the duties of an executive assistant is to maintain a calendar for recording appointments, conferences, reminders, and holidays.
7. The calendar should have all the pertinent information about an appointment (person's name, place of appointment, time, item of business, and telephone number).
8. The key ingredient in planning time wisely is the ability to predict how long a task will take.
9. The following guides are useful in planning to use time more efficiently: list your activities, break activities into component parts, and assign priorities.
10. Tasks can be accomplished most efficiently when they are scheduled according to the executive assistant's personal barometer. For example,

some people work best in the morning and should assign the most creative work to that time.

11. Stick with one job until it is completed.
12. Be flexible even though you have a written scheduled planned. If emergencies arise, you must be flexible and willing to change.

CHAPTER RECALL EXERCISES

1. Describe the top of an efficient executive assistant's desk.
2. List the reference books an executive assistant might have available.
3. List some items that might appear in these desk drawers:
   a. Executive assistant's wide center drawer.
   b. Top side drawer.
   c. Middle side drawer.
   d. Bottom side drawer.
4. What responsibilities should an executive assistant assume in maintaining a supply cabinet?
5. Describe how an executive assistant can overcome interruptions in trying to complete one job at a time.
6. What criteria would be used to assign priorities to tasks?
7. Work assignments are a personal consideration and should be planned on the basis of work habits and individual levels of competence and concentration. Explain.
8. A calendar is useful to remind an executive assistant of approaching deadlines. How would you use the calendar as a dated file?
9. Are calendars considered public information for anyone in the office to see? Why or why not?

PROBLEMS AND APPLICATIONS

1. You have just been hired as the administrative assistant to a radio talk show personality. The previous executive assistant left a few months earlier, and the parade of temporaries left the desk and assigned work area in a shambles. The in-basket was piled high with unanswered letters; file folders were stacked on the desk, along with assorted bits and pieces of papers and books. Describe your plan of action on your first day on the job.

2. Your job as administrative assistant to a radio talk show personality entails the following tasks:
   a. Transcribe letters from associate producer.
   b. Allocate other correspondence to assistants.
   c. Confirm guests via telephone.
   d. Make sure commercial copy to be read is in sequence.

e. Update and confirm facts on today's guest (3 × 5-inch biography card).

f. Read and clip any newspaper or magazine articles that are topical or newsworthy and alert associate producer.

g. Check appointment calendar and remind associate producer of special meetings.

h. Check out-of-town trips and arrange airline reservations and hotel accommodations.

i. Act as advance person to check out hotel and auditorium prior to guest appearance.

j. Send out press releases.

On a sheet of paper, type the order in which you would handle these tasks and estimate the amount of time it would take you to complete them. Design a chart that would be appropriate to incorporate these tasks. Use the following guidelines for your chart:

MAIN HEADING: DAILY ACTIVITY PLAN

Subheadings: Date: _____

Goals: 1. _____

2. _____

3. _____

Symbols for Priority Goals

a. do immediately

b. do today

c. do when convenient

d. do when present assignments are complete

Column Headings

Time	Assignment	Priority	Time Completed and/or Disposition

3. Jane has been asked to check some purchase orders. As she starts the job, however, someone phones to request some carbon copy sets. So she goes to her cabinet to check her supply but stops to glance at some new mailing labels in the cabinet. She forgets about the phone call, is intrigued by the new mailing labels, and starts for the supply department to inquire whether to use the new labels or the old labels for all future correspondence requiring a large envelope. On the way to the supply department she passes the cafeteria and decides to stop in for a cup of coffee. If you were Jane's supervisor and concerned about maintaining a reasonable work schedule, what would you say to Jane? What principles of time management does Jane's conduct violate?

4. Make a list of all the activities you have to accomplish tomorrow.
   a. Assign priorities to the tasks.
   b. Break the activities into component parts.
   c. Assign a time schedule to each of the activities.
   d. Compare your estimated time with your actual time to complete each task.
   e. Evaluate the items that took you more or less time than you originally estimated to determine what caused the discrepancies.

5. Make an appointment to visit three offices in three departments on your campus or three offices in the business community and casually observe the work area of the executive assistants in those offices. Write a brief description of the organization or disorganization of each of these offices. Note such things as:
   a. Your first impression of the office.
   b. The organization of the top of the desk.
   c. The tools and items the executive assistant keeps on the top of the desk and within easy reach of the desk.
   d. The use of a supply cabinet.

6. Study your own work area or study area at home to determine how you can rearrange it for more productive use. Make a list of how you can change it.

LANGUAGE SKILLS DEVELOPMENT

1. Using the number rules found in the appendix (page 503), choose the correct use of numbers in the following sentences:
   a. On (May 1st, May 1) the physician said Joan was not able to work.
   b. The (3-way, three-way) relationship was a threat to the security.
   c. Jim was stopped by the police officer for driving (56 miles per hour, fifty-six miles per hour) in a school zone.
   d. The company gave ($450,000, $450 thousand) to (2, two) schools.
   e. (Fifteen, 15) companies in the area said they did not know how the decision would affect them.

2. Consult your dictionary to define the following words:
   a. complimentary, complementary
   b. effect, affect
   Use each of the words in a sentence.
3. Proofread and correct the errors in the following paragraph:

   Lock crews along the St. Lawrence seaway obeyed a goverment order and allowed commerical shiping through. A offical said the ships were tyed up because of a job protect. The vessells were forced to tie up after midnight when workers left there jobs in a dispute over planes to reduse the size of the lock crews.

4. Put in commas in the following paragraph:

   Today national boundaries are becoming invisible. If a company is growing its expansion abroad is almost inevitable. Establishing a company abroad however demands a great deal of work expertise and knowledge in addition to creativity. A company that wishes to establish an overseas operation will find the prospect exciting rewarding and tiring.

HUMAN RELATIONS INCIDENTS

1. Nancy, the new messenger, has not been picking up work on schedule. You have seen her loafing in the building with some of the other new workers. Since you recommended her for the job, you feel she has let you down. Should you say something to her? If so, what?

2. You are executive assistant to Dr. Mayer, director of athletics at the university where you work. One of the fringe benefits of your job is that, with the permission of your supervisor, you can take a class each semester during working hours. The tuition for the class is free; and the administration of the university encourages staff members to take advantage of this opportunity to take courses to upgrade their skills. This semester the Office Services Department is offering a course in Records Management which meets three days a week from 10 a.m. to 11 a.m. Dr. Mayer signed your permission waiver to allow you to take the course. No problems occurred during the first two weeks of class, but after that time Dr. Mayer appeared to resent your being out of the office three days a week for that hour. He would give you "emergency" items to handle about ten minutes before class would start or "rush" items to be completed before you went to class. Because of these tasks you

have missed three of the last five class meetings. You've been able to make up the work missed in class, but you are concerned about missing any more class sessions. What should you do?

3. You keep your boss's calendar on top of your desk so it will be convenient to check dates and make appointments. Mr. Newland, a sales representative, usually visits your office unannounced and without an appointment. He always wants to know if Ms. Bert, your boss, has a few minutes to spare. While he talks with you, Mr. Newland always comes around to the side of your desk and glances at the calendar. You think Ms. Bert's appointments and schedule are private information. How can you handle this situation with Mr. Newland?

4. You are executive assistant to three people—Mr. David, Mr. White, and Ms. Case. Since all three people have a moderate amount of work to be done, you always stay busy but are usually able to handle the work because of keeping a daily and weekly time schedule. However, Mr. White considers most of his work as high priority and rush items. He usually puts off until the last minute any correspondence and reports he has to complete. Because he is so late completing his work, you are usually under a lot of pressure to complete his work on time. To do his work, you have to let Mr. David's and Ms. Case's work pile up for a couple of days. Is there any way you can help Mr. White complete his work on time? How should you handle this situation to take off some of the pressure?

INFORMATION PROCESSING

Executive assistants need a high level of technical skill to effectively operate office equipment and produce professional documents. In addition, they need up-to-date information about changes in office equipment so they can intelligently use this equipment.

The executive assistant must be highly skilled to interpret the input into an accurate and complete document. Sophisticated office systems have brought about drastic changes in paperwork processes. ■ Chapter 4 The Typewriter: Manual, Electric, Electronic, and Text Editing □ Chapter 5   Word Processing □ Chapter 6   Typing Techniques □ Chapter 7   Written Business Communications □ Chapter 8   Methods and Procedures of Input □ Chapter 9 Dictation/Transcription Equipment and Procedures □ Chapter 10 Computers

SECTION II

THE TYPEWRITER: MANUAL, ELECTRIC, ELECTRONIC, AND TEXT EDITING

One of the primary technical skills needed by the executive assistant is typewriting. Typewriters have changed tremendously during the past decade, and they are continuing to change now. This chapter will not only present a summary of the evolution of typewriters, but it will introduce you to some of the latest advances in typewriters.

Along with the introduction of new equipment comes the necessity of choosing the right equipment for the job. Some features of the new typewriters will be explained so you get an overview of what the newest typewriters can do.

An executive assistant needs to know what steps to take to keep the typewriter operating efficiently and effectively. In this chapter, we will list the procedures to follow in order to keep your typewriter in the best operating condition.

At the end of this chapter you should be able to:

1. Describe the evolution of the typewriter. ☐ 2. Name the criteria used for selecting typewriters. ☐ 3. Describe some of the electric models of typewriters. ☐ 4. List some of the features of electronic and text-editing typewriters. ☐ 5. List the ways to properly maintain your typewriter.

CHAPTER 4

HISTORY OF THE TYPEWRITER

The first idea for a writing machine surfaced early in the eighteenth century when Queen Anne of England awarded a patent to an engineer named Henry Mill to develop "an artificial machine or method for the impressing or transcribing of letters singly or progressively one after another, as in writing."

Many people worked on developing a practical typewriter during the eighteenth and early nineteenth centuries. William Austin Burt invented the typographer, the first machine to use typebars. Another inventor, Charles Thurber, devised a machine with a movable carriage in 1848. The main problem with all these early machines was their slow speed. In fact, a person with a pen could write faster than a person working on one of these typewriters.

The credit for inventing the machine that is the forerunner of today's typewriters is given to Christopher Sholes, a printer, editor, and inventor from Milwaukee. Sholes, working with Samuel Soule and Carlos Glidden, spent seven years perfecting a workable typewriter. To market their "Type-Writer," the three men contacted the firm of E. Remington & Sons, which at that time made sewing machines and guns. This firm produced the first successfully marketed typewriter, the Remington Model 1. The machine looked very much like more modern typewriters, but it was mounted on a stand similar to a sewing machine table; and the carriage was returned by a foot treadle. Remington advertised this typewriter as "an ornament to an

Figure 4.1
Oliver typewriter (Courtesy of Milwaukee Public Museum).

Figure 4.2
Mignon typewriter (Courtesy of Milwaukee Public Museum).

office, study, or sitting room" and said, "It is certain to become as indispensable in families as the sewing machine."

The main barrier to the growing popularity of the typewriter was the lack of trained operators. So, in 1881 the New York YWCA pioneered typing courses. The reaction to these classes was mixed. Many people felt women were too frail to survive a six-month typing course. Also, they felt business was a man's world and did not welcome the entrance of women. However, women survived the course, and eventually other schools began to offer instruction in typing. Within a few years, every major firm in the United States had at least one woman typist. By 1909 the typewriter and the typist had become so popular that 89 separate typewriter manufacturers existed in the United States alone.

The typewriter also became popular for personal use. Mark Twain, who is said to be one of the first writers to use a typewriter, typed this letter to his brother in 1875:

"Dear Brother:

I am trying t to get the hang of this new f fangled writing machine, but am not making a shining success of it. However this is the first attempt I ever have made, & yet I perceivethat I shall soon & easily acquire a fine facility in its use ... The having been a compositor is likely to be a great help to me,since o ne chiefly needs swiftness in banging the keys. The machine costs 125 dollars. The machines has several virtures. I believe it will print faster than I can write. One may lean back in his chair & work it. It piles an awful stack of works on one page. It dont muss things or scatter ink blots around. Of course it saves paper."

The typewriter has come a long way since those days. Improvements have come rapidly and have been dramatic. Today there are several categories of typewriters used in business: manual, electric typebar, proportional spacing, single element, self-correcting, electronic, and text-editing systems.

Manual machines are no longer in great use because they are slower than electric models, and they cause greater operator fatigue. However, they are still appropriate for use in small businesses or establishments where the typing volume is small.

ELECTRIC TYPEWRITERS

The next major improvement in the typewriter's development was the introduction of the electric typewriter which was introduced in 1925 by Remington. Also at that time, a firm called Electromatic Typewriters, Inc., was manufacturing an electric typewriter. In 1933 the International Business Machines Corp. (IBM) purchased the tools, patents, and production facilities of the firm. A year later, IBM began to market the Model 01 electric typewriter.

TYPEBAR MACHINES

Most typebar electric machines have the various characters, numbers, and punctuation on individual bars which press against the typing ribbon when the typist depresses the keys. Every character, regardless of its width, is given the same amount of space on the paper. In other words, an "i" is given the same amount of space as a "w."

On the other hand, typewriters with proportional spacing have characters of varying widths. The width of a character is measured in units of space, generally from two to five units. Most characters on these machines measure three units, but letters such as "f, l, i, t, and j" are two units, and wide characters such as "w" and "m" receive more space.

Proportional space typewriters produce documents that look like they have been printed. However, the proportional typewriter requires more skill on the typist's part since making corrections may require that the typist replace an "i" which uses two units of space with a "w" which uses four units of space. Once the typist has learned how to use this type of machine, it is possible to produce professional looking correspondence.

Figure 4.3
Executive typewriter (Courtesy of IBM).

SINGLE-ELEMENT MACHINES

Another development in the standard electric typewriter is the single-element machine. Instead of a series of type bars, each with an individual character on it, the single-element machine uses a typing ball called a font. All the characters, numbers, and punctuation are on this single ball or element which revolves to the proper position as the typist depresses the keys. Once the element is in the proper position, the correct character is pressed against the typing ribbon, making an impression on the page. On most single-element machines, the typewriter carriage does not move. Instead, the element moves across the page. The typist can choose among different types of balls to vary type size and style (pica, elite, standard, or script).

The single-element machine most familiar to executive assistant students is the IBM Selectric®. However, in the last few years, other manufacturers, such as Facit, Royal, Adler, Olympia, Hermes, and Olivetti have also introduced single-element typewriters.

SELF-CORRECTING MACHINES

The self-correcting electric typewriter uses a reel of tape which either covers up or lifts off the mistake (depending upon the type of tape used). The correcting tape is activated by a special correcting key (see Figure 4.5). The typist uses the correcting key to backspace to the last incorrectly typed character and then restrikes that character to delete it either by covering it up or lifting it off the page. If more than one character is incorrectly typed, the typist keeps backspacing with the correcting key until all the incorrect characters have been deleted. The typist can then type in the correct character or characters. If carbon copies are being typed, the typist must correct them in the traditional way (erase and correct).

Figure 4.4
IBM Selectric® typewriter (Courtesy of IBM).

Figure 4.5
Special correcting key.

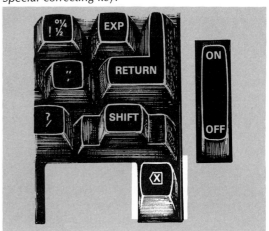

SPECIAL FEATURES

Every year typewriter manufacturers introduce machines with new and better features. Today, the standard office electric has a large number of useful features. The most important aspects of the keyboard are the number of keys, the shape and size of the keys, the distance from one key to the next, and the slope of the keyboard. The shape and size of the keys are important because they affect the speed and ease of the typing operation. For maximum typing speed, the shape of the top of the keys should be designed to accommodate the fingertips. They should also be the correct size since keys that are too large for the fingers often cause the typist to strike the key off center, which disturbs the typing rhythm. However, if the keys are too small, the typist may strike two keys at the same time.

The typist may also hit more than one key if the keys are too close together. On the other hand, if the keys are too far apart, the typist will have to stretch to reach them and this will slow her or him down. The keyboard should also be sloped at a comfortable angle so that the typist's fingers move in an arc with the wrist as the pivot point.

Almost every typewriter on the market has the traditional Q-W-E-R-T-Y arrangement of keys. Several years ago, however, a new keyboard configuration was introduced called the American Simplified Keyboard (ASK). This keyboard is said to be more efficient than the traditional key arrangement. It is based on methods analysis techniques and motion studies which determine the most commonly typed words. The proponents of ASK claim that 70 percent of the most commonly typed words can be typed on the home row. Since this would require less finger movements, it can, according to these studies, result in productivity increases of 30 percent or more. At the present time, this keyboard is not in common usage; but this may change in the future.

ELECTRONIC TYPEWRITERS

The electronic typewriter, also called the intelligent typewriter, is a mixture of the standard electric typewriter and sophisticated text-editing units (sometimes called word processors). The electronic typewriter has been projected to garner over 40 percent of the office typewriter market in the next few years. It is unique because it is usable by smaller organizations in a decentralized environment where larger, higher-priced offerings could not hope to gain a foothold.

The prices and capabilities of the electronic typewriters on the market cover a wide range; but their common base is their ease of operation, their compactness, and their ability to automate some of the repetitive manual functions of typing. Their general capabilities include automatic carrier return, error correction, underscore, and centering; electronic margins and tabs; format storage; line memory; decimal alignment; and phrase storage.

Figure 4.6
QYX® typewriter (Courtesy of Exxon Information Systems).

The electronic typewriter is the ideal alternative for the executive who is reluctant to give up his or her personal executive assistant and yet who needs faster, more efficient production of typed documents. The electronic typewriter provides a smooth transition between the old and the new in the advancing age of automation.

Some electronic typewriters are upgradable. It is possible to start with a basic electronic typewriter, and as you need new functions or as budgets allow for expansion of the system, you can add hardware and software by purchasing the necessary microprocessor chips, programs, and peripherals to upgrade the original machine.

Most users' perceptions of electronic typewriters are: (1) they simplify an executive assistant's typing tasks; (2) they save time; and (3) even though they sometimes cost more than a regular electric typewriter, they are worth the extra expense.

TEXT-EDITING TYPEWRITERS

Text-editing typewriters (also called word processing typewriters) evolved from automatic typewriters which were first introduced in the 1930s. Automatic typewriters typed the same document over and over by using a punched paper roller that was similar to the tapes used in player pianos. The holes in the tape instructed the typewriter to type certain characters.

In the 1950s the machines were enhanced with a punched paper tape that could be removed from the machine and stored. Still later, automatic typing machines could accept two punched tapes which meant that information could be merged. For instance, one tape could contain names and addresses, while the other tape stored a form letter. When the two tapes were merged, a person could have the machine produce form letters addressed to different people. However, these machines did have a number of drawbacks. The main one was that the paper tape could not be erased and updated. If changes in the text had to be made, a new tape had to be produced. Also, paper tapes could be torn.

This situation changed in 1964 when IBM introduced the Magnetic Tape Selectric Typewriter™ (MT/ST). The main advantage of magnetic tape over paper tape is that it can be recorded over in the same fashion as a tape recorder. With a tape recorder, the person records over the tape by talking over the old tape; on an editing typewriter, however, the typist records over the original characters by typing the new characters over them.

With this machine, and the other mag tape-editing typewriters introduced after it, the typist could type a document on the typewriter portion of the machine and see the characters print out on paper, the same as with a regular typewriter. However, if a mistake was made, the typist would just backspace to the incorrect character and type the correct character over it. The typist could also add and delete characters, words, lines, and paragraphs. This was possible because as the typist typed with the machine in the record mode, the keystrokes were recorded on the magnetic type. When the typist backspaced, the characters were erased. Then, as the correct characters were typed, these characters were recorded on the magnetic tape.

When the document was completed, the typist put the machine in the play mode, and the typewriter typed the document automatically "as keyed in" at a speed of 150 words per minute. After the letter was typed, the

Figure 4.7
IBM MT/ST (Courtesy of IBM).

Figure 4.8
Mag tape editing typewriter (Courtesy of Wang Laboratories Inc.).

magnetic tape could be stored and replayed at a later date. When there was no further need for the document, the tape could be reused for other documents.

Five years after the introduction of the magnetic tape-editing typewriter, the magnetic card machine was introduced. This editing typewriter operates on the same principle as the mag tape machine; however, instead of recording the keystrokes on magnetic tape, the unit records them on magnetic cards. Approximately one document page can fit on a mag card; and since many business letters are one page in length, the magnetic card machine became extremely popular. The cards were also easy to file and retrieve since they took up less room than an 8½ × 11-inch piece of paper.

The mag card machines were constantly being improved to make them easier to use and more productive. One dramatic improvement was the addition of communications capabilities. Communicating mag card machines could "talk" to one another through a telephone line or private wiring connection. The typist would insert a mag card, record a document, and then instruct the machine to send the document over regular telephone lines to another mag card machine with the communications feature. This is done by inserting the telephone receiver into a coupler on the communicating mag card machine which connected the originating machine to the tele-

Figure 4.9
IBM MC/ST (Courtesy of IBM).

phone wires, so that the information can be converted into signals that can then be sent and received by a similar machine at the other end.

The next major development in the text-editing typewriters was the introduction of machines with display screens. This was a big departure from the magnetic tape and card machines which used the regular Selectric™ typewriter for typing documents and printing out finished copies. With the tape and card machines, the keystrokes were printed by the typewriter on a piece of paper as the typist entered the information.

With display editing typewriters, the characters appear on the display screen as they are typed on the system's keyboard. Most of these screens are cathode ray tube (CRT) screens which look very much like television screens. Many of these video display terminals (VDT) show a full typewritten page; others show half a page or a few lines at a time. A few machines have displays which show only one line at a time—the line the typist is working on.

When the executive assistant makes a mistake while typing, he or she merely moves the cursor (a small lighted mark that moves around the screen to indicate the character that is being typed, deleted, or moved) to the

Figure 4.10
Visual display system, R-III (Courtesy of Burroughs Corporation).

incorrect character or characters and depresses the appropriate action key (insert, delete, or move) and then types the correct character or characters over the mistake. By using the cursor, the executive assistant can also underline portions of the text, move whole lines or paragraphs, change margins, and indent portions of the text.

The display text processing system has four main components: (1) the keyboard, which has the standard typewriter keys plus code and action keys that tell the machine what to do with the text; (2) the display screen, which is used instead of a piece of paper to type and edit the text; (3) the logic or "brain" of the system, which controls the text processor and houses the recording medium (usually a card, cassette, or diskette); and (4) the printer, which prints out the hard copy of the information recorded on the medium. Some printers used in display text processing systems type at speeds over 500 words per minute. Two of the latest types of printers are the ink jet printer and the laser beam printer; these two printers are nonimpact printers that print at speeds over 1,000 words per minute.

Display text processing systems may be standalone, shared logic, or shared resource. The standalone systems are completely self-sufficient and

Figure 4.11
Visual display system (Courtesy of Datapoint Corporation).

operate independently of any other systems. They are simply assembled and plugged into an appropriate electrical outlet.

Shared logic systems, on the other hand, are interdependent. One processor or brain is shared by two or more editing stations, which consist of

Figure 4.12
AMText 425, word processor (Courtesy of AM International).

Figure 4.13
IBM Office System 6 (Courtesy of IBM).

keyboard, display, and printer. In some cases, a printer is also shared by two or more keyboard/display stations. The number of input (keyboard) and output (printer) stations that can be used with one processor (intelligence or brain) will vary from one system to another. With very sophisticated

Figure 4.14
Lanier Shared Cluster System (Courtesy of Lanier).

systems, over a dozen input and output stations can be supported by one processor.

Shared resource word processors have their own intelligence (like stand-alone systems) but share some resources, such as files and printers, with other word processing machines in the system.

FUNCTIONS OF TEXT-EDITING TYPEWRITERS

Text-editing typewriters, no matter what kind they are, have four major functions: input, revision or editing, storage, and output.

During the input function, the typist keys in the original document using the machine's keyboard. As the operator types, the information appears either on a piece of paper (on a "blind" or nondisplay text editor) or on a video or display screen. The typist makes decisions regarding formatting and style. On some machines, once the margin is set, the machine moves to the next line automatically. This allows the typist to type at rough draft speeds without worrying about making end-of-line decisions or returning the carriage.

As the document is entered and corrections are made, the typist records the document on some type of magnetic medium for playout and future revisions.

The output function involves the production of the final copy of a document. The document is error-free (if it was typed in error-free) and is formatted according to the typist's specifications. On some text-editing systems, the output device is the same as the input device (a typewriter, usually a Selectric®). On other systems, there is a separate printer that allows the typist to begin typing the next document while the previous one is being typed by the printer. This is called simultaneous input and output.

Output devices print at various speeds. Most fall in the range of 150 to 540 words a minute, although computer printers, ink jet printers, and laser beam printers print out at much higher speeds because they are not limited by mechanical parts technology. The different output devices also have various type sizes and styles. Many have interchangeable typing and printing elements. Some output devices also justify the right margin so that the text looks as though it has been printed.

The revision function refers to changes that are made in the text after it has been entered and recorded. For example, when a letter has been changed by the executive, it is sent back for retyping. With a text-editing typewriter, only the changes have to be retyped, not the whole document. Once all the changes are made, the whole document can be typed out automatically by the system.

In the revision mode, copy can be deleted, inserted, changed, moved, and duplicated. The copy can be a letter, word, line, paragraph, or page. In addition, margins and tab settings can be changed, page numbers can be added, deleted, or changed, and information can be merged from two different media (two cards, tapes, diskettes).

There are four basic types of revisions that can be made: corrections, repetitive corrections, extensive editing, and format changes. Corrections are minor changes such as typographical errors. They usually involve only a word or two.

Repetitive corrections involve a change that has to be made throughout a document. For instance, there may be one word that appears 12 times in a particular document and has to be replaced in each case with another word. On some systems, the operator has to play through the document, finding each place where the word appears, and type the correct word in each place. Many text-editing typewriters have a feature called global search and replace. With this feature, the operator instructs the machine to find a particular word (or string of characters) wherever it appears in the document and replace it with a new word. The machine will then automatically search the entire document searching out that word and replacing it with the new word.

Some machines will automatically find the word each time it appears and then wait for the operator to indicate whether it should be replaced in each particular case. This is useful in applications where the operator wants to replace a particular word in most, but not all, of the places where it appears.

Editing changes involve extensive corrections, such as changing, deleting, or adding lines or paragraphs. It may also involve moving large blocks of copy on one page or from one page to another. Format changes are changes in the length of the line, in tab settings and alignment of columns, and in justification.

Every text-processing system has some way of storing documents for retrieval and revision at a later date. The typist's keystrokes must be stored on some kind of magnetic medium. The most commonly used storage media are mag cards, cassettes, and diskettes. Each has advantages and disadvantages for various applications, and each accommodates a different amount of text.

Magnetic cards store one to three typewritten pages (standard) $8\frac{1}{2} \times 11$-inch pages) and are adequate for standard business letters. They can be stored as easily as a piece of paper. Magnetic cassettes store from 25 to 125 typewritten pages depending upon the type of tape used. They are generally housed in special filing systems that are designed specifically for cassettes. A floppy diskette, which looks very much like a flexible 45 rpm record, may contain from 60 to 250 pages of text. Diskettes may be housed in special files, but they can also be stored in standard file cabinets. Very sophisticated word processing systems use hard disks as the storage media. These disks are large and expensive, and they can store thousands of pages of text.

Some text-editing systems are dual-media machines, employing two cards, cassettes, or diskettes. Other systems can accept two different media, such as a card and a cassette or a card and a diskette. Dual-media units permit the user to merge information from two different media to form one

Figure 4.15
Magnetic cards (Courtesy of BASF).

finished document. For example, addresses may be stored on a tape cassette while a form letter is stored on a mag card. When the card and cassette are put into the machine at the same time, the unit will merge the addresses and body of the letter to produce a series of personally addressed form letters.

Figure 4.16
Magnetic cassettes (Courtesy of BASF).

Figure 4.17
Floppy disks (Courtesy of National).

FEATURES OF TEXT-EDITING TYPEWRITERS

Today's text-editing typewriters provide executive assistants with a multitude of features to make their jobs easier. Some of the features commonly found on these typewriters are discussed below.

Display Screen Features. The display generally shows from one line to a full page of text. The number of characters that can fit on a horizontal line may also vary. The typewriter may feature vertical, horizontal, and page scrolling. Vertical scrolling is the ability of the system to move up and down through a page or more of text, one line at a time. Horizontal scrolling is the ability of the system to move horizontally along a line of text in order to access more characters than can be shown on the display screen at one time. Page scrolling allows the word processor to move backward and forward through the pages of a multipage document. Other features of the display are as follows:

Display highlighting either blinks or intensifies certain portions of the text to emphasize it. Underscored text may also appear on the screen.

Line justification permits the user to see on the screen how the justified text will look when it is printed out.

Prompts help the operator by displaying various actions on the screen, prompting the operator to take the next step.

In the **magnification mode,** characters are magnified on the screen larger than they will actually print out in order to make it easier for the typist to read the displayed text.

With **display reversal,** characters are displayed opposite the way they usually are. For instance, if, normally, white characters are displayed on a dark screen, with display reversal, dark characters will be displayed on a light screen.

Sub- and superscript display permits characters to be displayed above and/or below the line.

Editing and Operating Features. **Automatic carrier return** automatically returns the carriage to the next line when it reaches the last word that will fit on the line. This feature often is combined with **word wraparound.** Word wraparound automatically moves words to the next line when the right hand margin is reached and the word does not fit within it.

Forms mode displays various forms, such as invoices and bills, on the display screen; this allows the operator to fill in the appropriate spaces on the form. The machine moves automatically from one blank space to the next.

Automatic decimal tabulation permits the text editor to automatically align columns of figures on the decimal point. This allows the typist to type numbers without worrying about aligning the figures according to the decimal point.

Document assembly and merge refers to the capability of the system to assemble new documents by using portions of previously recorded documents.

Repagination automatically changes page numbers if copy is inserted into or deleted from a document, or if the user wants to change margins or page lengths.

File sort describes the ability of the system to do sorts on the various files, arranging them in numerical, alphabetical, or some other kind of order, such as ZIP code order in a list of addresses.

File selection allows the user to select various documents from the file based on certain criteria. For instance, the operator may want to find all employees who can type and have a degree from a junior or senior college. The system will search through the files and pull out all the names of people who fit in this category.

Footnote tie-in feature links a footnote with the copy to which it refers so that if the copy is moved to another page, the footnote is automatically moved with it.

Arithmetic capability is the ability of a text-editing typewriter to perform math functions, such as addition, subtraction, multiplication, and division.

The menu feature on a text-editing typewriter shows the typist what jobs are in the system. The typist can choose which jobs to work on first.

Message capability refers to the ability of the text editor to store messages electronically. When the user turns the system on, the messages appear on the screen.

A dictionary contains commonly used terms which can be retrieved when the operator types in one or two special characters. For example, a company's name and address might be retrieved by typing in two keystrokes, such as an ''n'' and ''a.''

Spelling verification dictionary checks the spelling of each word in a typed document against an internal dictionary and highlights misspelled words so that the operator can correct them.

Computer capability allows the text-editing system to be used to perform some data processing tasks.

Figure 4.18
Form feeder (Courtesy of Qume Corporation).

Figure 4.19
Twin sheet feeder (Courtesy of NEC Information Systems).

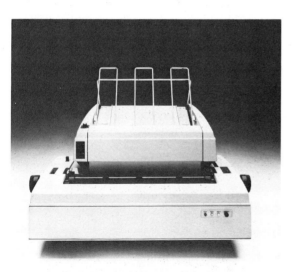

Printer Features. **Forms feeding device** inserts paper into the printer and advances it to the first copy line. It continuously feeds paper, forms, or envelopes into the printer. (Figures 4.18 and 4.19)

End-of-page stops the printer at the end of the page so a new page can be inserted by the operator.

Justification prints out a document with a right margin that is even or justified.

Bidirectional printers print both from left to right and from right to left across the page. This saves on unnecessary carriage returns and increases the productivity of the printer. Some printers check for the closest margin before deciding to print either left to right or right to left.

Queuing permits a number of documents to be lined up for printing in turn so that the operator can do other work.

Index creation prints out an index of documents that are stored on a particular medium.

COMPATIBILITY OF TEXT-EDITING TYPEWRITERS

Most text-editing typewriters are used to produce a printed copy of someone's thoughts; however, in some cases that printed copy is not the final result of the system. Many text-editing systems are compatible with phototypesetting equipment. In these applications, the medium (mag card, cassette, or diskette) is used to produce phototypeset copy. The operator merely keys in the codes that run the phototypesetter along with the text of the document. Then, the medium is put through a conversion process and run through the phototypesetter. In at least one instance, the diskette can be put directly into a compatible phototypesetter without going through a conversion process.

On the input side, text-editing equipment is compatible with OCR (optical character recognition) equipment. OCR has the ability to read written, typewritten, or other printed material directly from the source using a mechanical means. An optical page reader converts copy that has been typed on single element typewriters equipped with OCR elements into electronic signals that are suitable for entry into a text-editing system. In this way, the text editor can be used where it is most advantageous, in the revision stage, while standard single-element typewriters can be used as input stations when needed. (Figures 4.20 and 4.21)

SUPPLIES

Most typewriters use either an inked fabric ribbon or a film ribbon or both. The different types of ribbons are designed for various applications. Fabric ribbons can be reused so they are more economical than film ribbons which can be used only once. However, the quality of film ribbons produces sharper images. Fabric ribbons are ideal for routine typing of in-house doc-

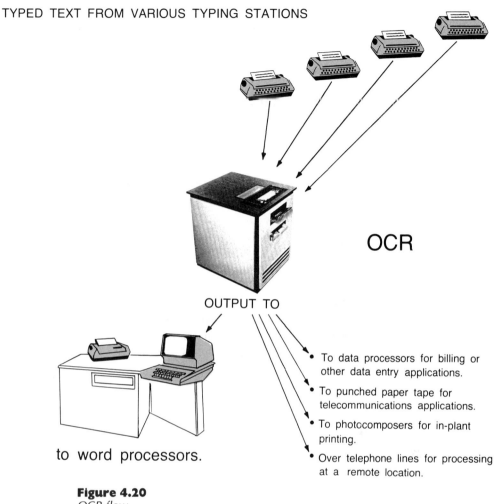

TYPED TEXT FROM VARIOUS TYPING STATIONS

OCR

OUTPUT TO

- To data processors for billing or other data entry applications.
- To punched paper tape for telecommunications applications.
- To photocomposers for in-plant printing.
- Over telephone lines for processing at a remote location.

to word processors.

Figure 4.20
OCR flow.

uments, memorandums, and forms. Film ribbons are most often used for documents sent outside the firm.

Ribbons in cartridges are used in most typewriters. These cartridges can be easily removed and replaced, without the mess associated with other types of ribbons. Since these ribbons are so easily replaced, the typist can switch ribbons according to the work being done. For instance, you may want to use different colored ribbons for different jobs.

Special purpose ribbons are also available. These include ribbons where the top and bottom are two colors (black and red, for example), ribbons with correction material on the bottom half, and ribbons for typing offset masters. Correctable film ribbons are becoming more popular.

Figure 4.21
OCR page reader (Courtesy of Compuscan, Inc.).

MAINTENANCE

When starting a new job, an executive assistant should always be familiar with the tools of the job. The most important of these is the typewriter. After learning about the capabilities of the particular machines you will be using, you should then learn how to take good care of those machines.

The most important step you can take is to keep the typewriter clean. This can be done by covering the typewriter at the end of the day to prevent dust from accumulating. You should also dust the typewriter at frequent intervals, using a brush to reach the hard-to-get places inside the machine. You should never use an eraser directly over the machine because the eraser crumbs may fall into the machine.

Cleaning the typebars or element is very important. This will prevent the characters from filling up with ink. Use a dry brush or a special cleaner frequently in order to produce crisp, clean copies. Type cleaners in sheet form can also be used. The sheet is inserted into the typewriter; the ribbon is set in the stencil position; and the typist strikes each character at least once. The chemical on the sheet picks up the dirt on the characters.

The typing platen or cylinder must also be cleaned periodically to prevent it from becoming shiny and losing its grip on the paper. In machines where the cylinder is removable, you can take it out and clean it with a cloth.

Equally important, be sure that the typewriter is serviced periodically by the manufacturer or dealer. This will ensure that the machine stays in good condition. If, however, you find that your typewriter is not working, quickly check the following procedures before you rush to call the repair department:

1. Be sure the electric cord is plugged into the outlet.
2. The "on" position of the motor control should be depressed.
3. Make certain that the ribbon position lever is not in stencil position and that the multiple copy control lever is appropriately set.
4. If the carrier will not move, turn the motor off for a few seconds and then turn it on. With the switch on, depress the margin release key or the tab key.

The printer is a separate component designed to produce quality documents at very high rates of speed. It is quiet and requires very little attention. However, the following cleaning service should be performed by the executive assistant to ensure maximum productivity. About once a week remove all paper fibers from inside the printer and clean the ink residue from the plastic card guide.

The printwheel will clog with ink and paper fiber over a period of time. Cleaning is indicated when printing quality decreases. You should never oil or lubricate the printer yourself. Call the service representative who will use the proper lubricants to ensure the best performance of your system.

TRAINING

If you are changing from a standard electric typewriter to a magnetic-media typewriter, learning to operate this new machine becomes more complicated. Because it has text-editing and memory storage capabilities, the new machine requires orientation and hands-on practice for you to become proficient.

Equipment manufacturers have organized training programs for executive assistants using the new equipment. A marketing support representative (MSR), a person employed by the manufacturer to train operators using the equipment, will provide training. Training sessions will usually be held at the branch office of the manufacturer or on the user's premises. Frequently, audio/visual programs are used to allow the executive assistant to learn about a machine at his or her own pace.

SUMMARY

The intelligent executive assistant has a curiosity that goes beyond the mechanical, repetitive tasks of operating a typewriter. Converting from a standard typewriting system to an automated typing system is a fascinating and drastic change. It challenges the executive assistant to understand the internal workings of the new system—the media, recording, playback, memory, and storage capabilities.

1. The typewriter has come a long way since the first machines were marketed in the nineteenth century; and these improvements are not at an end.
2. In recent years we have seen the introduction of single-element typewriters and self-correcting machines.
3. Text-editing typewriters were developed to relieve executive assistants of much of the work involved in typing, revising, and retyping documents.
4. Today's text-editing equipment includes magnetic card and tape cassette standalone units; card, cassette, and diskette standalone display units; and shared logic and shared resource systems.
5. Text-editing typewriters have four major functions: input, output, revision or editing, and storage. Each of these functions is handled through a variety of features and options that vary from one system to another.
6. Some text editors are compatible with other text-editing systems, and/or computers, and phototypesetters.
7. On the input side, single-element typewriters equipped with OCR devices can be used to input data into a text-processing machine.
8. You have a responsibility to learn everything possible about the typewriter you work with and to keep it in top condition.

CHAPTER RECALL
EXERCISES

1. Trace the historical development of the typewriter.
2. What effect did the typewriter have on the role of women in business?
3. What kinds of typewriters are used in today's offices?
4. What are some of the special functions available on electric typewriters?
5. How should executive assistants care for their typewriters?
6. Name some of the unique features found on electronic typewriters?
7. Name and describe two types of ribbons used on typewriters?
8. How did text-editing equipment evolve?
9. What is the purpose of text-editing typewriters?
10. What are the various types of text editors available?
11. What are the magnetic media available for use?
12. What is the difference between a nondisplay and a display text editor?
13. What is the difference between standalone and shared logic systems?
14. What are the four functions of text-editing typewriters? Describe each.
15. Discuss the various features available on today's text-editing typewriters.
16. What is a communicating text processor?
17. What does OCR mean? What does OCR have to do with a text editor?

PROBLEMS AND APPLICATIONS

1. Assume that you will be giving a report to high school students about some of the features of your correcting Selectric® typewriter. Choose five features of the typewriter and write a description of them.

2. You were just promoted to be the executive assistant to a new department that is being formed in your company. The new department, the Research Department, will have three persons whose primary job responsibilities include writing research proposals. These research proposals and reports will contain many scientific notations. You are asked to recommend the purchase of a typewriter for this new department. The only limitation is that the typewriter must cost less than $7000. What procedure should you follow to make this recommendation? What questions would you ask about the work done in this new department?

3. Choose a company that manufactures an electronic or text-editing typewriter with which you are not familiar. Find out as much as you can about this piece of equipment (features, cost, specifications, dimensions, service contract, training needed). Write a memorandum report about this piece of equipment. Give an oral report to the class about your findings.

4. Write a research report on one of the following topics. Limit the report to no more than five pages (double-spaced). Follow the proper report writing principles.
   a. American Simplified Keyboard
   b. Entrance of Women into the Office
   c. History of the Typewriter

5. Assume that your office will be purchasing new typewriters, and you are responsible for making the final recommendation. Design a matrix or an evaluation form to use to rate the specific kinds of typewriters you research and see demonstrated.

LANGUAGE SKILLS DEVELOPMENT

1. a. Learn to spell the following words:

   accessible   circuit
   accommodate   dependent
   business   familiar
   calendar   spontaneity

   b. Using the word division rules, divide each word.

2. Consult your dictionary to define the following words and use each word correctly in a sentence.
   a. formally, formerly b. later, latter c. device, devise

3. Proofread and correct the following paragraph:

   On the eve of the County National Banks opening it's new head quarters down town 2 groups charged that they had not been meeting the credit needs of the community. The two comunity groups refuced to sent representatives to a meeting with officals of the Bank. A public meeting is planed for Wednesday June 4th.

4. Punctuate and correct the following sentences:
   a. So far this equipment has performed satisfactorily.
   b. Group insurance is often paid for at least in part by your employer.
   c. Medical expenses for example can ruin a family's budget.
   d. Keep the list in an accessible place and put a copy in your safe deposit box.
   e. Word of mouth reputation is probably the best indication of an items worth.
   f. Not only will you escape the installment costs you'll also earn interest on your money.
   g. When you shop for sunglasses find out how much light the lenses transmit.
   h. Metal frames should be light plastic frames should have metal rods.
   i. The part you need to make your project work is a wing bolt but you don't have one of the correct size.
   j. Cover the grate with paper or foil place the object in the center and turn the grate with one hand.

HUMAN RELATIONS INCIDENTS

1. You are executive assistant to Dave Brennen, the supervisor of office services. Mr. Brennen has been exploring the possibility of replacing some older typewriters with electronic typewriters which have a limited amount of text-editing ability. This equipment replacement will not affect anyone's job and will require only a limited amount of training to learn how to use the new equipment. While you were in the lounge this morning, you heard two of the other executive assistants talking about this new change (which was supposedly confidential). The executive assistants had misinformation about the projected change and were passing on their own fears and mistrust of the new equipment. How should you handle this situation? Should you ignore the situation, explain the facts to them, or talk to your supervisor?

2. Barbara is a rank-conscious person. She turns her manners and charm on and off like a faucet, depending on the status of the person with whom she is dealing. She is pleasant only to someone on a higher level. Since you have to work very closely with her, how can you cope with this type of person?

WORD PROCESSING

The introduction of the typewriter in the 1800s proved to be more than just a fad. It disrupted the way companies did business: In fact, the typewriter revolutionized the office by providing a fast, practical way to communicate with large numbers of people.

The initial reaction to word processing was not unlike the reception given the first typewriter. Company officials questioned the purpose of word processing. Comments such as "It will disrupt our office;" or "It will replace our executive assistants" were heard in offices.

Many people were scared off by the name "word processing." They visualized a room filled with robot-like executive assistants working at strange-looking machines. This chapter will give you an overview of word processing—what it is and how it can be used. At the end of this chapter you should be able to:

1. Define word processing. ☐ 2. Describe the four components of word processing. ☐ 3. Determine the place word processing has in the electronic office.

CHAPTER
5

DEFINITION OF WORD PROCESSING

Word processing is a very simple concept with the same goal as every other office machine or procedure—to help a business run more efficiently and economically. It achieves this goal by automating part of the process involved in getting ideas on paper in an acceptable format.

When word processing first appeared on the business scene, it did not receive rave reviews: In fact, it got very little attention of any kind at first. The idea grew slowly, evolving from the automatic typewriters that were used to type form letters to the MT/ST introduced in 1964 by IBM. The MT/ST was the first word processor or text-editing typewriter. Since that time, the market has grown tremendously as more and more business firms realized the importance of word processing or text-editing typewriters. The reason for the growth in the popularity of text-editing typewriters in the last few years is simple; it is mainly a matter of economics.

The cost of a business letter keeps rising, mainly because the salaries and fringe benefits paid to executives and executive assistants keep rising. (See Table 5-1.) Since constantly rising salaries seem to be a way of life in American business, the only alternative way of keeping costs down is to make people more productive so that they can produce more work in the same amount of time. This enables companies to get more work for their money and reduces the need to hire additional personnel as frequently.

Figure 5.1
MT/ST (Courtesy of IBM).

TABLE 5-1
COSTS OF BUSINESS LETTERS, 1930–1980

1930	$ .30	1974	$3.41
1935	$ .52	1975	$3.79
1940	$ .72	1976	$4.17
1953	$1.17	1977	$4.47
1960	$1.83	1978	$4.77
1964	$2.32	1979	$5.59
1968	$2.54	1980	$6.07
1973	$3.31		

Source: Dartnell.

COMPONENTS OF WORD PROCESSING

While word processing equipment, such as dictation/transcription machines and text-editing typewriters, plays an integral part in any word processing operation, the concept involves much more than machines. Word processing requires a combination of four elements: people, procedures, equipment, and the work environment.

PEOPLE

Word processing could not work without people. Those who think that it will result in the eventual obsolescence of people are mistaken. Machines cannot think, no matter how complex or advanced they may be; machines do what people tell them to do. Of course, word processing does automate many routine typing functions, which frees the executive assistant for more creative thinking work.

Just as the scribes of the last century had to be retrained to use a typewriter, so today's executive assistant has to be trained to use the new equipment and procedures involved in word processing. Word processing does change the executive assistant's job, but it does not eliminate it. In fact, in many cases the executive assistant's job is enriched since much of the routine and repetitious work is performed by machines, and extensive typing projects can be delegated to correspondence specialists.

Homemakers do not feel threatened by labor-saving devices such as dishwashers and vacuum cleaners. They know they are not going to be replaced by a machine because their main skills are organizational. Homemakers keep the home running; and if a machine can help them accomplish that goal quicker and easier, they are all for it. Executive assistants, on the other hand, often look upon labor-saving devices such as the text-editing typewriter or dictation/transcription equipment as threats to their jobs. Executive assistants should learn to welcome labor-saving devices which free them for more productive and creative work.

Word processing does make changes in the executive assistant's function.

Figure 5.2
IBM Displaywriter System (Courtesy of IBM).

In fact, many changes have already taken place, and more are sure to come in the future. The degree of change, however, varies from one company to another. Some companies still have the traditional one-to-one executive/executive assistant arrangement. However, more firms realize that this is an inefficient and expensive method of operation.

Having a private executive assistant gives an executive status in the same way a private office does. However, many of today's executives are realizing that status does not mean very much if you cannot get your work done correctly and on time. So, a change in priorities is occurring. Business people are choosing efficiency and practicality over executive trappings that appeal mainly to the ego.

The disadvantages of the private executive assistant arrangement are becoming obvious. Consider this hypothetical office situation. One executive assistant may be loaded down with work, while another one is reading a book because the boss is out of town. One executive may be typing because the executive assistant is out sick. Down the hall, the vice-president's executive assistant is letting work pile up because of a dozen two-page letters that need to be typed. The letters are all the same, except for the names and addresses; but the vice-president insists that the letters be individually typed to give them the required personal touch. The vice-president's executive assistant should be doing research for a marketing report, but the vice-president will have to do the research because the assistant will be tied up all day with the letters.

What is wrong with this office? In short, there is a very inefficient and nonproductive use of everyone's time. What is needed is a better distribution of the workload, based on needs and not status.

Businesses that convert to word processing modify the one-to-one relationship between the executive and the executive assistant. Some divide the functions of an executive assistant into two distinct areas: correspondence (typing functions) and administrative (nontyping functions). Other companies do not have such a sharp division of functions and allow some overlap.

Correspondence Assistant. The correspondence assistant works in a word processing center or work group. A center is generally a large area that services several departments or possibly the whole company. A work group usually is dedicated to a particular department or a few small departments. In either arrangement, the correspondence assistant reports to the supervisor of the center or group, not to an individual executive. The correspondence assistant may do typing and transcription work for a number of people or may deal exclusively with a few individuals. This, again, depends on the individual company.

In general, the correspondence assistant works with two primary pieces of equipment: a transcribing machine and a text-editing typewriter. When an executive has work to be typed, it is either written in longhand and sent to the center or dictated into a machine. The correspondence assistant then transcribes the dictation by typing at rough draft speed on a text-editing typewriter. Mistakes are easily corrected; the correspondence assistant merely backspaces to the error and types the correct character over it. Because of this ease of correction, the assistant does not have to worry about mistakes and can type at much faster speeds.

When the document is completely transcribed, the assistant proofreads it to check for misspellings, errors, and incorrect punctuation. When the document is perfect, the assistant directs the machine to print the letter out automatically. This is done at very high speeds and does not require the correspondence assistant's help. In fact, on many editing typewriters, the assistant can begin working on the next document while the typewriter's printer is typing out the previous document. This enables the correspondence assistant to produce a lot more work in the same amount of time, and all documents are free of erasures.

In many companies, correspondence assistants are also responsible for seeing that a letter is polished. They may contact the author to verify or clarify certain points or to suggest changes which would improve the letter. Therefore, the correspondence assistants must be more than good typists and transcribers. They need to know how to interface with people effectively. They must be good proofreaders and be able to detect misspellings and incorrect grammar and punctuation. Also, correspondence assistants should know how to format letters and other documents since appearance is important. They should work well with machines and enjoy seeing a project through to completion.

Good correspondence assistants will find word processing a rewarding career. First, salaries for assistants who know how to operate the more popular types of editing typewriters are constantly rising, and correspondence assistants can command good salaries. They will also find it easy to change jobs since companies are looking for trained word processing operators. In addition, there are part-time and free-lance opportunities for word processing correspondence work.

Also, since the work of a correspondence assistant is easily measured (in words or lines completed each day or week), the assistant can rise on his or her own merits. With a traditional executive and executive assistant arrangement, the assistant often is tied to the executive's success, or lack of success. Correspondence assistants, however, get promotions and raises based solely on their work performance.

Where can the correspondence assistant go in the organization? You can become the supervisor or manager of the word processing center or work group. The word processing supervisor or manager hires and fires, monitors workflow, measures the assistants' work performance, buys equipment and supplies, controls the budget, and attends management meetings. You have a chance to be a manager with a salary to match the job title. In addition, there are related lateral job opportunities in data processing, graphics, and telecommunications.

Administrative Assistant. With the correspondence assistant in a word processing center or work group, that leaves a vacuum in the executive support area. The executive still needs administrative support, even though the typing functions are being taken care of by the correspondence assistants. In a word processing setup, these duties are handled by the administrative assistants.

Basically, administrative assistants perform all nontyping functions, including handling the mail and phone, arranging travel and meetings, filing, dictating letters, doing research, and performing other administrative support duties for the executive. They may also handle small typing jobs such as addressing envelopes or labels or doing confidential typing. People who become administrative assistants should be good at handling details, should like dealing with people, and should be well organized. The administrative assistant acts as a right hand to the executive, relieving her or him of some jobs and responsibilities. Administrative assistants have the time for this since they have been relieved of most typing jobs. In fact, they can use the word processing center for some of their own correspondence.

Administrative assistants also have career options. As they assume some of the executive's tasks, they learn how a business operates and how an executive handles job tasks. This could eventually lead to a job at a middle management level. It could also lead to a supervisory job where the administrative assistant not only serves as an assistant to the executive or to several executives but supervises a number of junior administrative assistants as well.

In most companies, the jobs of correspondence and administrative assistants are equal in status and pay. Of course, once a person is hired for either position, the raises will vary according to the individual's ability. It is important to realize that both these positions are essential to the efficient operation of the company; neither is more important than the other. In fact, one could not exist without the other.

The separation of typing and nontyping functions accomplishes specialization. It allows people who are good typists and transcribers to dedicate themselves to that function. In the same way, people who are good at handling a number of administrative details in an efficient manner can specialize in that area without having to worry about the typing function.

Word processing gives executive assistants an alternative to the traditional role. It permits them to make a choice, deciding on the job function that they enjoy and do well. It also provides some career paths independent of the success of the executive. And since both the correspondence and administrative assistants usually provide services for more than one executive, they get the chance to interact with a number of people.

Of course, every company is different and handles the word processing function in a unique way; but the basic patterns remain the same. Word processing changes the executive assistant's function. It may mean a division of the various typing and nontyping tasks, or it may just mean that you are given a transcribing machine and an editing typewriter to help you handle the typing work more efficiently. But, no matter how a firm handles the division of labor, the executive assistant is still the most important element in the word processing environment. Editing typewriters do type out the finished document, but only after the executive assistant has keyboarded (typed and recorded the keystrokes on some type of magnetic card, tape, or disk) the information. Without someone to operate it, the text-editing typewriter is useless.

PROCEDURES

People and equipment are obviously essential elements in any word processing system. Another not so obvious, but important, element is the area of procedures. When a business operation changes, it is also necessary to change its procedures. It is no different with word processing.

If a firm has a center that serves the correspondence needs of the entire company, it must set up procedures for getting copy and dictation to and from the center. Questions that need to be asked include: Will we use the mail distribution system or have separate messengers dedicated to the word processing center? If cassettes or magnetic belts are used for dictation, how will they be logged in and out of the center? How will the center's supervisor distribute the work and keep track of the flow of traffic? How will the supervisor measure the productivity of the correspondence assistants? These are just a few procedures that have to be set up to handle a word processing center.

Without procedures for receiving dictation and delivering typed copy, there would be chaos. Without some way to measure the flow of traffic in and out of the center, as well as the productivity of the correspondence assistants, the center's supervisor would be at a loss when it came time to hire additional people or to promote some of the assistants. Without measurement procedures the supervisor would not be able to justify expenditures or guarantee a certain number of hours turnaround.

This is extremely important because an improperly run center will not be able to produce work in a reasonable period of time. And if people have to wait two days to get a letter back from the word processing center, they are just not going to use it. They will go back to their old way of doing things. Therefore, procedures for running a center are necessary if that center is to provide fast, efficient service to end users.

Procedures for the administrative assistants need not be as strict as those for the center because these procedures do not involve the whole company, only the assistant and the one or more people the assistant works with. Therefore, there is more room for variety. A word processing center that services an entire company must have one set of rules for everyone, but administrative assistants can work out a set of procedures based on their needs and the desires of the executives they serve.

This is fairly simple when the assistant is working for only one person. However, in a word processing environment, the administrative assistant may work for two or more people. This means that the assistant must set up procedures that are satisfactory to everyone involved. For example, the assistant and the executives must decide how the mail should be handled. Is it a top priority item or can it wait until more pressing work is completed? Should the assistant go through the mail for important items as soon as it comes in and distribute them immediately, leaving the rest of the mail for a later time? All these details must be decided so the assistant has a clear idea of the procedures to follow and the priorities that are acceptable to the executives.

Many companies do not leave procedures to chance or to the whims of the employees. They set up standard procedures and often create one or more manuals to explain these procedures in detail. A manual might include such items as types of work accepted by the center (longhand, typewritten drafts, dictation); procedures for getting work to and from the center; average turnaround time; what to do about priority work; and how to request reproduction and distribution of copies.

The procedures manual may also include a chapter on how to dictate, an art that is becoming essential for both executives and administrative assistants. Proofreading and proofreader's marks may also be included in another chapter. The correct way to fill out the request forms needed to have work done by the center may be explained in detail. The role of the administrative assistant may be discussed in general terms.

In addition to this manual, some companies will offer classes for both the executive and the executive assistant. These classes will explain the concept of word processing and will elaborate on the topics covered by the manual. Most will have question-and-answer sessions to clear up any topics that are not perfectly understood.

Firms interested in word processing want it to work, but it will work only if all the elements are included. Procedures provide the groundwork for an efficient operation. They will vary from company to company, but the goal is the same—to ensure an efficient, cost-justifiable operation.

Good executive assistants learn and use their company's procedures. In that way, they will be doing their part to ensure the success of the word processing operation in particular and the company in general.

EQUIPMENT

The third element, equipment, was discussed in Chapter 4.

WORK ENVIRONMENT

The fourth element involved in a word processing arrangement is the work area or environment. The administrative assistant and the executive assistant, who handles both nontyping and typing functions (with the help of dictation/transcription equipment and an editing typewriter), may be situated in a traditional office environment. Generally, this means the executive assistant is located in an area just outside the executive's office. In the case of an administrative assistant who works for more than one person, he or she will generally be located in an area that is convenient for all the executives. This type of assistant will often have a standard desk, one or more file cabinets, and possibly a bookcase or additional work surface.

The correspondence assistant, on the other hand, is usually located in the center of an open office environment. The open office environment is discussed in more detail in a later chapter, but its main advantages when used in a word processing center will be covered here.

Of course, the administrative assistant may be located in an open office environment, too. In fact, many companies are converting all but top executives' offices to this type of arrangement; but the characteristics of the open office make it especially beneficial for use in a word processing center.

First, a center has to accommodate a number of people and machines in an area that may not be spacious. Yet, because of the noise of the machines and the need of the correspondence assistants to be able to concentrate on transcribing tapes, there has to be some kind of barrier to keep the noise level down to an acceptable level. When a firm has a number of typewriters and printers operating simultaneously, it can become almost impossible to work unless steps are taken to lessen the noise in some way.

The use of modular work stations, which incorporate acoustical screens, is a very effective noise absorber. These acoustical screens absorb much of the noise made by both people and machines, rather than bouncing it back the way metal surfaces do. In a noisy area where intense concentration is

Figure 5.3
Word processing work station (Courtesy of Westinghouse Electric Corporation).

needed, acoustical screens can mean the difference between productive assistants and assistants who cannot concentrate because of the noise.

Another way to reduce noise is to add on acoustical covers to machines. Some firms will put carpeting on both the floor and the walls to reduce noise even further. Other firms play soft music in the background or use "white noise" (a system that makes a humming sound) to diffuse machine noise.

Aside from reducing noise, which may be the greatest benefit modular work stations offer to the word processing center, these work stations provide enough room to work in without using a lot of space. This is accomplished by hanging components such as work surfaces, files, and shelves on the screens rather than on the floor. Since everything is hanging on screens, less floor space is needed, yet the assistant still has the same amount of working and walking space.

The modular work station does something else for the executive assistant. In addition to noise, the assistant must also contend with visual distractions. Every time someone walks past your work area, whether it is to deliver a tape to be transcribed, to ask a question, or to hand in a finished document, you are momentarily distracted from your task. These minutes can add up during a day and can make quite a difference in your output. This is critical in a word processing environment where productivity is the goal and the number of lines you produce is constantly measured and used as a guide in determining raises and promotions.

Because the correspondence assistant spends most of the day in the word processing center, most firms go to great lengths to make the center a pleasant place to work. Modular work stations are quiet, private, and attractive. Each work station is almost like a private office and gives the assistant a sense of having his or her own territory.

These work stations come in a variety of colors and designs or graphics to warm up and brighten the environment. There may also be live plants and music to add to the attractiveness of the environment. Some work

Figure 5.4
Compatibility between furniture and equipment (Courtesy of Steelcase, Inc.).

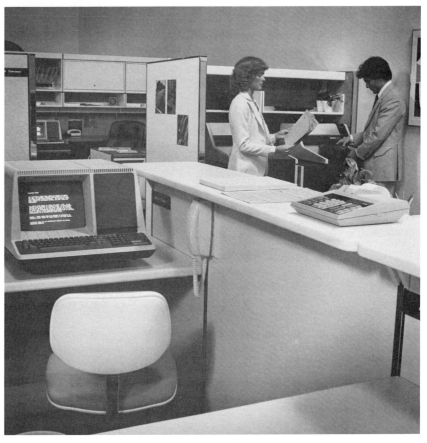

stations also include task and ambient lighting (a form of lighting that provides enough light to perform a job without overlighting the environment, a situation that results in glare and can cause headaches).

Special attention is also given to the correspondence assistant's chair. Since the assistant spends so much time sitting, firms are realizing the importance of good, comfortable seating. The chairs are designed to provide proper back support, which helps to eliminate the backache that frequently plagues typists.

WORD PROCESSING IN THE ELECTRONIC OFFICE

Word processing is one part of a much wider and more encompassing concept known as the electronic office, which includes data processing, electronic mail, micrographics, reprographics, and records management, as well as word processing. Word processing is the first step in the direction of the electronic office. Word processing automates much of the routine typing work performed by secretaries, but in the electronic office, the routine work performed by executives will also be automated.

The goal of word processing is to increase the productivity of the executive assistant. It makes even more sense to increase the productivity of the high-priced executive, but this is not as easy to do. However, some major companies are already starting in this direction. For example, there is an experimental program called the Electronic Office Project that is designed to automate the work of executives as well as executive assistants. Both executives and executive assistants work with specially designed work station systems that have cathode ray tube (CRT) displays. The executive can use the system to send messages electronically to other people who have the system, to call up on the screen any messages that have come in, to access files on a computer which may be located many miles away, and to find out what the daily schedule is (an electronic calendar). The executive's and executive assistant's systems are tied together so they can communicate with one another and have access to the other's files.

Of course, not every company will have a system like this; but many will have one that is similar to this type of system. Even this system will change over the years as new technology is introduced and added to the system, but the idea behind the system will not change. No matter what form the system takes, the goal will remain the same—to increase the productivity of the office worker, whether that worker is an executive or an executive assistant.

Today, the electronic office is in its infancy. It is growing every year as new technology is introduced and as the constantly-rising salaries of office workers make some kind of labor-saving device a financial necessity.

Word processing is here today, however. It is not yet in every office, but

Figure 5.5
The Office Automation System from Prime Computer combines the features of word processing, electronic mail, filing and retrieving information, and management communications. (Courtesy of Prime Computer Inc.)

it is making great strides. The smart executive assistant will try to figure out how to take advantage of word processing to make it work to produce higher salaries, job enrichment, and career paths. The main point to remember is that word processing is not the enemy; it is merely a weapon in the war on inefficiency.

SUMMARY

Word processing is more than a fad or a passing fancy. It is a practical concept to improve the productivity of executive assistants, making their time more valuable and saving the company money. The goal of word processing is to help a business run more efficiently and economically. It achieves this goal by automating part of the process involved in getting ideas on paper in an acceptable format.

1. Word processing combines four elements: people, equipment, proce-dures, and work environment.
2. Word processing cannot work without people—people to run the ma-

chines and tell them what to do, people to set up the necessary procedures, and people to provide the proper work environment.

3. In a word processing environment, the executive assistant function is changed, but it is not eliminated.

4. The executive assistant position is generally divided into the correspondence or typing area and the administrative or nontyping area. In some companies there is not this sharp definition of job functions.

5. Administrative assistants perform all nontyping functions. Correspondence assistants do typing and transcription work.

6. Procedures for running a word processing center are necessary if that center is to be successful.

7. Most companies develop procedures manuals to be used in a word processing center to make sure that standard procedures are followed.

8. Correspondence assistants are usually located in an open office environment.

9. Modular work stations are quiet, private, and attractive.

CHAPTER RECALL EXERCISES

1. What is word processing and what is its goal?
2. What four elements are necessary in a good word processing system?
3. How does word processing affect the executive assistant function?
4. What equipment is used in a word processing environment?
5. Why is a change in procedures necessary when a firm begins using word processing?
6. How does a word processing environment differ from a traditional work area?
7. What is the electronic office? How does word processing fit into this concept?
8. Should the executive assistant consider word processing as friend or foe? Why?
9. What can an executive assistant do to take advantage of the word processing movement?

PROBLEMS AND APPLICATIONS

1. Play the devil's advocate and list some of the disadvantages of word processing.

2. Assume you are developing the procedures manual for the word processing center. Write the section of the manual that will go at the beginning on the rationale behind the word processing center.

3. a. Go to your school library and prepare an annotated bibliography of the books found on word processing.

b. Make an alphabetical listing of the word processing periodicals to which your school library subscribes.

4. Research the professional organization IWP (International Information/Word Processing). Determine the goals of the organization, the membership requirements, the cost of membership, the benefits associated with membership, and the location of the local chapter of IWP.

5. Equipment is more important in a word processing environment than people. Defend or dispute this statement.

6. Find out the following information:
a. Cost of a business letter today.
b. Average salaries of correspondence assistants and administrative assistants.

7. Consult the classified ads in your local paper to determine what jobs are available for working in a word processing center. Make a list of the job requirements for these jobs.

8. Find a definition of "Ergonomics." Write a paragraph which describes how ergonomics is related to the office.

LANGUAGE SKILLS DEVELOPMENT

1. Consult the dictionary for meanings for the following words. Write a summary of each definition.
discrete
empirical
transient

2. Proofread and edit the following letter. Type a corrected copy.

June 22nd, 19—

Mildred Pelman, Claims Adjustor
Universal Insurance Co.
8888 Heath Drive
Cleveland, Ohio, 44111

Dear Madam,

Yesterday I recieved your letter dated June 2nd. Since it is now June 22 I wonder how eficient you company is.

As you told me to do, I had my car aprasied by 3 people and I have enclosed the three prices $784.00, $687.00 and $650.00.

I await your decision eoncerning my next step and remaine
Yours Truely

---

3. Choose the correct usage of numbers in the following sentences.
   a. The (100-character, one hundred-character) line can be scanned in (1 second, one second).
   b. This guide is now available to administrators for the low price of ($18, $18.00, eighteen dollars).
   c. The display was viewed by over (1 million, 1,000,000) people during the past (3, three) years.
   d. School begins a little later than usual this year—on (September 12th, September 12).
   e. The demonstration of the new equipment will start at (2 p.m., 2:00 p.m., two p.m.).
   f. We offer an ordering system with a (36-hour, thirty-six hour) turnaround time for shipping.
   g. We have been meeting the equipment needs of offices for over (10, ten) years.
   h. To update the file, please order 150 (3 × 5, three by five) sets.
   i. (12, Twelve) copiers are now within the price range of our company.
   j. In (10 to 15, ten to fifteen) years every person can afford to own a home computer.

HUMAN RELATIONS INCIDENTS

1. You are a correspondence assistant in a small word processing center in which two other persons work. You work in a bullpen environment where there are no walls or screens to separate the work stations. All the desks in the room are facing the door. Every time someone brings work into the center, all three operators stop their work for a few seconds to check out who entered the center. Many times the visitors will stop and chat for a few minutes. The work production is suffering because of all these disturbances. How can you discourage visitors from stopping to chat when they come into the word processing center. How can you arrange your work area to help discourage visitors from disturbing your work?

2. You have been working as private executive assistant to Paula Spring, vice-president, for about eight months. You were so pleased to finally make it up to executive row; you have your own private office and some exciting new responsibilities and privileges in your new job. This morning Ms. Spring came into your office in a very agitated mood and told you that she had just learned that the company is going to install a word processing center and that everyone from the vice-president on down will be using the center to have work completed. She also told you that you will have a

choice of being a correspondence assistant or administrative assistant. You like your present job; even though you know very little about word processing, you decide that you will leave the company before you ever go back to working in a "typing pool" again. What should you do? What are your options? Could Ms. Spring have handled the situation better? What could she have done?

TYPING TECHNIQUES

How many times have you eaten in a restaurant and had a discourteous waiter or waitress spoil your meal? Or, have you ever had a disrespectful or indifferent salesperson dissuade you from a purchase? These are unfavorable first impressions. Whether they occur in restaurants, retail stores, or business offices, they can make or break a business organization's reputation and good will. An organization's first contact with the public—a courteous greeting, a well-groomed sales representative, or an attractive letter—can go a long way toward creating a favorable first impression.

Perfect letters are essential for all companies. A perfect letter results when you take the time and effort to type a well-balanced letter with clean, even type, and which is free of smudges and fingerprints. Such a letter will encourage the recipient to read the letter in a positive frame of mind. A letter with typographical errors or smudges may fail to command the attention it deserves. Your responsibility as an executive assistant not only involves typing the letter correctly in the first place but making sure it is absolutely mailable (perfect) in every aspect.

At the end of this chapter you should be able to:

1. Describe the techniques for typing a professional document. ☐ 2. Know the steps in making carbon copies. ☐ 3. Be able to make professional corrections not only on the original copies but on the carbon copies. ☐ 4. List the features that make text-editing typewriters unique in making the corrections and doing editing. ☐ 5. List the steps involved in performing special typing applications, such as drawing lines on the typewriter and underscoring backwards.

CHAPTER
6

TECHNIQUES FOR PROFESSIONAL TYPING

The executive assistant should develop high personal standards and proofread each document with a keen and critical eye. Here are some points to consider when completing a typewritten document.

1. The side and bottom margins should be well balanced.
2. The placement of the letter parts should be consistent with the company style manual.
3. Corrections should be neat and inconspicuous.
4. The document should be clean; there should be no smudges.
5. The type should be even and clean.

Some of the techniques a professional executive assistant should adopt to develop mailable copy are given below.

EXPECT A PERFECT JOB

Don't anticipate making mistakes. If you expect to do perfect work, you will usually achieve it. If you approach every job with this positive attitude, you will reduce your error rate considerably. A positive mind set will perpetuate high-level performance unconsciously.

KEEP A NEAT WORK STATION

Although this phase of executive assistant performance was discussed in detail in an earlier chapter, it is important to mention this factor as a means to help produce perfect typing. Keep your desk-top clear; put away everything except the one item on which you are working and the materials needed at that time. This will keep you from being distracted.

PROOFREAD WITH CARE

Don't be in a rush to send your letter or other projects out. Doublecheck everything before you remove it from the typewriter. In fact, it might be a good idea to have a second person proofread important documents, reports, or letters. Someone who has not worked on a project is more likely to see errors than the person closely involved with it.

CORRECT ERRORS PROFESSIONALLY

Aiming for perfection will certainly reduce the number of errors; but since no one is perfect, you will still make occasional mistakes. When that happens, don't panic. First, correct the error, using an appropriate technique; then analyze how you can avoid making a similar error in the future.

GET INSTRUCTIONS RIGHT

One of the best ways to avoid mistakes is to get instructions right the first time you hear them. It is not always easy, but here are some guidelines that may help you.

1. *Listen carefully.* Communication is a two-way street. Listening is an important part of communicating. Do not daydream or become sidetracked when listening to instructions. Have a clear mind and do not try to think about other thoughts while listening to instructions. Self-consciousness and preoccupation with other thoughts interfere with your concentration.
2. *Take notes if it helps you concentrate.* There are many people who feel more secure when they write instructions on paper. If the instructions are complicated, for instance, it may be a good idea to take notes. Good notes will ensure that you understand the instructions and will build your own confidence.
3. *Ask if you are not sure.* Don't be shy about asking questions if you are not sure about instructions. It is far better to ask before you start a project than after the project is complete. If there is any doubt at all in your mind, check with your boss to be sure you have everything right.

KNOW YOUR TYPEWRITER

Typing skill can be easily transferred from one typewriter model to another. The ability to touch type is ingrained in early training and does not diminish much when an executive assistant uses another brand of typewriter. There are occasions when the company purchases newer models with additional "bells and whistles," and an orientation or familiarization period must precede its productive use.

If it is the case of one standard electric model replacing another, carefully reading the operator's manual should acquaint you with the various new keys and service mechanisms. These booklets can be very reassuring if you are working on a particular typewriter for the first time. It is a good idea to keep a copy of an operator's manual in your desk. If one is not available, you can write to the manufacturer for a copy.

MAKING CARBON COPIES

Most business communications that are typed require at least one copy for retention in the company's files. Some companies use the copying machine to make extra copies; however, there are many companies that use carbon paper for making extra copies of typing. Proper assembly and insertion of a carbon pack (an original letterhead, carbon paper, and copy paper) will facilitate typing productivity.

To insert a carbon pack, assemble the original sheet, followed by a piece

Figure 6.1
Carbon pack.

of carbon paper, and a second sheet for each copy. The carbon side of the carbon paper should face toward you as you are inserting the pack into the typewriter and away from you when you begin to type. Straighten the pack by tapping the sheets on the desk before inserting them into the machine.

To prevent slippage of loose carbons and copy paper, you might try placing the top edge of the assembled carbon pack into the flap of an envelope with the back of the envelope and the back of the pack facing forward. Place the envelope carrying the carbon pack behind the platen and roll or index (a special key that allows you to space vertically from any point on the writing line to any line on the page) the entire assembly into place. Remove the envelope and position the pack to begin typing. Or, you can fold a piece of paper in half and place the pack inside the paper.

In order to save production time, many companies use preassembled carbon sets, sometimes in tablet form. The executive assistant either selects the number of sets needed or simply tears off the number of carbons and copy sheets required, places the original letterhead on top of the pack, and inserts all items into the typewriter. When the document has been typed, the pack is removed; and the carbon paper is discarded.

Carbon copies prepared on odd-sized stationery should be prepared using standard-sized carbons and second sheets because of their ease in filing.

MAKING CORRECTIONS

Use of the proper correcting implements and techniques is essential to productive typing. The true test of a good correction is whether the corrected error is noticed within the body of the text. A high level of skill in correcting errors can be achieved by selecting the appropriate correcting tools and by making careful corrections.

CORRECTION TOOLS

Many manufacturers now include correctable ribbons in their machines, but the traditional correction tools remain the eraser stick, correction paper, and correction fluid.

Erasers come in a variety of textures and shapes. It is best to use a hard eraser for originals and a soft eraser for carbons. A soft eraser might be used first to take off excess ink. Then the hard eraser may be used to take off the remaining ink. To make sure the top of the eraser is clean before erasing, simply rub the tip on an emory board or stiff card. Keep the eraser handy while typing so that erasing time can be reduced by not having to hunt for the eraser.

Here are some of the mechanics of correcting errors:

1. Move the carriage of the typewriter to the extreme left or right to prevent erasure particles from falling into the typewriter mechanism. If you have a nonmovable carriage, move the element or carrier away from the area to be erased.
2. Insert a solid plastic card or cardboard square (this acts as a shield) between the original paper and the carbon paper (not between the carbon paper and the carbon copy as might be expected). This prevents the original from picking up carbon smudges on its back since the shield will accumulate ribbon smudges from constantly making contact with the carbon paper.
3. During the erasing process, to protect surrounding words or lines from becoming smudged, use a plastic or metal shield with cutouts. Place this shield directly over the error or errors to be erased. Make sure you have the erasing shield readily available whenever erasures are to be made.
4. Erase with short strokes. Do not scrub; friction and heat which come from extreme pressure may cause holes to appear in the paper. It is generally best to erase only in one direction or in small circular motions; smooth over the erasure with your fingernail to straighten out ruffled paper fibers. After completing the erasure, blow eraser particles away from the machine.
5. Remove the solid shield behind the first carbon copy and erase that copy using a special soft-tip eraser designed especially for carbon copies. Again, place the cutout shield over the error.
6. Continue to erase all carbon copies.
7. Return the paper to typing position and type the corrections. Try to match the ink of the corrected letter by tapping the key several times until the corrected letter is as dark as the other letters on the page. Most advanced electric typewriter models have a touch-regulator dial to help achieve the desired shade automatically.

When the error occurs at the bottom of the page, you can turn the cylinder knob towards you. This will bring the carbon pack to the top of the page. Gently bend the paper over the cylinder, separate the carbon pack sheets,

Figure 6.2
Variable spacer.

insert the shield, lean on the frame of the typewriter, and erase in the usual manner.

Manuscripts stapled across the top can be corrected without removing the staples. Insert a blank sheet of paper around the platen leaving the paper bail in upright position. Select the sheet to be corrected and place the bottom edge of that sheet behind the top of the paper in the machine and in front of the platen. Roll the sheet down into the front of the machine to the desired point.

Always proofread before removing the carbon pack from your typewriter. If, however, an error is detected after the paper is removed from the typewriter, erase the error on the desk and reinsert the paper in the typewriter to strike the correct letter. Errors found on carbon packs will have to be corrected individually when the pack has been removed from the machine.

You should know the relationship of your typing line with your typewriter alignment scale. When you reinsert the paper, make sure you reposition your line to be corrected on the same line as the alignment scale. You can do this by turning the cylinder knob to the position nearest the line to be corrected.

To reposition the line exactly even, you must then push your variable line spacer (located in the middle of the left cylinder knob). The variable spacer disengages the gears to permanently change the position of the writing line or to realign a page for corrections or additions.

Knowing the exact spatial relationship of your typing line to your aligning scale saves time in repositioning. It helps if you have a visual memory of the exact distance between the bottom of the typed line and the alignment scale. Does the bottom of a letter touch the alignment scale? Is it slightly above?

Once you have established the correct position for vertical alignment, you must be concerned with horizontal alignment. The correct position is to place the typewritten letters directly above the vertical guides on the alignment scale. Pick a word that has an "i" or an "l" and try to place it correctly. You can move your paper horizontally by pulling the paper release forward and moving your paper to the desired point.

When you make a typewritten error, you usually know immediately; you do not have to look at the paper to prove it. When this occurs, the best technique is to stop typing and make the correction immediately. Do not

Figure 6.3
Alignment scale.

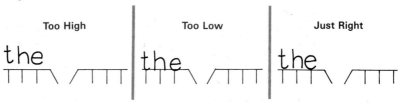

Too High   Too Low   Just Right

Figure 6.4
Alignment scale.

finish typing the word, the line, or the paragraph and decide to go to the error later.

If you make an error in a letter, a word, or maybe a few words, you would correct them. But what if you inadvertently positioned your fingers on the wrong home keys and typed an entire line wrong or failed to release the shift lock and typed a line of all capitals or transcribed from the wrong place in your shorthand notes, and as a result, typed one or more lines incorrectly? Obviously, erasing under these circumstances would be impractical. You would remove the paper, assemble and insert a new carbon pack, and resume typing.

Ideally, you should correct all errors whether they appear on the original and/or carbon copies. In some offices, however, carbon copies are prepared and filed for the executive assistant's eyes only. In the interest of saving time, eliminating the correcting of carbon copies may be both practical and realistic. Common sense and evaluation of your own applications should determine your decision.

If failing to correct errors on carbon copies does not alter the meaning of the word in the context of the sentence and the copy is retained for your file only, correcting errors on carbons may be unnecessary; and it is not practical with correcting ribbons. This decision must not be made lightly; there may be future occasions when the executive assistant's file copy might be retrieved and used as evidence in a judicial hearing. All errors on carbon copies should be corrected when the carbon copy is to be retained in the dictator's file or sent to a third party.

CORRECTABLE RIBBONS

Many typewriters now incorporate a built-in correcting feature. A correctable film ribbon with special lift-off tape allows the operator to lift the error off the page. With this procedure, erasures, strikeovers, and messy corrections on originals are a thing of the past. During the correcting cycle the typing element stays in place after the incorrect character is deleted with a special backspace or correction key. The correct character can be typed immediately without wasted motion. It is necessary, however, to match the appropriate tape and ribbon.

Making corrections with this special correctable film ribbon requires the following steps:

1. Press the special correcting key to backspace to the last incorrectly typed character. This key is usually automatic so you can quickly backspace to correct any character toward the beginning of the line. If you space forward after backspacing with the correcting key, the correcting process is deactivated.
2. Restrike the last incorrectly typed character to delete it from the paper.
3. Backspace with the correcting key to the next incorrect character and restrike it to delete it from the paper. Repeat until all incorrect characters are deleted.
4. Type the correct character(s).

Correcting errors using this method applies to originals only. If you are typing carbon copies, correct them in the usual way after deleting the character(s) from the original.

CORRECTION PAPERS

Correction papers are chalk-coated strips of paper. To correct with this method, use the following steps:

1. Backspace to the letter or word typed in error. Place the special correction paper for carbon copies over the carbon copy error with the coated side down. Place the special correction paper for originals over the original copy error with the coated side down.
2. Retype the same error using exactly the same letters and typing on the correction papers. Remove all sheets of correction paper for carbons and the one correction strip for originals. You will notice that the chalklike chemical has covered the error(s) with a special coating.
3. Type the correct word. Usually you must retype the character two or three times to overcome the chalk substance and match the surrounding characters.

You should be aware that one of the disadvantages in using correction paper is that the correction lacks permanency. If the original document is retrieved after a year or more, the chalk may flake off and the error may show through. The quality of the correction paper is important or the chalk may flake off immediately. Also, with this type of correction, if it is read so that light comes in from behind, the correction will show as a strikeover.

CORRECTION FLUIDS

This method employs the use of quick-drying enamel that is brushed over an error. Correction fluids are best used when typing with a carbon ribbon, typing an original for photo offset, or making a carbon only for your files. When used correctly, this method can do an effective job of covering up

Figure 6.5

Executive assistant making a correction (Courtesy of Liquid Paper).

an error so that it is undetected by the reader. To use the correction fluid method, simply:

1. Roll your paper forward to position the error for correction.
2. Shake the bottle well to mix the fluid thoroughly.
3. Check the fluid's consistency by dotting some of it onto a sheet of scratch paper.
4. Add, if necessary, a few drops of thinner if the correction fluid appears too thick.
5. Dot the fluid over the outline of each individual character. Correct one character at a time; do not paint out whole letters or words. Too much fluid above or below the typed line attracts attention to the correction.
6. Allow the fluid to dry thoroughly (about eight to ten seconds). Type the correct character.

Some additional tips for using the correction fluid method are:

1. Recap the bottle securely after each use.
2. Maintain the original consistency of the fluid by adding a few drops of thinner with the aid of the transfer bottle.

"FOR YOU, MARY, CORRECTION FLUID."

Figure 6.6

3. Keep your brush clean and soft by switching the correction fluid and thinner caps. Allow the brush to soak in the thinner until clean.
4. Clean the bottle neck of any excess correction fluid buildup with a tissue dampened with thinner.
5. Adjust the typewriter's impression setting according to the number of copies you are typing. This will prevent the errors from being "cut" into the paper.

If you have colored stationery, you can order correction fluid that is specially blended to match the color of paper you use so you can make undetectable corrections on typed or written errors.

With the proliferation of photocopies, a special opaque fluid has been developed specifically for correcting photocopies or pen ink errors. This fluid has a special waterbase formula that goes on smoothly, dries quickly, and covers copies so effectively it is undetectable. Since it won't streak copier toners, it is a boon for the executive assistant in helping to eliminate paper waste and save valuable time on the job. Although it dries quickly, it does not dry as quickly as the fluid for typed originals.

CORRECTION TAPES

Correction tape is a white, self-adhesive paper that is available in one-line or more widths. The tape is packaged in a small box with an opening and cutting edge. The executive assistant pulls the tape out of the box to the desired length, tears off the strip at the blade, and tapes over the corrected area. Corrections are then typed on top of the tape. This correction method is best used for photo offset masters or other documents where appearance may not be important since the correction (tape) is visible.

ERROR CORRECTION AND EDITING IN AUTOMATED TYPING

With automated magnetic media typing systems, the executive assistant is freed from the bother of correcting and fussing with erasers, correction paper, liquid corrections, and starting the page over again. Editing and error correction are two of the main advantages of using automatic typing equipment. In nonautomated typing, the typist's errors alone cause the average word per minute of actual typewritten output to be somewhere between 10 and 20 words a minute. Typists' errors thus cause output to be slowed because:

1. The executive assistant must make the correction or repeat the entire process.
2. To avoid making an error, the typist keyboards at a much slower rate. However, typists make errors not just because of their own keyboarding or stroking failures but also because they misinterpret the source material, do not understand instructions, and/or are confronted with spelling and grammatical mistakes.

CORRECTING TYPOGRAPHICAL ERRORS

To correct an error on a line before it is recorded, simply backspace to the error, type over the error with the correct material and continue typing the rest of the material.

EDITING (AUTHOR CHANGES)

Almost without exception, anybody who creates a written document will find that he or she could have worded it better once it is typed. What determines whether the document will get changed is the importance of the document and whether the author has the capability to change it. Authors may think twice about changing the document if they know the bothersome job executive assistants go through to make any change using a standard (nonautomated) typewriter. The question, therefore, is: Does the author have the typing power, and does the executive assistant have the time to redo it?

On the average, every document is revised at least once. Very often this revision accounts for the author's handwritten changes. Documents are rarely revised totally. Therefore, much of the information that was in the author's original copy remains unchanged. With nonautomated typing this information must be retyped with the author's corrections. This means a duplication of key strokes which have already entered through the typewriter keyboard.

While correcting typographical errors usually occurs before the errors are recorded, editing is the process of making changes in previously recorded material. These changes may be minor or major. They may be the result of typographical errors or changes made by the author of the document. Changes include additions, deletions, or substitutions. These corrections often affect the way the page looks; paragraphs are eliminated, combined, or separated; words, phrases, and sentences are added and/or tab positions are rearranged.

FEATURES AND TECHNIQUES OF AUTOMATED TYPING SYSTEMS

When executive assistants convert to automated typing systems, retyping documents ceases to exist. All the best features of more productivity, greater versatility, and advanced electronic design are incorporated into automated typing systems. If letters contain smudges or documents appear unbalanced, all you need do is insert a clean sheet of paper, activate the playback key, and you get a perfect letter typed at a high rate of speed.

Some of the special features found on text-editing typewriters to help executive assistants produce high-quality, accurate documents are discussed below:

1. *Setting and adjust zone.* If you wish to play back on special-sized stationery, you can play back the document in "adjust" mode to any side margins to accommodate special stationery. By resetting the side margins and pressing a special key, the system automatically prints within the margins specified by you.
2. *Automatic underlining.* Special code keys will automatically underline a word, a phrase in word-by-word underline, or continuous underline.
3. *Single and double spacing.* Single and double spacing can be produced in playback by coding special keys. Simply press a special key in recording mode and the system will automatically change the line spacing both while recording and again during playback. This is a vast improvement over the manual system of having the operator stop and manually move the line lever on the typewriter accordingly.
4. *Automatic centering.* In standard electric typewriter operation, the executive assistant moves to the center point of the paper and backspaces once for every two characters to center material. Using automatic typing systems, the executive assistant instructs the system to automatically

center words on a line by coding a special centering key. This occurs during playback operation. To record a centering instruction, the executive assistant spaces or tabs to the desired centering position, codes the special centering key, and then types the word to be centered. After typing the words and returning the carrier, the system has been instructed to automatically center during playback operation. This same procedure can be used to center headings over columns in tabulation projects.

5. *Automatic tab.* An automatic tab can be coded by instructing the system during recording mode. This is used when the same tab position is needed on two or more consecutive lines. It is ideally suited when a number of sentences or possibly paragraphs are always indented from the left margin to the same position. The special automatic tab key instructs the system to set up this temporary left margin. This tab code is not used for a single paragraph indention or for columnar indentions; use a regular tab in those circumstances. Obviously, this feature can save the executive assistant a great deal of time in typing because once the instruction is recorded, at every carrier return the system will automatically move in to the indicated tab position.

6. *Stop code.* The stop code feature on automated typing systems makes it possible to reproduce the same letter over and over again and give each copy an originally typed appearance. This type of form letter has a much higher degree of acceptance by the recipient than a duplicated or an offset-reproduced letter. When using stop codes, the system is automatically instructed to stop at a certain point during playback to insert variable information manually, such as dates, names, addresses, or amounts of money. The executive assistant simply presses a special stop code during recording mode. During playback the typewriter will stop at the point specified. To resume playback, simply depress another key for continued printout.

7. *Right margin justification.* To heighten visual quality even further, automatic systems may include automatic right margin justification. By coding a special key during recording, the system will fully justify an attractive right-hand margin during playback.

8. *Attractive finished documents.* One unique feature of automated systems is the appearance of the finished document. Sophisticated systems may employ special elements or electronically driven print wheels with one type character on each spoke. The wheel precisely imprints every selected character with uniform density and maximum clarity. Interchangeable elements and wheels are available in a wide range of type styles and pitches.

Visual display systems often employ diskette (floppy disk) media and may offer sophisticated routines to automate pagination, hyphenation, and global changes. The operator can utilize the screen during initial keyboarding instead of the paper. Since you see every word on the screen, corrections are easy; striking over the error leaves only the correction on the screen in full view for instant verification.

Whether updating a report or proposal, making major revisions on a lengthy document, adding or deleting a few words or lines from a memo, or just correcting typographical errors, editing is simple on visual display systems. With instant access to any line, page, or document on the diskette, the system eliminates sorting stacks of mag cards and waiting for slow search speeds.

Some systems employ a special hyphen scan feature. This means the system rapidly reads every line, stopping only when a word will not fit into the specified margin. The executive assistant sees all hyphenation on the screen before playback on paper. The result is the straightest possible margins the first time.

Many automated typing systems go far beyond the relatively simple functions described in the preceding sections.

SPECIALIZED TYPING TECHNIQUES

Two examples of specialized typing techniques are drawing lines and underscoring backwards. For more information about specialized techniques, you should consult a typing book.

To draw lines, place a pencil or pen in the notch of the card holder and move the carriage from left to right or roll the platen up and down depending on whether you are drawing vertical lines or horizontal lines. When drawing vertical lines, disengage the line finder. Remember to return the line finder to its home position for normal line spacing. Consult your operator's manual to make horizontal lines on nonmovable carriages.

To underscore backwards, tap the backspace and the underscore at the same time. Think of the many times you've typed a heading, returned the carriage, and then had to turn the platen down one line before you could underscore. Now, you can start underscoring and backspacing as the very next step after you type the last character in the heading.

SUMMARY

The choice of typewriters and related office equipment is a very important consideration in the tasks of executive assistant. Also of major importance is the focus on typewriting techniques to get the most out of your equipment. The intelligent use of typing systems (electric, electronic, and automated) allows the executive assistant to type, revise, and retrieve information in a lot less time—which, in turn, allows the executive more time to create and perfect documents.

1. It is important for the executive assistant to set high standards for mailability of documents.

2. Some techniques for producing professional-looking documents include: expecting to do a perfect job, keeping an organized work area, proofreading carefully, correcting errors professionally, following instructions carefully, and being familiar with your typewriter.
3. Proper use of a carbon pack will facilitate typing productivity.
4. A carbon pack consists of the original sheet, the carbon paper, and a second sheet.
5. A professional correction is one that cannot be detected by the reader.
6. Correction tools include the eraser, correction paper, correctable ribbons, correction fluid, and correction tapes.
7. Automatic typing equipment frees the typist from many of the time-consuming jobs of correcting and revising copy.
8. Some of the features on automated systems which help the executive assistant to produce professional documents include setting and adjust zone; automatic underlining, centering, and tab; stop code; and right margin justification.
9. A pencil or pen placed in the notch of the card holder facilitates drawing lines on the typewriter.
10. Underscoring backwards involves using the backspace and underscore keys simultaneously.

CHAPTER RECALL EXERCISES

1. Define the following terms:

carbon pack	right margin justification
correction paper	second sheet
eraser shield	soft eraser
index key	stop code
platen	

2. What is the difference between correction paper and correction tape?
3. Name the criteria you should use to determine if a document is mailable.
4. Explain the procedure to assemble and insert a carbon pack.
5. What does thinking positively have to do with producing perfect copy?
6. Why is it important to keep the operator's manual for your typewriter?
7. How can you prevent slippage of carbons and copy paper?
8. List the steps to make a professional correction using an eraser.
9. To assure that copy is typed perfectly, what are some ways to ensure perfect proofreading?
10. Give the correct procedure for making corrections with correction fluid.
11. When would you use an opaque correction fluid?
12. Describe five of the features found on most automated typing systems to help executive assistants correct and edit copy.
13. Describe the procedure to draw vertical lines and horizontal lines.
14. Describe the procedure to underscore backwards.

PROBLEMS AND APPLICATIONS

1. Assemble a carbon pack and type the following memorandum, making one carbon copy. Correct your errors on the original and the copy. Use an eraser to make the corrections. (Make sure that you make at least five errors.)

```
TO:        The Staff                    Date: (current)
FROM:      Graham Anchor
SUBJECT:   BUSINESS SHOW IN SIX MONTHS

Yesterday, I attended the planning conference for this year's
Business Show which will be held from September 15–18.
Each exhibitor has approximately 200 square feet this year
in which to display products and equipment. Please submit to
me by June 1 any suggestions you have for this year's ex-
hibit.
```

2. Type the following paragraph four times. Correct the errors using the following tools: eraser, correction tape, correction paper, and correction fluid.

    a. Use an eraser.

Eastern Colllge is an acadimic institution with a reputetion for qualiiy education. There if an atmosphere of freindliness and good taste. Considor us when you are ready to choose the plase to sent your childrin.

    b. Use correction tape.
    c. Use correction paper.
    d. Use correction fluid.

Now insert a sheet of paper into a typewriter that has a correctable ribbon. Type the paragraph, making the corrections using the correctable ribbon.

Compare the quality of the corrections and the amount of time it took you to make each correction. Which correction has the highest quality? Which took the least amount of time? Which would you prefer to use on a regular basis?

3. Read the following instructions to a friend. See how many of the facts the person can remember five minutes after the exercise.

I meant to call earlier but got tied up in traffic and trying to find a parking space here. I'm going to have to write a memo to describe how difficult it is to get a parking space at the corporate headquarters. Why don't you talk to Beth, Dave, Doug, and Janet to see if anybody else has as much difficulty parking here; ask them if they would like to contribute to the memo. Did you have an opportunity to talk to Rod about changing that meeting to later in the week? Yes, Thursday afternoon is fine for me, so call and confirm that time. I won't be back until about two o'clock tomorrow, so that means I will miss the staff lunch. Better tell Rod that I won't be there. See you tomorrow.

4. Read the following set of instructions to the same person you used in question 3, and ask that person to take notes. See how many facts are recalled five minutes later. The person can refer to the notes taken earlier to recall the information.

My rental car has mechanical problems so it looks like I won't be able to get another car for a few hours, so please call:

a. Mr. Barber and cancel my appointment and try to arrange another for tomorrow morning.
b. Ms. Deal and tell her I'll call her tomorrow and try to arrange a meeting.
c. The airline and try to arrange a return flight for some time on Friday for late afternoon.

I'll try to call you later when I know more about what is going on here with this car. Oh yes, if you get a chance, will you call my husband and tell him that I will be staying an extra day and ask him to change my dentist appointment scheduled on Friday morning. I'll try to call him later this evening.

5. If you had received the two telephone calls in questions 3 and 4, make notes of what you would record to remind yourself about things to do.

6. Consult the operator's manual of your present typewriter. Review all the instructions found in the booklet. Did you learn anything new or recall an important point that you had forgotten?

7. Assemble a carbon pack with three carbons. Insert the carbon pack using the flap of an envelope, using a piece of folded paper, and using no aids. Which was easier to keep the papers lined up?

8. a. Type the following lines (including the errors):

Every month we guve you poonters to hepl you acheive your every gaol. There is no need to sent ane money now. We"ll bill you lattr.

b. Note the placement of the characters with your typewriter alignment scale.

c. Take the paper out of the typewriter.

d. Insert the paper and make the corrections, using an eraser.

9. Type the following sentence on vertical line 60 of your paper:

Few poeple know aboot the origens of this machnie.

Position the paper to make the corrections by turning the cylinder knob toward you.

10. Type the following paragraph using a four-inch line of type:

More and more people are beginning to realize how important it is for professionals to use their time wisely every day. Numerous companies and professional organizations are sponsoring seminars on time management. Recent studies indicate that the productivity of professionals can be improved as much as 30 percent with the application of time-management principles.

a. Using an electric typewriter, justify the right margin of the paragraph.

b. If you have access to a text-editing typewriter, justify the right margin using the justification key.

c. If available, justify the right margin using a proportional space typewriter.

11. Insert a sheet of typing paper and using a pencil, draw the following figures:

a. A square that is 2 inches on each side.

b. A rectangle that is 2 inches in length and 1 inch wide.

LANGUAGE SKILLS DEVELOPMENT

1. Punctuate the following sentences:
   a. Because the court records reveal a change in attitude the judge asked the department to examine the transcript.
   b. Edward Batty Bureau Chief told the reporters about the change at headquarters.
   c. A report on the Coast Guard prepared by the General Accounting Office found that there are not enough dollars to support the mission properly.
   d. In addition the city will have to pay about $50,000 in back taxes.
   e. John Haynes said it was premature to think about the new product but called on staff members for suggestions.
   f. Although mistakes have been made and poor judgment has been exercised it is better to move ahead on the construction of the road.
   g. Harrison who bought the parking lot operation from International three years ago has expanded the operation.
   h. Urban parking is the dominant part of the business however airport revenues are expected to increase.
   i. After 40 years in the grocery business the last 15 years in a modern store the owner has no plans to sell.
   j. For a vast majority of Americans the car is the only way to get to work.

2. Proofread the following paragraph for errors:

   Its harvest time on America farms. For many people whose are not familar with the process harvest is a mysterous think. For the farmer however, harvest means hard work, frequent frustration and renewed commitment. Harvest is a race against rain, wind, heat and insects.

3. a. Check yourself on the spelling of the following words:

compatible   forty
computer   privilege
digital   similar

    b. Use each word correctly in a sentence.
    c. Divide each word in the preferred place, using the word division rules.

4. Here are some words that are easily confused. Look up each of the words in the dictionary for the proper meaning; then use each of the words correctly in a sentence.
    a. already, all ready
    b. allude, elude
    c. minor, miner
    d. site, cite, sight

HUMAN RELATIONS INCIDENTS

1. You have been working as an executive assistant to Chris Page, sales manager of Byrne's Department Store, for the past five months. Yesterday Ms. Page told you that the store will be going through inventory on Wednesday and Thursday of this week, and she needs you to stay late for those two nights to help her coordinate the job. Since you use public transportation, you do not want to stay after 5 p.m. because of the inconvenience of trying to arrange alternate transportation home. Should you:

    a. Explain to Ms. Page about the inconvenience of staying late and hope she understands what a sacrifice you would have to make to stay late?

    b. Explain the situation very politely to Ms. Page and tell her you will help as much as possible before 5 p.m. but just cannot stay after 5 p.m.?

    c. Put on your "Well, there's-another-insurmountable-problem-face" and agree to stay?

    d. Let Ms. Page know right away that you don't resent the request. Arrange for alternate transportation and consider the job an opportunity to show you are interested in learning about this new phase of your job?

Do you have another solution to this problem? If so, how would you handle the request?

2. This morning while you were making copies of a report, you overheard two other executive assistants talking and learned that the

company is about to launch into a reorganization. Jim Miller, executive assistant to one of the vice-presidents, mentioned that it is just a matter of time until most of the executive assistants will be replaced with automated equipment. Jim said that the vice-presidents have already purchased the equipment and it will be installed at the first of the year. What should you do?

a. Keep the rumor to yourself and try to forget what you overheard.

b. Go to your supervisor immediately, repeat what you heard, and demand an explanation.

c. Start looking for a new job.

d. Go to Jim Miller and try to obtain more details about the reorganization.

e. At the first opportunity, explain to your supervisor what you heard and ask if he or she has any information about the change.

If you have a better solution, what is it?

WRITTEN BUSINESS COMMUNICATIONS

Some executive assistants may feel that it is not necessary for them to be able to compose letters; they may feel their job is to transcribe another person's words. That is not enough. Good executive assistants should be able to correct and improve their bosses' letters, even if they do not have to compose letters from scratch.

The executive assistant turns out a finished product. It should be a matter of pride to turn out the best possible letter and that includes a letter that is grammatically correct with the proper spelling and punctuation; in addition, the format should be one established by the company. The executive assistant should be concerned also with the tone of the letter, the way it sounds to the recipient.

The language skills of the executive assistant have always been important. Whether typing from longhand or shorthand notes, the executive assistant had to polish the original material and turn it into a mini masterpiece. Today, with more firms turning to dictation/transcription equipment, the executive assistant's language skills are more important than ever. Many executives are unnerved by dictation equipment. Other executives have mastered the art of dictation but must dictate into a portable machine while they are on the run. The result is that dictated letters are not always as well thought out as they should be. That's where a good executive assistant can really make the difference. You can take very rough dictation and turn it into something the executive will read and sign without making a single change.

The executive assistant can learn to turn out a good finished product every time by learning some basic rules about good business communications. At the end of this chapter, you should be able to:

1. List the principles of good writing. ☐ 2. Name the criteria for selecting stationery. ☐ 3. Know how to place a letter attractively on a page. ☐ 4. Know the parts of a letter. ☐ 5. Name and describe the most popular letter styles. ☐ 6. List the principles of writing effective memorandums and business reports.

CHAPTER 7

PRINCIPLES OF WRITING

The purpose of a business communication, whether it be a letter, memo, or report, is to inform. The writer should not try to impress the recipient with his or her knowledge of big words or ability to write long, involved sentences. A business document should be written so that the person receiving it can read it quickly, yet understand it thoroughly. There are a number of steps you can take to ensure that your communication is clear, complete, concise, and courteous.

DEFINE THE PURPOSE AND AUDIENCE

Is the purpose of the communication to give the recipient some information or to make a request? Is the purpose to offer someone a job or turn down someone's request? Is the purpose to order a product or find out why something was not received on schedule? In other words, what are you trying to say to the reader—what is the main idea of the communication?

Once you decide on the purpose of the letter, define your reader. What is the reader's job background? For example, is the recipient a technical or nontechnical person? Knowing your reader is important because you should write on the right level for your reader and adjust your writing so that the letter means something to the reader.

The terms you use should mean the same thing to you and your reader. This applies particularly to technical terms. Will your reader understand them? You should not write over your reader's head; however, you should not write down to the reader either. Both of these approaches are insulting.

USE SHORT WORDS AND SENTENCES

Limit your use of long and unnecessarily technical words. Don't use a long word when a short one will convey the same meaning. This does not mean you should use only short words. You should use long words occasionally to enhance your writing.

Use nouns and verbs as much as possible; they are objective, concrete words that give exact information. Adjectives and adverbs, on the other hand, are subjective and mean different things to different people.

The same principle holds true for sentences. A mix of short and long sentences eliminates monotony, but the average length of your sentences should be 17 to 20 words. Short sentences are easier to read. The recipient can glance at the sentence and understand it quickly. With long sentences, by the time the reader gets to the end of the sentence, he or she may have forgotten the beginning.

Avoid run-on sentences. A run-on sentence is one that is really two or three sentences strung together. Reading a run-on sentence is like trying to find your way out of a maze. The purpose of business communication is not to confuse or frustrate the reader; it is to make a point clearly and simply.

ORGANIZE YOUR WRITING

Once you have the sentences written, they have to be organized into paragraphs. Paragraphs are designed to make reading and understanding easier by separating ideas—one idea for each paragraph. In other words, each paragraph should cover a single subject.

The main idea should be stated clearly somewhere in the paragraph. It may be in the first sentence of the paragraph with the remaining sentences giving details to support the main idea. Or, one or more sentences may be used to lead up to the main topic sentence, which could be in the middle or at the end of the paragraph.

The sentences should be organized in logical order within the paragraph without skipping around. The sentences should flow smoothly and logically so the reader is carried along without abrupt changes in direction. When a new idea or topic is to be presented, the writer should begin a new paragraph.

The paragraphs are the final components that go into the making of a letter, memo, or report. They, too, must be arranged in a logical sequence. Every communication should have a beginning, a middle, and an ending. The beginning (introductory paragraph) introduces the subject or topic and explains why it was written. The middle of the communication, which may consist of one or more paragraphs, gives all the details that explain or back up the introductory paragraph. The ending may summarize the previous paragraph, suggest future action, bid the reader a courteous goodbye, and/ or ask the reader for help.

GATHER THE FACTS

Before preparing any business communications, you should line up all the facts that have to be included. List all the points you want to make and then organize them into main and subordinant points. Then, when the communication is written, read it over to be sure you have included all the points. If an executive assistant is composing the message, he or she should ask the executive what points should be covered in the communication. The executive assistant should write them down and later check the communication against them.

A good business writer includes all pertinent information without being long-winded. The author should avoid using unnecessary words that result in roundabout, overloaded sentences. Short and to-the-point business letters and reports are easier to read and comprehend. Such an approach also takes into account the fact that the recipient is a busy executive who does not have time to read long, involved letters. The executive wants to get to the point of the business communication fast.

A letter can follow a standard business format; the spelling, punctuation, and grammar can be correct. Yet, the letter may be a good example of how not to write a letter because it does not have the proper tone and is not courteous. Courtesy is as important in the business world as it is in social situations.

The tone of a communication is the overall impression it makes on the reader. Notice the tone of the following letter; it is negative and abrupt.

Dear Mr. Hill:

I'm sorry to tell you that your book has been rejected by our company. It is just not the type of book we publish.

The rejected manuscript will be returned to you under separate cover.

Very truly yours,

Letters, even those containing bad news, should stress the positive aspects of the situation. For example, the above letter could have been written in a more positive, courteous way:

Dear Mr. Hill:

Thank you for sending the manuscript of your book; we feel it shows a lot of promise. However, after careful consideration, we feel that we are not the right publisher for this type of book.

The manuscript will be returned to you under separate cover so that you can send it to another publisher.

We wish you the best of luck with your book, Mr. Hill, and feel sure you will find the right publisher for it in the near future.

Sincerely,

WRITING LETTERS

A letter represents the person and the company from which it comes. If the letter is courteous, well written, and factual, it projects a good image. Even form letters can be personalized to some extent by changing a few words so that they relate to the recipient and project a warm, courteous feeling.

The importance of a good letter is evidenced by the impression and motivating force it has on the reader. Every letter should be an envoy of good will, a friendly personal messenger to customers, clients, and business associates. This makes the contents, form, and general appearance of your letters vitally important.

LETTER SUPPLIES

Letterheads should be designed to reflect the image of the company. This is the age of the designer, and first impressions that are visually attractive enhance the image of the company. Evidence of this shift in graphics is that advertising agencies, designers, art studios, freelancers, and creative printers are producing more letterheads than ever before. Recent studies have shown that over one-third of the letterheads being produced on premium correspondence papers are now being created by professional designers, and this percentage is rapidly increasing.

When a client, a customer, or a prospective buyer receives a business letter from a firm, an impression is formed about the sender. The appearance of the letterhead is an important part of this impression. The graphics become an integral part of the message.

An executive assistant might very well have some input into the elements of designing a letterhead for an organization. The design must be thought of in terms of application and need. What are your company's communications requirements? In a small office, for instance, one size of letterhead and envelope might be sufficient. On the other hand, larger organizations might need the services of a graphics designer.

Most correspondence papers are letter size, or $8\frac{1}{2} \times 11$ inches with a matching No. 10 envelope. That seems to be the upper limit as it is standard business size and anything larger is difficult to file. But, there may also be need for executive stationery. The most prestigious sheet is called monarch size, $7\frac{1}{4} \times 10\frac{1}{2}$ inches, with matching envelopes available. Other items that should be considered are note pads, memo forms, folders, and business cards.

Basically, the elements that should be included in a letterhead are name of company, address, and telephone number. Optional elements to include might be company logo, advertising slogan, regional offices, products, and names of officers of the company. The letterhead should also include telex or cable address, if appropriate.

The major cost of producing a letterhead is in its design and production. It is rarely in the cost of paper. Paper selection, therefore, is the last place to economize. The most expensive paper contains 100 percent cotton; this paper makes the best impression. Costs climb, of course, when you add color printing, embossing, or engraving.

Figure 7.1
Letterhead sizes.

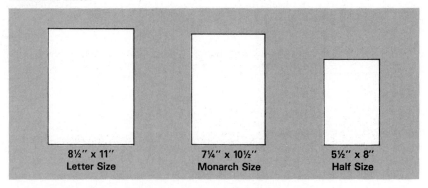

8½″ x 11″
Letter Size

7¼″ x 10½″
Monarch Size

5½″ x 8″
Half Size

JOHN W. WYDLER
FIFTH DISTRICT, NEW YORK

MINORITY FLOOR MANAGER
COMMITTEE ON COMMITTEES
N.Y. REPRESENTATIVE

DISTRICT OFFICE:
150 OLD COUNTRY ROAD
MINEOLA, NEW YORK 11501
TELEPHONE: CH 8 7676

Congress of the United States
House of Representatives
Washington, D.C. 20515

COMMITTEES:
SCIENCE AND TECHNOLOGY

SUBCOMMITTEES:
AVIATION AND TRANSPORTATION
RESEARCH AND DEVELOPMENT
ENERGY RESEARCH, DEVELOPMENT
AND DEMONSTRATION
SPACE SCIENCE AND APPLICATION

GOVERNMENT OPERATIONS

SUBCOMMITTEE:
INTERGOVERNMENTAL RELATIONS AND
HUMAN RESOURCES

 TWA

605 THIRD AVENUE, NEW YORK, NEW YORK, U.S.A. 10016

SMITHSONIAN INSTITUTION
Washington, D.C. 20560
U.S.A.

 **International Word Processing Association**

Maryland Road, Willow Grove, Pa. 19090   215-657-3220

 **American Federation of Teachers** AFL-CIO

11 Dupont Circle, N.W.
Washington, D.C. 20036

 EXCELLENCE: A Hunter Way of Life

THE HUNTER COLLEGE SECOND CENTURY FUND

Hunter College / 505 Park Avenue / New York, N.Y. 10022

 **HILLEL**

COUNTRY DAY SCHOOL
33 WASHINGTON AVE. · LAWRENCE, N. Y. · (516) 569-3370

The John F. Kennedy Center
for the Performing Arts
Washington, D.C. 20566

 The American Film Institute

Citibank, N.A.   **J. B. Ryan**
399 Park Avenue   Vice President
New York, N.Y.
10022

CITIBAN<0

WNET/13
356 WEST 58 ST.
NEW YORK, N.Y. 10019
EDUCATIONAL
BROADCASTING
CORPORATION

 **VYDEC**®

Vydec, Inc.
9 Vreeland Road
Florham Park, New Jersey 07932
Telephone: 201-822-2100
Telex: 136385

Figure 7.2 *Letterheads.*

The selection of a premium correspondence paper gives the organization a number of important advantages. Cotton-content papers, also called rag papers, have the look and feel of quality even before they are printed or engraved. The cockle finish provides a snap to the paper that feels like a crisp dollar bill. Cotton content paper provides the company with a wide array of choices—letterpress, offset, or any other forms of printing, as well as embossing and engraving. Cotton content papers can be watermarked, die-cut and folded to enhance the graphic effect.

The watermark is an ancient art form that has long denoted quality in paper. For the most part watermarks have consisted of logos, names, or seals positioned on the paper with little relationship to the overall letterhead design. But in recent years some designers have embraced this subtle graphic device and have given it new stature by integrating it into their overall graphic concept. Watermarks are also very personal. The fact that the user must have the paper manufactured to specification often appeals to the vanity of the executive, the organization, or more important, the reader and makes an impression of prestige and quality that no other letterhead art form can achieve.

When preparing carbon copies, the executive assistant has the choice of using the following types of carbon copy "second sheets."

1. Yellow second sheets, sometimes called railroad manila, are usually heavy quality paper.
2. Tissue sheets have a smooth surface and do not have a watermark. This paper is well suited for all carbon copies of letters, memorandums, and reports between the original copy and the yellow file copy. Tissue sheets may be plain, or the company name and address and the word "copy" may be printed on them.
3. Onionskin paper often has a cockle finish and a watermark. It is a higher grade paper and more expensive than the regular tissue paper sheets. This paper is sometimes called fidelity. Onionskin paper may be used in place of regular tissue paper when the report or special letter will have heavy usage or circulation.
4. Sometimes plain, white bond paper may be used as carbon copy paper; it is used usually when a joint letter is written to two or three people.

LETTER PLACEMENT

The dictator of business correspondence and the executive assistant who transcribes the final document must work together to produce an accurate and attractive business letter. All the factors of letterhead design, quality of stationery, placement of letter, quality of type, and correct content form an image of your company in the reader's mind.

Organizations may establish different policies for the preparation of written communications and letter styles. You must be prepared to adhere to company policy and be flexible in your thinking. The mechanics of business correspondence are usually determined by the organization and are spelled out in the company procedures manual provided for all executive assistants.

The patterns of letter style and placement and the individual parts of a business letter in this chapter are presented as general guidelines. Remember, style and placement of business letters may vary from company to company. They are formulated, however, for the sake of consistency and fast typing output.

Table 7-1 shows the placement scale that might be used in a company. These margin settings assume that the left edge of the paper is at zero. The right margin should be set so the bell will ring at the space indicated on the right. For example, if your machine will lock at the right margin seven spaces after the bell rings, you would set your right margin seven spaces after the right margin indicated in the table.

Another approach may provide settings for side margins as well as the spacing for the dateline (see Table 7-2).

Although letter placement tables are helpful, experienced executive assistants are able to use eye judgment in positioning letters on the page. The tables are an aid to beginning executive assistants and will probably be abandoned once they develop a sense of confidence in judging placement visually. These tables should be used as an approximate guide, and the settings should vary depending upon other elements included in the letter, such as attention lines, subject lines, or special tables. Such space-consuming special features should be considered by adjusting the space before and after the dateline or by adjusting side margins.

LETTER PARTS

It is important for the executive assistant to know the correct placement of all letter parts. A sample of all the possible parts of a letter follow.

Dateline. The dateline should contain the month, day, and year and should appear on the line specified in your company's correspondence manual.

Some companies prefer that the dateline be typed on a specific line from the top edge of the paper, perhaps on the twelfth line. Other companies prefer the dateline two or three lines below the last line of the printed

TABLE 7-1
LETTER PLACEMENT SCALE

	XYZ Company			
	Pica Type		Elite Type	
Words in Body	Typing Line	Margins	Typing Line	Margins
Under 100	40 spaces	22 and 62	50 spaces	25 and 75
101–200	50 spaces	17 and 67	60 spaces	20 and 80
Over 200	60 spaces	12 and 72	70 spaces	15 and 85

TABLE 7-2

LETTER PLACEMENT SCALE

	ABC Company	
Words in Body	Side Margins	Dateline
0 −100	2 inches	Line 20
100–200	1½ inches	Line 16
201–300	1½ inches	Line 13
301–350	1 inch	Line 12
Over 350 (Two-page letter)	1 inch	Line 12

letterhead. Or, the dateline can be aligned with the printed letter-head—starting at the left, blocked, or aligned at the right.

Inside Address. The inside address should be typed at the left margin and single spaced. Again, the placement of the inside address is optional depending upon company policy. It may be placed from three to eight lines below the date, or it may be typed a specific distance from the dateline, usually four lines.

An extreme placement of the inside address is for it to be typed at the bottom of the letter after the sender's name. The placement of the inside address at the bottom of the letter is usually reserved for very formal letters.

Always spell out words such as street and avenue and the names of cities. If the names of cities, streets, or other geographical areas are not spelled, consult a dictionary or ZIP Code Directory when you are not sure of the correct spelling of these proper nouns. If both street address and box number are given, always use the box number.

When the letter is addressed to one individual, the name of the person should always appear on the first line. If a title follows the name of an addressee, it is written on the same line, except when either is unusually long. In such a case, the title is placed on the next line.

Mr. Fred Swerdlow, President
Sentry Supply Company
837 River Road Boulevard
Columbus, OH 12345

The Honorable John R. Brown
Attorney General of New York
Albany, NY 12202

Attention Line. If the writer addresses a letter to a company, but wishes a specific person in the company to receive the letter, an attention line is typed two lines below the last line of the inside address and two lines above the salutation. The trend, however, is to avoid using attention lines. If a letter is to be directed to an individual, his or her name should be placed at the beginning of the inside address.

There are various ways to type an attention line within a letter. The word "Attention" may be spelled out, followed by two blank spaces and the name of the person or department:

```
Office Systems News
123 Oak Avenue
Coral Springs, FL 12345


Attention  Mr. Henry Marcus
```

The attention line may be centered:

```
Office Systems News
123 Oak Avenue
Coral Springs, FL 12345


              Attention  Mr. Henry Marcus
```

The attention line may be typed with the word "Attention" in all capitals:

```
Office Systems News
123 Oak Avenue
Coral Springs, FL 12345


ATTENTION  Mr. Henry Marcus
```

Or, the entire attention line may be underlined:

```
Office Systems News
123 Oak Avenue
Coral Springs, FL 12345


Attention  of Mr. Henry Marcus
```

Salutation. The salutation in the business letter should be in harmony with the personal relationship between the writer and the recipient. It is typed a double space below the address or attention line. The body begins a double space below the salutation. The first letter of the first word of the salutation is capitalized, as are the first letters of the addressee's courtesy title and surname.

Use of the person's name, as in Dear Mr. Smith, gives the letter a personal tone. A dilemma arises when the name or the sex is not known. As a result of the strong national interest in the Women's Rights Movement, the conventional titles of Gentlemen or Dear Sir are offensive to recipients if they are women. Alternate salutations include Ladies and Gentlemen or Dear Sir or Madam.

Also, there is the controversy over the titles Ms. versus Miss or Mrs. The use of all three may contribute to controversy among recipients who are particularly sensitive to their marital status. Since women constitute a greater portion of the workforce than ever before, companies are moving toward greater consistency in salutations. It is particularly expensive to change name plates, name tags, registers, telephone directories, and employee rosters. One alternate is to use Ms. This simplifies procedures and takes the guesswork out of deciding whether to use Miss or Mrs.

Some progressive companies are solving the problem by eliminating the salutation in letters. They have adopted the AMS Simplified letter form which omits salutations and closings. Other companies suggest a compromise: either one salutation for all or no salutations at all, such as M. Jones or M. Smith.

Subject Line. A subject line focuses the reader on the central point of the message. Its phrasing is short and direct; and it emphasizes the key topic of the letter.

A subject line is typed a double space below the salutation and begins usually at the left margin:

Ms. Jane Thomas
Manufacturers Life Insurance Company
200 Bloor Street
Cleveland, OH 44112

Dear Ms. Thomas

Subject: Regional Conference

It can also begin at paragraph point, if the paragraphs are indented, or be centered on the page, or begin at the center of the page. The word "Subject" when used in the subject line is followed by a colon and may be typed with initial capitals, with all capitals, or omitted altogether.

Reference Line. A reference line is included in a letter if correspondents refer to a file or case number. Some companies provide a printed position for this information in the letterhead. A reference line may be typed above the salutation or below it. The word "Reference" may be spelled out, abbreviated to "Re," or omitted. Reference or Re is followed by a colon and two blank spaces. If the reference information takes more than one line, the second line aligns with the first word of the reference.

Ms. Joan Lewis
California State College
9001 Stockdale Highway
Bakersfield, CA 93309

Dear Ms. Lewis:

Reference: Report No. 8-135
          Executive Assistant's Salary Survey

Body of the Letter. The body of the letter is single spaced with double spacing after the salutation and between paragraphs. Paragraphs may be indented.

Complimentary Close. The complimentary close is typed a double space after the body of the letter. Its page placement depends on the general letter styling being used, block style or modified block style. The complimentary close and the date start at the same horizontal point on the page. In the block style, the date and complimentary close begin at the left margin. In the modified block style, they begin at the horizontal center of the page. Only the first word of the complimentary close is capitalized. If the person dictating does not specify a complimentary close, use one of the following: Sincerely, Sincerely yours, Cordially, Cordially yours.

Company Name in Closing Lines. If the policy is to include the company name in the closing lines, it should be typed a double space after the complimentary close in all capitals.

Sincerely yours,

FMC CORPORATION

Ruth M. Dunne

Ruth M. Dunne

If printed letterhead is being used, the name of the firm should not necessarily appear below the complimentary close. The trend is away from using the company name in the closing.

Signature Line and Title. The originator of the letter signs his or her name between the complimentary close and the typed name. The typed name appears on the fourth line below the complimentary close. By typing the sender's name, no problem is caused by a poorly written signature.

Sincerely yours,

Julia T Ebeling

Julia T. Ebeling
Vice-President

When you type your employer's name, no personal title is necessary before the name, such as Mr. or Dr. A woman, however, may request that her legal name be typed—her own first name, middle initial, and married last name; and also place Miss or Mrs. before it. The title Miss or Mrs. may be typed either with or without parentheses. Since this may be a sensitive area for some women executives, find out exactly how they want their names to appear and comply. The following examples illustrate the variety of closing signature lines for women:

SIGNATURE WITH NO TITLE	SIGNATURE OF AN UNMARRIED WOMAN	SIGNATURE OF A MARRIED WOMAN OR WIDOW
Sincerely,	Sincerely,	Sincerely,
Barbara Drucker	*Barbara Drucker*	*Rosalie Kaufman*
Barbara Drucker	Miss Barbara Drucker or (Miss) Barbara Drucker	Mrs. Rosalie Kaufman or (Mrs.) Rosalie Kaufman

A divorced woman may use her maiden name if it has been legally retained, along with the courtesy title Ms. or Miss enclosed by parentheses, or she may omit the title. Or, she may use her maiden name and her former husband's surname with Mrs.

Cordially yours,

Barbara Dragatta

(Ms.) Barbara Dragatta
(Miss) Barbara Dragatta

Cordially,

Mrs. Morton Blum

Mrs. Morton Blum

If your employer is not available to sign his or her name, you may be authorized to sign the name and mail the letter. If you are requested to do this, be sure to initial the signature.

Cordially yours,

Donald Robins (B. R)

Donald Robins

Executive assistants may also be requested to write letters for their employers, such as making reservations or answering simple inquiries. In this case, the executive assistant should sign his or her name and include a courtesy title.

Sincerely yours,

Alice Gallworthy

Alice Gallworthy
Assistant to Mr. Mielton

Reference Initials.   Reference initials or identification initials are usually typed a double space below the sender's name and title. If you use the writer's initials followed by your own, type a colon or a diagonal between them. The more modern style is to use only your own initials. Some organizations place the reference initials at the very end of the letter, after all closing notations have been typed.

Enclosure Notation.   An enclosure notation alerts the reader that something is enclosed in the envelope in addition to the letter. Enclosures should be noted at the end of the letter. This is a reminder to include the enclosure with the correspondence. It is also a service to the addressee who can quickly check to see if the material is included in the envelope. The enclosure notation can be typed a single or double space below the reference initials. The person dictating often omits this information, and you must remember to add the proper notation at the end of the letter. If there are multiple enclosures, indicate their number. Typical enclosure notations are:

enc.   enc. 2
enclosure   enclosures 3
Enclosure   Enclosures 2
Enclosure—Annual Report

When a letter refers to material to be sent in a future mailing, you should type the proper notation at the left margin, two lines below the last enclosure line, or two lines below the reference initial line if there are no enclosures. Items that are sent separately are termed "Separate Cover." Examples of separate cover notations are:

Separate Cover 3
Separate Cover—REA Express
Separate Cover—Ryder Truck Delivery
Separate Cover—19—— Catalog

Copy Notation. A record of every piece of communication that leaves the office must be prepared and filed. Carbon copies may be prepared, or your company may use the copying machine to make extra copies of letters.

When you prepare a carbon copy for the information of a person other than the addressee of the letter, the notation cc is typed at the left margin, a double space below the reference initials or enclosure notation. If more than one person is to receive a copy, type the names in a column, either in order of importance or in alphabetical order. The most common examples are:

cc: Phil Nicholson   cc Jack Adams
                                      Mary Bahntge

Some organizations keep a record of their correspondence by preparing a photocopy of outgoing communications. The following notations may be used:

pc: Rosemary Motter (photocopy)
xc: David Brandenberg (Xerox copy)

A blind carbon copy notation is prepared if you are planning to send the letter to a third party and do not want the addressee to know that it is being sent to another person. The reference notation bc (blind copy) or bcc (blind carbon copy) should list the name of the recipient on all carbon copies, but not on the original letter. It may be typed in the upper left-hand corner of the page or where the regular cc notation would have been. To save time the notation may be typed before the letter is removed from the machine by placing a card or piece of paper over the notation position on the original copy.

Postscript. A postscript is used to emphasize a special point by setting it apart from the rest of the letter or to relay a personal message to the recipient of the letter. A postscript should be typed as a single-spaced paragraph a double space below the last notation. The letters PS are not needed. Indent the paragraph if the paragraphs of the letter are indented.

Second Page Heading. A letter that is longer than 300 words will usually take more than one page. Plan for a bottom margin of 1 to $1\frac{1}{2}$ inches. In typing a multipage letter, do not end a page with a divided word. Leave at least two lines of a paragraph at the foot of a page and carry at least two lines to the next page. Use plain paper of the same color and quality as the letterhead for the second and subsequent pages of the letter.

Type a second page heading 1 inch from the top of the page in either horizontal or vertical style (see the example shown). The heading should include the name of the recipient, the page number, and the date. Leave a triple space below the heading.

BLOCK STYLE OF SECOND PAGE HEADING

Dr. Albert Donor
Page 2
October 6, 19—

HORIZONTAL STYLE OF SECOND PAGE HEADING

Dr. Albert Donor   2   October 6, 19—

LETTER STYLES

Office personnel should learn how to evaluate alternative letter styles so they can arrive at an intelligent decision regarding the best style for a particular organization. Ordinarily, decisions will already have been made and placed prominently in manuals. Many companies use a standard style throughout their offices; in other companies, the person dictating the letters will decide the style to be used. In the following paragraphs, only the most modern letter styles and their variations will be illustrated.

Block Style. The block style letter, also called a full block style letter, is typed with all lines beginning at the left margin. Paragraphs are never indented. Because the letter can be typed without using tabular stops, it is easier to type. It is modern in style and is gaining in popularity in many offices.

Modified Block Style. A letter in the modified block style has the dateline, the complimentary close, and the sender's name and title beginning at the center of the page. Paragraphs may be indented, or they may begin at the left margin.

Figure 7.3
Block letter.

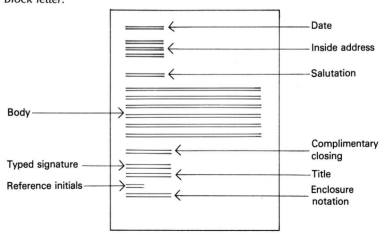

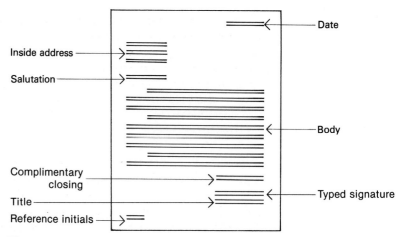

Figure 7.4
Modified block letter.

Simplified Style. The simplified style, also known as the AMS (Administrative Management Society) simplified letter, is perhaps the most radical of all the styles. This style eliminates the salutation and the complimentary close. All lines begin at the left margin. The primary advantages of this style are that it reduces the cost of business letters and increases the productivity of typists.

Research by the AMS has demonstrated that typists increase their correspondence output by about 20 percent using this style as opposed to a traditional letter style such as the Modified Block. Thus, if a typist normally

Figure 7.5
Simplified letter.

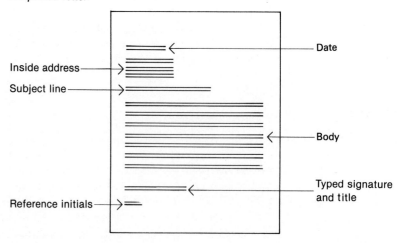

produces 60 letters during a working day, he or she can expect to produce 72 by using the simplified letter style.

Like the block style, the reason for this style's success is its simplified format which tends to reduce mechanical and typewriting errors. The more tab stops and decision making there is in vertical spacing and changing margins for various letter lengths, the greater the chance of a typist's error.

A summary of the characteristics of the simplified letter style are:

1. All lines begin flush with the left margin. There is no need to set tabs. Number items are also typed even with the left margin.
2. This letter can be styled to conform to uniform line length. Organizations can adopt uniform side margins (one inch, for instance). The margin stops can remain the same for all letters. Also, the spacing between the parts of the letter can be standardized regardless of the length of the letter.
3. The inside address can be typed on line 15 of the letterhead or within very light markings on the letterhead, regardless of the length of the letter, so the letter can be mailed in a window envelope. Using window envelopes saves time and money and increases efficiency as it eliminates the need to type the address twice—once in the letter and again on the envelope.
4. The elimination of the salutation can save typing time. Although it has been established as part of the amenities of letter writing, it is now waning in favor of the more streamlined approach.
5. The subject line replaces the salutation. It pinpoints the thrust of the letter, and the person reading it is immediately aware of the central idea.
6. To counter the claim of opponents of the simplified letter that it is too cold and abrupt, include the name of the addressee in the first and last paragraphs. This gives the letter a warm and personal touch.
7. The writer's name and title should be typed in all capitals four spaces below the last line of the body of the letter, allowing sufficient space for the personal signature.
8. As with traditional letters, include the reference initials of the typist in lower case, a double space below the writer's name and/or title. Omit the initials of the writer of the letter.

WRITING MEMORANDUMS

Interoffice memorandums are usually less formal than business letters. Letters and memos have one thing in common—they are both concise and to the point. Memos may be directed to more than one person within the organization.

Memos are written for a number of reasons: to pass along information to a number of people in the company, to discuss what went on at a meeting, to confirm an agreement or decision, to set up a conference, to tell personnel about new policies or directives, or to ask advice or approval for a project.

Interoffice memorandums are usually sent to personnel within the company or organization and are typed on special preprinted forms. These forms permit departments within a company to communicate with each other rapidly and conveniently. Titles, such as Mr. and Mrs., the salutation, the complimentary close, and the formal signature are usually omitted. The use of the subject heading is included, however, because it immediately tells the reader what is discussed in the memorandum. The subject line is also an aid in filing the communication.

The style of an interoffice memorandum form may vary from one office to another, but the approach to typing memos is always the same. In offices that do not have printed forms, you can follow the same general procedures to transcribe a memo on a sheet of plain typing paper.

Memo Stationery.   Memorandums can be typed in both full-sized and half-sized memo forms. The printed head on these forms will usually show these key words: To, From, Subject, and Date. The heading might also contain other items such as telephone extension, department, and copies to.

Placement and Margins.   Set a left margin even with the headings or two spaces after the printed colons. Set a right margin approximately equal to the left margin.

Plain Paper.   If no printed forms are available, the memo should be typed on standard-sized plain typing paper. MEMORANDUM or INTEROFFICE MEMORANDUM should be typed in all capitals and centered at least one inch from the top of the paper, with at least two blank lines below. Use the company's standard format to set up a heading. The person dictating the memo may not give you the information in correct order.

Spacing.   Triple space after the last line of the heading to begin transcribing the body of the memo. Generally, memos should be typed in block form and single spaced with double spacing between paragraphs.

Closing.   There is no complimentary close and no signature. Sometimes the sender will sign the memo at the bottom, depending on the nature of the memo and/or the policy of the organization.

Typist's Initials.   The typist's initials and other notations such as enclosures and carbon copies are typed a double space below the body of the memo at the left margin.

Second Page.   The second and subsequent pages of a memo are typed on plain typing paper of the same size and color as the first page. Use the same side margins as on the first page and type a second page heading as you would for a two-page letter.

Carbon Copies. Use standard-sized carbon paper and second sheets to make carbon copies of a memo, even if the original memo is transcribed on a smaller memo form.

There are special memorandums printed on three-part forms which provide space at the bottom for the addressee to respond. The original message is typed or written on the top portion. If a reply is necessary, it is written or typed on the bottom portion. The first sheet is kept by the original recipient, the second copy is kept by the sender, and the third copy is returned to the original sender.

While most memos are short, some are very long and may contain tables, charts, or graphs. Memos, especially long ones, should be organized in a way that makes it easy for the reader to absorb the information presented. Long memos can be broken up with headings and subheadings, using letters and numbers to break up different categories. For example, notice the use of headings in the following memorandum:

MEMORANDUM

TO: All Employees   DATE: August 8, 19—
FROM: James Crew
SUBJECT   Sick/Personal Days

I.   Number of Sick/Personal Days Allowed
Each employee is entitled to ten sick and/or personal days each year. Five may be taken between January and June, and the remaining five between July and December.

II. Reasons for Taking Sick/Personal Days
Any employee may take a sick and/or personal day for any of the following reasons:
    a. illness or accident
    b. death in the family
    c. doctor's or dentist's visit
    d. illness of spouse or dependents
    e. court appearances
    f. tests for driver's license
    g. children's school-related activities

III. Procedure to Follow
If you know in advance that you will be taking a sick and/or personal day, give your supervisor as much notice as possible. When you are too ill to come to work, you or a family member should

---

call your supervisor before 10 a.m. so that temporary or fill-in help can be arranged.

Following these rules will ensure a smooth running operation and a pleasant working environment for all of us. If you have any questions or problems, stop by the Personnel Department, and we will endeavor to help you.

WRITING REPORTS

Some long memos may actually be reports. Business reports serve several functions: they may present or explain a situation, analyze one or more solutions in detail, or recommend a course of action. Some reports merely present information and let the reader draw his or her own conclusions. Other reports explain a problem and present various solutions.

An executive assistant may have to do research for a report or take notes at a conference and turn those notes into a report. Research and handling meetings will be discussed in later chapters. What is emphasized here is the final step: preparing the information for consumption; in other words, organizing the data into a logical, readable format.

Here again, the executive assistant can follow the basic rules discussed under letter writing: short words and sentences; well-organized paragraphs; correct grammar, spelling, and punctuation; and proper style and tone. However, since reports are generally much longer than either letters or memos, the executive assistant will have to pay even more attention to organization. Therefore, it is usually helpful to make an outline, following the format for memos: headings, subheadings, letters, and numbers. Arrange the data in the clearest way: an introduction, the body of the report, and a summary, conclusions, and/or recommendations.

SUMMARY

Being able to write good business letters, memos, and reports is a valuable asset for any executive assistant. Increasingly, it has become an absolute necessity for many executive assistant jobs and is often considered a skill as essential as typing. Therefore, an executive assistant should learn the basic rules of business communications and should keep reference tools such as a dictionary, thesaurus, and grammar book handy.

An executive assistant should be able to correct letters when necessary and compose his or her own letters when that is part of the job. The executive assistant is a specialist who uses skills—writing, spelling, grammar, and sentence structure—as well as a basic knowledge of the styles and formats of a variety of business documents to produce a finished document that is accurate, attractive, and consistent with company style.

1. The purpose of business communications is to inform.
2. An author should decide on the purpose of the communication and define the reader.
3. Long, technical words should be used sparingly in communications.
4. Sentences and paragraphs should be organized according to a plan.
5. Courtesy and proper tone are important components in a letter.
6. The letterhead reflects the image of a company.
7. Style and letter placement may vary from company to company.
8. Parts of a business letter include: date, inside address, attention line, salutation, subject line, reference line, body, complimentary close, company name, signature line and title, reference initials, enclosure notations, copy notation, and postscript.
9. A two-page heading of a letter contains the name of the recipient, the page number, and the date.
10. Executive assistants should learn to evaluate alternative letter styles so that they can arrive at an intelligent decision regarding the best style for a particular organization.
11. Memos are usually written to people within an organization.
12. Reports are written to inform, explain, analyze, and recommend.

CHAPTER RECALL EXERCISES

1. Why is it necessary for an executive assistant to know how to write business letters, memos, and reports?
2. How will the ability to write enhance an executive assistant's career potential?
3. How can an executive assistant learn the necessary writing skills?
4. Should the executive assistant correct the executive's grammar or spelling if it is incorrect? How can this be handled diplomatically?
5. What are the principles of effective communication? Explain each in your own words.
6. How is a memo different from a letter?
7. Why is tone so important in a business communication?
8. What are the basic elements in writing a report?
9. How can the executive assistant begin to compose letters if the executive does not suggest it?
10. Describe some changes in producing letters that can lead to cutting costs.
11. What impact, if any, does a well-designed letterhead have on recipients?
12. Briefly describe types of paper used in stationery.
13. What source does the executive assistant turn to for company letter styles?
14. Why is a letter placement table helpful to an executive assistant?

15. Identify the elements of the following letter by writing in the name(s) of the parts.

_____   October 18, 19—

              | Mr. Ted Helweg
_____ | Integrated Word Processing
              | 420 Lexington Avenue
              | New York, NY 10017

_____ Dear Mr. Helweg:

              | Your presentation to my medical workshop class was
              | informative and interesting.
_____ |
              | Thanks for taking your free time to share your
              | expertise with me and my students.

_____   Sincerely,

_____   Lillian Swanson
_____ drf

16. What are some choices (alternatives) regarding titles for women when marital status is unknown?
17. How should reference initials be typed? Where are reference initials placed in the letter?
18. Briefly describe the purpose of a blind carbon copy. Where is it typed?
19. List the advantages of the simplified letter compared to traditional styles. Do you see any disadvantages in the simplified letter style?

PROBLEMS AND APPLICATIONS

1. Ruth Chester was excited about her new position in the communication and office services department of a medical center. After graduating from a local college, Ruth was involved in the planning and implementing of the correspondence center. The center, which served a group of five doctors specializing in rheumatology and arthritis, was equipped with text-editing and dictation equipment. Two correspondence assistants handled the medical reports and correspondence. Ruth was the supervisor but often pitched in on the typing during busy periods.

The correspondence was uniform and consistent, thanks to Ruth's creation—a simplified correspondence manual which served as a guide for all documents.

As time progressed, many of the member doctors became more involved in research and actively participated in professional foundations and the preparation of medical papers for publication in the *Journal of the American Medical Association*. As the volume of paper work increased, it became

Ruth's job to increase productivity without increasing equipment and/or personnel. Perhaps a solution might be to streamline and modernize the preparation of correspondence and documents. This would involve, of course, the approval and cooperation of the doctors (word originators) as well as orientation of the assistants to the new procedures. What are some of the changes you would suggest to improve the correspondence preparation? Outline a plan of action.

2. Write to a business forms or stationery company and request sample copies of their stationery.

3. Design a letter placement scale, using the margins that apply to your typewriter. Determine how many spaces there are after the bell rings and compute the spaces for your right margin. For example, if your typewriter is pica and there are eight spaces after the bell before your carriage locks, your margins for a 50-space line would be 17 and 75 ($42 - 25 = 17$; $42 + 25 = 67 + 8 = 75$).

4. Correct and type the copy in the right column as directed in the left column.

a. Address and salutation. Use open punctuation.	ms peggy c. keenan customer service advisory service damart thermawear 1811 woodbury ave portsmouth nh 03805
b. Second page heading. Use block form.	ann mayfield, 2, current date
c. Second page heading. Use horizontal form.	mr. jim bruno, 2, current date
d. Address with attention line. Use mixed punctuation.	management information systems 140 barclay center cherry hill nj 08034 attention mr. lawrence feidelman
e. Letter with blocked subject line. Use open punctuation.	dear mr. becklye subject good will

5. When Barbara started her new job as administrative assistant to Ms. Johnson in the marketing department, she was a little nervous but was confident that she could handle the job. After all, she had been an executive assistant for over two years, and her typing and transcribing skills were excellent. This was a step up for Barbara, and she was anxious to do an excellent job.

When Barbara came in on her first day of work, she familiarized herself with her work tools and then asked Ms. Johnson if she had anything for her to do. Ms. Johnson looked up from a large stack of mail and said, "Yes, you can help me answer the mail. I've just come back from a business trip and the mail is really backlogged."

She then gave Barbara a tape cassette to transcribe. "There are about a dozen letters on this side of the tape, Barbara; I was in a rush, so they are a little rough," Ms. Johnson explained. "Polish them up for me, please, because they are very important letters and I want them to sound just right."

"When you're done with those, you can begin on this stack," Ms. Johnson continued, as she handed Barbara a pile of letters. "I jotted some notes on the top of each letter explaining how I want to answer it. Will you compose the letters for me?"

Barbara was paralyzed. She had never written business letters before; in fact, she had done very little editing before since her previous boss had preferred that letters be typed exactly as they were dictated. What should she do? How should she handle this situation? Is there any way Barbara can prepare herself to be more competent in this area?

6. a. Using the AMS letter style, type the following letter:

current date, Ms. Susan Fidel, Director, Bend Foundation, 139 State Street, Rochester, NY 10016. Put in an appropriate subject line for the letter. Put in the salutation, and sign your name in the closing.
BODY: Thank you for sending the information concerning grants available through the Bend Foundation this year.

We are planning to send in a proposal for funding for the Community Development Program which has been going on for the past three months. The two-year program will provide parks for each of the apartment complexes.

You can expect to receive our proposal by the deadline date of April 1.

  b. Type the letter in blocked style.
  c. Type the letter in modified block style.
  d. Set the letter up as a memo and type it.

7. Choose one of the following topics and write an outline of what you would include if you were writing a report on the topic.
  a. Principles of Written Communication
  b. Good Study Habits
  c. Careers for Women in Business

8. How would you present the following bad news in a positive way? Write each of the paragraphs the way you would present them in a letter.

  a. You don't have the time to fill out a questionnaire for a graduate student.

  b. Refusal must be made to a college student for granting credit at your store. You never grant credit to college students.

  c. You hired someone else for the job because that person had more work experience and now you must write a letter giving the decision.

LANGUAGE SKILLS DEVELOPMENT

1. Improve the following sentences:
   a. The study is nearly complete at this point in time.
   b. Your request is on file at the present time awaiting assignment for determination and execution.
   c. After a comprehensive appraisal of all the circumstances pertaining to the case. . . .
   d. If one does a little digging, you will find the treasure buried in the backyard.
   e. Because he does not have a sense of balance, the shark bit Jim's leg as he fell into the water.
   f. Let me take this opportunity to congratulate all the employees whom made it to work during the recent blizzard.
   g. Its a known fact that those plants all have very high stacks to carry there smoke above the surrounding countryside.
   h. Your the right person for this job, alright.

2. a. Learn to spell the following words:

accidentally	methodology
concede	previous
convenience	recommend
intuition	society

   b. Divide the words in the best place.

3. Define the following easily confused words and use each word in a sentence.
   a. capital, capitol
   b. stationary, stationery

4. Proofread and correct the following paragraph:

   The finale census figures should show that manny citys in the US have loss people. That may be becauce familys and household sizes have decreased during the pass decade. Their is expected to be a large increase in the number of elderly person and and increase in the number of persons over thirty-five years of age. Theres also a continued hi rate of divorse in American. Complete counts will not be availabal until early nextyear.

HUMAN RELATIONS INCIDENTS

1. Gene has been working as Mr. Sikora's executive assistant for the past year. Mr. Sikora is a perfectionist and demands that all correspondence be perfect in every detail. Mr. Sikora takes the time to dictate all the paragraphs and punctuation marks, even though

---

Gene feels he is competent enough to put in the correct punctuation. There are times, in fact, when Mr. Sikora does not follow the punctuation rules given in handbooks. Gene has changed the punctuation on these occasions, but Mr. Sikora always changes it back. Is there a way Gene can tactfully educate his boss about the proper use of some of the commas? How would you suggest doing this?

2. To save time and money, the supervisor of the correspondence center decided to start typing all correspondence in the AMS simplified letter style. There are a few of the very traditional word originators who are balking at this so-called innovation in letter styles. How can the supervisor convert these die-hards to the simplified letter style? Should the supervisor refuse to type the letters in any other style, or should the word originators make the decision about the style of letter?

METHODS AND PROCEDURES OF INPUT

The professional role of the executive assistant is exemplified most keenly within the dictation cycle. Two techniques are important in the dictation cycle: (1) the ability to take dictation, and (2) the ability to produce a mailable copy of the dictation the first time.

This chapter will analyze the comparative merits and applications of the methods of input. It will explore the ways in which ideas are originated, and the skill and responsibilities of the executive assistant to accurately take and transcribe input.

At the end of this chapter, you should be able to:

1. Compare the methods of input, giving the advantages and disadvantages of each method. ☐ 2. List dictation supplies necessary for the executive assistant. ☐ 3. Discuss techniques for taking shorthand dictation. ☐ 4. Discuss techniques for taking machine transcription.

CHAPTER
8

METHODS OF INPUT

The workflow through an office system is from the word originator or word author (both terms refer to the individual originating ideas) to the typist where it is put on paper (transcribed) and sent back to the originator for revision and/or distribution.

The originator or author inputs (originates ideas) work to the executive assistant or typist by one of several methods: longhand, rough draft typed copy, dictation at the typewriter, shorthand, or machine dictation.

LONGHAND

Longhand continues to be the most frequently used method of input. Several surveys[1] conducted by office systems and professional word processing consulting organizations reveal the following classifications of input:

Longhand	75 percent
Shorthand	8 percent
Machine dictation	12 percent
Other	5 percent

Longhand is so popular because executives can see the document being created and thus can reread it and make any final changes before releasing it for transcription. Many people feel totally comfortable when writing something on paper. They can think, compose, and organize their thoughts by using simple tools like a pen and a writing tablet, instead of manipulating machines. Thus, the advantages of simplicity, convenience, and visibility make longhand the most frequently used form of origination in offices today.

Legibility can be a problem as valuable time is consumed by the tran-

Figure 8.1
Office systems workflow.

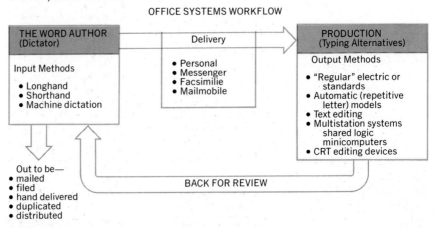

OFFICE SYSTEMS WORKFLOW

[1]International Information/Word Processing Association (IWP).

Figure 8.2
Three methods of input.

scriptionist in trying to decipher poor handwriting. When you consider that time is money in terms of salaries and productivity of both executive and transcriptionist, it is evident that longhand is, perhaps, the least desirable means of origination.

SHORTHAND

Shorthand is another method of origination involving the interaction of two people. Shorthand has been considered one of the basic tools in office work. The executive, the creator of ideas, who dictates on the run or who needs instant transcripts, finds this method of input more convenient than long-hand. The executive simply calls his or her executive assistant into the office and dictates the correspondence. The executive assistant is responsible for catching any omissions, errors, and ambiguities. The executive assistant usually reads back the dictation for possible revising and final polishing, and then types the dictation in final form.

Dictation supplies should be readily available so that you can respond immediately to the dictation call. When your employer requests assistance with dictation, take the following necessary supplies:

1. *Stenographic notebook.* Stenographic notebooks are standard size and are constructed of spiral-bound pages that lie flat. The covers are stiff so that the book will stand alone for transcription.
2. *Pen.* For writing shorthand, select a reliable pen with a good point. Avoid using pencils for taking dictation as the thickness of the point tends to vary as you write, and a pencil is more difficult to read than a good pen.
3. *Miscellaneous supplies.* Colored pencils, rulers, paper clips, and elastic bands are other supplies that may be necessary in the dictation/transcription cycle.
4. *Dictation folder.* All of these supplies can be assembled in a work folder or binder that has a stationery pocket inside each cover. The stenographic

notebook will fit easily in the right-hand pocket. The left-hand pocket can be used for reference copies of correspondence, reports, or other items related to the day's dictation. These related items consist of information about telephone calls and additional appointments. Place several pens, colored or black pencils, and a small ruler in the pocket of the folder beside the stenographic notebook.

The following dictation techniques will provide guidelines for promoting efficient and accurate recording of dictation:

1. Sit in a comfortable position and place your notebook on a firm surface.
2. Use the thumb and forefinger of your left hand (right hand for the left-handed writer) to push the page upward gradually and thus avoid writing near the bottom of the notebook in a cramped position.
3. Write the beginning date of use on the notebook cover. Label each notebook cover with the name of the dictator if you take dictation from more than one person.
4. Use an elastic band, paper clip, or triangularly folded notebook page corner to help you find the first blank page on which to write.
5. Use special coding symbols to remind you of some special direction, such as clearing up an error, a question, or an omission.
6. Use pauses or interruptions in the dictation to your advantage by writing in special transcribing instructions in colored pencils or rereading your notes to improve your outlines.
7. Mark rush items appropriately. Print the word "RUSH" in capital letters at the beginning of a letter. A number may be assigned to each letter. This may be helpful if you are asked to transcribe particular letters in any special order.
8. Allow several lines between items of dictation to provide room for insertions, changes, and special instructions. If you find that the dictator normally makes quite a few changes after the dictation, you may want to leave the entire right column blank to make the changes to the dictation.
9. Write difficult words, technical names, or proper names in longhand if you are not sure of the shorthand symbol.
10. If you are unsure about a word, phrase, or special instruction, do not be afraid to ask the dictator. Obviously, executives prefer not to be interrupted while dictating, but it is better to interrupt the dictator to ensure accuracy rather than to guess and transcribe an incorrect word or phrase or misinterpret instructions.
11. Indicate the end of the dictation by marking your notebook with a line across the column after the last word or sentence transcribed.
12. When the dictation is complete, listen carefully to any last-minute instructions.
13. Present the letters for the dictator's signature after you have transcribed and proofread them.

MACHINE DICTATION/ TRANSCRIPTION

Machine dictation is perhaps the most efficient method to move words along the communication cycle. Machine dictation allows the dictator the freedom to dictate wherever and whenever he or she wishes. The dictator is not locked into any schedule and does not have to wait for the executive assistant to finish another task. Also, there is a greater sense of freedom, for the executive assistant no longer has to wait around with pad and pen while the word originator finishes a phone conversation. It does not tie up the time of two people. Using dictating and transcribing machines means that only one person is needed for each of the two functions which, in turn, results in lower cost per unit of work than longhand and shorthand.

Machine transcription is the production of typewritten copy of dictated material using a transcribing machine. It is transcribing from sound—from a recording of someone else's voice, not from visual materials, such as

Figure 8.3

shorthand notes or handwritten copy. This is a unique skill, and it takes learning and practice to develop.

It is a misconception to think that if you are skilled as a typist, you will be equally skilled in machine transcription. There is an added dimension to the machine transcription skill, which is the ability to retain (in the mind) a group of words while momentarily releasing the foot pedal to stop the machine and continue to type. As you type the last few words, you must restart the foot pedal to stop the machine and continue to type. Soon, an ear-foot-finger coordination develops and a momentum builds for smooth typing.

Here are some suggested techniques for efficient machine transcription:

1. Prepare the machine (transcriber) by inserting the media (belt, cassette, or disk). Listen and adjust the controls for proper tone, volume, and speed.

Figure 8.4
Dictaphone Thought Tank System 192 (Courtesy of Dictaphone).

2. Preview the material (scan) to locate corrections or special instructions found on the index slip or LED (light emitting diode), an electronic display panel. The index slip is a record of dictation that helps determine the length of documents and number of items; it also shows the location of corrections and special instructions within the body of the documents. The new LED electronic display panels do essentially what the index slip does. The electronic display will indicate the approximate length of each item dictated and the indicator scale will show total dictation time.

An additional preview aid is a special index tone. This is a sensor that permits you to scan the media electronically. By activating the foot pedal or fast-forward control, the unit will scan at high speeds. At each electronic index tone the unit will stop momentarily, and a tone will be heard in the headset. This feature permits rapid scanning forward and backward to locate urgent memos for priority transcription. It also permits the dictation to be scanned rapidly for special instructions.

3. Organize your work before you start. Use the proper stationery and

Figure 8.5
Executive assistant transcribing (Courtesy of Lanier).

business forms as instructed by the dictator. Keep media to be transcribed and any correspondence or attachments in individual correspondence folders. This allows you to refer to these materials if necessary as you transcribe dictation.

4. If a letter doesn't make sense, don't transcribe it; ask the dictator about it. The dictator will appreciate your concern. However, if a grammatical error has been dictated, transcribe the correct word or phrase.

A good transcriptionist also needs a thorough knowledge of syllabication and word division. On-the-spot decisions must be made to maintain continuous typing and to produce as even a right-hand margin as possible. Maintaining an even right-hand margin can be a challenge, but you can do it easily if you learn some basic word division rules. When in doubt, you should consult a dictionary. Word division rules appear in the appendix.

In addition to word division, a sound knowledge of the rules of capitalization, numbers, abbreviations, and punctuation marks will help you apply them correctly and quickly during transcription work. Your value and confidence as a skilled office worker soars when you become proficient in these important skills. Some basic rules for grammar and style appear in the appendix.

5. If you miss a word or phrase because the dictation sounds garbled or distorted, you should do the following:

a. Adjust the tone for more clarity.

b. Adjust the speed control to the normal setting and use your foot pedal as a source of word or phrase retention. There is a misconception that if you adjust the speed control to the lowest setting, it will slow the voice speed. It only distorts the voice by dragging out the syllables. A good transcriptionist should not consider excessive speed an insurmountable problem. Simply activate the foot pedal to compensate for the high rate of speed, thus transcribing shorter phrases at a time.

c. Turn your volume up or use the headphone, rather than an earpiece, if you are working in an area in which there is considerable noise.

The dictator may not speak distinctly. You may backspace by depressing the backspace part of the foot pedal and listen to the word or phrase several times. If, after this is done and the word still cannot be understood, you can ask someone else to listen. Or, you can review the context of the sentence and insert a word that would make sense. For instance, in this recording, "The snow and sleet have made driving. . . . (inaudible)" Instead of reporting back to the dictator and perhaps interrupting the executive who dictated the message, you should be given the authority to insert an appropriate word that would best complete the sentence. In this case, words like hazardous, dangerous, or slippery might be used.

Although the policy for inserting words by the executive assistant may vary, executive assistants should be given the authority to insert words or phrases that are not discernible in the recording and will not change the context or meaning of the sentences. This responsibility saves valuable time in the communication process.

Technical words, proper nouns, amounts of money, and dates that are not transcribed precisely may change the meaning of the sentence and may be very costly or embarrassing to the company. Any of these terms, if unclear, should be checked with the dictator.

If the dictator uses trite expressions, redundant or awkward words, the policy of allowing the executive assistant to make changes that will improve the dictation might not be as clear-cut as a gross error in English or an obvious error in fact. An understanding should be reached between executive assistants and dictators about what changes can and cannot be made. Some executives want their dictation transcribed word for word, while other executives trust their assistants to make any necessary changes that would enhance the quality of the document.

Before you make a change, make sure there is really an error in the first place. If you keep a reference book on English usage handy, you can check to be sure you are right. In addition to English usage books, you should keep a dictionary, thesaurus, reference manual, ZIP Code Directory, and company correspondence manual at your desk.

6. Erase the cassette or file the media after transcription (whichever is company policy).

7. The final step in the transcription process is proofreading. It is your responsibility to check the material before it leaves the office. Each document of the final copy is proofread word for word and figure for figure. It is not enough to check all work for typographical errors. It is imperative to read the content for sense as well. Once the errors are spotted, they should be corrected neatly.

OTHER FORMS OF INPUT

Sometimes it is easy for an executive to dictate to an executive assistant and the material is then typed on the spot. Short memos or informal letters are sometimes transcribed in this way. There are circumstances where an executive has a typewriter available at his or her work station. Brief documents are typed by the executive as final or may be given to the executive assistant in rough draft form to be retyped. Although these input methods are used rarely, there may be times when these simple methods are appropriate. Good judgment and a judicious use of time will influence the choice of which method to use to process words.

Table 8–1 gives a listing of the advantages and disadvantages of the various methods of input.

SUMMARY

There are many options available for the executive concerned with the processing of ideas. The executive assistant must be highly skilled to interpret the input, no matter what form it takes, into an accurate and complete document. This requires skill, training, practice, and a spirit of cooperation between the dictator and the transcriptionist.

TABLE 8-1

COMPARISON OF METHODS OF INPUT

Type of Input	Advantages	Disadvantages
Longhand	Simplicity More natural Visibility (aids in composing and editing)	Poor legibility Time consuming Not economical
Shorthand	Faster than longhand Reliance on personal contact with executive assistant for support while composing Can be used for taking telephone messages and other personal jobs Good for highly confidential dictation	Ties up time of two people Slower than machine dictation Outlines may become illegible with time
Machine Dictation	Convenient Fast Economical Freedom to dictate anywhere, any time Easier to transcribe Compatible with word processing center	Absence of personal contact may be resented by both parties Dictator must be encouraged to use machine and must be trained to use effective dictation techniques
Other Methods	May be more appropriate for certain short documents	Volume of work and type of application may not justify slower method

1. The workflow through an office system is from the word author to the typist where it is transcribed and sent back to the word author for revision or distribution.
2. The author inputs by using the following methods: longhand, rough draft typed copy, dictation directly at the typewriter, person-to-person dictation, and machine dictation.
3. Longhand is the most frequently used method of input.
4. Shorthand lends itself more to on-the-spot and confidential dictation.
5. Machine dictation is the most efficient input system.

6. Stenographic notebook, pen, and dictation folder are some of the necessary supplies needed by the stenographer.
7. It is a misconception to think if you are skilled as a typist, you will be equally skilled in machine transcription.
8. The index slip is a record of dictation that helps determine the length of documents, number of items, and location of corrections and special instructions.
9. The policy of allowing the executive assistant to make changes in the transcription depends upon the dictator.

CHAPTER RECALL EXERCISES

1. Name three methods an executive may use to communicate his or her thoughts.
2. In spite of the inefficiency of using longhand to communicate, why is this method used most often?
3. Why is machine dictation more economical than alternate methods of input?
4. Describe some circumstances when shorthand would be the most appropriate means of dictation.
5. A skilled typist may not necessarily be a skilled machine transcriber. Explain.
6. How does the index slip help the transcriptionist?
7. Some words may be inaudible during transcription. Describe the options you may use regarding the insertion of words while transcribing.
8. What factors determine the correct stationery and letter style to use during transcription.
9. Why is it particularly important for the transcriptionist to possess excellent language arts skills?
10. Name some reference sources you might use during transcription.

PROBLEMS AND APPLICATIONS

1. Your employer dictated a letter in which several of the phrases were garbled and others seemed to fade out. You have reviewed the tape several times and cannot understand the missing phrases. What can you do?

2. Your supervisor calls you in for person-to-person dictation. In the midst of the dictation session, a colleague of your supervisor drops in and begins discussing the latest baseball scores. This exchange goes on for ten minutes. What should you do?

3. One of the executive assistants who works in the same office with you called in sick for the day. Your boss desperately needs a series of letters

transcribed that were recorded by the executive assistant who is out ill. You find the stenographic notebook and attempt to transcribe the shorthand outlines, but you cannot read many of them. What can you do?

4. Do a research report comparing three methods of shorthand: symbol shorthand, alphabetic shorthand, and machine shorthand. Look at such factors as:

    a. history of the shorthand system
    b. time required to master each system
    c. speeds usually attained with each system
    d. how widely each system is used in the United States
    e. advantages and disadvantages of each system.

Present your information as a memorandum report. Use proper headings and footnotes.

5. Visit or call ten offices in your area to determine the method of input most frequently used by these offices.

6. Go to the library and read a recent article on methods of input. Type up a summary of the article. Be prepared to give an oral report to the class about your findings.

7. At your typewriter, compose answers to the following questions. Make your answers complete sentences. Use proper punctuation; proofread and correct your errors.

    a. What is today's date?
    b. What is your name and address?
    c. What are your favorite activities?
    d. What do you plan to do after you finish school?
    e. Write a brief summary of a book you have recently read or a movie you have recently seen.

8. Have someone dictate the following short memo to you as you type it at your typewriter. Make one carbon copy. Correct your errors.

To the Staff; From your boss; Use today's date; Subject is Travel Vouchers.

Effective July 1, the new travel vouchers must be turned in three days prior to an out-of-state trip. This will allow the Accounting Department enough time to process cash advances.

You can pick up the new travel vouchers in Room 215 any time after 1 p.m. on Friday.

9. Type the following letter written in longhand. Use an appropriate letter style. Make two carbon copies of the letter and address an envelope.

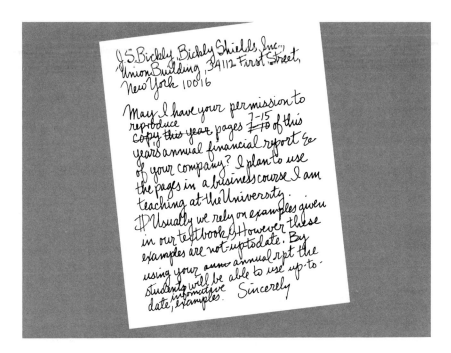

LANGUAGE SKILLS DEVELOPMENT

1. Insert the proper punctuation in the following sentences:
   a. Fred Reeves a small time thief decided not to show up for his trial last December.
   b. This was a potentially expensive situation for Keith Frank who signed his name on a $2,000 bond to get Reeves out of jail.
   c. The Commission ignored the advice of its lawyers and allowed the recipients to continue receiving the tax abatement.
   d. If the union fails to reconsider their position this becomes a question of strong wills and endurance.
   e. Already 25 children have been hospitalized for undernourishment and treated with a liquid nutrition substitute according to the morning paper.
   f. There may be far reaching consequences unless this situation is resolved by Friday November 15.
   g. The two storms at 9 a.m. and 5 p.m. dumped two inches of rain on the city.
   h. Meanwhile there were 33,000 homes without power and there were 1,000 homes without telephone service.
   i. Although the downtown tours will end in October the city hopes to continue the tradition next year if available funds come through.
   j. Increasingly the law is recognizing that sexual harassment between

coworkers is the responsibility of management to stop however many companies are doing nothing to stop this injustice.

2. Proofread the following paragraph and correct any errors.

You can gain knowlege to advanse in you job or change carrers with out leaving your home by using a home study corespondence cource. For example men and woman with all types of back ground thruout the US are learning too become electricians, technisians, and specialist. There classroome may be a kitchen, a den or a bedroom. Where they study. Where they study is not nearly as important as what they learn. After a lessen is completed and returned to to the school it is checked by a qualifeid instructor whom is available by phone for additional disucsssion.

3. a. Learn to spell the following words:
   commitment
   discreet
   ninetieth
   novelty
   optimal

   b. Divide each of the spelling words in the preferred place, using word division rules.

   c. If you are not familiar with the meanings of the spelling words, look them up in the dictionary and construct sentences using each of the words.

HUMAN RELATIONS INCIDENTS

1. As executive assistant to Mr. Beckman, Robert has many opportunities to use his shorthand skill because Mr. Beckman prefers face-to-face dictation so he can try out ideas and sentences on Robert as he dictates. Mr. Beckman is usually out of the office about two days a week, and the workload during those two days is much lighter for Robert.

Ms. Marsh, a colleague of Mr. Beckman's, has an adjoining office. Ann, who is a good friend of Robert's, is executive assistant to Ms. Marsh. Ann does not take shorthand, and Ms. Marsh usually gives correspondence to her in longhand to be typed.

A couple of times during Mr. Beckman's absence, Ms. Marsh has asked Robert to take some dictation for her. Because he wasn't particularly busy and because he was a little surprised at the request, Robert took the dictation and transcribed the letters. Now, Robert wonders if he should be taking dictation from Ms. Marsh when his first commitment is to Mr. Beckman. Also, Robert is afraid that Ann will think he is after her job and misunderstand when Ms. Marsh asks him to take her dictation.

Should Robert refuse to take Ms. Marsh's dictation? What should be his response to Ms. Marsh? How would you handle this situation?

2. Terri and Roberta sit at adjoining work stations in the correspondence center. Both of their work stations are equipped with reference books (dictionary, thesaurus, procedures manual). Terri has a problem with her spelling. When she first started working for the company, Terri would check the dictionary for spelling; but since that took so much time and since she had so much difficulty using the dictionary, Terri started asking Roberta how to spell certain words.

At different times during the day Terri interrupts Roberta's work to asking the proper spelling of a word. Roberta's concentration is then broken, and her productivity is beginning to suffer.

Roberta is becoming annoyed with Terri's interruptions. Other than this one problem, the working relationship between Roberta and Terri is good, and Roberta wants to keep it that way. How can she handle this situation without harming the working relationship?

DICTATION/ TRANSCRIPTION EQUIPMENT AND PROCEDURES

The use of dictation/transcription equipment in the office has increased dramatically in the last few years. The reasons for this change are threefold. First, the cost of producing a business letter continues to rise; and a large portion of this increase is directly attributable to the higher salaries paid to office employees. Dictation/transcription equipment helps cut the cost of producing a business letter by reducing the amount of time involved in the dictation and transcription processes.

Second, the introduction and acceptance of word processing concepts have resulted in a much greater utilization of input (dictation machines) and output (transcribing machines and text-editing typewriters) equipment.

Third, the type of dictation/transcription equipment available to today's user is technologically superior to older models in terms of appearance, construction, voice quality, ease of operation, and variety of equipment.

What this means to today's executive assistant students is that they should be prepared for a business world that relies more and more on dictation equipment. A brief tour of the classified ads will reveal an increasing number of jobs calling for machine transcription skills.

The ability to dictate into a machine is particularly important in firms that have established word processing centers. Since these centers are often some distance from the executive, it is imperative that the executive be able to generate correspondence remotely, without having to send for a stenographer from the center.

At the end of this chapter, you should be able to:
1. Describe the kinds of dictation/transcription equipment. ☐ 2. Describe how to measure productivity of input. ☐ 3. Describe standard features on dictation equipment. ☐ 4. List the media used in dictation equipment. ☐ 5. Define administrative dictation. ☐ 6. List the techniques for good dictation.

CHAPTER 9

Figure 9.1
Executive assistant dictating (Courtesy of Lanier).

TYPES OF EQUIPMENT

Today's executive assistant will find current dictation/transcription equipment different from the bulky, complicated machines of the past. Present machines are designed with the user in mind. They have controls that are clearly identified for ease of operation; they are built to last, yet are compact and attractive.

The quality of voice rendition makes it much easier for the executive assistant to transcribe dictation quickly and accurately, and the variety of equipment available means there is a machine to fit almost every need.

Dictation/transcription equipment can be divided into three basic categories: portable models, desk units, and central systems.

PORTABLE DICTATION MACHINES

Portable dictation machines range in size from pocket models to units that can be carried in an attache case. Business people using dictation equipment for the first time often start with portable machines because they are compact and extremely easy to operate. They are especially popular with people who

Figure 9.2
*Sanyo TRC 3500 Ultra compact cassette recorder
(Courtesy of Sanyo Electric, Inc.).*

need to dictate away from the office; for example, on planes, in cars, or at home. Correspondence that is dictated on a portable model can later be transcribed in the office as long as the portable and the transcribing machine use the same medium.

A dictation medium is the magnetic device on which the dictation is recorded. It may be a belt, cassette, cartridge, disk, endless loop, or reel-to-reel tape. Portable units generally employ a cassette of some type, a standard cassette or a smaller mini- or microcassette. In fact, cassettes have recently become the most popular medium in all sizes of dictation equipment.

If the portable model uses a standard cassette, the dictation must be transcribed on a transcribing machine that uses a standard cassette. If the portable uses a mini- or microcassette, the transcriber must use the same medium. Sometimes, an adapter will enable a standard cassette transcriber to accommodate a mini- or microcassette.

Most of today's portable models feature one-finger control of the basic dictating functions: record, playback, fast forward, and rewind. This makes operation extremely simple and encourages executive use.

Volume and speed controls allow you to adjust the speaking voice to your preference, while fast forward and reverse allow you to back up or speed ahead when necessary. Other standard controls include start, stop, playback, erase, and eject.

One feature of particular importance is indexing, which tells you how

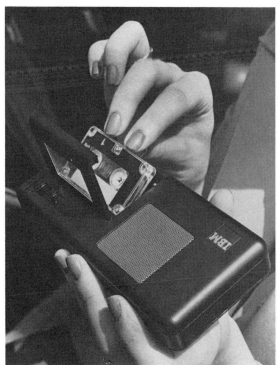

Figure 9.3

Pocket-size minicassette recorder (Courtesy of IBM).

Figure 9.4

Sony Model BM 12 Portable (Courtesy of Sony Office Products).

long each segment of dictation is and how many individual letters or documents are included on the medium. It also lets you keep track of how far you are into the transcription and alerts you to special instructions or priority items. These special instructions and/or priority items can be indexed in various ways: by placing an audible tone on the tape; making visible marks on an index strip; or electronically cueing the tape so that ends of letters and special instructions are shown on the transcribing machine's display panel. Audible signals, or cue tones, can be heard as you play the tape through at high speeds.

When an index strip is used, it is inserted into a slot on the machine. As words are recorded, a needle moves across the index strip. When a special instruction or end of letter signal is given, a button is depressed and a visible mark is made on the strip. When dictation is completed, this strip is removed and sent with the medium to be transcribed. The strip can also be used to identify the dictation on the medium. In some transcribing equipment, the machine will automatically stop at points cued on the system.

DESK-TOP UNITS

Desk-top units use various media. Users have a chance to mark special instructions, end of document, or important changes. The transcriptionist

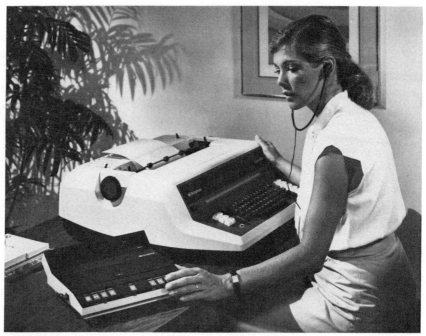

Figure 9.5

Dictamation line of cassette desk-top transcription units (Courtesy of Dictaphone).

can find these special notations immediately by hitting the cue or index button on the office transcribing machine.

Desk-top units are designed for in-office use. The dictation machine is put in the executive's office while the transcriber is placed on the executive assistant's desk. After dictation is complete, the magnetic medium is removed from the dictation machine and given to the executive assistant for transcription.

Some machines serve a single purpose, either dictation or transcription, while other models accommodate both functions in one piece of equipment. When used as a dictation machine, a microphone is attached. When the unit is utilized for transcription, the microphone is removed, and a headset and foot pedal are plugged in.

Desk-top units are more sophisticated than portable models and offer a number of convenience features for both the executive assistant and the executive. However, as in the case of portable units, the trend is toward units that are compact and easy to use. Many units feature instant-on and automatic-off functions, as well as one-button control of major functions.

Some microphones are shaped like telephones to make the user feel more comfortable with them. All controls are located on the microphone so they can be operated easily with standard, mini-, or microcassettes, as well as cartridge-loaded magnetic disks.

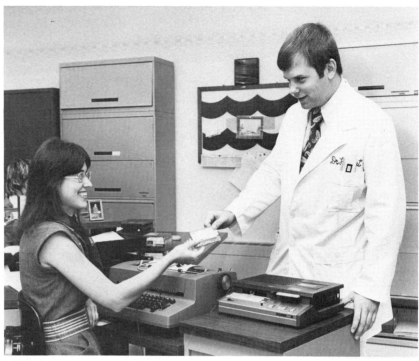

Figure 9.6
Doctor handing cassette to executive assistant (Courtesy of Sony Office Products).

Figure 9.7
Norelco desk-top model (Courtesy of Philips Business Systems, Inc.).

Figure 9.8

Doctor dictating, using telephone handset (Courtesy of Sony Office Products).

Another advantage of the desk-top dictation equipment is its ability to record conferences and telephone conversations. Models with built-in speakers allow a group to listen to recorded material.

Aside from standard dictation, this type of equipment may be used also

Figure 9.9

Lanier Action line desk-top dictation machine (Courtesy of Lanier).

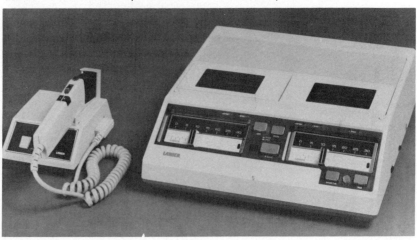

as a communication device between the executive and the executive assistant. For instance, an executive assistant may record phone calls and other messages for the executive who is out of the office. The executive, on the other hand, may record instructions or job assignments for the executive assistant. In addition, some models are designed to serve as an intercom between the executive and the executive assistant.

CENTRAL SYSTEMS

Work group configurations are becoming popular because more firms are taking a distributed approach to word processing. The executive dictates into a remote recorder, which is located in a work group that services the executive and others in the department.

Firms that have set up word processing centers, whether they take the form of one large center or a number of smaller satellite centers, may opt for a central dictation system. Central systems range in size from configurations involving a few people to arrangements involving hundreds of dictators and transcribers.

This type of system is most often used by firms that have large numbers of people who occasionally need transcription services, yet do not require private executive assistants. Central systems allow many users to share dictation facilities. They provide 24-hour-a-day dictation capabilities without the need for constant supervision.

Central systems usually involve the separation of the executive assistant function into two parts, correspondence (transcribing and typing) and ad-

Figure 9.10
Dictaphone's thought center system 293 (Courtesy of Dictaphone).

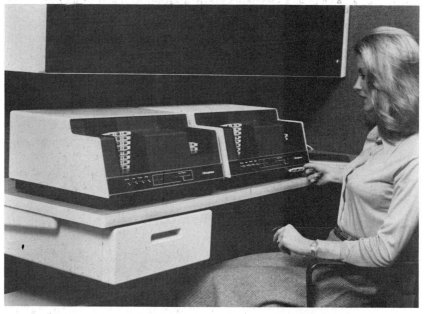

Figure 9.11

Time Master Word management computer (Courtesy of Dictaphone).

ministrative (nontyping) functions. In such cases, administrative assistants would also make use of the services provided by the word processing center.

In a central system, the dictator uses a microphone or telephone that is hooked into the word processing center. When the executive dictates into the microphone or telephone, the dictation is recorded on machines located in the word processing center. This is called remote dictation since the recording device is located at some distance, rather than on the dictator's desk.

If a person uses the system infrequently, it is possible to dictate into the center via a standard office telephone. A person who dictates a large volume, on the other hand, will probably have a separate telephone primarily for dictation.

The most common kinds of central dictation systems are tanks (endless loops) and multiple cassette systems. Tank systems have a loop of tape that provides many hours of continuous recording. Multiple cassette systems use a series of cassettes that are loaded into the system in sequence. When one cassette is filled with dictation, the unit automatically begins recording on the next cassette.

MEASURING PRODUCTIVITY OF DICTATION

An executive assistant working in a word processing center will service many different people, yet will report to the supervisor of the center. The supervisor is responsible for judging the quality and quantity of the work. This is usually done by counting the number of lines or pages produced by each typist in a set period of time. With some central systems, this is done manually, by logging in the amount of work transcribed by each typist; for example, how many cassettes or belts were transcribed.

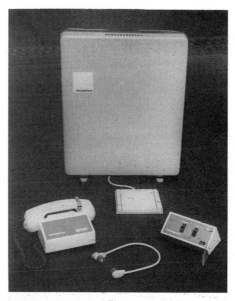

Figure 9.12
Dictaphone's Thought Tank System (Courtesy of Dictaphone).

Figure 9.13
Dictaphone's Thought Tank System 193-MARK II (Courtesy of Dictaphone).

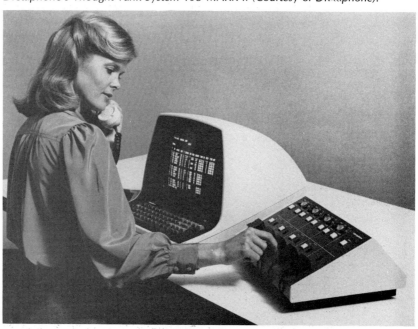

Figure 9.14
Dictaphone Master Mind (Courtesy of Dictaphone).

Figure 9.15
Dictaphone's Time Master produces summary reports of word processing activities (Courtesy of Dictaphone).

Other central systems include a computerized monitoring device which tells the supervisor how much work each typist has transcribed, as well as how much dictation is left to be transcribed. Some models also compute the speed of each of the typists, and this information can be used by the supervisor to determine who should be given the next assignment, based on the speed of each typist and the amount of work each one has to complete.

ADMINISTRATIVE DICTATION

Although administrative assistants sometimes handle creative dictation— dictation that is planned, fully developed, and lengthy—most executive assistant dictation is administrative dictation. Administrative dictation is not a creative process; rather, it is communication for the purpose of completing tasks. Examples of administrative dictation would be appointment scheduling or delegating assignments. Most often, an executive would dictate instructions to an administrative assistant telling the assistant to author a letter to a certain party. The executive would give specific data, such as amounts of money, time, dates, and product names, to be included in the letter. The executive assistant then creates the letter based on the facts supplied by the executive.

There may be occasions, even though the letters may have been addressed to the executive personally, when the executive refers certain letters to you

Figure 9.16
Executive assistant dictating (Courtesy of IBM).

or other associates in the company. This is another example of the executive assistant assuming the dictator's role in correspondence.

The executive assistant may draft a reply for the executive's signature, even though the executive has been asked to reply. When this happens, it may not be readily understandable to the person who receives the reply. In fact, the person may resent not hearing from the executive addressed. When a letter is answered under these circumstances, it is important to avoid giving the impression that the person addressed was too busy or too uninterested to reply.

The efficiency of any company communications network depends greatly on the ability of the word originator to dictate proficiently. More and more corporations are discovering that word originators do not dictate well because of lack of knowledge in the use of equipment, lack of skill in composing and dictating, and lack of a positive attitude toward learning.

Companies are allocating valuable time for teaching dictation skills to executives and executive assistants by means of learning packages, manuals, classroom demonstrations, and simulations. A good dictator can work with a central recording transcription system and can dictate to an executive assistant as well. The message should be audible, simple, and to the point. If correct techniques are followed, dictation will be transcribed accurately the first time; and better letters will result.

TECHNIQUES OF
GOOD DICTATION

Sophisticated office systems have brought about drastic changes in paperwork processing. Perhaps the most significant is the streamlined network of communications, processing the work faster, easier, and more accurately than ever before. This, coupled with the expanded role of the executive assistant to assume more creative work, makes good dictating skills essential for the well-rounded executive assistant. A well-trained executive assistant can dictate routine correspondence into a machine or directly to another executive assistant taking shorthand and thereby relieve the executive of many daily activities. As executive assistants gravitate upward into the mainstream of corporate activities, they undertake more responsibilities that involve creativity, composition, and origination of business correspondence.

Although they are not the prime users of office dictation systems, there is a growing number of administrative assistants who originate dictation. The executive assistant is perhaps more aware and more sensitive to the importance of good dictating techniques than many other people within the corporation. This awareness has been nurtured by the executive assistant's basic groundwork and experience in working on the other side of the microphone. A transcriptionist can understand the exasperation and frustrations that result when confronted with the following problems:

1. The dictator forgets to indicate a correction. The transcriptionist races ahead unaware, types the incorrect version, and then must waste time correcting or retyping.
2. The dictator neglects to indicate carbon copies. When the letter is finished, the individual dictating begins to rattle off the names of people who are to receive copies.
3. The dictator uses a word like epimorphosis and does not spell the word. More time is lost as the transcriptionist ponders over the dictionary.

These are just a few examples of poor dictation techniques. There are others, of course, that can make the calmest transcriptionist smolder, such as when the dictator rustles papers while doing some last-minute research in the middle of dictation.

Whether the executive uses a shorthand dictation system or chooses machine dictation, careful planning and an empathy for the transcriptionist are necessary. Following are some suggestions that an originator of business communications can practice to help the transcriptionist do a better job:

1. Prepare your dictation machine by inserting the media (belt or cassette) and adjusting the controls of your machine. An index slip or indicating device should be used to help the transcriptionist plan for letter length and margins during transcription.

Figure 9.17
Transcriber finding it difficult to transcribe words.

Figure 9.18
Executive dictating a memo into the recorder (Courtesy of IBM).

2. Organize your thoughts before you dictate so that you know what you are going to say. Specifically, this can be done by following a logical pattern:
   a. Select a quiet location.
   b. Schedule dictation early in the day.
   c. Try to prevent interruptions while dictating.
   d. Decide the purpose of the communication.
   e. Select points to meet your objective.
   f. Gather appropriate reference material.
   g. Briefly outline points in sequence.
   h. Develop ideas into paragraphs.
   i. Visualize your reader.[1]
3. Do not shuffle papers while dictating. This sound can be picked up and can disturb the transcriptionist.
4. Before dictating, identify yourself, your department, and your telephone extension.
5. Indicate the type of document to be transcribed—a letter, memo, report—so that the proper stationery can be assembled.
6. Let your transcriptionist know how many carbons you want before you start dictating.

[1]Mona Casady, "Teaching Administrative Secretaries to Dictate," Unpublished report.

7. Indicate any unusual formats beforehand, such as long quotes, graphs, or enumerated items.
8. If the job is a rush, notify the supervisor beforehand or as soon as the correspondence is dictated.
9. Dictate numbers slowly, numeral by numeral—that is, zero, two, five, seven (0,2,5,7).
10. Indicate capitalization before you say the word you want capitalized.
11. Mention paragraphs, underlining, and unusual punctuation.
12. State corrections to alert the transcriptionist. Preface your remarks with the words "correction please" or "change that to . . . ."
13. Talk clearly in well-modulated tones, not too loud or too soft. Use your normal conversational tone. When reading material, speak at a normal rate. Avoid mumbling, smoking, and chewing gum or a pencil.
14. Use technical terms with which the transcriptionist is familiar. If you feel there will be a problem with correct transcription, spell technical or difficult words.
15. Be concise. Stick to your plan. Avoid side remarks unrelated to the dictation.
16. Release the talk button during a long pause or break in the dictation.

A good dictator recognizes that the transcriber is part of a team and that effective communication is a two-way street. The dictator should compliment the transcriber for good work, encourage the transcriber to ask questions about items that are not clear, and welcome suggestions for improved dictation.

You can use all of these techniques in developing the following example of a properly dictated letter:

Ellie, this is Anita Kaskel of the Interior Design Department. My telephone extension is 5432. I have a letter requiring two carbons. Please address the letter to Mr. Shep (S-h-e-p) Forrest (F-o-r-r-e-s-t), 901 Surf Avenue, Portland Oregon, ZIP 97331.

Dear Mr. Forrest:
    The preliminary drawings (correction, Ellie, change that to sketches) have been completed, and I know you will be excited to show them to your staff. You will note the decor (d-e-c-o-r) of the lobby is a soft beige color reflecting the same color scheme as the guest rooms. Period. Paragraph.
    The front desk will have a counter-top made of marble imported from Carrera (C-a-r-r-e-r-a), Italy. The (capital M) Manager's (capital O) Office (capital B) Banquet (capital O) Offices will be situated at the rear (correction, Ellie, change rear to northeast) section of the lobby. Period. Paragraph.
    Everything is progressing on target (correction, Ellie, change that to

Figure 9.19
Executive preparing to dictate (Courtesy of Lanier).

schedule), and we see no problem in completing the job by July 23. Please give my best regards to your family. Period. End of letter.

Sincerely, Anita Kaskel, Interior Designer. Send a copy to Laurie Frankel in Sales.

SUMMARY

Sophisticated office systems have brought about drastic changes in paperwork processes. Perhaps the most significant change is the streamlined network of communications—processing the work faster, easier, and more accurately than ever before.

The use of dictation/transcription equipment has increased dramatically in recent years. Today's executive assistant student should be prepared for a business world that relies more heavily on dictation equipment. Executive assistants should think of dictation/transcription equipment as a tool that will allow them to utilize their time more efficiently.

1. The three basic types of dictation/transcription equipment are (a) portable machines, (b) desk-top equipment, and (c) central systems.
2. Dictation equipment uses such different kinds of media as belts, cassettes, cartridges, disks, endless loops, and reel-to-reel tapes.

3. Indexing can be done with a paper strip or electronic cueing.
4. Standard features of dictation equipment include the following functions: record, playback, fast forward, and rewind.
5. Measuring productivity of transcription is usually done by counting the number of lines or pages produced by each typist in a set period of time.
6. There is a growing trend for more administrative assistants to originate dictation.
7. Whether the executive uses shorthand dictation or chooses to dictate into a machine, careful planning is essential.
8. The organization of thoughts by a dictator is an important preliminary step in good dictation techniques.
9. The dictator should encourage the transcriber to ask questions about items that are not clear and welcome suggestions for improved dictation.
10. Dictators do not dictate well because of lack of knowledge about the equipment, lack of skill in composing and dictating, and lack of a positive attitude toward learning.
11. A well-trained executive assistant skilled in proper dictating techniques can make a valuable contribution to the company.

CHAPTER RECALL EXERCISES

1. Name three types of dictation/transcription equipment.
2. What is the function of dictation/transcription equipment in the modern office?
3. Why has dictation/transcription equipment gained in popularity in recent years?
4. How does the speed of machine dictation and transcription compare to shorthand and longhand?
5. What are some of the standard controls found on dictation/transcription equipment?
6. What is a recording medium?
7. Name the various types of media used in dictation/transcription units.
8. How does indexing help the executive assistant?
9. What type of needs do central systems fulfill?
10. How are central systems monitored?
11. Are there similarities in dictation techniques between machine dictation and person-to-person dictation? Explain.
12. Why would the newly promoted executive assistant be sensitive to the importance of good dictation techniques?
13. Describe one example of poor dictating habits.
14. Briefly describe some of the preliminary steps necessary to prepare for dictation.

15. What is administrative dictation? Why does this type of dictation more readily lend itself to the executive assistant dictator?
16. If an executive assistant is instructed to reply to a letter addressed to someone else, what precautions must be taken to avoid giving the impression that the person addressed was too busy to answer?
17. How can companies upgrade dictating techniques among their staff?
18. What role will dictation equipment play in future office systems?

PROBLEMS AND APPLICATIONS

1. As an administrative assistant, you have been asked to reply to letters even though the letters are addressed to your executive. What precautions are necessary to make your letters understandable to the people who receive the replies?

2. Sue Kasten was promoted to administrative assistant. Part of her responsibilities included attending staff meetings, checking news releases, and dictating correspondence. It was this latter task that Sue dreaded the most. She tried using the desk-top dictation unit provided her; but when she picked up the microphone, she froze. The words simply did not want to come out. And, as a result, she reverted to taking pen in hand and writing her thoughts out in longhand. The company was trying to encourage its executives to dictate into machines, and Sue did not want to create the impression that she was unwilling or unable to use dictation equipment. What suggestions can you offer Sue to help her develop machine dictation skills? Is there anything the company can do to help Sue?

3. a. Practice dictating the following paragraph to improve your techniques. Notice the sections of dictation where words are spelled, capitalization is indicated, and special typewriting instructions are given:

These are quotes from the (capital S) Section (capital C) Chief's (apostrophe s) memo of June 17: (colon; space down twice; indent left margin 5 spaces; quote) All secretaries attending (capital W) Workshops in Albuquerque (A-l-b-u-q-u-e-r-q-u-e) must have their estimated travel expense forms completed by June 1 and attend the briefing in the (capital C) Chief's (apostrophe s) (capital O) Office at 9:45 a.m., June 2." (period; unquote; resume original margin; paragraph) Please study carefully the material in your training folders before reporting to your first session.

b. Dictate the paragraph to someone in your class, using either dictation/transcription equipment or face-to-face dictation. Ask the stenographer for suggestions for improvement in your dictating habits.

4. a. Dictate the following letter, using some type of dictation/transcription equipment:

This is a letter on our company's letterhead. Please prepare four copies, an original and three carbons on white onionskin. Dr. Donald E. Robbins (R-o-b-b-i-n-s) 15 Haverford (H-a-v-e-r-f-o-r-d) Road, Utica, New York 13503.

Dear Dr. Robbins: Arthritis (A-r-t-h-r-i-t-i-s) is called (quote) "everybody's disease" (close quote) and with good reason. This widespread (one word) crippler (c-r-i-p-p-l-e-r) affects every one of us in some way-- (dash) directly or indirectly, (comma) physically or economically. (period) Yet most people have only hazy ideas, (comma) or incorrect ideas, (comma) of what arthritis is all about. (period, paragraph)

b. Transcribe the letter from the dictation/transcription equipment.

5. Your employer received a letter from a prospective customer requesting information about the heat pump your company sells. Since the company has brochures printed with this information, you were asked to reply to this customer, enclosing the requested information.

a. Write the letter in longhand, following the principles of good writing. Sign the letter with your name as the executive assistant to Ms. Stone, your employer.

b. Dictate the letter, using dictation/transcription equipment.

c. Transcribe the letter from the equipment, setting it up in a correct letter style.

6. Using the same information given in problem 5:

a. Make an outline of what you will cover in the letter.

b. Dictate the letter, using only your outline as a guide.

7. Visit a dealer that sells dictation/transcription equipment or write or call a manufacturer of such equipment. Prepare a short memo report of the latest features available on the equipment. If possible, include copies of photographs of the equipment.

8. The word processing center where you work is developing a new procedures manual for the word originators in the company. You are responsible for writing the section on effectively using the central dictating equipment in the center. Write an outline of what you would include in this section.

LANGUAGE SKILLS DEVELOPMENT

1. Consult the dictionary to find the meanings of the following words and then use each word correctly in a sentence.

   a. advice, advise
   b. altar, alter
   c. council, counsel
   d. except, accept

2. Using the word division rules, divide the following words in the preferred place:

alter	$1,000,000	business	elude
through	John M. Yellen	commendable	logical
available	Chapter 10	self-respect	yesterday
required	product	claret	yearly

3. Choose the proper use of numbers in the following sentences:
   a. The cost of the folders has increased to (25 cents, $.25).
   b. Almost (11,000, 11 thousand) or (13%, 13 percent) of the city's students failed this year.
   c. Keith complained of having to pay ($10.00, $10) for the item.
   d. More than (60, sixty) of the free passes go to the city's (20, twenty) legislators.
   e. The admission fee is $3.25 for adults, ($2.00, $2) for students, and ($1.00, $1) for senior citizens.
   f. (Nine, 9) of the (twelve, 12) defending champs were dethroned yesterday.
   g. Game wardens began shutting down the area on (July 22, July 22nd).
   h. The collision cost the Port of New Orleans ($1 million, one million dollars) in lost business.
   i. The fair will be open every day from (11 a.m., eleven a.m.) to (9:00 p.m., 9 p.m.).
   j. An applicant must have (2, two) years of professional experience.

HUMAN RELATIONS INCIDENTS

1. Bruce is executive assistant to Mr. Union, who is a director of the community playhouse. At Mr. Union's request, Bruce wrote a thank-you letter to a patron who had sent in a $100 donation for the playhouse. Two days after he sent the letter, Bruce received a call from the angry patron. The patron was furious that Mr. Union did not take the time to write the letter himself and assured Bruce that this was the last time any money would be sent to such a rude organization. What should Bruce's reaction be to the telephone call? Is there a way to salvage this situation?

2. Carol transferred from her job as executive assistant in the purchasing department to the word processing center as a correspondence assistant. During her first day on the job, Ms. Russell, the supervisor of the word processing center, explained the center's procedures for measuring productivity. Carol was surprised that her work would be measured and resented the fact that someone would be looking over her shoulder and counting the number of lines she typed each day. What should Carol do? How should Ms. Russell handle this situation?

COMPUTERS

Many office workers are intimidated by computers and want nothing to do with them, mainly because they do not understand them. This attitude is understandable since most people have never seen a computer in operation. Computers are just machines; they are collections of electronic components that must be operated by people.

A computer is a piece of hardware that is programmed by an individual to process data (information) by performing various computations, such as sorting and summarizing. A computer is a tool to help today's managers run their businesses more efficiently by providing fast, accurate information on which to base business decisions.

At the end of this chapter, you should be able to:

1. Name the types of computers. ☐ 2. Describe the primary functions of the main types of computers. ☐ 3. Define the processes involved in a computer system. ☐ 4. Describe the methods of data input. ☐ 5. Describe the methods of data output. ☐ 6. List the modes of operation. ☐ 7. Describe the software used by computers.

CHAPTER
10

TYPES OF COMPUTERS

Executive assistants should be familiar with computers since it is highly likely that they will be dealing with them at some point in their careers. There are hundreds of models of computers available, but they all fall into four main types, based on size and capability: microcomputers, minicomputers, midicomputers, and mainframes or maxicomputers.

MICROCOMPUTERS

Microcomputers are very small computers that use a microprocessor, which is a tiny chip of silicon that contains the arithmetic and logic of the computer. These microprocessors, which are also used in electronic games and home computers, perform thousands of computing functions at a very low cost. This means that even very small companies can afford to purchase á microcomputer today.

According to International Data Corp., a Massachusetts-based research firm, sales of microcomputers for data processing are expected to reach over $600 million by the mid-1980s. This means that executive assistants will have an increasing amount of on-the-job contact with computers in the coming years.

Figure 10.1
The desk-top IBM 5120 Computing System has the power of a computer that twenty years ago would have filled a 20 × 30-foot room and weighed a ton (Courtesy of IBM).

Figure 10.2
TRS-80 Microcomputer System (Courtesy of Radio Shack, a division of Tandy Corp.).

Figure 10.3
The B91 is one of two models in Burroughs B90 series of small computers (Courtesy of Burroughs).

Figure 10.4
Honeywell's Level 6 minicomputer, the Model 57 (Courtesy of Honeywell).

MINICOMPUTERS

Minicomputers offer more capabilities than microcomputers and have a correspondingly higher price tag. A mini may be used as a general purpose computer, performing a variety of business functions such as accounts payable, inventory, and payroll, or it may be dedicated to a specific type of work, such as science or engineering.

MIDICOMPUTERS

Because the power of minicomputers is limited, many growing companies have traded in their minis for the next step up the data processing ladder, the midicomputer. Midis have more processing power than minis, which means they can handle more jobs at faster speeds. This makes them the logical step up for firms that have outgrown the capabilities of their minicomputers.

Micro-, mini-, and midicomputers can be located within the office environment since they do not require a special room.

MAINFRAMES

A mainframe or maxicomputer is a large-scale system that can perform thousands of computing jobs at tremendously fast speeds. Only large companies can afford these mainframe computers because the cost is very high, and small- and medium-sized firms would not need all the capabilities these machines offer.

Unlike small computers, the large-scale computer must be installed in a special computer room that is free of dust and dirt and is kept at a specific temperature. Access to this room is generally limited to the data processing professionals who run the system. Small computers are often operated by office personnel, but this is not the case with mainframes.

PROCESSES OF COMPUTERS

The three main processes involved in any computer system are input, processing, and output. Input involves getting information into the computer in a form the computer can understand. Processing involves the calculations and manipulations that are performed on the information. Output is the way information comes out of the computer.

INPUT

Data can be input into a computer in either one or two stages. In the one-stage method, information is entered into devices that are connected directly to the computer. In the case of small computers, this is usually a keyboard that is part of the computer. With larger systems, the input device is a terminal of some sort.

Figure 10.5
The IBM System/32 Computer offers up to 13.7 million characters of direct access fixed disk storage and can accept input from IBM magnetic card typewriters through the IBM 5321 Mag Card unit (Courtesy of IBM).

Figure 10.6
Burroughs B90 system is suited for use as a standalone data processing system or as a remote processor in distributed data processing and data communications networks (Courtesy of Burroughs).

Most computer systems include a number of peripherals, which are devices that work with, but are external to, the main computer. Peripherals can be either on-line or off-line. On-line peripherals are electronically connected to and under the control of the main computer. Off-line peripherals are not connected to the main computer and operate independently of it.

On-line terminals are connected directly to the computer (on-line to the computer) and can be used both to input data into the computer and to obtain data from the computer. Therefore, they can be both input and output devices.

Some terminals merely send data; others only receive data. Still others both send and receive information from the computer. Some send and receive terminals perform the send and receive functions alternately (one after the other). This is called half-duplex operation. Others send and receive data simultaneously—a full-duplex operation.

Terminals can be either dumb or intelligent. Dumb terminals perform specific functions, such as sending and receiving information, when con-

Figure 10.7
Wang's Virtual Storage multi-user/multi-job computer features virtual memory to deliver the equivalent of a one-megabyte computer at each of up to 32 work stations (Courtesy of Wang Laboratories Inc.).

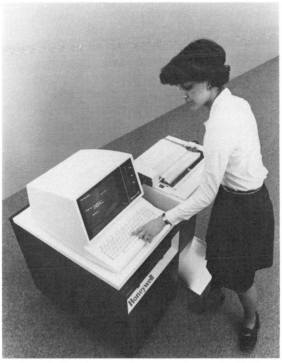

Figure 10.8

Honeywell's entry-level mini, the Model 23. Included in the thirty-inch high cabinet is a Model 23 processor with up to 128 K bytes of main memory, and up to four drawers of double-sided diskettes giving a maximum of two million bytes storage. Also shown is the VIP 7200 console and the 160-character-per-second, bidirectional matrix printer (Courtesy of Honeywell).

nected with a computer system. They do not have any intelligence of their own so they cannot perform any computing functions.

Intelligent terminals, on the other hand, do have intelligence built into them so they can perform some processing functions. In fact, some of these terminals are as intelligent as minicomputers and can perform the same functions.

All terminals have a keyboard and a printing device. Some also have limited storage capabilities. The more sophisticated terminals have a CRT (cathode ray tube) display screen similar to the one on a display word processor. The screen makes it easier for the operator to see the information as it is keyed in. The operator can also check the information to be sure it is correct before sending or storing it.

CRT display terminals are also commonly used for on-line inquiries. For example, if an operator in an insurance company receives a customer account inquiry, the operator can call the information up on the display screen. The operator can then read the information to the customer; if the customer wants to see a hard copy of the information, the operator can instruct the computer to print out a copy of the information that is displayed.

Terminals with screens may also prompt the operator, telling him or her what steps to follow when entering or correcting information. In some cases, if the operator enters wrong information, the terminal will notify the operator that an error has been made. This only works in certain situations, such as when alphabetic characters are entered in a spot where there should be numeric characters only—in a ZIP code, for instance.

In the two-stage method of data input, data is recorded in machine readable form and is then read into the computer. With this method, a person has to read the information and then type it on a keyboard device that converts the information into a format that the computer can read (understand). These input devices include keypunch, key-to-tape, and key-to-disk machines.

Keypunch machines make perforations on paper tape or cards. These perforations represent the data and are read by the computer's tape or card reader.

Key-to-tape and key-to-disk devices use a magnetic rather than a paper medium. When the operator keys in the data, small bits or spots are magnetized onto the medium. These bits, which cannot be seen by the human eye, represent various alphabetic and numeric characters which can be understood by the computer.

Key-to-tape machines use a computer compatible magnetic tape as their medium. This tape is mounted onto a tape drive for entry into the computer. Key-to-disk units utilize a magnetic disk which is put on a disk drive that is directly connected to the computer.

Magnetic input devices are much faster than paper or card units since they are electronic. They also make it easier for the operator to correct mistakes since magnetic media can be erased and recorded over.

Another two-stage method of input involves the use of optical readers. With this method, the data is typed on a typewriter that is equipped with a special typing element. The information can then be read by an optical character recognition (OCR) device.

Data may also be printed in magnetic ink, which can be read by a magnetic ink character recognition (MICR) device. OCR or MICR devices then input the data into the computer.

PROCESSING

The computer itself (not the input or output peripherals) is the part that processes and manipulates the data. It is often called the central processing unit (CPU) and contains a control unit, an arithmetic or logic section, and internal storage or memory.

The CPU is the engine that drives the entire computer system. It processes data by moving information around (sorting, summarizing) and by performing arithmetic and logic operations. It controls its own operation and the operation of all equipment and peripherals attached to it.

Figure 10.9
OCR Systems Model 1205 (Courtesy of Burroughs).

The control unit of the CPU is the manager. It examines the various instructions given to the computer and determines the order in which they are to be executed. It also directs the other components of the computer. For instance, it tells the printing device when to begin printing.

A computer's arithmetic and logic section performs all the arithmetic operations and manipulates the data.

Internal storage houses the computer program (the instructions telling the computer what operations are to be performed and in what sequence) and sometimes stores the data as well.

OUTPUT

After the computer has finished processing the data that has been fed into it, the results may be output in one of a number of ways. As mentioned

Figure 10.10
3M "735" COM System (Courtesy of 3M).

previously, the information can be displayed on the CRT screen of a terminal or it can be printed out.

At the present time, a good portion of computer output is printed at speeds varying from 55 characters per second to hundreds of lines per minute. These printers produce reams of computer printout paper.

Some companies have tried to cut down on these reams of printouts by using computer output microfilm (COM). With a COM system, the computer data is output on microfilm or microfiche instead of paper. This results in a great savings in price. It also saves time since COM is a much faster operation than even the fastest computer printer.

Data processed by the computer may be stored off-line on a magnetic tape or disk drive. A tape drive stores information on reels of magnetic tape. Information is stored sequentially on the tape, which means that to find a particular spot, you must move along the length of the tape until you reach the desired piece of information.

A disk drive stores data by magnetically recording the information on disks or platters that rotate continuously. Disks can store a lot more information than tapes and can find a desired piece of information much faster because storage is random access. This means that the recording arm moves quickly to a desired location on the disk without having to move through all the previous information.

COMPUTER SOFTWARE

Computer hardware cannot run by itself. Something must tell the computer what to do and what steps to follow to perform a particular operation. This is where computer software comes in.

Software is a set of programs and procedures concerned with the operation of the computer system. The software includes a number of computer programs. A program consists of a series of instructions that the computer must follow to achieve a desired result. The program is written in a coded language that is acceptable to the computer.

Various programming languages have been written. The most commonly used ones are high-level (sophisticated) languages such as BASIC, COBOL, and FORTRAN. BASIC is the easiest language to understand because it is a human-oriented language (one that is very much like a human language). For this reason, even noncomputer people can write programs in BASIC.

COBOL is a more complicated programming language used for business applications, and FORTRAN is used for mathematical work. Executive assistants who run small business computers will probably work with BASIC.

Figure 10.11
Sperry Univac® BC/7 Computer (Courtesy of Sperry Univac).

MODES OF OPERATION

A computer mode is a method of operation. Computers can be made to operate in different modes to meet the needs of different companies and applications. Some modes of operation are batch, remote batch, multiprocessing, on-line, interactive, time-sharing, teleprocessing, and networking.

In the **batch mode,** a number of transactions or jobs are accumulated and then fed into a computer in a batch.

In **remote batch** or **remote job entry (RJE),** a remote site or office transmits a batch of transactions to the mainframe computer.

Multiprocessing or **multiprogramming** refers to a mode of operation in which a computer executes two or more programs at the same time.

In the **on-line operating mode,** all the terminals that are on-line to the computer can access and get results from the computer at any time. The computer handles the transactions of all the terminals immediately.

Figure 10.12
NCR I-8140 small business system provides interactive direct processing in which information entered into the system is immediately processed and used to update all affected files (Courtesy of NCR).

Interactive is similar to on-line operation but has the additional capability of being able to engage the computer in a "conversation." The terminal operator presents the computer with a problem; the computer answers the problem, and then the operator can ask the computer for an amplification of its answer. It is a give-and-take operation.

A **time-sharing mode** is like an interactive mode except that users from different companies can access the computer. In an interactive mode, the computer is dedicated to one company and all the terminal operators belong to that company. With time-sharing, the computer is usually owned by a time-sharing computer service bureau that rents out computer time to various companies. The time-sharing computer does just that—shares time among various users.

The **teleprocessing mode** utilizes special hardware and software that allows the mainframe computer to communicate with small computers or terminals over standard phone lines or special data lines. Teleprocessing (also called telecommunications) is necessary to connect geographically remote computers.

In the **networking mode,** geographically separated computers are linked together with transmission lines. This permits data to be transmitted from one computer to another on a regular basis.

DISTRIBUTED DATA PROCESSING

One of the most significant trends taking place in the data processing industry today is called distributed data processing. It is also a trend that will have tremendous impact on office workers.

Distributed data processing (DDP), also called dispersed or decentralized data processing, is a system that redistributes computer power from one centralized location (like a computer center) to a number of remote sites or branch offices. It is a way of bringing computer power to the people who need it, rather than keeping it "locked up" in a computer center.

With DDP, small computers or intelligent terminals are located in a firm's branch offices or departments. These small computers or terminals are linked to the main computer through phone lines or data lines (a teleprocessing network).

There are several advantages to this type of system. First, it gives computer power to branch locations, which means that these offices can perform some of their own computer operations without having to wait days or weeks to have the information processed by the main computer. This speeds the flow of information, giving managers instant access to data without placing undue pressure on the mainframe.

Local managers assume more responsibility for their own operations, thereby gaining better control. Yet, since the small computers and terminals

Figure 10.13
Burroughs B920 is a powerful, interactive, screen-based system designed for a broad range of distributed processing applications (Courtesy of Burroughs).

are easy to operate, the local manager does not have to employ professional data processing personnel to run the system. In most cases, executive assistants and clerical personnel are trained to operate the branch computer.

SUMMARY

The computer is one of the tools that an executive assistant uses in today's office and will continue to use in tomorrow's office. It is a tool that is used to provide fast, accurate information for managers to make business decisions. A computer is a piece of hardware that is programmed by an individual to process information by performing various computations on the data.

1. There are four main types of computers: microcomputers, minicomputers, midicomputers, and mainframes.
2. Three main processes involved in any computer system are input, processing, and output.
3. Terminals can be either dumb or intelligent and on-line or off-line.
4. The central processing unit or CPU contains a control unit, an arithmetic or logic section, and internal storage or memory.
5. A program consists of a series of instructions that the computer must follow to achieve a desired result.

6. Some modes of operation are batch, remote batch, multiprocessing, on-line, interactive, timesharing, teleprocessing, and networking.
7. Distributed data processing is a system that redistributes computer power from one centralized location to a number of remote sites or branch offices.

CHAPTER RECALL EXERCISES

1. What is a computer?
2. Describe the four basic types of computers.
3. What are the three main processes involved in any computer system? Describe each.
4. What is a CPU?
5. What is internal storage?
6. Describe some ways of inputting information into a computer.
7. Describe the processes of data output.
8. What is software?
9. Describe three computer programs.
10. What is distributed data processing?
11. What are some of the advantages of DDP?
12. What impact will DDP have on the executive assistant?

PROBLEMS AND APPLICATIONS

1. There are many applications for the use of computers in the office. Describe three uses that an executive assistant might have for the computer.

2. Recent periodical articles relate that because of the computer, many people will start doing more work at home.

a. Do you agree with this statement? Defend or dispute it.

b. How would the computer make it possible to do more work at home?

c. What would be the advantages and disadvantages of a large percentage of the work force staying at home to work?

3. Home computers (for personal use) are currently being marketed. What are four applications for home computers?

4. Visit a local firm that has a computer to determine how that company uses the computer to make its operations more efficient.

5. Find an article written in the last two years that talks about data processing for the executive assistant. Write a summary of that article. Be prepared to give an oral report of the article to the class.

LANGUAGE SKILLS DEVELOPMENT

1. Punctuate the following sentences:
   a. The paper was delivered after you left for work this morning.
   b. Robyn plans to travel by plane although I do not believe she will.
   c. He watered the plants for he was leaving for vacation immediately after work today.
   d. She looks as well in person as she does on television.
   e. The package cannot be delivered on Thursday no matter what the supervisor says.
   f. The company will not accept bids on Monday after the deadline has passed.
   g. The cake is for Len who has a birthday today.
   h. Pleased by the friendliness of the group we joined the Community Club.
   i. Also please close the door and the windows when you leave.
   j. Tired by the long day Mary Ann decided not to take the long walk.

2. Put in the correct capitalization for the following sentences:
   a. Chicago is known as the windy city.
   b. We live close to one of the great lakes.
   c. Michigan is next door to the buckeye state.
   d. According to the federal trade commission, these procedures are not legal. The commission lists the laws in its latest publication.
   e. My favorite salad dressing is french dressing.
   f. The meeting was called to order by chairman ross.
   g. I always enjoy visiting the farm because of aunt jane's and uncle jim's vegetables.
   h. The president of the United States will address the united nations today.
   i. The campus was crowded today because of parent's day.
   j. When visiting washington, d.c., we had an opportunity to meet governor flower.
   k. The accounting department will be moving to the third floor.
   l. We moved to the east side about three years ago.
   m. I took up skiing after I moved to the north.
   n. The new fall clothes are now in the stores.
   o. The twentieth century has certainly been full of changes.

HUMAN RELATIONS INCIDENTS

1. Frieda, Audrey, and Jerry work as executive assistants in the finance department. Frieda and Jerry have a personality conflict that

is causing everyone in the department some discomfort. They refuse to talk to each other but spend a great deal of time complaining to Audrey about each other. They spend so much time talking to Audrey that she is having a hard time keeping up with her work, and it also puts Audrey in the middle of the situation. Audrey tries not to take sides but does want to heal the rift. Do you know of any solutions for Audrey? How would you solve this problem?

2. On Friday mornings the data processing department has staff meetings that start at 8:30 a.m. One of Martha's responsibilities every Thursday afternoon is to order doughnuts for this Friday meeting. After these staff meetings, Ms. Barnes, Martha's boss and the head of the data processing department, always says to Martha, "Martha, there are a few of the doughnuts left over, so you and the other executive assistants in the department help yourself to what is left."

Martha and the other assistants resent the fact that they are offered leftovers from the staff meeting. They would occasionally like to have first choice or even order doughnuts for their group. They feel like second-class citizens who get to taste the leftovers, if there are any. How can Martha communicate these feelings to Ms. Barnes? Should Martha say anything at all to Ms. Barnes? What should Ms. Barnes do about the situation?

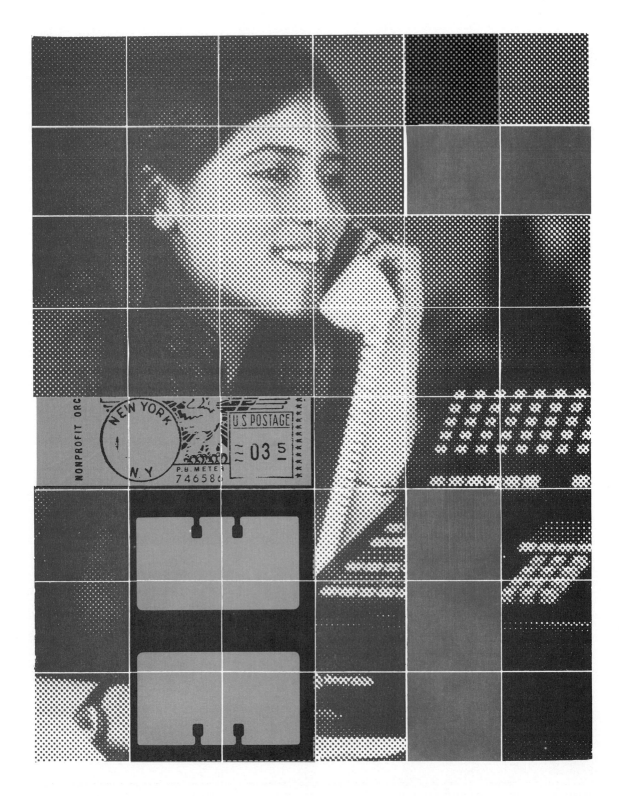

COMMUNICATION TRANSMITTAL SYSTEMS

Establishing effective communication transmittal systems is a vital function in any organization. Because of the increased cost of communications systems and the importance of fast delivery, many companies are considering or using alternative systems.

By understanding each of the available delivery systems, an informed executive assistant can utilize the most effective means of transmitting communications and, at the same time, cut costs. The executive assistant should know the speed, capabilities, and relative costs of all communication systems used by the company. ■ Chapter 11   Mail Handling Equipment □ Chapter 12   Techniques for Processing Mail □ Chapter 13   The U.S. Postal Service □ Chapter 14 Telecommunications □ Chapter 15   Telephone Techniques

SECTION III

MAIL
HANDLING
EQUIPMENT

One of the major responsibilities of almost every executive assistant is the processing of mail. To do this effectively, the executive assistant must be familiar with the various types of mail handling equipment that simplify the job. The major types of mail handling machines on the market today are covered in this chapter.

You need to be familiar not only with the mail handling equipment but also with the actual mailroom in the company. You should know the mailroom's capabilities and limitations—what it can and cannot do for you. If you know what capabilities the company mailroom has, you can use this information as a tool to help you perform your job more efficiently.

At the end of this chapter, you should be able to:

1. List and describe the equipment for processing incoming mail.

☐ 2. List and describe the equipment for processing outgoing mail.

CHAPTER
II

INCOMING MAIL

Most mailrooms are divided into two major operations: handling incoming mail and processing outgoing mail. Different types of equipment are needed in each of these operations. The type of equipment used depends largely on company size and the volume of mail handled.

The functions involved in processing incoming mail include sorting, opening, and distributing envelopes and packages. Equipment used to perform these functions may be single-purpose or multipurpose machines. Single-purpose machines are dedicated to handling one function, such as slitting the envelope. Multipurpose machines perform two or more mail handling functions; for instance, one machine may slit the envelope, remove the contents, check to be sure the envelope is empty, and then discard it.

SORTING THE MAIL

The most common method of sorting mail is by using racks which are divided into bins—one bin for each person, department, or other designation, such as special delivery or priority mail, which should be delivered immediately. The mail clerk goes through the incoming mail and puts each envelope and package into the appropriate bin on the rack.

Most racks have adjustable bins so people who receive large volumes of mail can have a large bin, while people who receive a few letters a day can have a small bin. The racks usually have a table in front where the mail clerk keeps the mail that has not yet been sorted. Some of these tables have a compartment or cabinet under the work surface which can be used for storing supplies.

Automated sorting equipment is also available. These systems are used to sort return address envelopes that have been electronically coded. For instance, when you return a payment on a charge account or insurance premium, the envelope supplied may have been electronically coded. The automated sorter scans each envelope, reads the bar code block, and sorts it into the appropriate bin. These units operate at tremendous speeds, sorting up to 30,000 envelopes an hour. Some of these systems also open, count, and batch envelopes by category.

OPENING THE MAIL

Machines used for opening mail include semiautomated and completely automated systems. A semiautomatic letter opener has a blade which slits envelopes that are fed into it. Generally, the blade can be adjusted to shave either narrow or wide edges from the envelopes. Some letter openers will accept only one size envelope, but most can handle mail of varying sizes and thicknesses.

Automated mail opening systems jog different sizes of envelopes and then automatically feed, open, and stack the envelopes. Some units also count the number of pieces of mail handled.

Automated mail extractors combine a number of functions involved in the opening of mail. These units slit the envelope on one or more sides

Figure 11.1
Open-back sorting rack (Courtesy of Friden).

(depending on the particular model), slicing as little as $\frac{1}{32}$ of an inch off the envelope. The units then pull the sides of the envelope apart so that the operator of the equipment can remove the contents. Some of these systems automatically remove the contents, without operator intervention. An optical scanner scans the envelopes to be sure all the contents have been removed and then discards the envelopes into a waste receptacle and stacks the contents.

Many of the mail extraction systems on the market are in the form of work stations, which allow operators to sit as they extract the contents from the envelopes. These work stations may be either single- or multistation systems.

Single-station work stations are designed to be used by one person at a time. Generally, these systems open mail on only one side. Since only one person is operating the unit, the speed can be adjusted to that person's working capacity. This is especially useful when new employees are being trained on the system. However, on some systems, the work station paces the employee by opening envelopes at a set speed regardless of the operator's readiness.

Multistation systems are operated by a number of people simultaneously. These units usually open envelopes on three sides and have higher through-put speeds than single station systems, handling thousands of envelopes per hour. Some mailrooms also stamp the time and date received on all incoming mail.

DISTRIBUTING THE MAIL

After mail has been sorted and opened, it must be distributed to the recipients. This can be done in a number of ways, including the traditional way of a clerk pushing the mail cart. In recent years, the distribution of mail has been automated through the use of conveyor systems, pneumatic tubes, and self-propelled mail delivery vehicles.

Mail carts can be used to deliver mail, packages, and office supplies. They come in various sizes to accommodate different mail volumes, and some have removable baskets and adjustable dividers.

Conveyor systems can be installed in buildings to distribute mail throughout the building. A horizontal conveyor distributes mail in various locations on one floor. A vertical conveyor system distributes mail to various mail stops on different floors in the building.

These systems operate in the following manner. The main station is the mailroom, where clerks load mail into bins. Each bin has magnets which are programmed to go to a certain mail station on a particular floor or section of a floor. The bin is placed on the conveyor and travels along the network of tracks until it reaches the mail station that has a magnet setting corresponding to the setting on the bin. It stops at that station and the mail clerk removes the contents from the bin and puts in outgoing mail that is going to the central mail station or to one of the other stations along the route.

Pneumatic tube systems can also be installed in buildings. With these systems, mail and other material is put in the tube and air pressure distributes it throughout the building.

Another type of mail delivery system is Bell and Howell's Mailmobile®, a self-propelled, battery-powered vehicle. This 550-pound vehicle is guided from one mail stop to another by following an invisible chemical line that is sprayed on the floor (see Figure 11.3).

Mail is sorted into the unit's delivery compartments, and packages and office supplies can be carried on top. Once the cart is loaded, it is started on its rounds by flicking a switch. The unit then follows the guide path on the floor and stops automatically at every mail station for a period of ten to twenty seconds. If a person wants to detain the unit for a longer interval, he or she depresses the red "stop" switch which runs along the top of the cart. To start up the unit again, the person depresses the green "start" switch.

Soft, pressure-sensitive bumpers automatically stop the Mailmobile® when obstacles are in its path. Motion is halted until the obstacle is removed. Then the unit resumes its rounds automatically. The system moves at a speed of one mile per hour, and an audible soft tone and flashing blue lights announce the unit's arrival.

OUTGOING MAIL

Functions performed in the outgoing mail process include addressing, collating, folding, inserting, tying, weighing, stamping, and sorting.

Figure 11.2
Mailmobile® vehicle (Courtesy of Bell & Howell).

Figure 11.3
*Mailmobile® proceeding on its way. Battery drawer is in lower front of vehicle
(Courtesy of Bell & Howell).*

ADDRESSING SYSTEMS

Addressing systems can be used to store all types of lists, including company names, addresses, and account numbers. Information is put in proper sequence and is then stored on metal plates, plastic cards, foil plates, or paper cards. The information on these address plates is imprinted on an envelope or label by an addressing machine.

Tabletop addressing machines include both manual and semiautomatic models. The simplest system in this group requires that the user hand feed address plates and material to be imprinted into the unit and then operate it by hand. Semiautomatic models combine manual imprinting with automatic feeding. The user loads the address plates into the unit and then imprints each one manually. With a different type of semiautomatic machine, the user has to feed the plates manually, and the machine imprints the addresses automatically.

Console addressing systems feature fully automatic operation and require little operator intervention. They can imprint between 5000 and 10,000 addresses per hour, depending on the model, compared with the 1000 to 5000 pieces per hour handled by tabletop units.

Console addressers often can be programmed to print various portions of a list automatically. In addition, they can perform functions such as document positioning, imprinting, plate transport and ejection, and stacking automatically.

The latest type of addressing system is high-speed ink jet printing. In this process, ink is jet sprayed onto the envelope, paper, or other material at speeds up to 18,000 documents per hour. That represents a speed of 1350 characters per second. The lists are stored on magnetic tape until they are needed.

Some systems are designed specifically to handle computer-generated mail. These high-speed, multifunction units take output directly from the computer, print it and then cut, fold, and insert documents into envelopes, seal the envelopes, apply postage, and sort according to ZIP code—all in one continuous operation.

COLLATING

Collators automate the process of putting stacks of document pages into their proper sequence. Manual and semiautomatic collators require some kind of operator intervention and are designed for small volumes. They are operated by a lever or an electric eye. With lever-operated units, the operator pulls the lever on the collator, and sheets from each bin are ejected so that the operator can grasp the complete set. The electric eye collator works on a similar principle. The operator pushes a button and one sheet is ejected from each bin. The electric eye signals when the sheets have been removed and ejects the next set.

Automatic collators are designed for large volume collating needs. They can be either on-line or off-line. On-line systems are attached to a copier or duplicator and collate copies as they are produced. With off-line models, the stacks are inserted into the collator, which is separate from the duplicating system.

Some collating systems include jogging and stitching options. The jogger/stacker jogs the collated sets into perfect alignment, and the stitcher puts a stitch into the corner of the set.

FOLDING AND INSERTING

Folding and inserting machines range from manual tabletop units to automated console models. Folders can produce many different kinds of folds, such as a single fold, double parallel fold, half fold, and accordion fold. Different units can also handle different paper sizes, ranging from $2\frac{1}{2}$ inches $\times$ 4 inches to 44 inches $\times$ 58 inches.

Once a sheet of paper has been folded, it has to be inserted into an envelope. A basic inserting unit will put one page or card into an envelope; more sophisticated models insert multiple pages of varying sizes and thicknesses. The most complex systems perform several functions, including collating, folding, inserting, sealing, and metering.

Where large packages must be handled, a bundle tyer is often used. These machines are adjustable so they can handle different package shapes and sizes. In addition, these tyers can be used to bundle groups of envelopes for bulk shipments or ZIP code sorts.

WEIGHING AND STAMPING

Postage scales weigh mail and tell the mail clerk how much postage is required. The clerk will then use a postage meter to put on the appropriate amount of postage.

Some systems combine the weighing and metering functions in one self-contained unit. Others perform weighing, imprinting, sealing, and stacking functions automatically.

The newest electronic scales contain a microcomputer and can be programmed to perform various functions. These units compute U.S. Postal Service (USPS) and United Parcel Service (UPS) charges based on either a single digit zone entry or a three-digit ZIP code entry. Weights are computed to within $\frac{1}{32}$ of an ounce for almost perfect accuracy. This, of course, means that the company saves on postage costs since the mail clerk knows exactly how much postage is required on each package.

Rates for special services, such as registered or certified mail and special delivery, can also be calculated by the unit when the appropriate data is input into the system. Rate changes can be made by inserting a new memory chip into the scale. On certain models, postage charges are shown on a display screen.

SORTING

Since the Post Office discounts charges on business mail that has been presorted by ZIP code, many companies have found it economical to sort

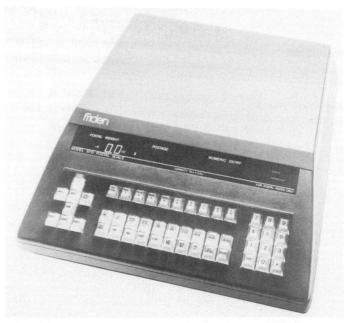

Figure 11.4
Model 8710 all-electronic postage computing scale (Courtesy of Friden).

their mail by ZIP code. This can be done manually or with automated sorting equipment that read the ZIP codes and then sorts the envelopes accordingly.

SUMMARY

Executive assistants should know the capabilities of their companies' mailrooms since they will have to interact with and use the mailroom to perform various phases of their jobs.

1. The mail handling operation is divided into two parts: processing incoming mail and handling outgoing mail.
2. The functions involved in handling incoming mail include sorting, opening, and distributing envelopes.
3. Machines used to perform these functions may be single-purpose or multipurpose devices.
4. Single-purpose machines are dedicated to a single function; multipurpose machines perform two or more mail handling functions.
5. Functions performed in the process of handling outgoing mail include addressing, collating, folding, inserting, tying, weighing, stamping, and sorting.

CHAPTER RECALL
EXERCISES

1. Why should the executive assistant know about the firm's mail handling operation?
2. Describe single- and multifunction mail handling machines.
3. What types of sorting equipment are used in the mailroom?
4. How is mail opened?
5. Describe a mail extraction system.
6. What is a mail conveyor system?
7. Describe a self-propelled mail delivery vehicle.
8. Discuss the different types of addressing systems.
9. Explain the various types of collators available for business use.
10. What does an electronic postage scale do?

PROBLEMS AND
APPLICATIONS

1. Visit your college mailroom or local post office and find out how it operates. List those machines discussed in this chapter which are used there.
2. Write to the U.S. Postal Service and ask for information on its discount for businesses that presort outgoing mail by ZIP code.
3. Look for information that gives principles for arranging the equipment and furniture in the mailroom. Make a list of these principles. Sketch out how you would arrange the mailroom.
4. Visit or write a manufacturer of mail equipment to obtain information about electronic postage scales.

LANGUAGE SKILLS
DEVELOPMENT

1. Choose the correct verb in each of the following sentences:
    a. In the folder (is, are) the letter and envelope to be typed.
    b. A majority of the students (want, wants) class to meet an hour earlier.
    c. The Hitton Corporation (is, are) expecting to announce a stock split.
    d. Neither the parents nor the children (is, are) happy about the new curfew.
    e. To learn to play an instrument, you need to (sit, set) aside some time to practice each day.
    f. None of the group (has, have) gone canoeing before.
    g. The data (is, are) shown in the findings section of the report.
    h. Is it the tulip tree or the ash tree which (grow, grows) so quickly?
    i. On my desk (is, are) the papers I graded for your class.
    j. Some of the family (plan, plans) to stay at the house.
2. Use the correct punctuation at the end of the following sentences:

a. I can count on you, can't I
b. When can we begin dinner
c. You are really clever
d. Will you please send me the trade brochure
e. I was asked whether the course will be offered this quarter
f. What! They still don't know where he is
g. Can I have a copy of your latest flyer
h. Dresses will be sold with savings up to 70 percent
i. Stop slamming that door
j. Will you please be on time for the next session

HUMAN RELATIONS INCIDENTS

1. Reba attended a seminar on mail handling equipment which was sponsored by her PSI chapter. At the seminar Reba realized how antiquated the equipment at her company was. She went back to the office the next day full of enthusiasm and good ideas. The first opportunity she had that day Reba talked to Mr. Ramsey about the seminar and what she had learned. Mr. Ramsey listened half-heartedly and immediately went back to what he was doing before Reba came into the room. Reba felt as if she, as well as her new ideas, had received a slap in the face. Do you have any suggestions for Reba? How should Mr. Ramsey have handled this situation?

2. Stephen was just hired as a correspondence assistant in the word processing center. Since Stephen was new on the job and wanted to make a good first impression, he worked continually throughout the day, skipped coffee breaks, and took a shortened lunch hour. Throughout the afternoon, other assistants in the center made remarks about how much work Stephen was producing. At the end of the day as the assistants were logging in the number of lines they typed that day, several people made comments about Stephen's high volume. Is Stephen creating a problem? Should he be concerned about keeping the status quo? Will he find himself alienated from the work group?

TECHNIQUES FOR PROCESSING MAIL

Intelligent processing of mail is a vital function in any organization. With the high cost of postage today, mail can be a significant expense. Because of this increasing cost and the importance of accuracy in mail handling, businesses cannot afford to be careless in organizing and controlling the mail function.

In some organizations the executive assistant's mail processing responsibilities are arbitrary and haphazard. The executive assistant may have vague mail processing instructions. Small, growing companies are faced with the problem of whether to continue to assign each executive assistant the mail handling tasks or to add a centralized mailroom to handle the increased volume.

The structure of the mailroom is determined by the size and needs of the organization. Smaller firms are generally able to function with each executive assistant handling the mail processing chores; in some cases, a company may assign one individual who has other responsibilities in addition to processing incoming and outgoing mail and delivering internal correspondence. In most small companies, there is not enough work volume for a full-time mail person.

If the mail volume in the company warrants it, the company should establish a centralized mailroom with a full-time, professional supervisor. The centralized mailroom personnel will process incoming and outgoing mail, provide internal pickup and delivery of mail, distribute internal correspondence, and receive shipments of parcels.

Whether or not a centralized mailroom is used, executive assistants are expected to perform efficient mail handling operations to speed the flow of communications. If a centralized mail system is used, they must work with and cooperate with the mail personnel. They must know the schedule for pickup and delivery and must prepare outgoing mail correctly.

At the end of this chapter, you should be able to:

1. Discuss the procedures for handling incoming mail. 2. List the methods of handling mail during your employer's absence. 3. Discuss the procedures for handling outgoing mail. ☐ 4. Describe addressing procedures. ☐ 5. Discuss the use of ZIP codes in mailing.

CHAPTER 12

PROCEDURES FOR HANDLING INCOMING MAIL

Handling incoming mail is one of the executive assistant's first tasks. The careful and intelligent disposition of incoming mail may very well affect high-level corporate decisions, depending upon the urgency and priority of the messages. The following techniques are generally applicable to mail processing in any size office.

SELECTING THE EQUIPMENT

Mail opening equipment, such as the devices discussed in the previous chapter, can help speed the incoming mail whether it is processed in a centralized mailroom or at the executive assistant's desk. If the volume is relatively small, you may need only an envelope opener, a stapler or paper clips, date or time stamp, and routing slip or tape. If the volume is large, you may use a small hand-fed unit that electrically cuts the edges of envelopes open as fast as you can feed envelopes into the unit.

Semiautomatic machines open envelopes of various sizes and thicknesses. With this type of equipment, you can trim two or three edges of an envelope by hand feeding from different angles. Care must be exercised not to cut the contents of the envelope. A good idea would be to tap the edges so the contents would fall to the bottom edge of the envelope and then insert the top edge in the cutting mechanism.

Figure 12.1
Desk-top electric letter opener (Courtesy of Carl Mfg. Co.).

SORTING THE MAIL

The executive assistant usually sorts the mail into categories based on the employer's needs. Since business mail (first class) usually requires immediate action, the first step would be to pull out the priority mail and separate it from advertisements and other low priority mail. As an experienced executive assistant, you will begin to know which letters are to receive top priority upon arrival. You will develop an awareness of customers' or clients' names and look for special priority items. A keen awareness of incoming correspondence will quickly crystallize in your mind during this sorting process. The following categories generally would receive priority sorting:

1. Personal or confidential mail.
2. Telegrams, mailgrams, special delivery, registered, or certified mail.
3. Regular first-class mail.
4. Parcel-post packages.
5. Second- and third-class mail, consisting of advertisements, magazines, and catalogs.

OPENING THE MAIL

After you have sorted the mail, use the proper implement to open envelopes. If you should accidentally cut a letter while opening it, use tape to put it together again. If a personal or confidential letter is opened inadvertently, place the letter back in the envelope, write on the outside "Opened by mistake," and add your initials. Check to see if there are any enclosures in each envelope. If a letter indicates enclosures and you find they are missing, make a note of this omission in the margin of the letter or clip a note to the letter stating that the enclosures were not received.

Do not dispose of the envelopes until you have examined each letter for the signature and the address. Sometimes you may receive a carbon copy of a letter typed on plain onionskin paper where the company's address is not printed. A good idea would be to attach the envelope to the back of the letter or make a notation on a scratch pad indicating the origin of the letter. Sometimes a check is received in an envelope without a cover letter. This is another example of the importance of attaching the envelope to the contents, as it may be the only source of identification available.

DATING AND TIME-STAMPING THE MAIL

After you have sorted and opened the mail, you should record the date and time it was received. This often serves as a reminder that the answer should be dictated as soon as possible. Recording the date and time can be done with a pen or pencil, a rubber stamp, or a time stamp machine. The date and time notations should appear on each piece of correspondence that comes to your desk in the white space at the upper left, right, or top edge. The hour that correspondence is received can be critical if the company's policy is to answer correspondence immediately.

READING AND ANNOTATING
THE MAIL

Some ways to assist the executive are reading, underlining, and annotating the contents of incoming mail. Underlining important passages and margin notations, such as "Refer to file," or "See invoice," expedites the answers to correspondence. You may also include other information for the executive that will help answer the correspondence. Various files pertaining to the customer or client may be particularly helpful.

Care must be exercised not to overdo underlining and marginal notations. Some executives ask executive assistants not to write on incoming letters because they may be photocopied and sent to third parties. Some letters may be used in lawsuits and writing on these letters would invalidate any claims. A safer approach would be to write important passages and re- minders on separate slips of paper and attach these papers directly to the correspondence.

ROUTING THE MAIL

If a piece of mail is to be brought to the attention of several people, it can be circulated by a routing slip. A routing slip is a small piece of paper, perhaps 3 × 4 inches, which contains the names of those people who should receive the items. The names are printed in a column. The item is sent to the first person, who reads it, checks it off by placing his or her initials on it, and sends the item to the next person on the list.

Letters and correspondence can also be photocopied and distributed. If time is of the essence, photocopying greatly expedites matters since routing slips may circulate slowly and may be misplaced.

USING A LOG

A log or record of incoming mail can be kept if company policy warrants such a practice. This practice confirms receipt of correspondence and doc- uments it if discrepancies arise at a future date.

HANDLING MAIL DURING THE
EMPLOYER'S ABSENCE

One of the most important communication ethics among business people is to answer letters and inquiries promptly. A good working relationship between executive and executive assistant will mean that the executive assistant will have the responsibility to acknowledge letters during the ex- ecutive's absence. It means that you have the responsibility to read and digest the contents of letters and then take appropriate action. It does not mean that you render high-level decisions unless specific instructions have been given. Here are examples of simple acknowledgment letters sent by an executive assistant during the employer's absence.

The executive, on the other hand, may wish to have the executive assistant

Dear Mr. Satenberg:

Thank you for your bid for construction of Arpex Plaza.

I am certain that you will be hearing from Mr. Davis shortly after his return from the Midwest (in approximately two weeks).

Sincerely,

Andrea Nichols
Executive Assistant

Dear Mr. Diaz:

Your price quotation for solid-state transistors arrived today.

Mr. Bruce Fastenberg is on an extended business trip. Your letter will receive prompt attention as soon as he returns.

Sincerely,

Marla Beth Southfield
Executive Assistant
  to Mr. Fastenberg

---

give urgent letters (requiring management decision making) to an associate for immediate action.

A mail digest can be prepared that summarizes all first-class incoming mail while the employer is away. If the employer is away on an extended trip, you might send the digest directly to the executive every week.

Processing incoming mail involves a combination of intelligence, good judgment, and utilization of appropriate methods and equipment. Experienced executive assistants play an important supportive role in this vital aspect of helping the executive to prepare and process the countless pieces of incoming mail.

PROCEDURES FOR HANDLING OUTGOING MAIL

When a centralized mailroom processes outgoing mail, the mailroom employees collect outgoing mail from special bins in each department. In some cases, mail is then brought to the central mailroom in a special mail distributing cart that is designed to accommodate both legal size and letter size hanging file folders. File folders enable the employee to sort, pick up, and deliver the mail. After the mail is delivered to the mailroom, it is weighed, stamped, sealed or packed, and sent directly to the post office.

In smaller offices, however, executive assistants usually attend to all mailing and shipping duties. Whether executive assistants handle some or all of their employers' outgoing mail, it is their responsibility to see that it is correctly prepared, ready to mail, and classified (first-class, second-class, or third-class).

SELECT THE PROPER ENVELOPES

One easy way to help ensure delivery of your mail is by using the proper envelopes. Too small envelopes may tear during processing; too large first-class envelopes may be mistaken for third-class mail. Keep an ample supply of various size envelopes on hand so you can match the envelope size to its contents. When you have to use large, flat, first-class envelopes, be sure they have a distinctive green diamond border design for easy first-class identification. Although green-diamond borders are recommended for larger envelopes (flats) for first-class mailings, they can be confused with flats sent at third-class rates.

An alternative to storing several sizes of envelopes adopted by the Weyerhaeuser Company in Tacoma, Washington, is that of stocking mailing labels printed in green with conspicuous green diamonds around the edge of the label. The first-class marking is carried also in large type in the upper right portion of the label.

The executive assistant should be familiar with the new postal regulations regarding size standards for envelopes, cards, and other pieces of mail. A penalty of a 7-cent surcharge will be levied for oversized and odd-shaped

Figure 12.2
Variety of mailing envelopes.

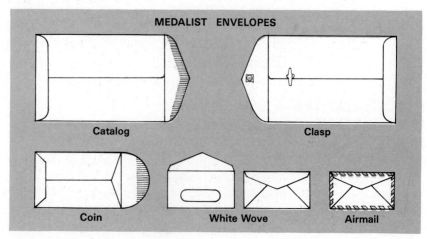

MEDALIST ENVELOPES

Catalog

Clasp

Coin

White Wove

Airmail

pieces of mail. The new regulations specify that pieces will be nonmailable if they are less than the following measurements:

$3\frac{1}{2}$ inches high

5 inches long

seven thousandths (.007) of an inch thick

Subject to the seven-cent surcharge will be first-class mail weighing one ounce or less and single piece, third-class mail of two ounces or less that exceed any of these dimensions:

$6\frac{1}{8}$ inches high

$11\frac{1}{2}$ inches long

$\frac{1}{4}$ inch thick

You should obtain current postal regulations pertaining to minimum and maximum dimensions for envelopes from your local post office.

SEPARATE AND PRESORT OUTGOING MAIL

Mail gets on its way faster if it is separated and marked before it reaches the post office. By separating first-class mail from other mail and local mail from out-of-town mail, you save the Postal Service steps in handling it. Further presorting by ZIP codes saves many additional steps. For those customers who are able to presort first-class mail, the cost of mailing a letter is 2 cents less than the rate for letters weighing one ounce or less. Presorting first-class mail provides a way for public agencies to demonstrate that they are concerned about reducing costs. With every piece of presorted mail showing that the agency paid 2 cents less per piece than for regular first class, the envelopes can represent a statement that the company respects the taxpayers' money.

Use wide rubber bands for banding bundles of presorted mail. Postmasters have been instructed to make rubber bands available to customers depositing presorted letter-size mail, including advertising material, without charge.

MAKE A MAILING SCHEDULE

Make a point of knowing when your post office dispatches mail and then arrange your mailing schedule accordingly. If you use a street or building lobby mail box, check the collection times listed. Often you can save a full day on delivery time by posting your mail just a little earlier. If you miss the last collection, take your mail directly to the post office because this extra effort will be rewarded by quicker delivery.

MAIL EARLY IN THE DAY

Late evening surges of mail cause problems for postal operations and hinder all attempts to schedule postal employees efficiently. Since post offices generally receive most of the day's mail around 5:00 p.m. to 6:30 p.m., you should pick up any signed correspondence at noon and mail it before going to lunch.

ADDRESS MAIL CORRECTLY

A ZIP code is a five-digit geographic code that identifies areas within the United States and its possessions for purposes of simplifying the distribution of mail by the U.S. Post Office Department.[1] It should appear on the last line of both the destination address and return address of mail, following the names of city and state.

In devising the ZIP code, the United States and its possessions were divided into ten large geographic areas. Each area consists of three or more states or possessions and is given a number between 0 and 9. This is the first digit in any ZIP code number. Special machines sort and read ZIP codes and automatically sort several thousand pieces of mail each hour. It is particularly important for you to use ZIP codes when addressing envelopes

Figure 12.3
Zip code national areas.

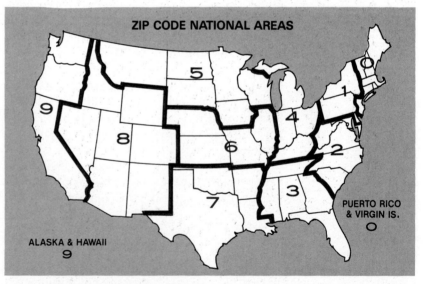

[1]The Postal Service began a nine-digit ZIP code system in 1981. This new program assists in holding down the amount of future rate increases by providing more economical and accurate sorting of mail and, in many cases, will speed up the delivery process. The key to anticipated savings will be the acquisition of new equipment that will sort mail into small delivery segments for carriers without the current need for distribution by memory.

since mail without them must be held for conventional sorting at slower speeds.

You may very well be the focal point of a large part of the company's communications effort. How well you function in the mail processing operation has a major effect on how your company looks in the eyes of its customers and how well it prospers financially. By making sure that mail is prepared for sorting by the Postal Service's computerized sorting equipment, you will promote better business, speed communications, and improve your own job performance.

Here are some additional suggestions that will expedite mail delivery:

Figure 12.4
Addressing for automation.

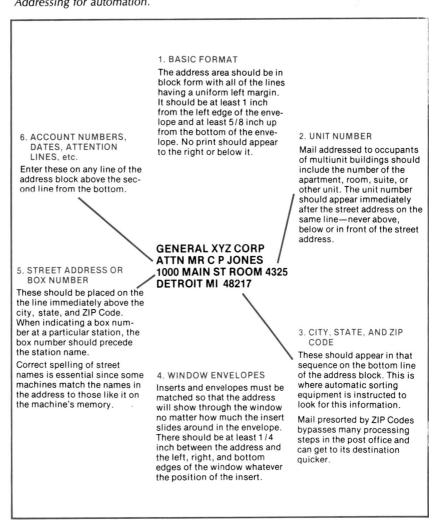

6. ACCOUNT NUMBERS, DATES, ATTENTION LINES, etc.
Enter these on any line of the address block above the second line from the bottom.

1. BASIC FORMAT
The address area should be in block form with all of the lines having a uniform left margin. It should be at least 1 inch from the left edge of the envelope and at least 5/8 inch up from the bottom of the envelope. No print should appear to the right or below it.

2. UNIT NUMBER
Mail addressed to occupants of multiunit buildings should include the number of the apartment, room, suite, or other unit. The unit number should appear immediately after the street address on the same line—never above, below or in front of the street address.

5. STREET ADDRESS OR BOX NUMBER
These should be placed on the the line immediately above the city, state, and ZIP Code. When indicating a box number at a particular station, the box number should precede the station name.

Correct spelling of street names is essential since some machines match the names in the address to those like it on the machine's memory.

GENERAL XYZ CORP
ATTN MR C P JONES
1000 MAIN ST ROOM 4325
DETROIT MI 48217

4. WINDOW ENVELOPES
Inserts and envelopes must be matched so that the address will show through the window no matter how much the insert slides around in the envelope. There should be at least 1/4 inch between the address and the left, right, and bottom edges of the window whatever the position of the insert.

3. CITY, STATE, AND ZIP CODE
These should appear in that sequence on the bottom line of the address block. This is where automatic sorting equipment is instructed to look for this information.

Mail presorted by ZIP Codes bypasses many processing steps in the post office and can get to its destination quicker.

☐ Use rectangular envelopes that will provide good color contrast with the address impression. The envelopes should be no smaller than $3\frac{1}{2}$ x 5 inches and no larger than $6\frac{1}{8}$ x $11\frac{1}{2}$ inches.

☐ Keep address plates clean to avoid filling in letters. Also, check plates that are leaving parts of letters blank to see if they need cleaning or replacing.

☐ Check printouts and labels for filled-in characters, characters out of register (parts not completely inked), or misaligned characters.

☐ Be sure all address plates include the correct ZIP code.

☐ Once you have prepared mail for machine sorting, do not mix it with other mail. Bundle it or place it in trays.

☐ If your firm wants to use a street location in its mailing address but wants its mail delivered to a post office box, the box number should be on the next-to-last line of the address. The ZIP code used should be the one for the box number, not the street address:

CHEVRON OIL COMPANY
8435 WESTGLAN STREET
PO BOX 36487
HOUSTON TX 77036

☐ Speed the movement of your mail and reduce the number of characters required in an address by using two-letter abbreviations for state names.

PREPARE PARCELS AND PACKAGES

Whether the executive assistant or the mailroom personnel handle parcels and packaging, it is important to prepare packages with care so that the contents will be delivered quickly and in good condition. All packages containing easily breakable articles should be marked "Fragile." Use appropriate labels for packaging.

The contents of the package should be surrounded with sufficient cushioning material to keep them from moving inside and to protect them against impact from the outside.

Excelsior, flexible corrugated fiberboard, or felt are commonly used cushions for heavy materials. Cellulose materials, shredded paper, or expanded foam are often used for lighter materials. Ask your local post office for the free pamphlet, "Packaging for Mailing," to give you step-by-step directions for packaging.

If you are using a postage meter, position the meter strip to overlap the corner of the address label.

If you wish to enclose a first-class letter in a parcel without paying first-class postage for the entire package, simply mark the package "First-Class Mail Enclosed" and add the first-class letter's postage to the parcel's postage; or, tape your first-class letter, with its own postage on it, to the front of the parcel.

34-105

34-101

34-762

34-118

34-109

34-764

34-760

34-761

43-201

43-202

43-203

VIA AIR MAIL
34-763

Figure 12.5
Mailing labels.

Figure 12.6
Metering parcels.

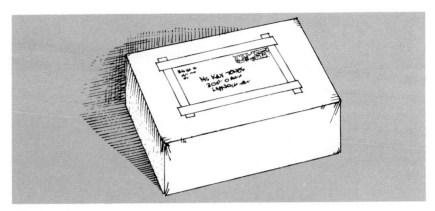

Figure 12.7
Piggyback (letter with package).

SUMMARY

This chapter was designed to help the executive assistant and the organization get the most out of the postal system and to present a number of suggestions to make mailing operations more efficient.

In some firms the initial sorting, processing, and routing of mail is done by workers in the company mailroom. In smaller offices where there is no central mailroom, the executive assistant is usually responsible for all mailing duties.

1. A centralized mailroom is usually established for companies that have large volumes of mail.
2. Centralized mail processing allows for (a) processing incoming and outgoing mail, (b) internal pickup and delivery of mail, (c) distribution of internal correspondence, and (d) receipt of parcel shipments.
3. The executive assistant must sort the mail into categories based on the employer's needs.
4. If a piece of mail is to be sent to several individuals within the company, the executive assistant attaches a routing slip to the correspondence.
5. An executive assistant should acknowledge letters in the absence of his or her employer by sending a letter acknowledging receipt of the correspondence.
6. In smaller offices, executive assistants will usually handle outgoing mail processing.
7. It is important for the executive assistant to know envelope dimensions because oversized or odd-shaped pieces of mail will be penalized.

8. Separating mail by classes expedites handling by the post office and provides a saving of postage cost.
9. All addresses should include a ZIP code, a geographic code that identifies areas within the United States and its possessions.

CHAPTER RECALL EXERCISES

1. What devices may an executive assistant use to open mail?
2. List the categories, in order of importance, that an executive assistant would use to sort classes of mail.
3. Why is it important to date and time stamp incoming mail?
4. Briefly describe one method of routing the mail.
5. Why is it necessary to separate and presort outgoing mail?
6. When is the best time to mail correspondence?
7. Describe the services a central mailroom might provide.
8. Where should the post office box number appear in the address?
9. Briefly describe how you would enclose a first-class letter with a parcel.
10. How should an executive assistant handle the mail if an employer is absent for several days?
11. Describe the function of a ZIP code.
12. Why is the size of an envelope important?
13. What is the correct way to prepare a parcel for mailing?

PROBLEMS AND APPLICATIONS

1. Your employer receives the following mail:
   Time magazine
   Brochure announcement for the latest industry conference
   1 mailgram
   3 regular first-class letters
   1 large, flat envelope marked "Personal"
Describe how you would sort these pieces of mail in proper order.

2. While opening the mail, you accidentally opened a letter addressed to the vice president. A check and several enclosures are included in the envelope. What should you do?

3. Your employer has complained to you that an important piece of correspondence that he asked you to distribute by way of a routing slip has not been returned. You noticed the correspondence sitting on the desk of one of the executives among piles of other paper. You recall that the correspondence has been out over three weeks. What should you do?

4. The following letter was composed by an executive assistant in answer to an inquiry during his or her employer's absence.

> Dear Mr. Gross:
>
> Thank you for sending us your letter inquiring about employment and your resume. Your credentials and experience seem very impressive. I am sure Mr. Hastings will be anxious to hire you. Your background certainly meets our requirements. As soon as Mr. Hastings returns from his business trip, I will have him call you.
> > Sincerely,
>
> > Marlene Steilman

Criticize the letter. How would you change it? Rewrite the letter making any necessary changes.

LANGUAGE SKILLS DEVELOPMENT

1. Form the plurals of the following words:

   attorney   half
   authority   handkerchief
   business   necessity
   cattle   notary public
   company   ox
   C.P.A.   woman

2. Punctuate each of the following sentences:
   a. The instructor previewed the examination and answered questions.
   b. The students enrolled in the class and those on the waiting list will meet in the library.
   c. The dog not only barked at the squirrel but chased it around the yard.
   d. If you wish to drive a car you must understand the rules of the road and you must be familiar with the car.
   e. Sweep the floor then you can ride your bike.
   f. When you finish reading the chapter please return the book.
   g. I would like to have an explanation when you have the time.
   h. The man who lives next door has a good garden this year.
   i. Television reruns which are often shown in the summer make it easy to turn off the television set.
   j. If however you had been more careful in your selection the product would have lasted longer.
   k. Call me on Friday when I will know the answer.
   l. The Franklins who are our next door neighbors are on vacation this week.

3. Learn to spell the following words:

   anonymity   conscientious
   avocation   eclectic

elude   negligible

illegible   obscure

a. Consult the dictionary for the meanings for any of these words which are not familiar.

b. Divide the words in the preferred place.

HUMAN RELATIONS INCIDENTS

1. Penny and Kaye are executive assistants in a small public relations office. The office has a postage meter to take care of the small volume of mail that goes out of the office.

Penny has noticed that Kaye uses the postage meter to put postage on her personal correspondence. Kaye also uses company paper and envelopes on occasion for personal correspondence.

Should Penny ignore Kaye's use of company supplies and postage? Should Penny talk to Kaye or her employer about this situation? How would you handle this problem?

2. One of John's responsibilities as executive assistant to Mr. Madison is to open Mr. Madison's mail and make notations in the margins of the correspondence. As John was processing the incoming mail one morning, he did not notice "Personal" marked on the envelope; and he began to read the letter. As he read the letter, John realized the letter was a very personal one from a woman friend of Mr. Madison's.

John immediately stopped reading the letter and put a note on the envelope that the letter was opened by mistake. Mr. Madison was furious with John for opening the letter. Since that time, there has been a barrier between John and Mr. Madison. Mr. Madison does not seem his usual friendly self, and John wonders how he can break down that barrier. What advice do you have for John? Should he ignore the situation or do something about it? What should he do?

THE U.S. POSTAL SERVICE

It has become fashionable to criticize government agencies, public utilities, and giant corporations in a decade of consumer awareness characterized by increased rates combined with decreased services. The U.S. Postal Service, along with telephone companies, public utilities, and other service-related organizations, has not been immune to these complaints.

Riding on the wave of this backlash, alternative delivery methods for packages and parcels that promise less expensive and faster service and other distinct advantages over the use of the U.S. Postal Service are emerging in cities across the country. This chapter reviews some of the positive features of the Postal Service and deals with the full cycle of postal services. By understanding postal rates, services, and products, an informed executive assistant can utilize the postal services more efficiently and, at the same time, cut mailing costs. This information is especially important for the executive assistant who works in a company that does not have a mailroom.

At the end of this chapter, you should be able to:

1. Describe the classes of mail. ☐ 2. List the special services offered by the Postal Service. ☐ 3. Explain how the postage meter is used by companies. ☐ 4. Define VIM (vertical improved mail). ☐ 5. Discuss the future of the Postal Service.

CHAPTER 13

CLASSES OF MAIL

Since postal rates have been changing so rapidly in the last few years, the executive assistant must know the current rates for letters and parcels. It would be impractical to list rates here; to keep current with postal rates, it is better to contact your local post office for a brochure of current rates. Executive assistants who handle outgoing mail should use the proper designation and classification of mail.

FIRST-CLASS MAIL

You can use first-class mail for postal cards and personal notes; it can also be used for the transmission of checks and money orders. First-class letter mail enjoys privacy and may not be opened for postal inspections. First-class mail is given the fastest transportation service available. The maximum weight for first-class mail is 70 pounds, and the maximum size is 100 inches in length and girth (the measure around anything, circumference) combined. If your first-class item to be mailed is not letter size, make sure it is marked "First Class."

PRIORITY MAIL

Priority mail is used when the fastest transportation and most expeditious handling is desired for any mailable matter weighing more than 13 ounces on which priority mail rates have been paid. The maximum size is 100 inches in length and girth combined.

When using priority mail, be sure to use special envelopes or stickers. Clearly mark the package or envelope "Priority Mail" in large letters on all sides to ensure it is handled properly.

SECOND-CLASS MAIL

Second-class mail is generally used by newspapers and other periodical publishers who must meet certain Postal Service requirements. You may use it for mailing individual copies of magazines and newspapers.

THIRD-CLASS MAIL

Third-class mail, sometimes called advertising mail, may be used by anyone; but it is used most often for large mailings. This class includes printed materials and merchandise parcels which weigh less than 16 ounces. There are two structures for this mail class, a single piece and a bulk rate. Many community organizations and businesses find it economical to use this service. Individuals may use third class for mailing light-weight parcels. A reduced rate for bulk third-class mail presorted is now available.

FOURTH-CLASS MAIL (PARCEL POST)

Parcel post service is provided for mailing packages weighing one pound or more. Parcels mailed between larger post offices in the continental United States are limited to 40 pounds and 84 inches in length and girth combined.

Parcels up to 7 pounds and 100 inches can be mailed to and from smaller post offices and between any post office from Hawaii to Alaska. Your post office has information about special mailing rates for books, records, materials for the blind, catalogs, and international mailings. For faster delivery of parcels over long distances, use special handling, priority mail (air parcel post), or express mail.

EXPRESS MAIL

Express Mail is the Postal Service's remarkable new overnight mail service. An item brought to an express mail office by 5 p.m. will be delivered in a network city by 3 p.m. the next day, or it will be available for pick-up at the post office by 10 a.m. if the customer prefers. Almost any mailable parcel up to 40 pounds can be sent Express Mail. The Postal Service has also installed special Express Mail collection mail boxes at key business locations in urban centers. All the customer does is fill out a Next Day Service label, attach it to the letter or package, apply the postage and drop it in the specially marked Express Mail collection box, to be delivered the next day.

For specific local information on how to effectively use Express Mail, you should contact your post office. In larger cities, call the customer service office; in small communities, ask the postmaster for assistance.

SPECIAL DELIVERY

Special Delivery may be purchased on all classes of mail to provide prompt delivery at the destination post office. Special Delivery is available at offices served by city carriers and within a one-mile radius of any post office. Certain local conditions sometimes make this service unavailable.

You should place a Special Delivery label (see Figure 13.1) on all parcels. On regular letters, fold the label over the top edge, at least 3 inches from the right-hand side. On smaller letters (7 inches or less in length), place the label over the left-hand edge (see Figure 13.2). Do not cover up the return address. On larger envelopes, fold the labels over the top and bottom edges. For packages (see Figure 13.3), fold labels over the top and bottom edges of both sides. Place the top label at least 3 inches from the right-hand side and the bottom label on the lower left-hand side.

SPECIAL SERVICES

The Postal Service offers many special services for the fast and efficient delivery of mail. The executive assistant should be familiar with each of these services.

MAILGRAM

The Mailgram® is a fast, effective communication service developed jointly by Western Union and the U.S. Postal Service and introduced in January 1970. Since then, millions of mailgrams have been sent as volume has continued to multiply.

Figure 13.1
Special delivery illustration.

Figure 13.2
Special delivery illustrations.

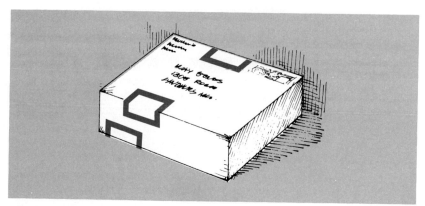

Figure 13.3
Special delivery illustration.

Mailgrams provide speedy and reliable delivery of important messages partly by eliminating most of the intermediate handling, routing, sorting, and transporting operations of the regular mail. Mailgrams are transmitted at the speed of light over Western Union's modern, computerized micro-wave communications network directly to a post office near the destination address. Mailgrams are delivered by regular postal carriers on the next business day.

PROOF OF MAILING AND DELIVERY

For a nominal cost, a certificate of mailing may be obtained if you need proof of mailing. It does not provide insurance coverage for loss or damage. No record is maintained at the post office.

Certified Mail provides a mailing receipt and record of delivery at the addressee's post office. Certified Mail is used for items of little intrinsic value and is dispatched and handled in transit as ordinary mail. A return receipt to provide the sender proof of delivery may be obtained for an additional fee.

The return receipt is your proof of delivery. It is available on insured mail of more than $15 value and on certified, registered, and COD mail. The return receipt identifies the article by number, by who assigned it, and by the date it was delivered. For a reasonable additional fee, you may obtain a receipt showing the exact delivery address. You may also request restricted delivery service by which delivery is confined to the addressee only or to an individual authorized in writing to receive the mail of the addressee.

VALUABLES SENT THROUGH THE MAIL

Insurance is available up to $200 for third-class, parcel-post, and priority mail (air parcel post) containing printed matter or merchandise. Insured mail is handled as ordinary parcel post. For articles insured for more than $15, a receipt of delivery is obtained from the addressee for the post office files. Irreplaceable articles, regardless of value, and all items of more than $200 value should be sent by registered mail.

Registered Mail is the safest way to send valuables. The full value of your mailing must be declared when mailed for security and insurance purposes. Included in the registration fee is insurance protection up to $10,000 for domestic mail only. You receive a receipt, and the movement of your mail is controlled throughout the postal system. For an additional fee, a return receipt may be obtained which shows to whom, when, and where the delivery was made.

Collect-on-Delivery (COD) service may be used if the recipient is to pay for merchandise when it is received, rather than by prepaying or separate billing. The amount due the mailer for the merchandise and postage, plus the money order fee, is collected from the addressee. COD service may be used for merchandise mailed via parcel post, first class, or third class.

Money orders are a safe way to send money through the mail. Domestic money orders may be purchased at all post offices in amounts up to $300. Should your money order be lost or stolen, it will be replaced. You can also obtain copies of paid money orders for two years after the date they are redeemed. Authorization to issue international money orders may be purchased at most large post offices in amounts up to $300 for most countries.

In the event you have a claim against the Postal Service because of lost or damaged mail, obtain the appropriate claim form from your post office and file it there. Only the mailer may file a claim for complete loss. Either the mailer or the addressee may file a claim for partial loss or damage. You are entitled to file claims for mail that has been insured, registered, or sent COD.

MILITARY PARCELS

Parcel Airlift Mail (PAL) is flown to the overseas destination. Packages up to 30 pounds and 60 inches in combined length and girth may be sent by PAL. You pay the regular parcel post rate to the U.S. exit port, plus a $1 fee for the air service.

Space Available Mail (SAM) is transported by surface means in the United States and flown on a space available basis from the United States to the overseas destination. Packages up to 15 pounds and 60 inches in combined length and girth may be sent by SAM for regular parcel post rates to the U.S. port.

CUSTOMS AND PASSPORT APPLICATIONS

Most imported goods are subject to U.S. Customs inspection and duty. Duty is collected for Customs by the Postal Service. For information about customs regulations you can write to U.S. Customs Service, Treasury Department, Washington, DC 20229.

You may apply for a passport at many post offices. The passport is issued by the Passport Office, U.S. Department of State. The passport fee must be paid by check or money order made payable to the Passport Office; cash is not accepted.

POST OFFICE BOXES

Lockbox and caller services are provided on a rental basis in many post offices. These services afford privacy and permit you to obtain your mail at any time the lobby is open.

SELF-SERVICE POSTAL CENTERS

The Postal Service has self-service centers at many locations throughout the country to provide basic postal service around the clock, seven days a week. Postal customers can mail letters and packages, buy minimum parcel insurance, stamps, postal cards, and envelopes at these centers. Each center has a direct-line telephone which customers may use to obtain mailing information or to request reimbursement (money or stamps) for money lost because of equipment malfunction. All stamps from the U.S. Postal Service machines are sold at face value.

Some of these units are located in post office lobbies; others may be at shopping centers, college campuses, and other places of convenient pedestrian access. These centers do not replace existing facilities but rather extend and supplement existing postal services.

Some postal machines are privately owned. The Postal Service, by law, must sell postage stamps at face value. However, they have no jurisdiction over those individuals in stationery or paper stores, for instance, who purchase postage stamps and then resell them at their own rates. The Postal Service assumes that the resale price will be based on the cost of vending and a reasonable markup.

POSTAGE METERS

A postage meter prints prepaid postage either directly on envelopes or on adhesive strips which are then affixed to packages. The metered mail imprint, or meter stamp, serves as postage payment, a postmark, and cancellation mark. It may be used for all classes of mail and for any amount of postage. Any quantity of mail in any size or shape may be metered.

A customer rents or leases a postage meter from one of several manufacturers and obtains a meter permit through the post office. The meter user sets the date shown on the postmark for each new day of use. The metered mail is then deposited in time for collection that same day. If metered mail is to be deposited too late for the last collection of the day, the meter date should be changed accordingly. There are, however, two special cases, third-class mail and business reply mail, in which a business firm might print metered mail in anticipation of mailing by its customers at some future date. These cases require no date when the meter impression is printed directly on the mail (without tape).

Use of a meter is limited to the user licensed by the post office except by special arrangement with the postmaster. Metered mail must be deposited in the area served by the post office issuing the license, except by special arrangement with the postmaster. Also, the mail must be bundled to be kept separate from other mail.

The meter user makes payment for postage in a lump sum at a designated postal location. The meter is set for that amount of postage in advance of the meter's operation.[1] Some post offices provide a meter setting service on the premises of the meter user for a nominal fee. A refund of 90 percent of the face value of unused meter impressions may be made if submitted within one year from the date shown on the postmark. Refunds of 100 percent of the face value of meter postage are made when the Postal Service is at fault or when meter malfunctions cause errors in printing postage.

Distribution of an electronic postage meter has been authorized by the U.S. Postal Service which utilizes a microprocessor and solid-state memory instead of the traditional mechanical controls.

AREA MAIL PROCESSING

Area mail processing is an efficient method of processing mail at central postal facilities. Letters do not have local postmarks but carry city identification where the mail is processed, the state abbreviation, and the facility's three-digit ZIP code number. Local postmarks can be obtained on request or by depositing mail in designated collection boxes.

MAIL PROBLEMS

Ordering merchandise through the mails can be time-saving and thrifty. If you are not familiar with the reputation of a company, check with the Better Business Bureau, Chamber of Commerce, or state or local consumer protection office before placing an order. If you later experience difficulty with the company, contact your postmaster or local postal inspector.

With the rash of pornography spreading from movies, books, and through the mails, some unsolicited, sexually-oriented advertisements may filter into your office mail. You can help stop such delivery by filling out Form 2201 at your local post office. Thirty days from the date your name is added to the reference list, mailers who send you unwanted, unsolicited mail, such

---

[1]A new mail processing system allows you to fill the meter with postage on the spot in 90 seconds or less with the use of any Touch-Tone® phone or tone generator available. You just call the computer, receive a special number code, and punch that code into your postage meter. The postage meter is then ready for service again.

as sexually oriented advertisements, subject themselves to legal action by the U.S. Government.

When you have a problem with your mail service, complete a Consumer Service Card, available from postal carriers and post offices. This will enable your postmaster to respond to your problem and simultaneously make the Postal Service Consumer Advocate aware of the problem.

The Postal Service Consumer Advocate is in Washington, D.C., to represent consumers at top management levels in the Postal Service. If your postal problems cannot be solved locally, write or call the Consumer Advocate, U.S. Postal Service, Washington, DC 20260, (202) 245-4514.

VERTICAL IMPROVED MAIL (VIM)

Your office building, in a special sense, is a mail manufacturing plant. The raw material, the product in process and the end product of most office work, is mail. Although mail is such a vital service for every business firm, its importance has been overlooked too often in the design of commercial buildings. Today's tenants, occupying steel and glass towers, demand fast, efficient postal service.

Vertical Improved Mail (VIM) is an improved mail service that makes the mail available to multistory office tenants at the start of the working day and provides more frequent outgoing dispatch. There are three types of VIM:

1. *VIM call window system.* Tenants pick up their mail at a call window from a post office carrier stationed in the mailroom. If not called for by a certain hour, mail is delivered to the tenants by the carrier.
2. *VIM lockbox system.* The mailroom is equipped with rear-loading lockboxes for all tenants, serviced by an onsite post office carrier. Tenants pick up their mail as they enter the building in the morning.
3. *VIM mechanical system.* Simultaneous delivery of mail from a central mailroom to all floors is accomplished with this system. It also handles tenant's outgoing mail automatically from a service mailroom on each floor. An additional benefit of the mechanical system is that there can be interoffice communication between floors for major tenants.

The sales and profits of business firms are affected by the prompt receipt and dispatch of mail. Similarly, mail delays drastically affect office routines and production schedules. Vertical Improved Mail (VIM) makes the mail available to every tenant at the start of the workday. With conventional office building mail delivery, it takes a carrier about one minute to make each delivery. With 100 companies in a multistory building, a carrier requires about two hours to deliver the mail. As a result, many tenants do not receive their mail early in the working day.

Getting a letter out of the building is also important. It costs over $7 to prepare an average business letter, and most business people cannot afford to have that letter delayed. Frequent VIM collections speed the mail to destinations.

VIM saves money and time. Companies can eliminate the costs of post office box rentals and mail messenger service. They save time by eliminating several daily trips to the post office.

For the owners of office buildings, VIM will keep their buildings competitive in the future. Traditional door-to-door delivery of office mail is becoming unsatisfactory in today's fast-paced business world and will not meet the demands of tomorrow. As the number of VIM installations continues to grow, tenants will expect this improved mail service in their buildings.

FORWARDING MAIL

If your company is contemplating a move, obtain a change-of-address kit from your local post office and promptly notify correspondents and publishers of your new address. Be sure the effective date of the change is on the form. First-class mail is forwarded free for one year. Contact your local post office about fees for forwarding other classes of mail.

MAIL SERVICE AND THE FUTURE

The Postal Service expects mail volume to climb to over 100 billion pieces in the next few years. This contradicts predictions by office systems consultants that mail volume through the postal system will taper off as more and more companies become disenchanted with the poor service and rising costs.

In an effort to speed up delivery, the Postal Service established a new set of delivery and collections standards for airmail and first class, the most commonly used mail.

Computer-based systems will be forwarding more than half of the mail that cannot be delivered as addressed within the next several years. The governors of the U.S. Postal Service approved a $10 million program to install computerized systems in the 50 largest metropolitan areas. This computerized system can offer more accurate handling of nondeliverable mail, and it is less costly than the various methods of forwarding mail. The new system represents another step by the Postal Service to provide better processing of the three billion pieces of mail annually that are undeliverable as addressed.

The new computerized system consists of a minicomputer, an operator keyboard with a video display, a label printer, and floppy disk file storage. It provides rapid filing and retrieval of customer change-of-address information and automatic printing of forward and return labels and endorsements, such as postage due.

In addition, the Postal Service hopes to keep its customers—both large and small mail users—from turning to private firms by drawing up additional

Figure 13.4
Computer-based system for processing mail (Courtesy of U.S. Postal Service).

new programs to deliver mail faster and to keep costs down. Some of the plans include:

☐ An international electronic message service utilizing satellites to transmit messages between the United States and overseas locations. This program will be in cooperation with the Communications Satellite Corporation (COMSAT), the pioneer in global satellite communications, and would involve five or six other nations.

☐ A computerized service for businesses that want to send the same letter, such as a recall notice, to thousands of customers across the country within two days.

☐ A courier service to deliver high-priority letters the same day in large metropolitan areas.

☐ An expanded nine-digit ZIP code number to enable the post office to automate the sorting of mail all the way down to a single letter carrier's route.

☐ Lower rates on parcels.

ELECTRONIC MAIL

Business people are continually exploring alternative methods to improve upon the cumbersome trail of rapid communications between two points in time—the moment an executive formulates a message and the moment

Figure 13.5
Self-dialing Xerox facsimile system (Courtesy of Xerox).

it is delivered. One alternative is facsimile, an electronic mail process whose wizardry lies in its ability to use telephone lines to transmit anything put down on paper. Within a matter of minutes, correspondence can be dispatched to a recipient thousands of miles away. That correspondence can include much more than a written or typed letter.

A facsimile unit operates like a long-distance copying machine. An executive assistant sets up the device next to a phone, plugs it into a socket, inserts the letter or document, dials the recipient's number, and places the telephone in an attached cradle. As soon as contact is made, the machine begins "talking" to a machine at the other end through use of optical scanners that read what is on the paper and breaks it up into thousands of tiny dots—dots that are translated into electronic sounds conveyed over the telephone line.

At the opposite end, another machine translates the sounds back into an exact duplicate of what was sent. The more dots you have, the better the reproduction of the facsimile.

Figure 13.6
QWIP System—Portable desk facsimile unit (Courtesy of Exxon Office Systems).

SUMMARY

The Postal Service is introducing many changes and innovations to help hold down costs and improve services. The growth of private competition (such as United Parcel Service) has set off the Postal Service's search for cheaper and more reliable delivery.

1. The Postal Service offers a wide array of services to business people.
2. Despite continuing automation, postage costs in the last few years have outstripped inflation by a large amount.
3. Special services for fast delivery are Express Mail, Special Delivery, and Mailgram.
4. Customers may insure valuables sent through the mail by insurance, registered mail, and COD mail.
5. Self-service postal centers provide postal service when the regular post office is closed.
6. Postage meters are a convenient alternate to the cumbersome method of postage stamps.
7. The Postal Service Consumer Advocate is available to solve problems with mail service.
8. Vertical Improved Mail (VIM) pertains to mail service in multistory office buildings.
9. An international electronic message service utilizing satellites to transmit messages between countries will help speed up international mail.
10. Facsimile is an electronic mail process that uses telephone lines to transmit documents to other recipients using a similar device.

CHAPTER RECALL EXERCISES

1. What are some reasons for complaints against the Postal Service?
2. Briefly describe the differences between first-, second-, and third-class mail.
3. How will Certified Mail assure the sender proof of mailing?
4. What can a mailer do if a parcel is lost or stolen in transit?
5. What service can the mailer use if the local post office is closed?
6. What are the advantages of using a postage meter?
7. What remedies can a mailer take if he or she has been subjected to unwanted, unsolicited mail, such as pornographic materials?
8. Briefly describe the three options for VIM.
9. Based on the projections of future mail service, what are your predictions for the future of the Postal Service?

PROBLEMS AND APPLICATIONS

1. You are employed by Lear Construction Company, manufacturers of high-speed trains used for mass transit. Your organization is submitting a bid to a city for the fabrication of 80 railroad cars. The bids are to be submitted by mail. What steps would you take to assure your organization that the bid is received by the proper person within the specified deadline?

2. As an executive assistant in a large retail store, you are helping your employer plan a large, storewide sale. The sale begins in six days. The newspaper ad that you placed has been canceled due to a newspaper strike. You need to "get the word out" to 500 special charge customers. If you use the Postal Service, what are your alternatives?

3. Your employer asks you to mail the following:
   a. 43 catalogs to Dallas, Texas.
   b. 1 basket of assorted fruit and candy to Fenton, Missouri.
   c. 12 coffee mugs to Washington, D.C.
   d. 1 real estate contract for the sale of the Nashville plant to Nashville, Tennessee.

What mailing instructions would you give to your mailroom for each of the items?

4. Find out if there are any multistory buildings in your area that use VIM. Visit one of the buildings and interview the person in charge of VIM. Be sure to find out which method of VIM is used.

5. Call or write a postage meter manufacturer to get some information and brochures on their postage meters.

6. Design a routing slip to use when circulating material so it will be returned to you for your files.

LANGUAGE SKILLS
DEVELOPMENT

1. Show the possessive of the following phrases:

   Example: dog of the boy   boy's dog

        pen of Charles

        dog of the boys

        toy of the child

        coat of Mr. Jones

        ponies of the children

        file of the employee

        guess of anybody

        house of Bruce and Sally

        goal of the sales repre-
   sentative

        front of the truck

        sale of Brooke Brothers

        a notice of three days

2. Hyphenate any of the following words that require hyphenation:

middle western sales representative	community college student
Tri Cities area	left and right hand margins
five inch card	part time job
letter that is up to date	12 dozen dresses
above mentioned address	one year guarantee
highly valued virtue	small town barber shop
New Jersey bridge	student magazine subscription
well known speaker	36 hour week
up to date news report	role playing activities

3. Choose the correct word in each of the following sentences:

   a. (Any one, Anyone) can operate this equipment.

   b. (Any one, Anyone) of us could make that same speech if necessary.

   c. We (always, all ways) try to get the work back to the originators in four hours.

   d. We have tried in (always, all ways) to get the work finished.

   e. The play was (almost, all most) one hour late in starting.

   f. We are (almost, all most) pleased with this new arrangement.

   g. The decision was (already, all ready) made.

   h. The group is (already, all ready) to go.

   i. This report is (altogether, all together) too messy to be mailed.

   j. The news team is (altogether, all together) in the newsroom.

HUMAN RELATIONS INCIDENTS

1. Ken is executive assistant to Mr. Young, manager of the research and development department. Mr. Young often circulates correspondence, notices, and periodical articles to members of the department with notations of "Let me have your comments, please" or "Please note and return with your suggestions." Very few of the letters and articles are returned to the office for Ken to file. Then, when Mr. Young wants to see the letter or article, Ken is unable to find it. Mr. Young usually says that the material must be misfiled and instructs Ken to find it as soon as possible. How could this situation be avoided? How can Ken tactfully tell Mr. Young why he can't find the correspondence?

2. Alice, who is an executive assistant in a small office, recently hired an 18-year-old assistant who had just graduated from high school. The new assistant types very well but does not do anything unless Alice first tells the assistant what to do and how to do it. One of the assistant's responsibilities is filing. Although Alice indicated that the filing was the assistant's sole responsibility, there never is time set aside for this important task. How can Alice help the assistant set aside time for the filing? Should Alice expect a young, inexperienced assistant to show initiative in assuming responsibilities in the office?

TELE-COMMUNICATIONS

Today's businesses depend on a fast, efficient flow of information in order to survive in the competitive environment. In the past, most companies had only one location or a few branches in close proximity to the main office. Now, however, all that is changed. Companies are expanding and are establishing branch offices in widely dispersed locations. The larger corporations have offices around the world.

The more offices a firm has, the more dependent it is on its communications systems. The telephone, of course, plays a vital role in these systems. But, many applications require a copy of a written document. In these situations, a phone conversation is not adequate, yet the mail system is too slow to handle documents that are needed almost immediately. In these cases, some form of electronic mail is necessary.

This chapter will look at the many varied features today's telephone systems offer to businesses. It will also introduce you to the electronic systems available for the transmittal of communications.

At the end of this chapter, you should be able to:

1. Describe the telephone systems available to today's user. ☐ 2. List and define the features available on telephones. ☐ 3. Describe the methods of electronic mail. ☐ 4. Discuss the future of telecommunications.

CHAPTER 14

TELEPHONE SYSTEMS

The business telephone was a fairly simple piece of equipment until the late 1960s when technological advances produced phones of increasing sophistication and complexity. An important event that occurred during that period was the Carterphone decision of 1968. This decision, which was made by the Federal Communications Commission (FCC), ended the exclusive right of the telephone company to provide phone equipment to its customers.

This meant that a business could buy telephones from a private manufacturer and interconnect them (hook them up) to the telephone company's lines. This type of arrangement is called an interconnect system or a private telephone system, since the phone equipment is privately owned by the business instead of rented from the telephone company.

Of course, the majority of businesses still rent their phone equipment from the phone company, but the popularity of privately owned telephone systems is growing, mainly because it is usually less expensive than renting phone company equipment.

Telephone systems, whether purchased or rented from the phone com-

Figure 14.1
Telephone instruments (Courtesy of AT&T).

pany, fall into one of two broad categories: key systems and private branch exchanges.

KEY SYSTEMS

A key system, designed for the small business or organization, consists of multibutton (key-equipped) telephones. Each person in the office who needs a phone is given an instrument with a number of buttons. Generally, one person in the office, usually the executive assistant, has the master phone station and is responsible for answering the incoming calls. There is no switchboard.

When a call comes through, a button lights up; and the executive assistant answers the call and finds out who is calling and the person the caller wants to reach. If, for example, the caller wants Mr. Jones, the executive assistant puts the caller on hold and notifies Mr. Jones that he has a call on line one. Mr. Jones would then depress the button for line one on his telephone instrument.

In a very small office, the executive assistant might just call to Mr. Jones or walk to his office to notify him of the call. In other cases, one of the

Figure 14.2
Telephone instruments (Courtesy of AT&T).

buttons on the phone might be used as an intercom. In such a situation, the executive assistant would put the caller on hold and then use the intercom line to notify Mr. Jones of the call.

Some companies have a separate intercom (intercommunication system) in addition to the regular phone system, which would be used only for external calls. An intercom is a communication system that is used only for internal calls. It permits one person in a company office to call another person in the office by dialing one or more digits.

PRIVATE BRANCH EXCHANGES

A private branch exchange (PBX), used by medium to large companies, is a small switching center. A PBX has a manual switchboard; a PABX (private automatic branch exchange) has automated switchboards or attendant stations using dial switching. Today, most companies have updated their equipment to PABX systems. The newer systems provide many convenience features such as direct outward dialing.

Direct outward dialing (DOD) allows the business person to pick up the phone and dial an access number to obtain an outside line. The caller can then dial the desired number. All this is done without going through the switchboard or operator attendant station. (On the older manual phone systems, a business person would have to call the operator and ask to be connected to an outside line.)

On this type of system, the employee can also call another person in the office by dialing his or her extension number, again without going through the operator.

Some phone systems, such as the telephone company's Centrex® series, also have direct inward dialing (DID). With a DID system, each person in the company has his or her own telephone number. When someone is trying to reach a particular person, he would dial that person's number; and the call would go directly to that person's phone, bypassing the switchboard.

On phone systems without DID, all calls come into the central station. The operator answers incoming calls and then switches them to the appropriate extension.

Companies that have direct inward dialing must also have at least one attendant to handle calls that come into the general company number. The caller may not know the direct number of the person he is calling, or he may just want to talk to someone in a particular department without knowing an individual's name.

FEATURES OF TELEPHONE SYSTEMS

In addition to DOD and DID, today's telephone systems offer a number of user convenience features. These features may make it more difficult for you to learn to use a particular system; but once you learn to use it, you will

Figure 14.3
Dimension® PBX system (Courtesy of AT&T).

Figure 14.4
Com Key® 416 key telephone system (Courtesy of AT&T).

find these features extremely helpful. Some of the more commonly used features follow.

Call forwarding permits a user to program the phone system to forward calls to another phone or to the operator. This can be done for all calls (if the user is out of the office, for instance), for calls that come in when the user's phone is busy, or for calls that are not answered after a certain number of rings.

Call pickup enables a user to answer any ringing phone in the system by picking up his or her own phone and dialing a certain number and the extension number of the ringing phone. For instance, if you hear a phone ringing in another department, you can pick up your phone, dial ''6'' (or some other predesignated number) and the extension number, and the call will be switched to your phone automatically.

Conference or consultation calling allows the user to set up a conference call among several people, both inside and outside the company, without the assistance of the operator. The consultation feature also makes it easy to get information over the phone from someone in the company while holding an outside call on the line. This eliminates call backs.

If an extension is busy, the caller can **camp-on** the line until the previous call is completed. The person on the busy phone will hear a signal indicating that someone is waiting to talk. This signal can be repeated at predetermined intervals, such as 10, 20, or 30 seconds.

If one person calls another person within the company and the line is busy, the caller can make use of the automatic **call-back** feature, which allows the caller to hang up and make other calls. When the busy extension becomes free, the system automatically rings the extension and the caller.

The call-back feature can also be used to gain access to outside lines. If the caller finds the outside lines are busy, the call-back feature will cause the phone to ring automatically when a line becomes free.

The caller can use **abbreviated dialing codes** (generally two or three digits) to call frequently dialed numbers.

Call timing signals the user at various intervals to indicate how long he or she has been talking.

Direct distance dialing (DDD) allows the user to place long distance calls directly without going through the operator.

A **speaker phone** allows the user to speak to callers without using a handset. The user can talk into the unit from anywhere in the room; the caller's voice is transmitted through the unit's loudspeaker. When privacy is desired, the user flips a switch on the unit, picks up the handset, and speaks into it as he or she would a regular phone handset.

The telephone company has **Picturephone**™, which allows people to see one another when carrying on a phone conversation. This feature is not available in all locations.

Paging allows the user to page individuals using the standard telephone.

Figure 14.5

Picturephone™, Mod II (Courtesy of AT&T).

By dialing the access code, you are automatically connected to the paging system.

The user can locate and talk to someone who is away from his or her desk. A page call, either a pocket pager or a low-level voice locating system, alerts the person that someone is calling. The person goes to the nearest phone and dials his or her own number, plus an access number. The system then automatically connects the person to the one who is calling.

Direct voice path is a direct connection between two phones. It is very useful for people who communicate frequently, such as the executive and the executive assistant, since the connection is made automatically and does not have to be dialed.

One feature that is used increasingly in phone systems is call routing, which is also called **automatic route selection**. This feature automatically routes all outgoing toll calls over the most economical route. The user just dials an access code and the number being called. The system then looks at the available routes, direct long distance lines, WATS lines, or tie lines, and picks the least expensive way to place the call.

The system may also be programmed to limit access to long distance lines to certain levels. For instance, clerks may only be able to place local calls, while executive assistants may be able to use WATS and tie lines, but not the direct long distance line, which is the most expensive way to place a call. Direct long distance may be reserved for management personnel.

The call routing system is usually part of the telephone system, but sometimes it is a separate unit connected to the phone system.

Very often the call routing feature is paired with a cost accounting system to help a firm keep track of its communications expenses by recording all details related to each call. These details include the name of the person who placed the call, the time of the call, the route, the number called, and the length and cost of the call. This allows a company to keep track of all calls made and to allocate costs to the various departments using the phone system.

TELEPHONE ACCESSORIES

In addition to the standard telephone, there are a number of accessories that help to increase the efficiency of telephones. These accessories include phone answering devices, call diverters, automatic dialers, voice amplifiers, privacy switches, and phone silencers.

Telephone answering devices serve two main functions. They can be used by the receptionist or executive assistant who has more calls coming in than he or she can handle. All excess calls can be answered and the message recorded, permitting the receptionist to respond to the calls when there is time.

Phone answering devices can also be used to record calls at times when the office is closed, such as evenings, weekends, and holidays. They can be used in the one-person office to answer calls when the executive assistant is away from the desk.

Answer-only models answer a ringing phone with a prerecorded message. For instance, the caller might hear, "The office closes at 5 p.m. Please call back after 9 a.m. tomorrow."

Answer-and-record models answer a ringing phone with a prerecorded message and then asks the caller to leave a message "at the sound of the beep." This message is recorded and can be played back at a later time.

Some answer-and-record models allow the user to set a time limit on the caller's message. For instance, they may give the caller 30 seconds to leave a message. Other units are voice activated, and they record for as long as the caller continues speaking, up to the end of the tape.

Generally, the business person will play back calls when he or she returns to the office. However, some systems are remotely activated, which means that the user can call the unit from outside the office and have the unit play back the calls.

Programmable systems that engage in simulated "conversation" with the caller are also available. These systems are designed primarily for taking orders and collecting information. The user programs a series of questions into the unit. The machine asks each question, then pauses to allow time for the person to reply to the question. All replies are recorded for later playback.

Call diverters divert incoming calls to a preselected location. This type of unit would be used in situations when the executive is working at home and wants all calls transferred there. The call diverter would transfer all incoming calls to the home number automatically, with the caller not even aware of the transfer.

Automatic dialers provide almost instant access to frequently called numbers. These numbers are programmed into the unit and assigned an access code. For example, the user dials the access code (which is generally one or two digits) and the dialer dials the entire number automatically. Many units also have an automatic redialing feature, which redials the last number until a connection is made.

Telephone amplifiers permit the user to have hands-free telephone conversations since the user speaks into a small microphone and hears the other person's voice from a speaker in the unit. Some of these systems have the capability to handle conference calls.

Phone silencers permit the user to turn off the ringing of the phone. This would be used in situations where a person was holding a meeting or was having an important discussion and did not want to be disturbed. The caller, however, hears the standard ringing so does not think the phone is

Figure 14.6
Touch-a-matic® (Courtesy of AT&T).

Figure 14.7
Hands free answer on intercom, Touch-Tone® service (Courtesy of AT&T).

out of order. The executive assistant can see the light flashing, which indicates the phone is ringing, and answer the call if desired.

Privacy devices allow the user to carry on a conversation with someone in the room without the person on the phone being able to hear anything. It is the same idea as putting your hand over the receiver, but it is more effective.

FUTURE DEVELOPMENTS FOR THE TELEPHONE

Future developments in telephone communications promise to bring even more advanced features. A hint of things to come has already been provided. Several manufacturers have introduced telephone systems with built-in microprocessors. This type of computerized telephone system provides the business user with several unusual features.

First, the phone has a display which shows the elapsed time on toll calls, the extension number that is calling you (on an internal call), the number dialed (on an outside call), the time of day, and the fact that another call is waiting or that a phone has been put on "do not disturb." The display also gives the user the ability to leave electronic messages on another person's phone. For instance, if the party called does not answer, the caller can leave the message "call 1456" on the display.

The system's memory provides a number of features, including speed dialing, which makes it possible to call commonly used numbers by depressing one, two, or three buttons (depending on the system). It also permits the user to enter account codes without interfering with an ongoing phone conversation. This feature is particularly important to businesses that charge their clients for phone usage, such as law firms, advertising and public relations agencies, and accounting firms.

In the future, business phones will be able to perform functions such as data entry and retrieval, word processing interface, electronic mail transmission, and credit card verification. In fact, phones that integrate voice and data in one unit are beginning to be introduced in the marketplace.

ELECTRONIC MAIL

Telephone communications play a tremendously large role in business; however, nonverbal communications are beginning to assume a large portion of the communications operations of companies. Nonverbal or message communications are essentially written communications that are transmitted over telephone lines. They fit in somewhere between telephone communications and mail handling. In fact, many firms call this type of communication *electronic mail*.

FACSIMILE SYSTEMS

One of the primary ways of transmitting documents electronically is through the use of facsimile systems. *Facsimile devices* (also called telecopiers because they combine telephone and copying technologies) can send copies of handwritten, typewritten, graphic, and photographic material to distant locations over telephone lines.

The facsimile transmitter converts the alphanumeric or graphic material into electronic signals that can be sent over telephone wires. The executive assistant inserts the document into the fax unit, dials the phone number where the document is to be sent, and then places the phone receiver into the coupler on the fax machine. The coupler couples or links the telephone to the fax machine.

At the other end, the facsimile receiver receives the electronic signals and converts them into a facsimile of the original document.

Some fax units only transmit; they are transmitters. Some only receive; they are fax receivers. Fax machines that transmit and receive documents are called transceivers.

Most facsimile machines currently on the market are analog units. Analog facsimile machines convert both image (textual matter and photos) and nonimage (white space) areas into audible signals. Digital models compress data and send only image areas, so these machines can send documents in much less time.

Standard transmission speeds for analog units are two, four, and six minutes for $8\frac{1}{2} \times 11$-inch paper. Digital machines can send the same $8\frac{1}{2} \times 11$-inch page in less than a minute; some models can transmit a page

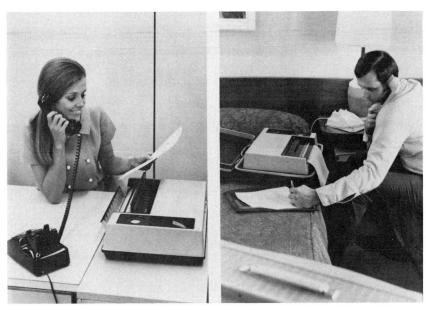

Figure 14.8
Portable Xerox 400 telecopier (Courtesy of Xerox).

Figure 14.9
Data Set 602A is used for FM transmission of facsimile signals on switched network or private lines. It provides for the transmission of analog information. (Courtesy of AT&T).

in as little as 20 seconds. This, of course, lowers the phone charge significantly. In high-volume situations, the higher price of digital units is more than offset by savings in telephone charges.

Facsimile units can also send documents that are either smaller or larger than $8\frac{1}{2}$ × 11-inch paper. Size limitations vary from one model to another.

You should be aware that slower speed machines provide a clearer copy than the high-speed units. Typewritten documents do not present a problem for even a sub-one minute fax; however, charts and graphs or complicated drawings would probably require a medium or slow speed unit with higher resolution.

Before you transmit a document over a facsimile system, you should be sure that the fax unit on the receiving end is the same model as, or at least is compatible with, the facsimile device in your office. Fax machines must be compatible if they are to communicate (send and receive documents) with one another.

Compatibility of fax units is a problem, but manufacturers in the industry have agreed to standardize their machines so that different types of fax

Figure 14.10
Dexnet™ networking capability links digital facsimile with high-speed analog equipment, enabling users to match equipment to message traffic requirements (Courtesy of Burroughs).

machines can "talk" to one another. This should eliminate the compatibility problem In the near future.

To solve this compatibility problem, many companies that use facsimile extensively establish facsimile networks in all their offices. In this way, all units in the network are compatible and can "talk" to each other.

Some networks use a polling procedure. The master station will poll all the fax units in the network on a periodic basis, picking up messages that are waiting to go out and distributing incoming messages. You can think of the procedure as an electronic mailman who picks up and delivers messages from all the fax units in the network. Unattended operation is often featured on these machines. This would allow a California office to transmit to a New York office without worrying about the time difference.

One of the major advantages of facsimile is that it can transmit exact copies of typewritten and handwritten documents, such as contracts, along with drawings, charts, and photographs.

Figure 14.11
Graphic Sciences dex 700 facsimile transceiver (Courtesy of Burroughs Facsimile Systems).

TELETYPEWRITERS

Teletypewriters transmit only alphanumeric information over phone lines. Some firms establish their own teletypewriter networks; however, many companies use one of Western Union's two commonly used teletypewriter networks, Telex and TWX. **Telex** means teleprinter exchange. **TWX** stands for teletypewriter exchange. Both systems permit a user to keyboard information and then send it to another Telex or TWX unit over standard telephone lines.

There are three types of Telex and TWX service: Automatic Send Receive (ASR) for tape operation; Key Send Receive (KSR) for manual operation; and Receive Only (RO) units for unattended operation. The type of system used will depend on the application.

For domestic transmissions, Telex and TWX are equally useful. For international transmissions, Telex may be more appropriate since Telex equipment used in the United States is almost fully compatible with Telex units used in other parts of the world. On the other hand, TWX machines used in this country may require operational changes when used to transmit messages abroad. Both TWX and Telex provide access to international carriers for sending cablegrams.

Western Union publishes an annual directory of Telex and TWX users. The executive assistant who has to send a message via one of these machines can look up the number of the recipient in this directory. If the transmission is a domestic one, it can be dialed directly.

To save on telephone transmission rates, you should prepare the message off-line by keyboarding the information on tape before transmission. In this way, the message will be error-free and ready for fast transmission before the number is dialed. This will also allow the machine to transmit at its full operational speed rather than at an uneven typing speed. You should also eliminate spaces wherever possible to cut down transmission time. Also, type the full width of the line to eliminate as many line spacings as possible.

For occasional overseas communications, a firm will generally use a telegram. For more frequent communications, a company will use Telex or TWX systems. Companies that have a high volume of messages to be sent abroad may lease an overseas communications channel. In these situations, the time differential plays an important role.

Overseas communications can be sent in a number of ways, including underwater cables, radio, and satellites. A cablegram is an international telegram that can be transmitted via cable, radio, or satellite. Full-rate cablegrams are delivered as soon as possible. Letter telegram (LT) cables are delivered during the following business day. The service chosen will depend on the urgency of the message, which must be weighed against the difference in cost between the two services.

COMPUTER-BASED MESSAGE SERVICES

One computer-based message service available is Mailgram®, a joint project of Western Union and the United States Postal Service. Western Union recently expanded its Mailgram® service. The new service, which is called Stored Mailgram, provides computer storage of a company's frequently used mailing lists, letters, and key paragraphs.

To access the information in the computer file, the company subscribing to this service dials an 800 toll-free number, gives the account number, and tells the computer what service it wants performed. For instance, the company can select a particular letter and request that it be sent to a portion of the mailing list.

Western Union gives high-volume users a special Mailgram® terminal which interfaces directly with the Western Union computer. The terminal operator would enter the company account number into the terminal and then keyboard transmittal instructions.

DATAPOST SERVICE

Other companies offer services similar to Mailgram®. One of these firms, Southern Pacific Communications, offers Datapost®. With this service, the subscriber faxes (uses a facsimile machine) messages to the Datapost computer, which prints out the appropriate message. The message is then taken to the airport; and from there, it is sent to the post office nearest the final destination. The post office then delivers the message the next day. The firm providing this service claims it is less expensive than Mailgram®, but it requires the sender to have a facsimile machine.

COMMUNICATING WORD PROCESSORS

Communicating word processing systems can also be used for electronic transmission of text. Copy is keyboarded and then stored on a magnetic medium. When the message is ready for transmission, the phone number is dialed and the receiver is placed in the word processor's coupler, and the message is transmitted over phone lines.

At the receiving end, the message can be either stored on the magnetic medium or printed out. Unattended operation permits the user to send messages at any time of the day or night, even when the receiving office is closed. This also allows a firm to take advantage of lower night rates on phone lines.

Some communicating word processors allow the communications function to go on in a background mode. This means that the word processing operator can continue to use the machine for text-editing functions while transmission of documents is taking place. This permits the most efficient and productive use of the system.

DATA COMMUNICATIONS

Data communications refers to the ability of computer systems to communicate over telephone lines or special dedicated lines. Telephone lines are used on a dial-up basis, which means that the user dials the appropriate number when a transmission is to be sent. In large volume situations, a

Figure 14.12
Telemail service provides instantaneous delivery of messages anywhere in the United States on a 24-hour basis. (Courtesy of GTE Telenet Communications Corp.).

dedicated line is more economical since it permits exclusive use of that line. In addition, the quality of the dedicated line is higher, making it more reliable and conducive to high data transfer rates.

Data communications usage is growing, especially because of the growing popularity of distributed data processing, which links remote terminals or small computers in a company's branch offices with the large computer in the main office. There is a constant exchange of information between the branch office computers and the main office computer.

Many businesses that do not have a distributed processing network do have an on-line computer system, which means that terminals communicate with the main computer in a question-and-answer mode. In other words, the terminal operator keys in a request to the computer and the computer responds to that request immediately.

FUTURE OF ELECTRONIC MAIL

The future of electronic mail is bright, according to most industry experts. This is due to several factors. First, the cost of mailing a letter through the U.S. Postal Service keeps rising. When you couple this with the increasing volume of business mail, you begin to understand why postal costs are becoming a major factor in the company budget. On the other hand, the cost of electronic mail is decreasing.

In addition, companies need information immediately if they are to operate effectively today, and the post office service is often too slow for business needs. For these reasons, many large companies are looking seriously at electronic mail. The U.S. Post Office itself is currently investigating the feasibility of establishing an electronic mail network.

At the present time, electronic mail is only practical for intracompany use because of the compatibility problem. For Company A to communicate electronically with Company B, they would both have to have equipment that is compatible; this is a serious drawback to intercompany communications. It would be like two firms trying to talk via the telephone when Company A's phone system cannot talk to Company B's system. Within a company, however, top management can ensure that all communications systems are compatible.

Before intercompany electronic mail becomes practical, on a wide scale, the industry will have to agree on a standard communications package that can be used by both large and small companies.

What will have to happen is intersystem compatibility among word processing, data processing, facsimile, and voice switching equipment. At this point, these various technologies are able to communicate with one another through a computer, but this is a very complicated and expensive procedure. The computer acts as a translator, accepting input from the sending system and converting it into a format that can be understood by the receiving equipment.

Figure 14.13
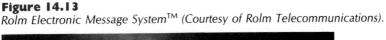
Rolm Electronic Message System™ *(Courtesy of Rolm Telecommunications).*

Currently, there are a few service companies that act as translators between noncompatible communications systems. These companies accept magnetic media from a text-editing system, convert them, and then read them into a different type of word processor or a computer or phototypesetter. This conversion process enables two different communicating systems to understand each other.

Another possible consideration is the development of a hybrid terminal that would combine the graphics capability of facsimile, the text-editing ability of word processors, and the terminal-to-terminal compatibility of message switching technology. It is even possible that this terminal could be used as a photocopier when it was not being used as an electronic mail system.

This type of system could probably be manufactured today, but the costs would be so high that few businesses could afford it. However, the cost of technology keeps dropping, so it is possible that this type of terminal will become economically feasible in the near future.

Advances in microwave and satellite transmission for business use are bringing the era of electronic mail even closer. With a microwave system, a firm can transmit voice and data from one microwave antenna to another by using radio beams. With a satellite system, voice and data communications are transmitted from one location to another via satellite.

SUMMARY

While many of the systems discussed in this chapter may seem more like fantasy than fact, the truth is that the executive assistant will undoubtedly be dealing with many, if not all of these systems, at some time. The question is not if these changes will occur, but when. For this reason, it is important for today's executive assistant to prepare to become tomorrow's executive assistant as well.

This can be done by finding out what types of communications systems the firm has and then using them when it makes economic sense to do so. Before deciding to use a particular communications service, the executive assistant should find out how important speed is.

In rush situations, speed—not cost—will probably be the determining factor. However, in most situations, the executive assistant should consider the cost factor as well as the speed of the various types of communications systems. For that reason, the executive assistant should know the speed, capabilities, and relative costs of all communication systems used by the company.

1. In 1968, the Carterphone decision of the Federal Communications Commission ended the telephone company's monopoly over telephone equipment installed on users' premises. Since that time, numerous businesses have purchased their own phone systems from private vendors and have interconnected them to telephone company lines.

2. Small firms have key systems in most cases, while larger companies generally have private branch exchanges.
3. Today's phone systems have a number of features including direct inward dialing, direct outward dialing, direct distance dialing, call forwarding, call pick-up, conference or consultation calls, and call-back of stations and trunks.
4. A number of phone accessories are also available for use with the telephone system. These accessories include phone answering devices, call diverters, automatic dialers, amplifiers, silencers, and privacy devices.
5. In addition to voice communications, businesses also use message communications (called electronic mail). Devices used to send message communications include facsimile systems, teletypewriters, computer-based services such as Mailgram® and Datapost®, communicating word processors, and data communications.
6. The future of electronic mail for intracompany business communications is bright, thanks to advances in office systems technology such as satellite and microwave communications.

CHAPTER RECALL EXERCISES

1. What is the Carterphone decision, and how did it affect business communications?
2. Describe the difference between a key phone system and a private branch exchange.
3. Name and describe five features available on business telephones.
4. What is automatic route selection?
5. Name and describe the use of three phone accessories.
6. Describe the differences between answer-only, answer and record, and programmable phone answering systems.
7. Define electronic mail.
8. What is facsimile?
9. What is the difference between analog and digital facsimile?
10. What is a teletypewriter?
11. Describe a computer-based message service.
12. How do communicating word processors fit into an electronic mail network?
13. What role does data communications play in a company's electronic mail network?
14. Discuss the future of electronic mail for business use.

PROBLEMS AND APPLICATIONS

1. Contact the telephone company and a private interconnect vendor and make a list of the telephone systems they have available. Compare the features available from each.

2. Check with three local firms to see what type of phone systems they use and what features they find the most useful.

3. Write or visit a local vendor of facsimile equipment and obtain as much information about the equipment as you can. Write a short summary of what you find out about facsimile equipment.

4. If your school has a text editor with communications capabilities, set up a network with a compatible system and exchange information over this system.

5. Write a letter to the U.S. Postal Service and ask about its plans for establishing an electronic mail service.

6. Your company uses electronic mail so communications can be sent and received more quickly. However, you have noticed that even though mail is received in a reasonable amount of time, it is sometimes two days before the communication is received by the proper person within the company. What can be done about cutting down on the delivery time of mail within the organization?

7. Using the information found in this chapter and also sources in your library, write a position paper about your predictions for the future of telecommunications for business.

LANGUAGE SKILLS DEVELOPMENT

1. Select the correct word in the following sentences:
   a. (Nobody, No body) in the group thought about taking an umbrella.
   b. (Nobody, No body) of students was more studious than yours.
   c. The sale appealed to (everyone, every one).
   d. (Everyone, Every one) of the employees attended the staff meeting.
   e. The word processing center can type the correspondence in (anyway, any way) that you choose.
   f. (Anyway, Any way), I'm glad you made it to the meeting.
   g. I will be home (everyday, every day) this week except Friday.
   h. Problems of (everyday, every day) living seem to crop up once in a while.

2. Choose the correct verb in these sentences:
   a. You (was, were) the first person to use this equipment.
   b. Our records of your banking account (do, does) not agree with the bank's records.
   c. One of my favorite places to go (are, is) the mountains.
   d. John is one of those who (rely, relies) on the weather report.
   e. Scrambled eggs and bacon (are, is) my favorite breakfast.
   f. Neither the manager nor the players (are, is) planning to attend the game.
   g. The Association of Bank Managers (was, were) planning to hold its annual meeting on Thursday.
   h. Part of the rooms of the house (are, is) to be closed for repairs.

3. Proofread the following sentences and make any needed corrections:
   a. It is easy to give advise to people.
   b. Leaving the party late, the driving was not easy for Beth.
   c. I would like to recommend that we hire 2 people for this job.
   d. I could see that the equipment was not working correctly, and that some changes needed to be made.
   e. In your first job you will become acquainted with office procedures.
   f. It took almost a hour to drive home.
   g. I accidently broke the vase.
   h. If Janet was here, she would take care of the complaints.

HUMAN RELATIONS INCIDENTS

1. Karl is an administrative assistant in a work area with two other administrative assistants. Karl's philosophy is that the telephone should be picked up immediately when it rings. The other two assistants sometimes will let their phones ring four or five times before they answer them, especially if they are involved in some other task. Even when they do not seem especially busy, the assistants will let the phones ring a couple of times before answering them. The ringing of the phones is a constant irritation to Karl. Is it his responsibility to educate the other assistants on the proper use of the telephone? Should he just keep quiet about the situation and endure the ringing? What do you suggest?

2. You work as a correspondence assistant in a word processing center with four other operators. Because there is only one outside line in the center, there is a rule that personal calls should be limited to three minutes. There is no rule on how many times you can use the phone during the day.

Leona is the only operator in the center who abuses the use of the telephone. She will sometimes spend as much as 10 to 15 minutes talking on the phone. This abuse is especially noticeable in the afternoons and all day during the summer when Leona's children are home from school. They will call several times a day.

The other operators in the center would like to say something to the word processing supervisor about Leona's abuse of the outside line of the telephone, but they are afraid they will only limit themselves because of the possibility of new rules for the telephone. Is there a good way to handle this situation? What do you recommend?

TELEPHONE TECHNIQUES

In spite of the dazzling array of computer hardware that is constantly being introduced into offices across the country, the development of future office technology will depend on telecommunications technology (telephone systems), not computer technology.

Telephone systems will continue to be the media through which the automated office will speed the flow of information. It will be a major part of the electronic office, merging the various segments together—word processing, teleconferencing, audio visual aids, reprographics, electronic mail, and micrographics.

To make this system work, the human factor remains the key component. Talking on the telephone with individuals outside the company—customers, sales representatives, suppliers, visitors, and various people soliciting or giving information—requires the good techniques and courtesies outlined in this chapter.

At the end of this chapter, you should be able to:

1. List the proper techniques for handling incoming calls. ☐ 2. List the proper techniques for making outgoing calls. ☐ 3. Discuss the methods available for making long distance calls. ☐ 4. Know how to handle emergency or annoyance calls.

CHAPTER 15

TECHNIQUES FOR INCOMING CALLS

Have you ever received a call and a voice said, "Mr. Kane? This is Mr. Askew's executive assistant. Just a minute, Mr. Askew wishes to speak with you." And three to five minutes go by until Mr. Askew comes on.

Have you ever telephoned a business office and the telephone rang approximately ten times before someone answered? Have you ever had someone keep you on "hold" for an extremely long time? Have you ever heard someone answer the phone in a discourteous or abrasive manner?

These are some of the irritating experiences that can create a negative impression of a company. An executive assistant has many opportunities to help the executive and the company. Mistakes and poor telephone techniques can influence the opinions customers have about the organization and about you as an individual. Your telephone job is doubly important because you represent your company. Your choice of words, tone of voice, and responsiveness on the telephone can be vitally important to customers, clients, and the general public because a telephone conversation is very often the first contact with the company. Here are a few suggestions for developing good telephone techniques.

ANSWER PROMPTLY

A prompt answer favorably impresses the caller. Then, your conversation is off to a good start. When you answer the telephone, greet the caller, identify your supervisor, and identify yourself: "Good morning. Mr. Stedman's office, Ms. Thomas speaking."

HAVE SOMEONE ANSWER YOUR PHONE

When you leave your desk, advise the person who is to answer for you where you are going, the telephone number where you can be reached, and when you will return. Give prompt attention to your telephone messages when you return.

Be cooperative with fellow workers. When you leave, you should be confident that your coworker will answer your phone. By the same token, you should be happy to answer your coworkers' phones when they are away from the office. Here are some hints for handling their calls:

☐ *Identify yourself.* It is helpful to have people know your name. For example, say "Ms. Baer's office, Mr. Hubbard."

☐ *Be helpful.* Offer what information you can. Tell the caller when your coworker will be back or whether the person can be reached somewhere else.

☐ *Be tactful.* Comments such as "She hasn't come in yet," or "She just stepped out for coffee" can give the wrong impression. It is better to say "Mrs. Viscosi is away from her office just now. May I ask her to call you?"

TRANSFER CALLS CAREFULLY

None of us likes the proverbial "runaround" so transfer calls only when necessary. Begin by telling the caller why and where you are transferring the call. Then transfer the call, using the method prescribed for your telephone system. Here is a good way to do it.

1. Explain why you are connecting the caller with someone else.
2. Be sure the party wants to be transferred. If not, offer to have someone call back.
3. If the caller agrees to stay on the line, check the instructions in your company's telephone manual, guide, or directory; then, transfer the person correctly.

ANSWER YOUR BOSS'S PHONE CORRECTLY

Answering the telephone for your boss is a vital and important part of your job, and your telephone manner plays a key role in communications. Be alert, friendly, and helpful. Some good examples of correct style include:

1. "She stepped out for a few minutes. May I take a message or ask her to call you?"
2. "He's talking on another phone. Would you care to wait?"
3. "She has a meeting in her office. May I help you?"

If your boss is in, ask the caller to wait a moment ("One moment, please"), depress the hold button, signal your supervisor on the intercom, tell him or her who's calling, and as soon as your boss accepts the call, hang up.

HANDLE WRONG NUMBERS EFFICIENTLY

Large organizations have thousands of extensions and receive many wrong numbers. If a person reaches you by mistake, help the caller reach the correct number by following the procedures below:

☐ First, apologize for the wrong number: "I'm sorry, but you have the wrong number."
☐ Next, find out whether the caller is inside or outside the company.
☐ If the caller is inside the company, tell him or her to please call company information for the correct number; or, if you know the extension number of the party, you can tell the caller the number immediately.
☐ If the caller is outside the company, here is a good opportunity for you to be extremely helpful. You can transfer the call to the company operator; or, if time permits, you can look up the number and then transfer the call.
☐ Tell the caller that you are going to transfer the call to the company operator.
☐ Contact the company operator by quickly pressing the plunger down,

once or twice, while you still have the caller on the line. When the operator answers, all you have to say is "Please transfer this call to. . ." and state the name and department of the party requested.

LEAVE AND RETURN TO THE LINE PROPERLY

Nothing infuriates a caller more than to be left hanging on the telephone. Do not neglect to say why you are leaving the line and approximately when you will return. Expressions such as "Hold on" or "Just a second" usually stretch into minutes and tell the caller nothing. Some companies feel that music piped into the phone when placed on "hold" soothes the caller. Sometimes it does the opposite. If you know you will be away from the telephone longer than a minute or two, offer to call back and say the approximate time you will return the call.

When leaving the line, depress the "hold" button for about two seconds. If your telephone is not equipped with a "hold" button, lay the telephone receiver down gently using a book or paper as a cushion. This will eliminate your caller hearing office noise while you are away from the phone.

When you return to the line, alert the caller that you are back by using a suitable introductory phrase, such as "Thank you for waiting" or mention the caller's name. If there has been an unavoidable delay, apologize.

TAKE MESSAGES CORRECTLY

Always keep your message pad handy and record the details accurately and completely while they are being given by the caller. Making a mental note often results in the message being incomplete, or in the rush of business you may forget to relay it.

Request, rather than demand, information. Such phrases as "What's your name?" or "Repeat that, I didn't get it," sound abrupt when compared to "May I have your name, please?" or "Would you mind repeating that information?"

If the name is an unusual one or contains letters which sound alike, verify the spelling through the technique of key letter spelling, such as "Is that b as in boy or v as in Victor?" Also, be certain to obtain the initials if it is a name like Smith or Jones.

It is especially important to be accurate if the message requires action on the part of your boss. Repeat the information to the caller to be sure that you have the correct information.

END CALLS GRACEFULLY

End the call in a favorable way. Thank the person if he or she has been helpful. Say "goodbye" pleasantly. After you say goodbye, let the caller hang up first. Then, replace your receiver carefully and quietly.

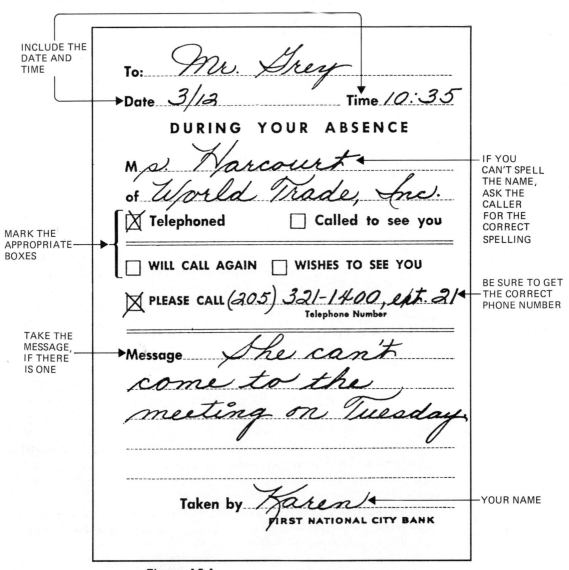

INCLUDE THE DATE AND TIME

To: *Mr. Grey*

Date *3/12* **Time** *10:35*

DURING YOUR ABSENCE

M *s* *Harcourt*

of *World Trade, Inc.*

IF YOU CAN'T SPELL THE NAME, ASK THE CALLER FOR THE CORRECT SPELLING

⊠ **Telephoned** ☐ **Called to see you**

MARK THE APPROPRIATE BOXES

☐ **WILL CALL AGAIN** ☐ **WISHES TO SEE YOU**

⊠ **PLEASE CALL** *(205) 321-1400, ext. 21*
Telephone Number

BE SURE TO GET THE CORRECT PHONE NUMBER

TAKE THE MESSAGE, IF THERE IS ONE

Message *She can't come to the meeting on Tuesday.*

Taken by *Karen*

YOUR NAME

FIRST NATIONAL CITY BANK

Figure 15.1
Taking telephone messages correctly.

TECHNIQUES FOR MAKING OUTGOING CALLS

The techniques for making outgoing calls are just as important to the executive assistant as the techniques for handling incoming calls. When you are making a telephone call for yourself or for your boss, you should be aware of the following suggestions:

☐ *Be sure of the number.* Before you dial, check the telephone directory or your personal call list in order to avoid wrong numbers.

☐ *Place your own calls.* It saves time and helps you show extra interest in the person you are calling.

☐ *Let the phone ring.* Give the person you are calling at least 45 seconds or ten rings to answer the telephone.

☐ *Identify yourself.* Others may not recognize you by your voice, so get the conversation off to a good start by giving your name right away.

☐ *Remember time differences.* When calling long distance, don't forget the four time zones in the United States. A map showing these areas is included in your telephone directory.

☐ *Be considerate.* Always stay on the line when you place a call. This will prevent irritation to the called person; it will also prevent tying up equipment unnecessarily, additional work for the company switchboard operator, and a waste of money by lengthening the call. By staying on the line, you can take immediate action if the number is busy or someone does not answer.

MAKING LONG DISTANCE CALLS

When you need to make long distance calls, there are several options available for your consideration.

Station-to-Station. Call station-to-station if you want to talk with anyone who answers. Station-to-station rates are lower than person-to-person ones. Charges begin when the called telephone number is answered.

Direct-Distance Dialing. For these calls, the caller dials the number directly and no operator assistance is required. Toll rates are lowest for direct-distance dialed calls.

Operator-Assisted Calls. Station-to-station calls that require operator assistance are charged at a higher rate than those that are completed without an operator's help. Higher rates are necessary to compensate for the costs of providing special services. These services include calls such as collect, credit card, billed to a third party, code billings, time and charges (including hotel guest calls), sequence calls, and calls placed by the operator at the customer's request.

Person-to-Person. If you wish to speak to a particular person, call person-to-person. Dial the operator and say you want to make a person-to-person call. Rates are highest for these calls even if you talk to an alternate person or extension. Charges start when the conversation begins. You can dial person-to-person calls by dialing "0" before the number.

Collect. You can call collect, either station-to-station or person-to-person, if the person or firm you are calling agrees to pay for the call. Charges start on station-to-station calls when someone at the called telephone agrees to accept the charges and on person-to-person calls when conversation starts with the person called. You can dial collect calls by dialing "0" before the number.

Credit Card. Customers who have Bell System credit cards may place calls and charge them to their credit card numbers. These calls require an operator's assistance to record the credit card number, but you can dial them by dialing "0" before the phone number. They may be station-to-station or person-to-person calls. Customers may apply for a credit card by calling their phone company's local business office.

Bill to Third Party. You may place calls and transfer the charges to another telephone number. This service requires an operator's assistance to record the number to be billed, but you can dial the number by dialing "0" before the phone number. The call may be either station-to-station or person-to-person.

Time and Charges. When placing calls, you may request from the operator the amount of time and the charges for the calls. This would be beneficial if you are dialing from someone else's phone. This service requires an operator's assistance. The call may be either station-to-station or person-to-person.

Directory Assistance. To obtain the telephone number of a person who lives in another community, dial access code "1" where applicable, the area code for the community you want (if different from yours), then 555-1212. When the operator answers, give the name of the city or town and then the name of the person you are calling. Make a note of the number for future use.

Wrong Numbers. If you should reach a wrong number, apologize for the call, then dial the operator and tell the operator of the error. No charge will be made for the wrong number reached.

COURTESIES AND ECONOMICS OF OUTGOING CALLS

1. When placing a call, stay on the line and be ready to greet your party. This avoids delay and resentment. It also demonstrates courtesy and respect for the person you are calling.
2. Place your own calls to save time and to show extra interest in the person you are calling.
3. Plan your call before you make it. Know beforehand what you are going to discuss so your call will be brief but effective. Planning saves time and money.
4. If you are connected to the executive assistant of the called person, announce who is calling—for example, "Mr. Diamond of XYZ Company is calling Ms. Wesson." If you reach the called person, announce your boss; for example, "Mr. Diamond of XYZ Company is calling you, Mr. Wesson. Here he is."

EMERGENCY CALLS

Certain states require you to hang up a telephone immediately when told the line is needed for an emergency call. An emergency call is defined as a call "to a police or fire department, or for medical aid or ambulance service, necessitated by a situation in which human life or property is in jeopardy and prompt summoning of aid is essential."

If an emergency occurs in your office, consult your company directory for the emergency numbers which are usually listed in the inside cover of your directory.

ANNOYANCE CALLS

It is rare to receive crank calls in a business office, but if you do, hang up; don't keep talking. That is what the caller wants. If the calls persist, contact your telephone business office. In difficult cases, a special Annoyance Call Bureau will work closely with you and police officials to catch offenders.

It is a crime to make a telephone call for annoying or harrassing purposes under federal and most state laws. In the case of federal law, it is a crime to knowingly permit a telephone under one's control to be used for such purposes.

CHANGING TELEPHONE PROCEDURES

As phone rates across the country continue to climb, a corresponding decrease in the time allotted to make calls usually occurs. This means a caller will have to say in three minutes what he or she used to say in five minutes.

A compulsory system of timed local calls for businesses, instead of the unlimited duration calls previously allowed, affects the way businesses conduct telephone communications. This is particularly true if they are concerned with the economics of telephoning. In simpler terms it means that people in companies will have to talk faster (initiate condensed conversations) if they want to avoid costlier bills.

As indicated earlier, higher postal rates are a source of frustration, and increasing phone rates are an additional frustration. The impact of higher bills makes callers resentful when they are told they will have to hold on before they can talk. Telephone etiquette is more important than ever in trying to implement cost-cutting telephone use. Higher phone rates may force changes in some of the more traditional office procedures. In order to economize,

1. People should make and answer their own calls, rather than operate through executive assistants.
2. Companies should schedule more employees to handle calls at busy times.
3. Operators should make sure that callers are switched promptly to a correct extension and should arrange to call back if a caller might have to await a response for some time. It is especially annoying to a caller using a pay telephone who is asked to hold on so long that he or she runs out of change.
4. Use the directory to find the correct numbers.

SUMMARY

The efficient executive assistant uses the telephone as one of the most important communication tools. It must be used with great skill, especially when talking with outside callers and with executives in a large office. Courtesy is the key to telephone effectiveness.

1. Greet callers pleasantly; be enthusiastic and sincere.
2. Use the person's name. There is no sweeter music to a person than the sound of his or her own name.
3. Treat every call as an important call. When customers feel you are giving them personal consideration, they will have more confidence in you and your company.
4. Be tactful. When it is necessary to refuse a request because of company policy, give a full and sympathetic explanation. Avoid expressions such as "you have to" or "you must." It is better to say, "If you will come in, we will be happy to check for you," rather than "You'll have to come in."
5. Apologize for errors or delays. Maybe things won't always be right, but you can still be courteous and sincere.
6. Keep sources of information about telephone services handy for quick

reference. The telephone company will supply you with several booklets that compare the different types of calls, rates, and applications.

CHAPTER RECALL EXERCISES

1. When an agent for a car rental company is talking on the telephone to a customer, he or she is acting not as an individual but as a representative of the company. Explain.
2. What are the essential elements to include in answering the telephone?
3. What provisions can executive assistants take to make sure their phones are answered during their absences?
4. When should you use the hold button in answering your boss's phone?
5. Describe how you could be helpful to a caller who reached you as a result of a wrong number.
6. What can you do to soothe a caller if a delay is anticipated?
7. Briefly list some preparations you can make prior to placing outgoing calls.
8. Compare station-to-station with direct-distance dialed calls.
9. List some emergency numbers that should be readily available to you.
10. Why is it important to know the correct time zone for the person you wish to call?
11. What changes in business procedures result in higher phone rates?

PROBLEMS AND APPLICATIONS

1. Assume you called an office and received the following responses. Improve each response.
   a. Hello, may I help you?
   b. Ms. Robyn is still at lunch.
   c. Mr. Randolph is in Chicago visiting the ABC Company.
   d. May I ask who is calling?
   e. Ms. Hale is on another line. I'll put you on hold.
   f. No, this is not the Purchasing Department.
   g. Hello. No, this is not Ms. James. She is away from her desk right now. I'm just answering the phone for her.
   h. Who is this?
   i. What did you say your name is?
   j. Good afternoon, Accounts Receivable Department of the ABC Corporation. Mr. James Andrews' office. This is Mr. Roberts speaking.

2. Choose another person in your class to role play the following situations. One of you will assume the role of the caller and one should assume the role of the person being called.
   a. Mr. Anderson, your boss, has been away from his desk for about

20 minutes. You don't know where he is or when he will return. He receives a call from the president of the company.

b. Ms. Rain gave you instructions that she is not to be disturbed by anyone. She is in her office working on a proposal to an important client, Ms. Swift. Ms. Swift calls and wants to talk to Ms. Rain.

c. While talking on the telephone on one line, another phone line rings.

d. You are talking to an important customer on the phone and you need to get important information which will take you about five minutes away from the phone.

3. Assume you have to give a talk to a local high school class on improving telephone techniques. The speech will last about 20 minutes. Outline the topics you would include in the talk.

4. You need to make long-distance calls to the following places. Note the time differences between where you live and where the persons to be called live.

a. Mr. Curry in San Diego, California.

b. Ms. Beech in Winston Salem, North Carolina.

c. Ms. Reston in Seattle, Washington.

d. Mr. York in Sarasota, Florida.

e. Mr. England in Chicago, Illinois.

f. Ms. Hewlett in Las Vegas, Nevada.

g. Mr. Sells in Boston, Massachusetts.

5. Assume you need to make some long-distance calls. What method or procedure would you use to make the following calls:

a. Call to an office in another state to find out their office hours.

b. Call to Mr. Frink whose company is about 500 miles away. You are not sure if Mr. Frink will be in, and you don't want to talk to anyone else.

c. A personal call that you want to charge to your home phone.

d. Call to a company which suggested that you let them pay for the call.

e. Call from a friend's house in which you need to know the cost of the call.

f. Call to a company in another state; you don't know the number.

LANGUAGE SKILLS DEVELOPMENT

1. Choose the correct usage of the numbers in the following sentences:

a. We hold sales (two, 2) times a year.

b. You will make your presentation at (nine, 9) a.m. at the opening general session.

c. The meeting is scheduled for (November 17, 17th).

d. The program committee has authorized me to offer you ($200, $200.00) for this talk.

e. We collected (twenty, 20) percent more this year than last year.
f. We would like to send you a (six-month, 6-month) subscription to *Business* for just ($15, fifteen dollars).
g. The newsstand price is ($1, one dollar) a copy.
h. Please add (50 thousand, 50,000) envelopes to our present order.
i. We will have to employ (300, three hundred) skilled mechanics.
j. We hold a promissory note for ($1,000, one thousand dollars) that was due the (15, 15th) of last month.

2. Insert the correct punctuation in the following sentences:
a. As you know all accounts do not carry the same risk and therefore should not be treated in the same way.
b. In addition there are agencies organized for the purpose of supplying data concerning the risk of failure.
c. The conference to which you referred in your last phone call will be held in San Francisco on March 10.
d. Congratulations Harriet on your new promotion.
e. To assist us in evaluating the product please keep a total of all the calls received.
f. Please fill out the enclosed card and return it immediately.
g. Do you know whether pencils pens or ballpoint pens are used most often by shorthand writers.
h. To support my view I recommend that you read the latest report published by the government.
i. Try to find out too who our competitors are.
j. He has handled a sales territory in Texas for the past year and is not a newcomer to our organization.

HUMAN RELATIONS INCIDENTS

1. You were talking to one of the company's most important customers when you had to leave the phone to get some information for the customer. You stayed away from the phone much longer than you had anticipated; and when you came back to the phone, the customer had the following to say:

Well, young lady, I hope you enjoyed your lunch! Do you realize how long I've been sitting here waiting for you?

How can you get out of this predicament without offending the customer any further? Can you do something to make sure this problem does not occur again?

2. Your boss, Mr. Stenbeck, likes to get his desk work done in the early morning and suggests that you hold his calls from 8 a.m. to 11 a.m. each day. Most of the people in the office respect Mr. Stenbeck's wishes. The only exception is Mr. Scott, who is one of Mr. Stenbeck's colleagues. He constantly calls Mr. Stenbeck in the mornings and says it is important or urgent that he speak to Mr. Stenbeck right away. Most of these calls could wait until 11 a.m. but Mr. Scott refuses to wait. Is there a way that you can help Mr. Stenbeck maintain his "quiet time" in the morning? How would you handle Mr. Scott's telephone calls?

ghijklmnopqrstuvwxyz
67890$.,-'':;!?*½¼¾–()[]=†/+%&@

xample of Univers, a precisely defined
reated by Adrian Frutiger for the IB
oser. It has an elegant simplicity of style,
type impression. Univers is a strong
aphical eccentricities. It is a practical fac
py used in advertising and technolog

Bold

EFGHIJKLMNOPQRSTUVWXYZ
fghijklmnopqrstuvwxyz
67890$.,-'':!2*½¼¾–()[]=†/+%&@

,s, a precisely de
an Frutiger for t
egant simplicity of
Univers is a st
cities. It is a practic
vertising and tech

ed sans-serif face,
e IBM "Selectric"
yle, giving a clean,
ng face, without
l face, appropriate
ological literature.

This example of U
was created by a
Composer. It has a
clear type impres
typographical ecce

ABCDEFGHIJKL
abcdefghijklmnop
1234567890$.,-'':

DUPLICATION AND PHOTOTYPESETTING EQUIPMENT

Because of the ease of operation, many companies are training and using executive assistants to operate phototypesetting equipment. This equipment is used to prepare company annual reports, brochures, and pamphlets.

Executive assistants usually are responsible for determining which machines are best for various types of applications of reprographics. They also must use and know how to maintain and operate reprographics equipment. ■ Chapter 16 Phototypesetting Equipment ☐ Chapter 17 Copying and Duplicating Equipment

SECTION IV

PHOTOTYPESETTING EQUIPMENT

Phototypesetting is a way of preparing textual matter so that it is ready to be reproduced (camera-ready) for eventual publication and distribution. Today, virtually all newspapers, magazines, and books are phototypeset. In addition, many companies use phototypesetting equipment to prepare annual reports, pamphlets, brochures, and newsletters.

Since the latest phototypesetting equipment is no more difficult to operate than most text-editing typewriters, a number of companies that install in-house phototypesetting equipment train their own executive assistants and clerical personnel to operate the equipment. For this reason, executive assistants should have a basic understanding of what phototypesetting is and how it works.

At the end of this chapter, you should be able to:

1. Define phototypesetting. ☐ 2. Describe the differences between typed material and material that has been phototypeset. ☐ 3. Define type font. ☐ 4. Describe the categories of typesetters used in the office environment. ☐ 5. Explain the integration of word processing and phototypesetting.

CHAPTER 16

DESCRIPTION OF PHOTOTYPESETTING EQUIPMENT

Since an increasing number of firms are using phototypesetting equipment, the executive assistant should understand the differences between typed material and material that has been phototypeset. There are some very distinct differences.

On most typewriters, all the characters, regardless of their width, are allotted the same amount of space on the page. Thus, both an "i" and a "w" are given one-tenth of an inch on a pica typewriter, even though the "w" is a wider character than the "i." The "i" just gets more white space around it.

Of course, this is not true of typewriters with proportional spacing, which gives each character a space commensurate with its size. With proportional spacing, an "i" might be given a space one-twelfth of an inch, while a "w" might get a space that is one-eighth of an inch wide. However, the majority of typewriters do not offer proportional spacing. Phototypesetters do.

One of the advantages of proportional spacing is that it permits the typist to justify perfectly the right-hand margin. To justify a margin means to make the margin perfectly even. Copy can be justified on the left side (flush left), as it is with most typewritten material; on the right side (flush right); or on both the left and right sides (flush left and right). Copy may also be centered.

FLUSH LEFT	FLUSH RIGHT
ABCDEFG	ABCDEFG
ABC	DEFG
ABCDE	BCDEFG

FLUSH LEFT AND RIGHT	CENTERED COPY
ABCEDFGH	ABCDEFG
ABCDEFGH	BCDEF
ABCDEFGH	CDE

TYPE STYLES AND SIZES

Typesetting also offers a much greater variety of type styles and sizes than is available on a typewriter. For example, a typewriter may offer 10 and 12 pitch or proportional spacing in several different styles, such as standard and script. However, the choices are limited.

With typesetting equipment, on the other hand, the user can choose from dozens of different type faces. Some are old-fashioned looking, while others are modern; some have thin letters and others have wide, heavy letters. The style of type chosen will depend on the application. A firm may use one typeface for annual reports, another for business forms, and still others for catalogs and brochures.

The size of the type will also vary. Type size is measured in points. Most typesetting systems offer a variety of type sizes in heights ranging from 6 point type to 72 point type. There are 72 points in an inch, so type set 72 points high would be one inch in height. Type set 36 points high would be half an inch, and type set 18 points is a quarter of an inch.

In addition to deciding on the size and style of the characters to be used, the typesetter also has to determine how wide the line is going to be. Most people would measure the width and depth of a line in inches. They might look at their favorite magazine and find that there are three columns and each column is two inches wide and ten inches long. Professional typesetters, however, do not measure lines in inches; they measure lines in picas.

The **pica** is the measurement used by typesetters and printers to measure the width and the length of a line. There are six picas to the inch, so a two-inch wide line would be 12 picas wide; and a 10-inch long column would be 60 picas.

A **type font** is a complete assortment of one size and style of type. It contains all the characters necessary to set type using that face and size, including both upper- and lower-case letters. Upper-case letters are capital letters. Lower-case letters are small letters. They got the name upper and lower case because printers used to keep capital and small letters in different cases, and the case with the capital letters was placed above the case with the small letters.

A particular type face is generally available in light, regular, italic, and bold faces. These can be mixed and matched within one piece of copy. For instance, the main headings can be set in bold face and the subheadings set in italic.

Generally, the operator of the phototypesetter does not determine the size or style of the type. The type is usually marked before it gets to the operator. On the other hand, many firms expect the phototypesetter to format the copy; that is, set it up on the page.

The executive assistant who is responsible for formating copy should see if the firm has a style manual. If not, he or she should discuss the possibility of creating a style manual. The manual would include various categories of jobs, such as newsletters, business forms, and catalogs, and each job category would be formatted in a particular way. Categorizing jobs in this way means the executive assistant does not have to format each individual job. This saves time, helps the executive assistant to visualize what each job will look like, and lends uniformity to the company's typeset documents. It also speeds up the entire typesetting process.

The executive assistant who operates a phototypesetter is also helped by the machine itself. The latest model machines have display screens and intelligence that either prompt the operator to make some formatting decisions or make the decisions automatically. For instance, the system may

Figure 16.1
AM Varityper's Comp/Set 4800 Area Composition Terminal (Courtesy of AM).

indicate to the operator where to end a line; or, it may make the line ending decision automatically.

Some machines can also determine what size headline is needed to fill a particular space. The display screen may show the depth and width of the page and tab locations. Of course, the number of operator prompts will depend on the type of machine.

STRIKE-ON TYPESETTERS

There are two general categories of typesetters that are used in the office environment: strike-on typesetters and phototypesetters. We will concentrate on phototypesetters since the executive assistant is most likely to find these machines in the office. However, it is worthwhile to mention other kinds of typesetting equipment.

Strike-on typesetters are similar to typewriters. The operator keys in the various characters the way he or she would with a typewriter, and the typesetter's printing bar strikes the paper, producing the character.

Strike-on typesetters are sometimes called cold type machines, as are phototypesetters. This category distinguishes them from hot type machines (linotype), which create characters out of molten metal that has been heated to over 500°F.

These hot type machines have lost popularity since cold type machines have been introduced. They are still used by some commercial printing establishments but are virtually never used by companies to produce in-house materials such as reports and brochures. The executive assistant is unlikely to come across a linotype machine unless he or she works for a printer.

The simplest type of strike-on typesetter is a machine with proportional spacing. With this kind of typesetter, the operator can right-justify the margin by following a two-step procedure. First, the executive assistant types a draft of the copy, ending each line as close to the right-hand margin as possible. Second, the executive assistant counts how many spaces have to be added to or deleted from each line in order to make the right margin perfectly

Figure 16.2
A type font is being inserted into the IBM electronic Selectric® composer. There are over 125 fonts available in eleven different type styles and in thirteen languages (Courtesy of IBM).

even. These adjustments are made by changing the unit spacing between the words in each line. In some lines, space is added between each word; in others, space is deleted. The copy is then retyped with the new spacing, producing a justified right margin.

Proportional spacing typewriters have limited type styles and sizes—10 and 12 pitch. Machines with typing balls rather than bars offer a greater variety of type faces, but many of these machines do not offer proportional spacing, making it impossible to have a completely justified right-hand margin.

More sophisticated keyboard composers offer a variety of interchangeable type fonts, permitting the operator to choose the type style most appropriate for each job. These machines offer proportional spacing, a range of type sizes, plus a variety of column widths. Justification is handled internally, eliminating the need for the operator to make justification calculations. The machine automatically adds the space needed to justify the right margin.

Some of these machines allow two or more different fonts to be in the machine at the same time, permitting the operator to switch from one to the other easily without removing the existing font and replacing it with a different one. Another feature permits the executive assistant to put different amounts of space (points) between the lines. The amount of space between lines of copy is called leading.

An internal memory is featured on a few of these composing units. Copy is typed and stored in machine memory until all revisions are made; then the copy is played back from memory automatically. Other systems store text on an external medium such as a paper tape or a magnetic card rather than in internal machine memory. A separate module reads the tape or card with its formatting instructions, and the copy is printed out.

PHOTOTYPESETTERS

Phototypesetting machines are more sophisticated than strike-on composers, offering the operator more advanced features and ease of operation. This process is called phototypesetting because it uses photographic principles to typeset copy. The easiest way to describe a phototypesetter is to compare it to a camera—a camera that takes pictures of type characters.

Phototypesetters differ in many ways, but they all have three elements in common: a master character image, a light source, and a light or photosensitive material. The character image is positioned in front of the light source, which projects the image onto the photosensitive material.

A phototypesetter must store its master character sets, which include all the characters and symbols for a specific type face. Some machines store the master sets on disks; others use grids, film strips, or drums. In some machines, a number of these master sets can be stored on-line in the machine for immediate use. In other cases, the sets are stored off-line and the operator must change the masters whenever a different type style is desired.

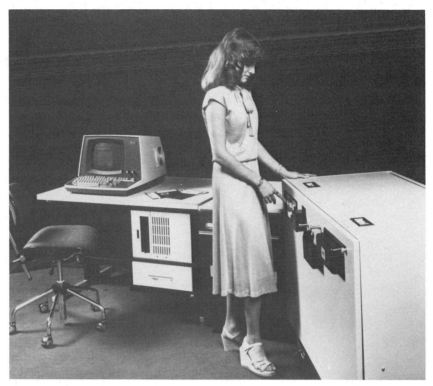

Figure 16.3
Wang Typesetter 44 and 48 Photocomposer (Courtesy of Wang Laboratories, Inc.).

Copy to be typeset can be input into the system in two basic ways: through direct entry keyboarding and through some intermediate or peripheral device. With the direct entry process, the operator keys the characters and machine instructions directly into the phototypesetter via the machine's keyboard. In models with a display screen, the characters appear on the screen as they are being keyboarded. This permits the operator to view and correct the copy before it is typeset.

When an intermediate device is used, the copy is keyboarded on some other type of machine, such as a typewriter or a text editor, and the keystrokes are recorded on a paper or magnetic medium. This medium is then input into the phototypesetter, usually through an interface device which translates the text and instructions for the phototypesetter. Two commonly used intermediate devices are optical character recognition (OCR) systems and text-editing typewriters.

An OCR machine reads copy that has been typed on a single-element typewriter equipped with a special OCR type element. The OCR device reads the copy, converts it into codes that can be understood by the phototypesetter, and then produces a paper tape or magnetic medium that can

Figure 16.4
Hendrix Typereader (Courtesy of Hendrix).

be input into the phototypesetting system. This eliminates the need to re-keyboard the copy.

Copy typed on text-editing typewriters can also be input into a photo-typesetter without rekeyboarding the copy. The executive assistant records the keystrokes and codes on the text editor's magnetic medium, and then inserts the recorded medium into a phototypesetting interface device. This device reads the word processing codes into the phototypesetting machine, instructing the machine on how to set the type.

When an executive assistant uses a phototypesetter, she or he must input machine instructions or codes as well as text. These codes instruct the typesetting system, specifying what size and style of type to use, what spacing to put between lines, and whether to set copy flush left, flush right, or flush left and right. In short, the operator has to give the machine formatting instructions.

On many machines, these codes are entered through the use of dedicated, special function keys. Dedicated keys are used to enter formatting instructions rather than text characters or numbers. For example, one key may be used to set line lengths only. Another may be used to tell the machine what point size to set the type.

Once the operator has given the formatting instructions to the phototypesetter, she or he can begin entering text. As the operator hits a character or number key, "a" for example, the machine searches for that character on the master image set. The intelligence in the phototypesetter cannot read the various characters, so it locates the correct character by counting lines or marks along the edge of the master set. So, when the "a" key is depressed, the machine knows that the "a" is the first position on the set and counts to the first line or mark. This positions the "a" before the machine's lens.

Once the correct character is in position before the lens, a light flashes, and the image of the character is projected onto photosensitive material.

As the operator continues striking character keys, the unit adds up all the unit values of each character until there are enough to fill a line. Then the machine determines the number of units remaining at the end of the line and divides the units evenly among the word spaces on the line. This results in a precisely justified line.

In some cases, it is necessary to hyphenate a word in order to justify a

Figure 16.5
AM International's Varityper Division has introduced a telecommunications interface option that enables comp/set and comp/edit phototypesetting systems to "talk to" word processing systems (Courtesy of AM).

line. Some phototypesetters leave hyphenation decisions to the operator; however, most offer some type of machine hyphenation.

Machines that have a hyphenation logic program hyphenate words according to logical word breaks. The problem is that the rules of the English language are not always logical. Therefore, there will be errors in any hyphenation program based on logic.

Very sophisticated phototypesetters use exception word dictionaries in addition to standard logic programs. The correct hyphenation for all words that do not follow logical hyphenation rules is stored in this dictionary.

Once the copy has been entered into the phototypesetter (either through direct entry keyboarding or an intermediate device), the exposed photosensitive material—either paper or film—is taken from the typesetter and put into a processing unit.

When the processed material emerges from the processor, the operator should check to see that the type is of uniformly high quality. Long pages of text should be cut into manageable pieces, preferably according to jobs or some other logical division. The material is then ready to be pasted up, producing camera-ready art—that is, copy that is ready for the printing process.

PHOTOCOMPOSERS

Photocomposers differ from phototypesetters in one important way. They not only set text and headlines, but they also set them as complete pages rather than strips of copy. This is in-machine page makeup, and it simplifies the paste-up process since the page can be pasted on a board as a unit, with all components, such as headlines and text matter, intact.

PARTNERSHIP OF PHOTOTYPESETTING AND WORD PROCESSING

Today, many companies are marrying their word processing and phototypesetting equipment to save time and money and to produce more professional looking documents and reports. For many of these firms, the marriage is a natural one. They feel that phototypesetting is an extension of word processing and, therefore, belongs in or near the word processing operation.

The partnership between text-editing and phototypesetting equipment eliminates redundant keying of information. Instead of rekeying information that has already been keyed on a word processor, the phototypesetting operator can transfer the information already recorded on the word processor into the phototypesetter.

In most cases, an interface device is needed to integrate the word processor and phototypesetter. This interface translates the coded word pro-

Figure 16.6
AM Varityper's Comp/Edit 5810 system features a 40-line text screen and 50 to 70 lines per minute typesetting speed (Courtesy of AM).

cessing text into a code that will be recognized by the phototypesetter. This eliminates the need to rekeyboard and then proofread material that has already been keyboarded and proofread.

SUMMARY

More and more companies are using phototypesetting equipment to prepare their annual reports, pamphlets, brochures, and newsletters. Because of the increase in the use of phototypesetting equipment in the office, executive assistants need to have a basic understanding of the process.

1. With phototypesetting equipment, it is easy to justify perfectly the right-hand margin.
2. Typesetting allows the user to select from a wide range of type styles and sizes.
3. Many phototypesetters prompt the operator to make format decisions or make those decisions automatically.
4. With strike-on typesetters, the print bar strikes the page, producing each character.
5. Phototypesetters use photographic principles to produce finished copy.
6. Copy can be entered directly into the phototypesetter or can be keyboarded on an intermediate device.

7. Once the copy has been entered into the phototypesetter, the exposed photosensitive material is taken from the typesetter and put into the processing unit.
8. Photocomposers set copy as complete pages rather than strips of copy.
9. The partnership between text-editing and phototypesetting equipment eliminates redundant keying of information.

CHAPTER RECALL EXERCISES

1. How does typewriting differ from typesetting?
2. What is camera-ready copy?
3. How do word processors and phototypesetters work together?
4. Describe justification.
5. What are points and picas?
6. What is a strike-on typesetter?
7. How does a typesetter differ from a phototypesetter?
8. Describe the two methods of inputting copy into a phototypesetter.
9. How do typesetters hyphenate words?
10. What is a photocomposer?

PROBLEMS AND APPLICATIONS

1. With a proportionally spaced typewriter, practice right-justifying a page of copy using the two-step method described in this chapter.
2. Take a standard 12-inch ruler and draw in the markings for picas. Use the pica measurements rather than inches until you become familiar with them. If possible, obtain a pica ruler and compare the two rulers.
3. Visit an office products trade show or the sales office of a phototypesetting manufacturer to see a demonstration of the equipment.
4. Read through several office products magazines and make a list of the different models of typesetters that are mentioned in the magazine. Describe their features and methods of operation.

LANGUAGE SKILLS DEVELOPMENT

1. a. Check the dictionary for the meanings of the following words:
   confident, confidant   envelop, envelope
   confirm, conform   quiet, quite
   b. Use each word correctly in a sentence.
   c. Using the word division rules, divide each of the words.

2. Write the correct letters (ei or ie) in the blanks.

a. rec____ve
b. aud____nce
c. bel____ve
d. cash____r
e. p____ce
f. handkerch____f

g. r____gn
h. y____ld
i. perc____ve
j. f____ld
k. n____ther
l. profic____nt

3. Write the plural for each of these words:

a. man
b. life
c. forty
d. child
e. quantity

f. foot
g. study
h. business
i. himself
j. news

4. Insert any apostrophes needed in the following sentences:

a. After a weeks vacation, I will be ready for work again.
b. Womens clothing usually is more expensive than mens.
c. Jason won the game because of beginners luck.
d. The citys finest recreation spot is the lake.
e. The paper was Bryans.
f. Sweet and Dickens clothes are the finest in this area.
g. She has three years experience in teaching.
h. The childs bicycle cluttered the driveway.

HUMAN RELATIONS INCIDENTS

1. Jeannette has been working as an executive assistant for about five years for the Jenkins Company. The company is purchasing new typesetting equipment. Because Jeannette is one of the most proficient operators of the text-editing equipment, she was chosen to be trained on the new equipment. Some of the other operators who have more seniority than Jeannette resent the fact that Jeannette is gaining this new skill. They talk behind her back about her ambitions. Should Jeannette turn down the job? Should Jeannette say something to the supervisor about the hostility in the company? Should Jeannette do something special to get along with the other workers in the department?

2. Robert is new in the word processing center. He has noticed that the other two operators stop working every day from 5 to 20 minutes early. Should the operators be expected to work until closing time every day? What type of work could be done during the last few minutes of the day without starting a new job? Is it Robert's responsibility to say something to the other operators about stopping early?

COPYING AND DUPLICATING EQUIPMENT

Most typed documents require one or more copies, and the responsibility for making those copies usually belongs to the executive assistant. Since the use of carbon paper is rapidly decreasing, especially for jobs involving more than one copy, most documents are reproduced on copying and duplicating equipment.

To effectively utilize these machines, executive assistants must understand the different kinds of copiers and duplicators used in offices today. Executive assistants should know which machines are best for various types of applications and how to operate and maintain the copying equipment.

At the end of this chapter, you should be able to:

1. Describe the types of reproduction equipment. ☐ 2. Describe the duplicating processes. ☐ 3. Discuss how the print shop can aid the executive assistant. ☐ 4. Describe the collating process.

CHAPTER
17

TYPES OF REPRODUCTION EQUIPMENT

There are three major categories of reproduction equipment: convenience copiers, centralized high-speed copiers, and duplicators. All of these categories, as well as the subcategories within each, will be discussed in detail.

CONVENIENCE COPIERS

Convenience copying machines are intended for low-volume applications, generally up to 10,000 copies a month. They are called *convenience copiers* because they are situated in scattered locations around a company and are conveniently near those people who will be using the machines.

A convenience copier may be limited to a particular department, or it may be shared. It depends on the volume of copies produced by each department on a monthly basis. For instance, a department that makes many copies, such as the legal department, may need two or more copiers itself.

Convenience copiers may be either desk- or table-top models or consoles. Desk- and table-top copiers are machines that are small enough to fit on the top of a desk or table, while console copiers are floor models.

Convenience copiers are available in various speeds, ranging from 3 to 50 copies produced per minute. The slower machines cost less and are suitable for applications where the volume of copies produced each month is less than 5000. In situations where 10,000 copies are produced each month, a higher speed machine is needed to avoid long waiting lines. In

Figure 17.1
Minolta EP 310 plain paper copier (Courtesy of Minolta Corp.).

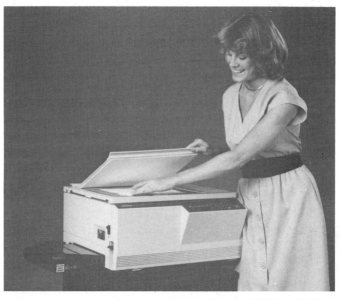

addition, a machine designed to produce 5000 copies a month will break down frequently if it is used to produce 8000 or more copies.

Coated Paper Copiers. In coated paper copiers, the machines make copies on coated and electrostatically charged paper. The document being copied is projected directly onto the coated copy paper, and the charge is erased from the areas on the paper that are exposed to light. This leaves an invisible charged image on the dark areas where the type is.

The image of the type is developed by putting the copy paper in a solution that is composed of toner particles that are dispersed in a liquid. The toner sticks to the areas on the paper where the invisible charged image remains, forming a permanent image on the copy paper.

Because the paper used to make the copies is coated, it does not feel like standard bond paper. For this reason, many companies use coated paper copiers (which are usually less expensive than plain paper copiers) for reproducing documents for intraoffice distribution or for files. Documents to be sent to customers or clients usually are reproduced on plain bond paper since these copies look and feel more like the original documents.

Before making any copies, find out your firm's attitude about using coated versus plain paper copiers and then comply with the firm's wishes.

Plain Paper Copiers. Plain paper copiers produce copies on plain bond paper. These machines have a drum or a belt inside to transfer the image of the original document onto the copy paper. The toner adheres to the image that is formed on the drum or belt and then the image is transferred to the plain copy paper and fused to the paper with heat.

Aside from the superior look and feel of the plain paper copies, other advantages of these machines are that the executive assistant can make copies on different colored paper, special paper such as company letterhead, and various kinds of business forms. The executive assistant can use address labels also to make multiple copies of mailing lists. None of this can be done on coated paper copiers since they can reproduce only on the specially treated copy paper.

Roll- and Sheet-Fed Copiers. Another major difference between the various types of copying machines is the way the copy paper, whether plain or coated, is fed into the machine. Some copiers use rolls of copy paper, while others use individual cut sheets.

Roll-fed machines make copies on paper that is cut from a roll, which means that a variety of different size copies can be produced. For instance, some copiers make only $8\frac{1}{2} \times 11$-inch (letter) and $8\frac{1}{2} \times 14$-inch (legal) size copies, while others make $5\frac{1}{2} \times 8\frac{1}{2}$-inch (statement) size copies, as well as letter and legal sizes. A few models make up to 40 different sizes of copies.

A roll-fed copier is especially suitable in applications where different sizes or odd-size copies are frequently used. For instance, the executive assistant who works in an accounting office may have to make numerous

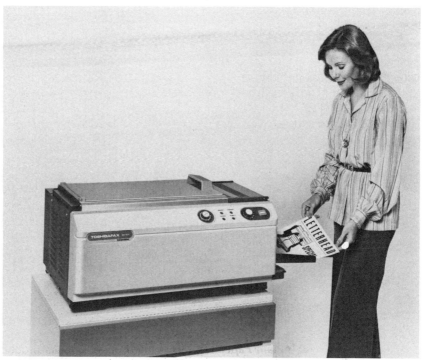

Figure 17.2

Model BD-601/Desk-top plain paper copier (Courtesy of Toshiba).

copies of invoices that are $5\frac{1}{2} \times 8\frac{1}{2}$-inches in size. In this case, it would be better to use a roll-fed copier that would cut the copies to statement size. This will keep the executive assistant from having to cut down letter-size copies and will result in a paper savings for the firm. With the cost of paper rising every year, this can be a significant savings.

In sheet-fed copiers the copy paper comes already cut into sheets and is loaded into the machine's paper tray or cassette. These types of machines use paper cassettes which snap in and out of the copier for loading and unloading paper.

Many sheet-fed copiers make only letter and legal size copies, but some models make several different sizes, including statement, letter, legal, and oversize copies—11 × 17 inches and 18 × 24 inches. This oversize capability is useful when copying newspapers, large drawings, and other oversize documents. The executive assistant merely removes the letter or legal size paper tray and inserts the tray with newspaper size paper.

CENTRALIZED HIGH-SPEED COPIERS

While most companies have one or more convenience copiers scattered throughout their premises, medium and large firms may also have a centralized copying facility that contains one or more high-speed copiers. These

Figure 17.3

Xerox 9700 Electronic Printing Systems (Courtesy of Xerox).

machines make from 50 to 120 copies per minute, so they are generally used for jobs involving more than five copies per original.

Many firms will dictate how many copies per original can be made on convenience copiers; anything over that amount should be sent to the copy center. For instance, if you have a ten-page document and need one copy of each page, you would make the copies yourself on a convenience copier. On the other hand, if you need ten copies of a ten-page document, you might send it to the central copy facility to be reproduced.

There are several reasons why firms divide the reprographics workload in this fashion. First, the centralized copy center has high-speed machines which can handle the big jobs much faster than the convenience copiers. This means the job can get done faster without tying up a convenience copying machine and taking up an inordinate amount of the executive assistant's time. By handling large volume jobs in the copy center, the convenience copiers are freed for small jobs so that people do not have to wait in long lines to use these machines. In addition, the executive assistant does not have to waste 15 or 20 minutes making copies but can simply send the job to the central facility through the interoffice mail system.

Another reason firms institute this type of policy is economic. The cost per copy is much lower on high-speed machines than it is on convenience copiers. A job that might cost 5 cents per copy on a convenience copier would cost 2 cents or 3 cents per copy on a high-speed system.

Also, the high-speed copiers are very expensive; some of them cost approximately $100,000. For that reason, companies want these machines to be utilized to their fullest capacity. A $100,000 machine that is idle for an hour or two a day is wasting money. On the other hand, convenience copiers that are used to make more copies per month than they were designed to handle will break down frequently.

It is your responsibility to follow company guidelines when utilizing any reprographics equipment. By utilizing the copy center as much as possible, you will be helping to keep the company's copying costs down and will also be freeing yourself for other tasks.

Of course, there will be situations where you may have to deviate from standard company policy. For example, if the executive has a job that has to go out immediately and the copy center is backlogged and cannot get any more work out that day, you should do the job yourself. However, before you start, you should check with the person responsible for the convenience copiers and explain your predicament. That person might tell you to use a particular copier that is not being used at the time.

There are other situations where you might not follow company policy. If you have a 100-page document and need only one copy of each page, you would make these copies yourself under company guidelines. However, if you have an urgent task to perform and cannot spend the time making copies, you should send the job to the copy center. And, if the 100-page job has to be copied on 50 pages using the front and back of the page, you would send the job to the copy center if it had the equipment that could copy onto both sides of a sheet of paper.

You should understand that company guidelines are just that—guidelines. They are meant to guide you in typical situations. When special cases come up, you must use your own judgment or check with your supervisor. The main rule to follow is to make the most effective use of both people and equipment.

When you determine that sending a job to the copy center is the most efficient and economical approach, you should then take the following precautions to ensure that the job gets done properly.

First, you should make sure that all the pages to be copied are in proper sequence. You should then fill out a request form. If your firm does not have a request form, you can create your own, which should include the following information:

1. Executive assistant's or executive's name and department.
2. Number of original pages.
3. Number of copies per original page.
4. Size of original document (letter or legal).
5. Kind of paper to be used (bond or letterhead).
6. The type of special functions required: collating, stapling, folding, or copying on both sides of the paper.
7. When the job is required. Be realistic when you tell the copy center when you need the job. If you want ten copies of a 500-page document, don't expect it back in an hour. On the other hand, if the job is urgent,

mark it "Top Priority. Please Rush." In this type of case, it is more effective for you to bring the job to the copy center to explain the special situation. Remember, a top priority job bumps someone else's work, so don't say it is urgent unless you are sure it is.

8. Write the name of the person to whom the finished job should be sent.

AUTOMATED FEATURES

You should be aware of the capabilities of the equipment in your company's copy center. Many high-speed copiers used in copy centers have automated features that get the job done faster. Some of these features also perform jobs, such as collating and stapling, that you would normally do yourself.

Automatic Document Feed. With this feature, which is also available on some of the more sophisticated convenience copiers, the machine operator does not have to position the original document on the glass platen. The operator just stacks the documents in the feeder tray and the machine automatically feeds in one copy at a time. This is a real time-saver, especially on jobs involving a large number of originals. Also, the machine feeds the documents much faster than the operator can feed them manually.

Figure 17.4
Thirty-copy per minute Minolta EP 710 Copier includes a document feeder and a 1000 sheet capacity cassette paper system (Courtesy of Minolta Corp.).

Recirculating Feeder. This capability automatically cycles original pages to produce finished sets in the proper sequential order, eliminating the need to manually collate documents.

Collating. Some copiers have collators attached so that as copies of a multipage document are produced, they are automatically sorted into the correct bins. You get collated sets without any work on your part; all you have to do is remove the collated sets from the bins.

Stapling. In addition to collating, some copiers jog the collated sets and staple them, eliminating another manual step in the copying process.

Duplexing. A feature that is becoming very popular is duplexing, which means copying on both sides of a sheet of paper. This saves on paper and cuts down on postage when the document is to be mailed. It also reduces filing space requirements.

Reduction. Another way of cutting down on paper usage is by using the reduction feature available on some copying machines. This capability allows the executive assistant to reduce a document by a certain percentage. For instance, some machines reduce a legal size original to letter size for ease of filing and distribution. Or, an 11×17-inch document can be reduced to either $8\frac{1}{2} \times 11$- or $8\frac{1}{2} \times 14$-inch size, depending upon user requirements. The reduction ratios vary from one copier to another, but the purpose is the same: to cut down on paper usage and to produce copies that are easy to handle, mail, and file.

Job Recovery. This feature automatically remembers the point at which a copying job has been interrupted and then picks up where the job left off. For instance, if the operator is in the middle of a large job (ten copies of 50 pages) when a rush job comes through, the operator can stop the large job, do the rush job, and then continue the large project. The machine remembers where it left off and automatically makes the remaining number of copies.

Return to Position. This useful feature returns all controls to the first position within a certain number of seconds after the last copy has been made. If the last job involved making five copies, the controls would return to one so that the next person using the machine does not get five copies by mistake. This prevents costly waste.

SPECIALIZED COPYING MACHINES

In addition to the copiers already discussed, there are also specialized copying machines. These include color copiers, fiber optics copiers, and intelligent printers.

Figure 17.5
Minolta EP 520 has its own integrated sheet bypass tray (Courtesy of Minolta Corp.).

Color Copier. Almost all copiers make black and white copies of original documents, no matter what color the originals are. A color copier, on the other hand, makes full color reproductions of a color original. It can also be used to make copies using one or more of the primary colors: blue, yellow, and red. The operator can combine colors to produce another color. (Blue and yellow make green.)

Color copiers are particularly useful for reproducing charts, drawings, graphs, maps, and other graphic materials for use in meetings and presentations. They are often used by advertising agencies to make copies of ads.

The cost of copies on color copiers is much higher than black and white copies. However, in applications where the graphic element is an important consideration, the extra cost may be justified since color helps to communicate more effectively. If your firm has a color copier, you should consider using it for making charts and graphs or other documents where the use of color will aid in understanding the material. You might also want to consider sending the job out to a color copying center.

Fiber Optics Copier. One of the newest arrivals in the copier marketplace is the fiber optics copier. This machine uses a fiber optics system to make copies instead of the three mirrors and one lens used in conventional copiers. By simplifying the optical system in this way, the manufacturers of these machines have been able to produce copiers that are smaller and lighter, with less maintenance problems and reduced energy consumption.

Intelligent Printer. The most recent advance in copier technology is the intelligent printer. This device is linked to a text-editing typewriter and can produce high-quality copies of the text that appears on the display screen of the editing typewriter. This eliminates the steps of printing out a copy of the text displayed on the screen and then reproducing that hard copy. With the intelligent printer, you can go right from displayed text to multiple copies without waiting for the text editor to print out the original document.

KEY OPERATORS

Almost every company that has copying machines trains a number of employees to be key operators. Key operators are responsible for the following duties, as described by Toshiba America: routine maintenance, adding paper, changing paper rolls and cassettes, adding toner and developer, and cleaning paper jams.

Usually, the manufacturer of the copiers will train some of a firm's em-

Figure 17.6

IBM 6640 Document Printer accepts up to 200 cards recorded on IBM magnetic card typewriters for continuous printing at speeds up to 92 characters per second (Courtesy of IBM).

ployees as key operators. They will also supply instruction booklets explaining each of the maintenance procedures. Generally, at least one person per department is trained as a key operator.

Adding paper is a fairly simple operation. The key operator is shown how to change both sheet-fed and roll-fed machines. With sheet-fed machines, the paper is stored in trays or cassettes that snap into and out of the machine. When paper is low, the light on the top of the machine will flash, telling the operator that more paper is needed. The key operator then removes the trays or cassettes and adds more paper, making sure the correct side of the paper is facing up. The operator also fans the paper and then jogs it until it is aligned. The tray or cassette can then be snapped back into the machine.

With roll-fed machines, the roll must be removed from the machine and a new roll inserted. The beginning of the roll of paper should be fed into the machine. The operator should then make a few copies to be sure the roll is feeding into the machine correctly.

On occasion, a user may want to produce copies on letterhead rather than on plain bond paper. This can be done on sheet-fed copiers. The key operator merely removes the tray or cassette, takes out the bond paper, inserts the letterhead, and replaces the tray or cassette.

Toner is a liquid ink or dry powder (depending on the make and model of the copier) that forms the image on the paper copy. Toner must be added fairly frequently by the key operator if the copier is to produce crisp, black copies. A machine that is producing light or gray copies usually needs more toner. It is the key operator's responsibility to check toner levels to be sure there is enough toner to produce good copies.

Toner comes in cartridges and bottles, again depending on the type of

Figure 17.7

Toner being added to copier by key operator (Courtesy of Toshiba).

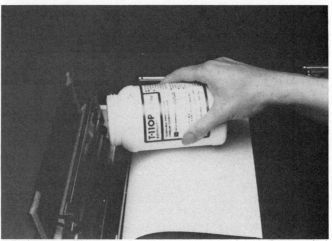

copier used. The cartridge is a self-contained unit that is inserted into the copier. When toner runs low, the cartridge is removed and a new one is inserted in its place. This operation is easy and neat.

With bottled toner, the toner must be poured into the toner well when it runs low. This can be messy, so the key operator should be very careful when pouring.

Toner is an extremely lightweight substance, so it cannot travel from the toner well to the copier paper by itself. It needs the help of the developer, which consists of larger carrier particles onto which the toner is coated. The developer helps to deposit the correct amount of toner needed to form the image on the paper.

Repairs are usually made by outside maintenance personnel, but small adjustments can be performed by the key operator. The most common problem is clearing paper jams that occur periodically in all copiers.

Because the copy paper must travel through the machine so that the image can be fused into the paper, paper jams are apt to occur, especially if the paper has not been loaded into the copier properly. When a paper jam occurs, a light will flash on the copier panel, indicating that paper is jammed somewhere in the machine. The key operator should then turn off the copier, open the front panel, and remove the jammed paper. Because the method of unjamming will vary from one machine to another, it is often demonstrated during the vendor's training session.

Some newer copiers are equipped with self-diagnostic features that indicate the cause of a machine breakdown. They will indicate such things as a paper jam or a lack of toner or developer. They will also signal the operator to call a service person if the malfunction is too complicated for the key operator to handle.

COPIER MONITORING SYSTEMS

Since copiers are located throughout a company, one cannot keep track of who is making copies and for what purposes. Since copier abuse (making unnecessary copies or copies for personal rather than company use) is widespread, copier costs have been increasing dramatically over the last few years. Many firms have become very concerned about this situation and have instituted copier monitoring programs.

Some companies have manual logging systems. With this type of approach, each time someone uses the copier, the person writes in his or her name and department, the number of copies being made, and the reason. This type of honor system is difficult to enforce since a person may forget or may deliberately neglect to fill out the form. This undermines the validity of the whole program.

Firms that want accurate and precise information on copier usage turn to copier monitoring systems. With these systems, a copier cannot be activated unless the monitoring system approves the operation. The monitoring system not only activates the copier, it also keeps a record of the copies that are made and the person or department making them.

To make a copy or copies, the user must insert the copier use device (a cartridge, key, or plastic card that has been authorized for copier usage) into the monitoring unit attached to the copier. This unit is linked to a central control system which scans the copier use device to see if the holder of that device is authorized to use that particular copier. If not, the monitoring device will not activate the copier, and the user will not be able to make any copies. If the user is authorized to make copies, the monitoring system will activate the copier so that it can be used and will record the name of the person and department making the copies, the time and date, and the number of copies made.

At the end of the month, the monitoring system prints out a report of the number of copies made by each department and by whom. A copy of that report is usually sent to every manager so he or she can see how many copies were made by each person in that department. Any excessive copying can be checked on.

Many companies spend thousands of dollars every month on producing copies. Naturally, they are anxious to keep these costs as low as possible. Copier monitoring systems help accomplish this goal by cutting down the production of unnecessary copies and reminding employees of the importance of controlling copier costs. Some firms frown on any use of copiers for personal reasons; others are more flexible and permit occasional use of the machines for personal copying. All companies object to excessive personal use of copying machines since this can add tremendously to copying costs.

The executive assistant should be aware of the company's policy on making personal copies and should not take advantage of it. One person making extra copies may not seem to make much of a difference, but if every employee makes only a few copies a week, the total amount can be quite high. The cooperation of all employees (especially executive assistants since they make the bulk of all legitimate copies) is required if a firm's cost-controlling efforts are to be successful. For instance, some firms ask their executive assistants to use carbon paper whenever possible rather than making a photocopy.

DUPLICATORS

The third major category of reprographics equipment is the duplicator. The duplicating process involves a number of different kinds of machines. The main types of duplicators are spirit, stencil, and offset machines.

All three duplicating machines differ from copying equipment in one important respect. Copiers use a direct, original-to-copy process, while duplicating machines require an intermediate step. The intermediate step varies depending upon which duplicating process is used—spirit, stencil, or offset.

Spirit Duplicators. Spirit duplicators require a master and a moistening solution to produce copies. A master set consists of a top white sheet and a second sheet of carbon dye.

When the master is typed or written on, the dye produces a mirror or negative image of the typed or handwritten impressions on the top sheet. Corrections can be made by removing carbon images from the master with special correction materials or with a knife. If a large area of the master has to be corrected or changed in some way, the executive assistant can cut out that section of the master and splice in a new piece with the corrected copy.

Once the master is prepared, the two sheets are separated and the sheet with the carbon image is attached to the master cylinder of the spirit machine. Blank sheets of paper are moistened in the spirit solution and are then pressed against the master. The surface of the moistened paper absorbs a small portion of the carbon dye from the master, and the negative or mirror image on the master becomes a positive image on the sheet of paper.

Since all images are formed by taking dye from the master, different colors can be used. The master sets used to produce copies come in various colors, including purple, black, blue, green, and red. Drawings and graphics can also be reproduced in color. The executive assistant merely draws on the master, using whatever aids are needed. These aids include lettering guides, templates, and wheels.

The carbon dye on the master is depleted with each copy made, so the number of copies that can be produced from a master is limited, generally to between 100 and 500 copies, depending upon the quality of the master set and the machine itself. Also, each copy produced will be slightly lighter than the preceding copy. For this reason, spirit duplicators are used more for their economy than for the quality of the image produced.

Stencil Duplicators. Stencil (also known as mimeograph) duplicators produce copies from a plastic coated sheet called a stencil. When the executive assistant types on the stencil sheet, she or he cuts into the plastic coating and creates a path through which ink can flow.

When the stencil is completed, it is mounted on the stencil machine's cylinder, which contains an inking pad (single cylinder) or is fastened onto an inking screen belt that is supported by two cylinders (dual cylinder). Ink is transferred from the pad or belt through the holes in the stencil and onto the paper which is pressed against the master. Up to several thousand copies can be run off from one stencil.

Stencils can be prepared on typewriters or with ball point pens or pencils or with a special stylus. Corrections are made by coating over the error with a special correction material and then typing or writing over the error. The executive assistant can also cut apart and patch together various parts of the stencil with a special cement.

Offset Duplicators. While spirit and stencil duplicators can be used either in the office or in the print shop and can be operated either by the executive

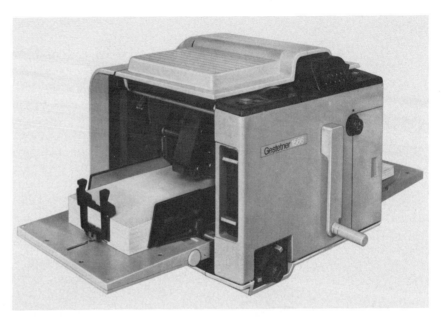

Figure 17.8
Gestetner 1566 Duplicator (Courtesy of Gestetner Corp.).

assistant or print shop personnel offset duplicators must be run by trained operators.

Offset duplicators use three cylinders and either paper or metal masters that have image areas which are receptive to ink and backgrounds which are receptive to water. The master plate is inked on the first cylinder, and the image is transferred from the master onto an intermediate blanket cylinder. Next, the image is transferred or offset from the blanket cylinder onto a piece of paper which is forced against it by an impression cylinder. Some machines in this category employ direct, rather than offset, lithography. These machines do not have the blanket cylinder, so the image on the master plate is transferred directly onto the paper.

Offset duplicators come in three basic types: manual and semiautomatic table-top models; more sophisticated console (floor) machines; and completely automated duplicating systems that include a master making device which automatically produces a master and loads in onto the offset press.

Table-top models generally produce between 60 and 125 copies per minute in paper sizes from 3 × 5 inches to 11 × 17 inches. Console models, which may include operator convenience features such as preset copy counter and automatic shut-off, can handle many paper sizes up to 20 × 25 inches. Speeds on these units also vary, with a maximum speed in excess of 250 copies a minute on some models.

Fully automated offset duplicators perform many functions such as automatic document feeding, mastermaking, and duplicating, in addition to producing a variety of copy sizes at very high speeds (up to 250 copies per

Figure 17.9
Gestetner 319 Mark II (Courtesy of Gestetner Corp.).

minute). Some offset presses also produce color reproductions, while others print on both sides of a sheet of paper.

USE OF THE PRINT SHOP

How does the company print shop affect your ability to perform your job efficiently? The print shop can provide you with high-quality copies of multipage documents. For instance, if you need 50 copies of a 25-page report, you can turn it over to the in-house print shop. This saves you from having to do the job or from having to send it out to be printed. Most in-house print shops can produce a job faster than an outside printing establishment and at less cost—a factor that is of great interest to executives.

In addition, the print shop can perform a number of other functions that you might otherwise have to do. The major examples of these are collating and binding or stapling, tasks that could take you hours on large volume jobs.

COLLATING

While some copiers and duplicators include collators, many do not. In those cases, separate collating devices may be used. If you must do the collating manually, you should place stacks of material requiring collation on a desk or table in sequence and then gather the material together sheet by sheet. This is a tedious and time-consuming task at best, and it is one that can be handled more quickly by machine.

According to recent estimates, the maximum speed at which a person can collate material is roughly 2000 sheets in an hour. When a collator is used, upwards of 12,000 sheets can be collated per hour. And, instead of spending work time collating, you can be performing more important and more interesting tasks.

Collators come in manual, semiautomatic, and completely automated versions. Manual models are mechanical devices designed to handle low-volume collating needs and are generally located in the office environment rather than in the print shop. To begin collating, the operator pulls down the lever and one sheet from each bin is automatically ejected from the unit. The operator then grasps the sheets and removes them from the collator, jogging them into a set and then stapling or clipping the set together. Manual collators are desk-top units and usually have from 8 to 12 bins. This means that documents with that number of pages (8 to 12) or less can be easily collated on these units.

Semiautomatic collators usually are pushbutton operated. The operator depresses the button, and one page is ejected from each bin. An automatic cycling feature (in some cases, an electric eye) monitors the bins; and when the ejected sheets have been removed, the next set of pages is ejected. This keeps the operation running smoothly.

Semiautomatic units may be either desk-top models or floor units. Some floor models may be controlled by a foot pedal. While desk-top units generally have between 8 and 12 bins, floor models may have 32 or more bins, each with a capacity of several hundred sheets of paper.

For large-volume collating requirements, such as those handled by an in-house print shop, automated collators are needed. These may be either on-line or off-line systems. On-line collators are tied directly to the copier or duplicator and automatically gather and collate copies at the same speed as they are produced on the copier or duplicator. Off-line collators operate independently of the copying machine. The copies must be physically removed from the copier or duplicator and loaded into the collating unit.

Automated collators may have hundreds of bins and offer a number of automated features. These include a feed control device that regulates the number of copies produced to ensure an accurate quantity. This monitoring feature may also scan the sheets being fed into the collator to prevent the feeding of extra sheets of paper. Bin conversion capability, which allows the user to create fewer bins with large sheet capacities or more bins with less capacity, is also featured on some models.

Different options are also available, and these, too, can relieve the executive assistant of a tedious chore—jogging and stitching the collated sets. A collator with these capabilities will take the collated sets, jog them, and then place a stitch in the corner or on the side. This saves the executive assistant from having to staple or clip all the collated sets together.

BINDING

In addition to the stitching and stapling options already discussed, collated sets may be bound. The executive assistant should be familiar with different methods of binding documents. Binding a document gives it a professional appearance that makes a good impression on the recipient; and in situations involving important presentations or reports, you might want to suggest binding rather than stitching or stapling.

The major types of binding are plastic comb binding, spiral binding, adhesive binding, and padding. With plastic comb binding, a series of holes are punched into the pages along the binding edge. Cylindrical combs made of plastic are then inserted into these holes. Spiral binding is similar to this process; however; instead of plastic combs, coils are inserted into very small holes along the binding edge of the paper.

Adhesive binding machines utilize a hot melt adhesive that is applied to the edges of the document pages with a brush or a roller. Then the pages are held together firmly with a clamp or a press, while heat is applied to speed the drying process. To increase the strength of the binding, strips of gauze may be placed on the spine of the pages between two layers of adhesive. Padding is very similar to adhesive binding except that a different adhesive substance is used. Also, this adhesive is applied more thinly and gauze is not used. Another binding method utilizes a tape that is heated and then adheres to the pages and the front and back covers of the report to form a spine.

The type of binding you select should depend on the ultimate use of the bound document. For instance, if the report or presentation is to go to the board of directors or to an important customer, it should look impressive.

You should also consider how long the document will be used. This will determine how durable the binding process should be. All bindings should be able to stand some abuse without weakening or releasing individual pages; but in cases where extremely long use is expected, the durability of the binding may be of primary importance. Some binding applications are permanent, while others allow documents to be taken apart, so that some pages can be removed, and then the remaining pages can be rebound.

In other cases, speed and economy may be the primary considerations. For instance, if you are supervising the production of a large number of multipage catalogs, you would probably select the binding process that could produce the greatest number of catalogs in the shortest period of time, at the least possible cost.

Another binding factor to consider is visibility. Does the bound volume lie flat when opened so that all type can be read? Or, does the binding cover the print that is close to the binding edge, making it unreadable? The size and shape of the binding (coils and combs) affect the way the finished, bound document can be stacked and stored. If space is limited, a binding that does not take up more space than the document itself may be the best choice.

These are just some of the points you should consider when choosing a binding for a particular document. If there is a print shop on the premises, the executive assistant can go to the supervisor of the shop and ask for help when it is needed. Such cooperation can yield a finished product that is not only neatly typed and carefully written but also professional looking. A professional looking document must be neatly typed, reproduced on good paper with crisp, sharp tones, carefully collated, perfectly aligned, and neatly bound.

SUMMARY

Executive assistants are generally the people most involved in making copies of the documents they type. Not only do they make the copies, but they are often responsible for maintaining the copying machines as well. For these reasons, executive assistants should be familiar with the firm's reprographics equipment.

1. The executive assistant should know about the three types of reprographics equipment: convenience copiers, centralized high-speed copiers, and duplicators.
2. The executive assistant should know the difference between coated paper copiers and plain paper copiers, as well as the advantages of roll-fed copiers and sheet-fed copiers.
3. Many companies divide the copying workload between convenience copiers and centralized copying facilities.
4. An executive assistant who is familiar with the specialized features available on copying machines can save a lot of work. Some of the automated features are automatic document feed, recirculating feeder, collating, stapling, duplexing, reduction, job recovery, and return to position.
5. Executive assistants should know how to operate their firm's copying machines, especially if they are the key operators.
6. Copier monitoring systems are used to help control the number of copies made and to determine who made the copies and why.
7. While the executive assistant is not as directly involved in the duplicating process, she or he should have a working knowledge of spirit, stencil, and offset duplicators.
8. The print shop offers many services to the executive assistant, including the collating and binding operations.

CHAPTER RECALL
EXERCISES

1. Discuss the different applications for which convenience copiers and copy centers are used.
2. Describe the differences between plain and coated paper copiers and roll- and sheet-fed copiers.
3. As a key operator, what are the executive assistant's duties?

4. What are copier monitoring systems? Why do firms use them?
5. What is the executive assistant's responsibility with regard to controlling copier costs?
6. What automated copier features relieve the executive assistant of some copying chores? Describe what each of these features do.
7. Describe the spirit, stencil, and offset duplicating processes.
8. How do the duplicating processes differ from the copying process?
9. Aside from printing, what other functions does the print shop perform to relieve the executive assistant of some of the work?
10. Describe the different types of collators and explain why machine collation is better than manual collation.
11. How can binding improve the appearance of an executive assistant's work?

PROBLEMS AND APPLICATIONS

1. Susan Green's company has a strict policy regarding copier usage; all jobs requiring more than ten copies per original must be sent to the copy center. Susan has an eight-page document and needs 15 copies of each page. The job is a rush one; her boss told her it had to be in the mail that afternoon. Susan's boss has left town for the rest of the day.

Susan called the copy center to see if they could finish the job in two hours, but one of the machines was broken and the other one was being used to produce a large volume, top priority job that could not be bumped. Susan could do the job herself on one of the firm's convenience copiers, but she could get in trouble for doing it. What should Susan do to resolve this problem?

2. Marcy Scheckman works in the public relations department of her company. At the beginning of every year, the department puts together the company's annual report, which is researched and typed in-house. In the past, the report was sent to an outside printer, but this year Marcy's employer is considering printing the job in-house. She gives Marcy the job of finding out what facilities the in-house print shop has and then writing a report on the subject. Make a list of the questions Marcy should ask the print shop. Write a detailed outline of what Marcy should include in her report.

3. Determine which duplicating process you would use for the following situations:

a. 2000 copies of new travel guidelines to be distributed to all employees.

b. 30 copies of a course outline to be taught by your supervisor in the company's training program.

c. 2000 copies of a form that is sent out to customers of the company.

d. 250 pages of a three-page report.

e. 50 pages of an article that appeared in the local paper.

f. 20 copies of a colored graph.

4. Construct a review sheet of the content of this chapter. Type a copy of the review sheet and duplicate it using the spirit and stencil processes. Make enough copies to distribute to class members.

5. Visit the print shop in your school or in a local company. Make a list of the equipment used in the print shop and what features are available on this equipment.

6. Construct a request form that might be used by the centralized copy center in your company. Type the request form and make enough copies for all the students in your class.

7. Arrange for the key operator of a copying machine in your school to show you how to change the paper, add toner and developer, and clear paper jams in the machine.

LANGUAGE SKILLS DEVELOPMENT

1. Learn to spell the following words:

absence	permissible
boundary	phenomenon
comprehensible	transferred
manageable	unanimous
necessitate	variable

Divide each of the words at the preferred place.

2. Put in the correct punctuation in these sentences:
   a. Mary was a quiet efficient student in class.
   b. I can go to the office either by bus or by the rapid transit.
   c. Mail the letter directly to Knoxville Tennessee.
   d. The more you practice your shorthand the higher the speeds you will attain.
   e. The exam as I pointed out yesterday will cover the entire book.
   f. The letter said The shipment is not to be sent COD.
   g. The classroom was stifling the students did not mind though.
   h. The following colors will be used in the room green yellow and beige.

3. Write the possessive form for each of these words:
   a. its
   b. everyone
   c. U.S.S.R.
   d. General Products
   e. gentleman
   f. city
   g. men
   h. executive assistants
   i. lady
   j. publishers

HUMAN RELATIONS INCIDENTS

1. Tony Garcia works for a large accounting firm. One of his duties is to make copies of the many accounting forms produced by his employer. Tony's girlfriend asked him to make a copy of a 50-page term paper she did for school. He explained his company's policy against personal use of copiers and said he could get in trouble for copying her term paper. She reminded him that he makes many copies during the day, so he probably would not even be noticed if he mixed her work in with the company's. She also pointed out that the company could afford to pay for the copies easier than she could. How should Tony handle this situation?

2. Connie works in a department that has one copier for ten executive assistants to use. All of the executive assistants use the copier a great deal; therefore, there is usually a line of people waiting to use it. Allen, one of the executive assistants, hates to stand in this line and wait. Therefore, he will usually tell the person at the head of the line that he has only a few copies to do and ask if he can go ahead and do the copies? Most of the executive assistants will allow Allen to go ahead in the line, but the others standing in line are usually furious about this arrangement. Should those executive assistants who have only a few copies be permitted to go ahead rather than waiting in line? What arrangement would you suggest? Should something be said to Allen before the situation gets out of hand?

RECORDS MANAGEMENT

The paperless office may exist in the future, but we are still very much a paper-based society. Most of the paper that is generated in the office must be stored for future reference. Executive assistants must be aware of the filing procedures and the types of office filing equipment that will most likely be used.

As more and more companies convert their paper files to microforms (to save space and facilitate retrieval), executive assistants will find themselves using this medium with increasing frequency. ■ Chapter 18 Filing Equipment □ Chapter 19   Filing Procedures □ Chapter 20 Micrographics Equipment

SECTION
V

FILING EQUIPMENT

The proliferation of automated office systems has not yet been effective in reducing the enormous amount of paper used by business. There is currently a lot of talk about the paperless office of the future, but that is a long time away, according to most reliable estimates. In the meantime, we remain very much a paper-based society.

Much of the paper that is generated must be stored for future reference; and, even when firms use storage media other than paper, this media generally has to be filed as well. These other storage media include magnetic cards, tapes, and diskettes, as well as microforms, such as roll film, microfiche, and aperture cards. This chapter describes the types of filing equipment that the executive assistant will most likely use in the office.

At the end of this chapter, you should be able to:

1. Define centralized and decentralized files. ☐ 2. Describe the types of filing equipment available. ☐ 3. Determine which filing equipment would be most appropriate for various applications. ☐ 4. Define automated filing systems. ☐ 5. Describe computerized filing. ☐ 6. Describe word/data processing filing systems.

CHAPTER 18

DEFINITION OF A FILING SYSTEM

A file is a way to store documents or other materials in an organized and standardized fashion so that they can be retrieved by following some logical procedure.

Files can be centralized or decentralized. Centralized files are stored in one central location, usually called a records center. The center may contain records for one or more departments, or it may hold the records for the entire company. Generally, the records center is managed by the records manager and file clerks, who are responsible for filing, retrieving, and organizing files, as well as checking files in and out of the records center and keeping a log of who borrows the files.

Executive assistants should be familiar with the operation of the records center and should know what procedures to follow to obtain files from the center. They should also be aware of the types of documents to send to the center for storage, as distinguished from those kept in the office. Executive assistants should keep files that relate to their principals and must be accessed on a very frequent basis. They should not keep records that are no longer active unless the records are of a confidential nature.

Files that the executive assistant, or some other person, maintains for personal use are decentralized files. These files are kept in or near the work area of the person using them.

TYPES OF FILING EQUIPMENT

Whether a firm maintains centralized or decentralized files, it must use some kind of filing equipment to store these materials. In the past, about the only choice the office manager had was the number of drawers in the filing cabinet. Today, there is filing equipment of every size and description, for every type of filing application. Since you are likely to use a variety of files, you should be familiar with the various types of equipment available.

VERTICAL FILES

Vertical file cabinets are standard in practically every business office. These files are called vertical because papers are filed upright (lengthwise) in the drawers instead of lying flat (horizontal) in the bottom of the drawers. When you stand in front of the cabinet and open the drawer, all the files are facing the front of the cabinet so it is easy to read the titles on the file folders.

File folders may be placed inside hanging file folders, which have hooks on each end so that the folders can be suspended from rods which have been placed in the drawers (Figure 18.6). The mechanics of setting up a vertical file drawer are explained in the next chapter.

Vertical filing cabinets come in a choice of heights with from one to six drawers. They are available in various widths depending on the size of the filed documents. The two most common widths are for letter size ($8\frac{1}{2} \times 11$-inch) documents and for legal size ($8\frac{1}{2} \times 14$-inch) papers. There are also vertical files for 3×5-inch cards as well as files large enough to hold blueprints and engineering drawings.

Figure 18.1
Courtesy of Esselte Pendaflex Corp.

"Then you're prepared to swear, Miss Farnsworth, that said contract leapt out of the file drawer and simply flew away?"

"I must warn you, Miss Woodbine, that your unfortunate predecessor made the fatal mistake of trying to sneak these documents into that corporate abyss known as central filing."

Figure 18.2
Courtesy of Esselte Pendaflex Corp.

LATERAL FILES

Lateral files are similar to vertical files except that they are sideways. Imagine a standard three-drawer vertical cabinet with its side instead of its back placed against the wall. Instead of the file folders facing you, they will be facing the front of the cabinet. You have easy access to every folder in the drawer since the whole side of the drawer is open. In vertical cabinets, you may have a hard time reaching folders in the back of the cabinet, even if

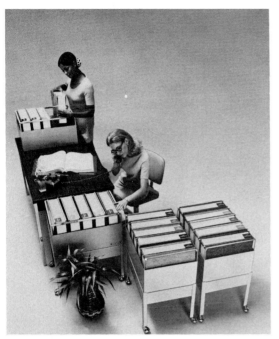

Figure 18.3
Decentralized files (Courtesy of Wilson Jones Co.).

Figure 18.4
Vertical files (Courtesy of Esselte Pendaflex Corp.).

Figure 18.5
Hanging folder (Courtesy of Esselte Pendaflex Corp.).

Figure 18.6
Hanging file folders are suspended from rods
(Courtesy of Esselte Pendaflex Corp.).

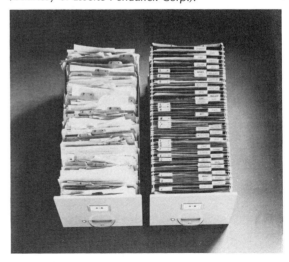

Figure 18.7

Lateral files (Courtesy of Esselte Pendaflex Corp.).

the drawer is fully extended. Since the drawer is only as wide as the widest document (generally 14 inches), less aisle space is needed than with a vertical file.

In vertical cabinets, all file folders must be filed from front to back, but in lateral file cabinets there is a choice. You can file the folders from front to back or from left to right. You can also combine front-to-back and left-to-right filing in one drawer, permitting you to store both letter- and legal-size documents in the same drawer without wasting any space. Legal-size documents would be filed front to back in part of the drawer, and letter-size documents would be filed left to right in a different section of the same drawer.

HORIZONTAL FILES

In horizontal files, documents are stored in a flat position in the drawer. These files are generally used to store maps, engineering drawings, and other oversized materials that must be stored flat. The length and width of the drawers are as large as the documents to be stored, but the height of each drawer is shallow since only a few documents are stored in each drawer. This expedites the retrieval of the documents.

BOX FILES

Box files can be made of cardboard or steel and can open on either the top or the front of the box. They come in various sizes, from small, desktop boxes designed to hold business cards or 3 × 5-inch index cards to large boxes used to store paper, magnetic media, and small parts.

Some box files are called transfer files because they can be used to transfer documents from one location to another. They are also frequently used to store inactive records that have been transferred from the active files. In these cases the boxes are generally stacked one on top of another or are placed in steel racks that go from floor to ceiling. These boxes may also contain tubes which are used to store rolled documents, one per tube.

VISIBLE FILES

Visible files make information visible at a glance. Cards are placed in see-through pockets that are arranged in trays or stands one on top of another. However, one part of the card (the bottom, top, or side) is always visible. The index or title identifying the information contained on the card is written on the part of the card that is always visible.

To find a particular piece of information, you would flip through the cards and read the index information until you find the card you need. The cards may be different colors or have colored strips (color coding) to aid in the retrieval process.

Figure 18.8
Visible files (Courtesy of Ring King).

TUB FILES

A tub file consists of a large tub or bin with legs. It either has a roll-back top or no top at all. This provides complete visibility of the filed documents and makes it fast and easy to file and remove documents.

In some cases the legs have casters so that the file can be easily rolled from one person to another and even from one department to another. Some tub files have a work surface next to the open tub so you have a convenient place to work without bringing the files back to your desk.

ROTARY FILES

Rotary files come in both desk-top and floor models. Desk-top models are generally used to store address cards. With these systems, holes are punched in the bottoms of the cards so they can be attached to a rod on the file.

In instances where the rod is shaped in a semicircle, the cards flip back and forth along the rod. Other models form a complete circle with the cards rotating around the circle when the knob on the side of the file is turned.

Desk-top rotary card files come with one, two, or three rotating banks of cards. Some also have covers to protect the cards when the file is not being used.

Carousel files are another type of desk-top rotary file. A small upright stand supports a number of panels that spin around the central stand when the knob on the top of the stand is twirled. These panels have pockets where

Figure 18.9
Tub file (Courtesy of Wilson Jones Co.).

paper, cards, magnetic media, and microforms can be inserted. The material filed in these pockets can be easily removed and reinserted. In addition, there is generally a label on the edge of each panel to identify the contents of the panel.

Floor model rotary files are used in applications where frequent access to large volumes of material is required. These systems consist of one or more tiers that revolve 360° around the central stand.

Since each tier revolves independently of the others, several people can access the file at the same time. Lower tiers can be accessed in a seated position, but it is necessary to stand to access the upper tiers.

In some instances, desks or other work surfaces are placed around the rotary file at specified intervals with the side of the desk touching the file unit. You can sit at the desk and can remove and refile documents without standing up.

Some of these systems are motorized so you can push a button and have the carousel revolve until the desired section is directly in front of you.

SHELF FILES

Shelf files are generally used in central filing areas since rows of shelves can hold a great many documents. This shelving, which is arranged in rows with aisles on each side for access, can hold file folders and/or boxes containing folders or other material. Most of the time these shelves are open

Figure 18.10
Carousel file (Courtesy of National).

Figure 18.11
Centrac file folder rotary (Courtesy of Acme Visible Records, Inc.).

Figure 18.12
Centrac centralized random access—total information work center (Courtesy of Acme Visible Records, Inc.).

so you can easily see and reach the documents. However, covered shelves are sometimes used to store confidential or sensitive records.

Color coding, which can improve the efficiency of almost any filing system, is particularly beneficial when used with shelf files since the eye can scan the long rows of shelves and quickly pick out the correct color. This enables the clerk to go quickly to that section and begin looking for the precise folder needed. This speeds up retrieval and cuts down on misfiles since a blue folder that is wrongly placed in a section of yellow folders will be obvious.

MOVABLE FILES

A refinement on the shelf file is the mobile shelf file. With standard shelf files, you need an aisle for every row of shelving. This requires a lot of space, so many companies have turned to mobile shelves which require much less space since only one aisle is needed for several rows of shelves.

With this type of filing system, there is one stationary or fixed shelf, a number of movable shelves mounted on tracks, and a floating aisle that moves around to permit access to one row of shelves at a time.

For instance, imagine that there is one stationary shelf (A) against the wall, plus three movable shelves (B, C, D) and one floating aisle (E) for all these shelves. When the file clerk comes to work in the morning, shelves A, B, C, and D are pushed together with the aisle on the end, next to D. The clerk sees that the first assignment requires documents from shelf C, so the lever on shelf D is moved and the shelf moves along the track until it is in the open space that had been aisle E. Now, however, the aisle exists between rows C and D, permitting the clerk to access documents from both these shelves.

When the clerk is finished with these aisles, she or he pulls the lever on shelf C and moves it into the aisle space next to shelf D, creating an aisle between shelves B and C. The clerk can also move shelf B into the open space next to C, creating an aisle between shelves A and B. This is why the aisle is called a floating aisle.

Mobile shelf files can be moved along the track that runs along the floor either manually or electronically. In manual systems, the file clerk pulls the lever on the shelf, causing it to glide along the track. In electronic systems, the clerk pushes buttons and the shelves move automatically, opening up an aisle in the desired location. All of these systems have safety devices which prevent the shelves from moving while someone is in the aisle.

LATERAL MOBILE FILES

Lateral shelf mobile files operate in a similar manner, except that instead of the shelves being placed side by side, one row of shelves is placed in front of another row. The back row consists of several stationary shelves, and the front row consists of movable shelves with one less shelf than the stationary row has. For example, if the back row has six shelves, the front row will have five, creating an aisle which can be moved about as needed to obtain access to the shelves in the back row.

OVAL TRACK FILES

For a third type of mobile shelf systems, the shelves are positioned around an oval track, rather than in rows. To access a particular section of the shelves, the clerk pushes buttons and the shelves revolve around the track until the desired section is reached.

AUTOMATED FILING SYSTEMS

Automated filing systems simplify the file clerk's job and reduce fatigue by automating a large portion of the filing and retrieval functions. This speeds up the process and upgrades the job since the file clerk is no longer just a clerk but the operator of a piece of highly sophisticated equipment.

In enclosed, automated filing systems, the records are stored within the file unit. The operator accesses a particular document by keying in that document's code number or name on the keyboard of the control panel. This instructs the machine to deliver a particular document or group of documents to the seated operator.

There are two main categories of enclosed automated files. The first type has shelves which revolve inside the unit like a ferris wheel. When the operator asks for a particular file, the unit revolves the shelves until the correct row is stationed in the opening facing the operator. The shelves may contain file folders and/or various types of magnetic media, microforms, or checks; or they may contain bins in which these items are stored.

The second type of automated enclosed file consists of a large square unit (sometimes as large as a room) containing many rows of shelves on which

Figure 18.13
Stratomatic power shelf filing unit (Courtesy of Acme Visible Records, Inc.).

bins are stored. The shelves are placed on both sides of an aisle. In the aisle is a moving platform which has a mechanism for removing and replacing bins. The file operator sits at the work station outside the opening of the unit. The work station contains a work surface and a control console. The operator uses the keys on the control console to instruct the unit.

When the operator keys in a particular bin number, the platform mechanism moves to the correct bin, removes it from the shelf, and brings it to the opening in front of the operator work station. There, the operator manually removes or replaces files and then instructs the unit to return the bin to storage. This type of system removes much of the drudgery of filing since the operator does not have to stoop or reach to get files. The machine brings the proper file right to the operator who just has to remove it from the bin.

COMPUTERIZED FILING

All of the file systems previously discussed have been for the storage of physical objects, such as paper, magnetic media for use in word processing systems, microforms, and x-rays. However, there is another type of filing system that does not store any kind of document or physical object; it just stores the information contained on that document. This type of system is a computerized file, and it is growing in popularity as we move toward the "paperless" office.

In a computerized filing system, the file clerk or operator enters the information from a document into a computer terminal. The terminal consists of a keyboard, which is similar to a typewriter keyboard but has additional keys for coding information, and a display screen, which is like the display screens on some text-editing typewriters.

As the operator keys in the information, it appears on the terminal. After the document is complete and the operator has checked its accuracy, it can be entered into the computer file where it is stored on magnetic tape or disk. The information is stored electronically; there is no paper involved.

The second part of the filing job, retrieval, is even easier. The operator merely keys in the number of the desired information. The computer scans through the files, finds the data, and displays it on the screen—all in a matter of seconds. The operator does not have to worry about where the information is located. The computer keeps track of all the files and can find any piece of information in a few seconds or less, even if the file contains thousands of electronic documents.

This type of file is often used by insurance companies to keep track of and update their customers' insurance policies. When a new customer is signed up, that person's name, address, account number, and other pertinent information is keyed into the system. This file would also include the various types of policies the customer had. Any correspondence from that customer would also be keyed into the system, and any policy changes would be noted.

Sometimes, a standard form appears on the screen and the operator merely has to fill in the blanks. A typical form for an insurance company might look something like this on the terminal's display screen.

ABC INSURANCE COMPANY

Type of Policy:_____

Name of Insured:_____

Address:_____

Phone Number:_____

Account Number:_____

Coverage:

Personal Liability_____

Property Damage_____

Personal Injury Protection_____

Comprehensive or Fire and Theft_____

When the file operator wants to add a new customer to the files, the keyboard would be used to call the correct form onto the screen. The standard entries, such as those listed above, would appear on the screen, with blanks where the operator has to fill in variable information. Sometimes, these blanks appear as lines; other times, they appear as bars that blink on and off.

With some systems, the computer moves automatically from one blank to the next. For instance, once the operator fills in the name of the insured, the system moves automatically to the blank area where the address is to be typed, and so on, down the form.

Most of these systems have built-in error detection to prevent the operator from typing information in the wrong area. For example, the system would not let the operator type the address in the blank area meant for the name. It would alert the operator that a mistake had been entered, sometimes by printing the word "error" on the screen.

Even this type of file system occasionally requires a paper copy. In this example, an insured person might request a copy of some correspondence. The file operator would call the desired information onto the screen and then use the keyboard to direct the computer to print out one or more copies of this electronic document.

Sometimes, the printer is right next to the operator's terminal. In other cases, the printer is located near the main computer, and the copy must be delivered to the operator. In either case, a paper copy can be made when desired.

WORD/DATA PROCESSING FILING AND MICROFORM FILING

Computerized files offer many advantages, but because of the expense involved in setting up a computerized filing system, they are not yet in great use. Paper filing systems are still the most common, but other types of media are gaining ground. The most common of these are magnetic media (used in word processing and data processing operations) and microforms. As these types of media become more popular in business offices, a variety of files are created to house them.

WORD/DATA PROCESSING FILES

Word processing and data processing media include cassettes and cartridges, magnetic cards, diskettes, and computer printout sheets, tapes, and disks. These media can be housed in standard file systems, but, increasingly, firms are storing them in files specially designed for a particular medium.

Some of these systems are desk-top units, such as three-ring binders with panels that have pockets for storing mag cards. Other desk-top units include

Figure 18.14
The multimedia storage carousel provides storage for up to 1500 mag cards (Courtesy of National).

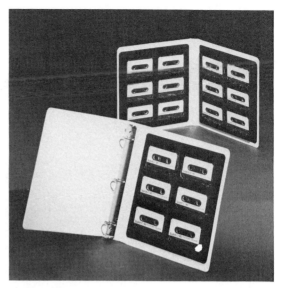

Figure 18.15
Ring King cassette binders (Courtesy of Ring King Visibles).

boxes and racks for storing cassettes and cartridges and rotary stands for storing cards, cassettes, and diskettes. Computer tapes and disks must be stored on shelves designed around the size specifications of a particular medium.

Computer printout sheets are often stored in binders and then hung on suspension racks that are made to accept the large size of the computer printout. Some racks are small, accommodating only a few binders. Many of these are modular, however, so that additional racks can be added as needed, eventually resulting in a huge system housing hundreds of printout binders.

MICROFORMS

There are also filing units specially designed to house one or more types of microforms. Microforms include rolls of film in spools or cassettes or cartridges, microfiche, ultrafiche, aperture cards, and jackets.

Some of these files are simple bins, drawers, or tubs. Binders and desktop rotary files with specially designed panels can also be used. A few of these systems combine work surfaces with file areas, creating a complete micrographics work station for the operator.

A number of microfilm readers feature a file and retrieval capability, which permits the operator to key in the number of the desired frame (page). The reader searches through the files, finds the desired document, and displays it on the screen of the reader.

Figure 18.16
Diskette display (Courtesy of Ring King Visibles).

Figure 18.17
Microfiche storage panels (Courtesy of National).

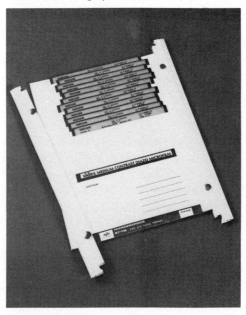

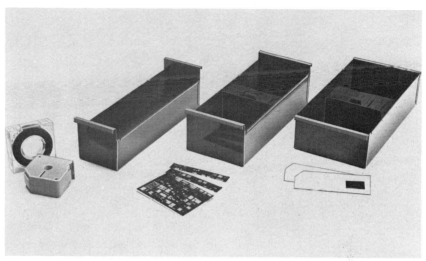

Figure 18.18
Filing microforms (Courtesy of National).

SUMMARY

There is a file for virtually every filing need. The filing manufacturers are quick to follow the lead of equipment manufacturers. For example, when the word processing manufacturers began producing text editors that used flexible diskettes, the filing manufacturers started to produce files for those diskettes.

No one knows for sure what new kinds of equipment will be created in the future, but one thing seems certain: if new kinds of media are created, there will be new types of files to accommodate them within a short period of time.

Since executive assistants come into very close contact with these files in the office, in the word processing center, in the computer room, and in the records center, they should have a working knowledge of the various kinds of files in use in business today.

1. Today's office is a paper-based society, and most of that paper must be stored in some kind of filing cabinet or system.
2. The executive assistant should be familiar with the files most commonly used by business today. These include vertical files, lateral files, horizontal files, box files, visible files, tub files, rotary files, carousel files, shelf files, movable files, automated files, computerized files, and specialized files.
3. Centralized files are stored in one central location, usually called a records center.
4. Decentralized files are kept in or near the work area of the person using them.

5. Transfer files are used to transfer documents from one location to another.
6. Color coding can improve the efficiency of filing systems.
7. Automated filing systems simplify the file clerk's job, reduce job fatigue, and speed up the filing process.
8. Computerized files are more expensive than other filing systems.
9. Paper filing systems are the most common types of filing systems.
10. There are specially designed filing units to house microforms.

CHAPTER RECALL EXERCISES

1. Explain centralized and decentralized files.
2. What is the difference between a vertical and a lateral file?
3. Which files provide the easiest and fastest access to filed documents?
4. How many types of rotary files are there? What are their applications?
5. Why is color coding especially useful with open-shelf files?
6. Describe the various types of movable files and their applications.
7. What are the advantages offered by automated filing systems?
8. What is a computerized file?
9. Describe some appropriate applications for computerized files.
10. Discuss the various types of specialized files and their uses.

PROBLEMS AND APPLICATIONS

1. Mary Ryan is the new administrative assistant to the vice-president of marketing at a large manufacturing company. The first thing she notices in her job is that the files are overflowing, and there is no room for new file cabinets. Mary sees that some of the documents are over ten years old. When she checks with the executive, she tells Mary that all documents must be retained; but anything over two years old can be transferred to the main records center in the basement. Mary decides to tackle the job and makes a list of things she must do. What should be on that list?

2. Harry Green is the supervisor of a word processing center. One of his main problems is storing all the magnetic cards and diskettes the equipment generates. The volume runs into the thousands. Harry finds standard filing cabinets very inefficient, so he decides to write to the manufacturers of word processing files to obtain some information about their products. After referring to several office systems periodicals, come up with a list of three manufacturers and compose a letter to send to these manufacturers. The letter should describe the needs of the word processing center and the type of files required.

3. What type of filing equipment would you choose for the following applications?

a. blueprints of the new office building.

b. alphabetical file of the personnel in the company. The file contains the names, addresses, and telephone numbers of the personnel. This information is kept on small index cards.

c. legal documents.

d. letters from customers.

e. documents to be stored in an area where there is very little aisle space.

f. computer printouts.

g. mag cards.

h. files which are going into storage.

i. files that will be moved from one department to another fairly frequently.

j. a large volume of documents, frequently used.

k. a filing system to lessen misfiles.

l. a system to help relieve the fatigue of file clerks.

4. Determine whether the following files should be kept in your office (decentralized) or in a central records center (centralized):

a. company travel policies.

b. departmental procedures manual.

c. bids your company sent out during the past year which were not accepted.

d. confidential letter to your boss from a customer.

e. sales reports for the past three years.

f. personnel records for the employees in your department.

g. personnel appraisals for the employees in your department.

h. copy of the budget for the company for this year.

i. blueprints of the building (which was built about eight years ago).

j. form letters for your word processing center which are stored on diskettes.

LANGUAGE SKILLS DEVELOPMENT

1. Punctuate the following sentences:

a. A new person is at the helm of the nations largest labor federation.

b. Theres plenty of good natured camaraderie among the members of the community of 4578.

c. The year long march began in March 1980.

d. Contracts were snagged after the industry rejected a new proposal.

e. Industry representatives have refused to negotiate smaller less controversial points.

f. The leaflet was distributed by an over eager supporter.

g. Jerry Valle president of the commission will call an emergency meeting to make sure the area gets the maximum benefits from the jobs program.

h. There is not one official in the state who knows whats going on he told the reporters in a news conference.

2. Choose the correct use of the numbers in the following sentences:
   a. More than (500,000, 500 thousand) of Ohio's (5,000,000, 5 million) workers were out of work this month.
   b. This number constitutes more than (10 percent, 10%) of the work force.
   c. In the (3, three) years she has worked there, she has met people from the surrounding neighborhoods and suburbs.
   d. Leap years are necessary because it takes the earth approximately (365¼, three hundred, sixty-five and one-fourth) days to travel around the sun.
   e. This (80, eighty) block-long sandbar is fraying at the edges.
   f. Traffic was backed up for more than (2, two) miles on the marginal road.
   g. Members of the maintenance crew have never missed a performance in (21, twenty-one) years.
   h. After (5, five) months, (55, fifty-five) hikers have survived the first (1000, one thousand) miles.
   i. (80, Eighty) hikers set out on May 21 with a sendoff from a crowd of (thousands, 1000's).
   j. The university has offered an (8%, 8 percent) raise over the current average of ($19,000.00, $19,000).

3. Correct any of these sentences which have errors.
   a. A lot of the people who come here say they never dreamt that they would loose there jobs.
   b. Its frustrating to see so many people standing in line.
   c. Most of the hikers are between 25 and 35 years old, 22 are women and 33 men.
   d. By the time they cross the mountains of Calif. and the desserts of Nevada the number had dwindled.
   e. The company is thinking of buying new uniforms, but won't buy safety shoes.
   f. The womens' weight class clinic will began at the community house on June 3rd.
   g. City officals yesterday dismissed a report saying the City had loss 19% of it's population, and is now ranked lower.
   h. Crowds jamed into down town yesterday creating traffic jams and filling up parking lots alot.

HUMAN RELATIONS INCIDENTS

1. One of Jan's responsibilities as executive assistant to Ms. Bohn is assigning and supervising the work to be done by the other office workers in the department. Jan always has opposition when she assigns tedious tasks, such as transferring files and preparing new filing systems. The other office workers never hesitate to remind Jan that they "always had to do the dirty work" and that "they did the filing jobs the last time." How can Jan help gain the cooperation of the office workers without complaining to Ms. Bohn? Do you think the office workers resent the fact that Jan, an executive assistant, is telling them what to do?

2. Geri had been executive assistant in the accounts receivable department for almost 11 years when she got a new boss, Mr. Rey. The correspondence had been filed geographically for as long as Geri had been working in the department. After a few days on the new job, Mr. Rey suggested to Geri that the files would be easier for him to use if they were filed alphabetically by company name rather than by geographic location because he was not yet familiar with the geographical locations of all of the companies. Since Geri is the person who uses the files the majority of the time, she is reluctant to change the filing system. How can this situation be resolved?

FILING PROCEDURES

Most people have a "junk drawer" in their homes and in their offices; it takes many forms. The contents are a mixed bag of articles and materials that we preserve with reverence. We save these things because we believe that someday we will need one or more of these items. When that moment occurs, we must rummage through the "junk drawer" to locate our prize quickly and easily.

The save-everything-in-a-junk-drawer syndrome can grow to unwieldly proportions. Is your file cabinet in your office similar to your "junk drawer" at home? It might be if it contains a hodgepodge of letters, carbons, invoices, and contracts filed in a haphazard manner. Most office filing systems contain a certain amount of deadwood—material that just lies there, never needed, never referred to. We have been conditioned to save every piece of paper that comes across our desks. The hard part is deciding what is deadwood and what is not.

Every office should have a uniform and systematic plan for filing its documents. This will obviously help the business to operate more efficiently. A good filing system is more than just putting a piece of paper or a microform (a reduced record on film) in a folder or a storage cabinet. It involves an important second step—the information must be found quickly when needed.

At the end of this chapter, you should be able to:

1. Name the procedures for effective filing. ☐ 2. Define name, numeric, and subject filing. ☐ 3. Describe desk drawer files and portable files. ☐ 4. List the guidelines for manual filing systems. ☐ 5. Explain the techniques of magnetic media filing. ☐ 6. Describe the open plan environment for filing.

CHAPTER 19

GUIDELINES FOR RETENTION OF FILES

To reduce unwanted and unnecessary paper, some common sense guidelines should be applied. If the executive assistant cannot visualize a future need for certain information or if it is available elsewhere, do not file it. On the other hand, if you are in doubt, play safe and file it. Here are some suggestions to help you decide what items to save and what items to dispose of:

Figure 19.1
Courtesy of Esselte Pendaflex Corp.

"You've heard the General refer to 'The Lost Patrol'?
Well, this is it."

☐ *Check records retention schedule first.*

☐ *If in doubt, ask your supervisor.* Do not guess or take anything for granted, especially if you are new on the job. Ask for guidance on what to keep, for how long, and what to throw out.

☐ *Use your experience.* Make suggestions based on your own observations. A lot of correspondence passes through your hands. You develop a knowledge of which kinds of things are referred to and which are not. You may realize better than your employer that there are a lot of things in the files which are never used, never referred to. Suggest what they are. Inquire if you may dispose of them, or at least transfer them to inactive files.

☐ *Dispose of useless paper.* Systematically go through the files and extract any documents that you are sure the company will never need or that no one will ever refer to. Dispose of them. It is a waste of time, money, and storage space to keep them.

☐ *Discard information duplicated elsewhere.* Before filing something, determine if the information is duplicated and/or stored somewhere else in the organization. Do not keep records in two places when one would suffice.

PROCEDURES FOR FILING

Today, a revolution in office procedures is occurring at the executive assistant's desk. The system of handling records and documents is on the threshold of change, from the cumbersome manual handling and storage of paper to the streamlined process of micrographics (the reduction and storage of information using the medium of microfilm).

Many offices still use the traditional method of manually indexing and filing paper in cabinets. However, by examining the newer methods of storing and retrieving by utilizing microrecords, you can better perceive and understand the changes taking place in the office. By understanding different filing systems, you can better follow the trend toward automation in records management.

SELECT THE CORRECT FILING SYSTEM AND MATERIALS

An executive assistant, if given the task of organizing an efficient filing system, must intelligently choose the correct filing materials.

There is an obvious need for different kinds of filing systems since there are so many different kinds of records. File usage is a prime consideration in deciding upon a system. Obviously, records that are infrequently referenced require a different type of housing than active files (those that must be constantly accessed by a number of people).

At the turn of the century, when roll-top desks were standard office equipment, it was considered sufficient for filing purposes to place the company's correspondence and documents in some kind of order and toss them into a drawer or into cubbyholes attached to a desk. Because the volume of correspondence and paperwork was minimal, storing records by crude methods was sufficient. Documents were bound together by strings or elastic bands and stuffed into bulky envelopes, or crudely marked and placed into a drawer or box.

Figure 19.2
Courtesy of Esselte Pendaflex Corp.

"Henceforth, Miss Birdsong, you will make twenty-six copies of everything and file one under each letter of the alphabet."

However, as the volume of paperwork in the modern office began to increase, a more efficient method of filing was a necessity. As offices began adding modern business machines and skilled personnel, a sense of logic and orderliness emerged in the conduct of business and office-related tasks. A new concept of filing emerged. Although the standard vertical file drawer was retained, a new method of file folders allowed the executive assistant to file documents with increased speed and accuracy.

There are thousands of business firms that use standard two- or four-drawer file cabinets for typical applications. However, it is what is inside the files that is of major concern to the executive assistant and the company. Proper equipment and accessories can help make the papers filed inside the cabinet accessible, can create a neat appearance, and can provide room for file expansion.

Suspended file folders are designed to be suspended from rails in the file drawer (rather than resting on their bottoms to stay upright); they can't slump or sag. The tabs that identify the contents of each folder are always at a uniform level and instantly visible. Since the folders slide effortlessly along the rails on which they are hung, they can be moved open or closed with a touch of one finger.

A **complete file drawer** is composed of the frame on which the folders are hung, the sliding folders, the interior manila folders (carriers) for use inside the sliding folders, and uniform-level, multiposition, color-coded tabs that identify the contents and sequence of the folders.

Figure 19.3
Suspended file folders (Courtesy of Esselte Pendaflex Corp.).

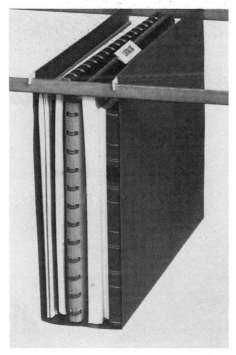

Figure 19.4
Box bottom folder (Courtesy of Esselte Pendaflex Corp.).

Sliding folders come in numerous sizes. The three most commonly used are the letter, legal, and invoice sizes.

Box bottom folders have a flat bottom of various widths to accommodate bulky materials such as catalogs, annual reports, and brochures; they come in letter or legal sizes.

Interior folders are lightweight manila folders placed inside sliding folders. They are used to hold materials that have been removed from the sliding folders from the drawers. Executive assistants may use one, two, or more interior folders inside each sliding folder, or they may not use any. Interior folders have tabs extending across the top for labeling; they come in letter and legal sizes.

The **drawer frame** holds the sliding folders and should be inserted in each file drawer. The frames come in six sizes and are adjustable to the drawer length. They are permanently rigid regardless of load and cannot warp or cause folders to stick.

Plastic folder tabs are necessary to identify the information placed inside each sliding folder. The transparent plastic tabs indicate information in three basic ways: by the labeling legend itself, by the position of the tab on the top of the folder, and by color celluloid windows, used with any tab for special signaling or for identifying certain records. All tabs should be

Figure 19.5
Drawer frame (Courtesy of Esselte Pendaflex Corp.).

slanted backward to permit quick visibility from above. They are easily positioned on either flap of the folder; when attached to the front flap, they allow the executive assistant to open the folder with ease.

Tabs come in various widths. The one-inch tab, for example, is used primarily for signaling, coding, and abbreviated indexing. Wider tabs are used for longer index legends. Other more specialized tabs are intended for such uses as follow-up files, in which action taken and to be taken is signaled by means of the tab itself.

Most papers come in many different sizes; unfortunately, most file folders do not. This means if the paper is bigger than a standard legal-size folder, you must fold it. When you retrieve correspondence from the file, you have to unfold it; and with refiling, the process begins again—fold, unfold, fold—until finally the paper is often damaged.

Unfortunately, the situation goes from bad to worse when the piece of paper is as small as a check or as large as a computer printout. The check soon disappears to the bottom of the standard folder never to be seen again or to be permanently crumpled. The large computer printout has to be folded so many times it soon becomes illegible.

The answer to filing odd-size papers is to select folders and equipment that match the size of your documents. Now, there are folders that come in a wide variety of sizes and can handle papers as large as computer printouts or as small as checks.

Special-sized folders—such as legal-sized documents—would require special-sized cabinets. Small-size folders can be placed in standard cabinets by manipulating (adjusting) the width of the frames or by the acquisition of special cabinets for small-size documents.

SELECT THE CORRECT INDEXING SYSTEM

Once the proper equipment and materials have been determined, an appropriate filing system should be chosen that would best meet the needs of your company. Filing systems are grouped into three classifications: name (alphabetic) filing, numeric filing, and subject filing. Name filing and subject filing are arranged in alphabetical order; numeric filing is arranged in numeric order.

If you wish to verify a person's record by name, as you do when you use the telephone directory, use name filing. If you wish to verify people by number, as you would where personnel records are arranged according to

Figure 19.6
Cabinets for small-size documents (Courtesy of Carl Mfg.).

*"I'm going to play a hunch.
I'll bet he filed the Washington office correspondence
under "M" for Mt. Vernon."*

Figure 19.7
Courtesy of Esselte Pendaflex Corp.

employee payroll number or where policyholders' records are arranged by insurance policy number, use numeric filing.

If you wish to look up something by subject, as you do when you use the Yellow Pages of the telephone directory, use subject filing. Materials should be filed according to the designation by which they will be sought and according to a method with an established procedure and set of rules understood by all who use the files.

These examples may be somewhat oversimplified, but they give the essential ideas. They include the three basic filing systems and have universal applications. Companies run into difficulty by devising their own special or unique systems, or by allowing a key executive assistant to control the files. Standard filing procedures should be practiced so that if there is personnel turnover, the filing procedures can be understood by all office personnel. Obviously, if a special filing system is known by a single executive assistant and if that executive assistant is absent for the day or leaves the company, retrieval of records can be a disaster.

You can master the skill of indexing, and it will be applicable from company to company if you learn and use a filing system that is accepted as standard throughout the business world.

NAME FILING Based on the principle of alphabetic filing, name filing is the most widely used indexing system of all. The names are arranged alphabetically; the sequence is based on the key name or word. In the case of individuals, the key name is the last name (Adams, Leslie not Leslie Adams). In the case of companies, it is the first name of the corporate title (Agnew-Belknap Corp., American Home Products). Each name has a separate file folder.

Name filing is based on names arranged according to the alphabet. A good example of this system is the telephone directory. There are hundreds of thousands of names listed in it. You find the name you are looking for by first looking at the top of the page. For example, page 225 of a directory

Figure 19.8
Name filing (Courtesy of Esselte Pendaflex Corp.).

might read, "Raines-Raue." If you are looking for Randy's Mobile Home Sales, you know you have reached the right page because "Ran" is between "Rai" and "Rau." The caption "Raines-Raue" is a signpost that tells you what is on that page. This brings us to the first law of proper filing: subdivide with an adequate number of signposts in each drawer.

In a large name file, a drawer might contain only folders beginning with the letter "M." You can see that a solitary signpost "M" in the front of the drawer would not help you locate material. So, every few folders, there are additional signposts reading "M," "Mc," "Mi," and so forth. You need look at the tabs of only a few folders to find the one you want. With just a little experience your eye locks onto the proper tab almost automatically.

Signposts are, of course, merely general guides. You can establish the exact sequence for all individual folders in name filing by following a few basic indexing rules:

☐ *Alphabetize last names first.* Arrange the last names in alphabetic order. If two or more last names are the same, it is the alphabetical order of the first name that counts. If both the first and last names are the same, it is the alphabetical order of the middle names that counts.
Hubbard, Arthur
Hubbard, Carl
Hubbard, William B.
Hubbard, William R.
Hubbard, William R., Jr.

☐ *Nothing comes before something.* A last name, when used alone, stands ahead of a last name with a first initial. This, in turn, precedes a last name with a full first name.
Baum
Baum, J.
Baum, John
Baum, John L.
Baum, John L., Jr.
Baumann, Mary
Baumann, Mary Ann

☐ *Prefixes are part of names.* Consider all prefixes as part of the name to which they are attached. Arrange them exactly as spelled.
Dellawuila, Larry
DeRoo, Edward
Donor, Albert
Fitzpatrick, Margaret
MacDonald, John R.
McFarlin, Doris, B.

☐ *Arrange firm names as written.*
American Automatic Typewriter Co.
American Pad & Paper Co.

American Word Processing Co.
Bowne Information Systems
Qume Corporation
Qwip Systems

☐ *Disregard "The" at the beginning of a name.* "The Arthritis Foundation" is indexed as "Arthritis Foundation (the)." "The Ohio State University Alumni Association" is indexed as "Ohio State University Alumni Association (the)." "Nick the Transmission Specialist" is indexed as written, however.

☐ *Arrange hyphenated names as written.*
Ben-Aroch, Anita
Ben-Aroch, Barbara
Ben Aroch, Kay

☐ *One word is better than two.* Any two words ordinarily written as one word should be treated as one word.
Interstate not Inter State
Southwest not South West

☐ *Two-word geographic names are considered one word.*
Benton Harbor
El Segundo
Huntington Beach
Mission Viejo
Upper Montclair

☐ *Numbers are treated as though spelled out.* "9 to 5 Secretarial Association" should be filed under "N" as if spelled out "Nine to Five Secretarial Association." "600 Fifth Avenue Corporation" should be fixed under "S" as if "Six Hundred Fifth Avenue Corporation." "2 Bees Service Station" should be filed under "T" as if "Two Bees Service Station."

☐ *Political divisions are indexed with major name first.* "The Department of Social Services of New York City" is indexed as "New York City, Social Services (Department of)." "U.S. Department of Health, Education & Welfare" is indexed as "United States Government, Health, Education & Welfare (Department of)." "Highway Department, Village of Scarsdale" is indexed as "Scarsdale (Village of), Highway Dept."

NUMERIC FILING Numeric filing can be useful to insurance companies, manufacturing companies, and professional organizations which assign a number for each project. The number becomes the basis for the numeric file. There is never a problem of spelling or sequence decisions.

However, the major disadvantage of numeric filing is that in order to retrieve information, you need a cross reference access book to find what each number refers to. A new executive assistant, unfamiliar with the system, would need to consult a card index to obtain the file number. The item is then located by number in the main numeric file. As new folders are required, new numbers in strict numeric sequence are added. New records

Figure 19.9
Numeric filing (Courtesy of Esselte Pendaflex Corp.).

are first kept in miscellaneous folders and maintained separately. Usually, there is a guide for every 50 or 100 documents.

SUBJECT FILING Subject filing is used when the name of the individual (name filing) is not as important as the subject of the record; thus, the subject unit becomes the filing unit for reference. It may appear that subject filing might be difficult to set up and administer. The guiding principle is easy to follow: Arrange your records according to *what* they are about rather than *who* wrote them or *to whom* they are addressed. The material filed may be to and from hundreds of people, both within and outside the company, but it is what the letters are about that determines the file headings used. A person experienced with company terminology should be put in charge of deciding what subject name to use.

"Contracts" would probably contain all the various contracts entered into, including such things as real estate acquisitions and publishing agreements. It would rate as a separate topic (or folder) if the company engages in several legal contracts. Once you have determined your topics, or file headings, you simply arrange them in alphabetical order.

A publisher of a magazine involved with modern office systems and automated text production maintains a file divided into five main categories:

Equipment

Events

Industry information

Management

Personnel and training

Each of these main headings has several divisions, such as:

EQUIPMENT
    Dictation

    Printers

    Text-editing

    Other

Subject filing means arranging records according to what they are about. One example of subject filing, already discussed, is correspondence—correspondence more often to be called for by subject rather than by the name of the writer or the person to whom it is addressed. For example, correspondence with a variety of educators dealing with manuscripts submitted for publication is more likely to be asked for as "Educators" rather than as letters to and from specific teachers in specific schools. So, it is

Figure 19.10
Subject filing (Courtesy of Esselte Pendaflex Corp.).

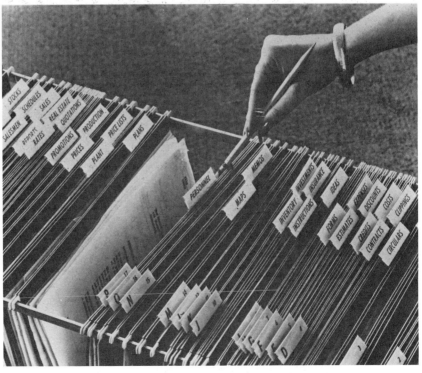

grouped under the subject heading, "Educators" or "Education."

Another major use is to group together records that would be too small for separate folders. A publisher of a monthly magazine, for example, may buy from many different suppliers. Yet, the volume of correspondence from individual companies may be small. Individual files would be cumbersome because of the hundreds of supplier names that would have to be provided for if alphabetic files were used. With subject filing, however, the files could be organized on a product basis with major headings, such as the following:

Acoustic covers

Adding machines

Baskets

Binders

Bulletin boards

Cabinets

Calculating machines

Cards, magnetic

Chairs

Cleaners

As you can see, the topics for subject filing depend entirely on the nature and needs of the business. No one knows these topics or subjects better than the people working with them. As part of your daily responsibilities, you undoubtedly will develop a thorough knowledge of the kinds of materials that are asked for by subject. Therefore, no one is better qualified than you to decide what the main topics are and how a subject file should be organized.

DESK DRAWER FILES

Most office workers who work at a desk have a least one desk drawer large enough to hold files. Unfortunately, they probably use it as a second "junk" drawer or to hold odd-sized items. However, there are many times during the day when it would be very handy to have information right at your fingertips. With your own personal file in your desk, you have got whatever you need right there.

The desk drawer can combine all three filing systems—name, numeric, and subject—or it can incorporate only one or two systems. It can even have a special reminder file (tickler) so you won't forget those important upcoming dates you need to remember.

A tickler file system is used as a reminder. A tickler card file is handy as a follow-up file since it contains reminders and copies of material that may be used in following up something (such as a meeting or special project). A tickler card file consists of 12 guides with the names of the months of the

"According to my follow-up file, your anniversary is yesterday."

Figure 19.11

Courtesy of Esselte Pendaflex Corp.

year printed on the tabs and 31 guides with 1 through 31 printed on the tabs to indicate the days of the month. The guide for the current month is at the front of the file with the 31 daily guides behind it.

As a reminder becomes necessary, a card is made out containing the required information; a reminder date is usually written on the top, and the card is filed behind that date. As you put information on cards, try to include information so that you will not have to look elsewhere in order to carry out the task.

The tickler file is of no value unless you use it. Each morning, refer to the tickler file and remove the reminders for the day and act upon them in appropriate sequence.

PORTABLE FILES

Most files are nearby, easy to reach, and stationary. This system works most of the time; but there are a lot of times when files are needed in different places, both inside and outside the office. In this case the answer is to have files that can travel. Those files that travel on wheels are called roll-arounds; and as the name implies, they can be rolled around the office.

In many offices files have to be used by different people in different places. The roll-arounds, which are simply files on wheels, fulfill exactly that purpose. They can be moved wherever they are needed. They can be whisked safely into a vault at the end of the day, or they can be used to sort out material before filing it in a central file.

There are portable files available if your business must be conducted out of the office. Portable files bring a sense of order to business papers and customer files for executives who travel a great deal.

Figure 19.12
Portable files
(Courtesy of Wilson Jones Co.).

Figure 19.13
Roll-around files
(Courtesy of Esselte Pendaflex Corp.).

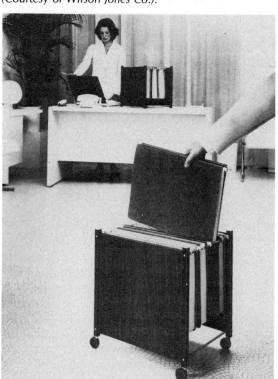

Portable files are available in the same size as a standard drawer file, and can easily slip in the back of your car. Temporary file boxes should be used to transfer files when moving.

GUIDELINES FOR MANUAL FILING SYSTEMS

After you have decided on the filing systems and selected the proper equipment, you are ready if you have set up the right routine and made sure it is working. This is not difficult if you establish a few simple rules and insist that they be followed.

KEEP PAPERS MOVING

In many offices, the search for needed records is a treasure hunt that starts with the files and then branches out to include desk trays and desk drawers. This happens when letters are not filed after they are received or because they are not returned to the files promptly after being used.

It is incumbent upon the executive assistant and the office manager to make sure that correspondence is placed into the appropriate file immediately after it is received and/or acted upon. In large offices, the best way to handle this is to require (a) that all incoming mail be stamped with date and time of arrival and (b) that all correspondence be answered or acted upon within a set time. There is no better way to make sure that correspondence is promptly and efficiently handled and that it reaches the files, where it can be located.

In a small office, time stamping may not be needed; but each executive assistant still has an obligation to check her or his employer's desk daily and make sure that papers are not accumulating there that should be filed.

Figure 19.14
Carryfile (Courtesy of Esselte Pendaflex Corp.).

USE CHARGE-OUT FORMS

When a folder is removed from the files, a record should be made so that others will be able to locate it. This record is known as a charge-out form and usually consists of a substitute card that serves as a replacement for the missing file (folder).

This form shows the name of the person using the record, the date of removal, and a description of the record. While a simpler form of charge-out may be used in smaller offices, it is still a good idea to make its use part of regular routine.

The charge-out form shows that the records are in use, instead of being out or misfiled. The charge-out system enables the file clerk to keep track of borrowed records, and it simplifies accurate return of the records when they are returned for filing. It is wise, therefore, to keep a supply of charge-out forms close to the file cabinet so they can be slipped into place when needed.

LIMIT BORROWING TIME

It is also wise to work out a system of following up on borrowed material, if it has not been returned to the files within a certain period, say five days. The longer records remain out of the files, the greater the possibility of loss. A file clerk should be asked to check through the charge-out cards at least once a week and to determine if the borrower still needs the record.

FILE REGULARLY

Provision should be made for a definite amount of time to be spent each day to meet filing needs. This is the most effective way to prevent records from piling up on desk tops and elsewhere.

DEVELOP A FILING MANUAL

The guidelines you developed for your files, as well as each individual responsible for each section of them, should be described in a filing manual. The purpose of such a manual is to give a clear description of your filing methods to any individual who may need to use the files. Additionally, it should serve as an authority when the proper procedure is in question.

The best form for such a manual is a loose-leaf hardcover notebook with typewritten, replaceable pages. It should be prepared and updated by the individual in charge of the files and should explain how the files are grouped, what systems are used for indexing each group, the location of the file cabinets, and the location of each section by drawers. Also, it should give the proper procedure for filing, refiling, charging out and following up the procedures, transferring of active files to semiactive status, storing, and destroying file papers.

AUTOMATED FILING SYSTEMS

As automated equipment continues to emerge in offices and as office functions begin to integrate, it is extremely important that the executive assistant and office manager understand document storage and retrieval systems in the automated office environment. Thousands of companies employ the technology and systems now available to better manage and understand the volume of information and documents necessary to conduct business competitively.

Information processing equipment with visual display terminals is increasingly being used to speed the storage and retrieval of information as well as to expedite revision, editing, and output functions. Sophisticated software systems make it possible to file documents by name electronically. The executive assistant simply codes an index onto the screen and then codes the desired document. This automated process allows files to come to the work station rather than the operator going to the files.

Confidentiality can be ensured by protecting diskettes or other magnetic media by assigning a password. This password protects the media against anyone trying to copy or alter the document because only authorized personnel would know the password. Confidential documents can each be given a code. If the code is not keyboarded, the document will not appear on the index, even though the operator has access to nonconfidential documents on the same disk.

In addition, an automated system of records management will be able to automatically search, retrieve, and assemble information from a given set of recorded files.

TECHNIQUES OF MAGNETIC MEDIA FILING

Just as paper documents must be stored and retrieved using a systems approach, so too must magnetic media be given proper storage facilities. Automated offices must plan for a cost-effective system for the efficient organization, indexing, filing, and retrieval of all types of word processing media, including mag cards, cassettes, and floppy disks.

MAG CARDS

The end value and usefulness of mag cards are determined by the user's ability to safely file, index, and retrieve them for the subsequent generation of hard copies. If the executive assistant cannot locate the exact mag card required or if it is subjected to mishandling or filing damage, the firm's original investment in time, labor, and supplies can be lost or even totally destroyed.

Mag card pockets are an efficient, cost-effective system for storage of

Figure 19.15
Mag card pocket
(Courtesy of Esselte Pendaflex Corp.).

Figure 19.16
Filing mag cards
(Courtesy of The Morley Co.).

mag cards. Original hard copy is typed right on the front of the filing pocket, and the related mag card is inserted in the slot at the top for safe filing or ready reference. The pocket stores in any standard ring binder and may also be adapted for filing in a file cabinet or deskside file drawer when used with a file bar. A file bar converts any pocket protector or sleeve for convenient filing in standard file cabinets, deskside file drawers, or revolving carousel.

If there is no need for hard copy to accompany the mag cards, a file panel within a loose-leaf binder is an excellent way to store a large number of mag cards.

CASSETTES

With the increased use of magnetic tape cassettes, there is also a growing awareness of the need to protect, index, file, and retrieve these valuable media because, like other magnetic media, dictating and digital cassettes are subject to environmental and handling hazards that call for special safeguards.

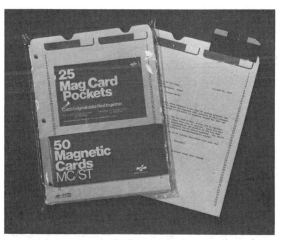

Figure 19.17
Mag card pockets
(Courtesy of National).

Figure 19.18
Loose-leaf binder for storing mag cards
(Courtesy of Ring King).

For example, it is strongly recommended that cassettes be filed in such a way that the magnetic tape is locked into a safe position to prevent unwinding and to protect against contaminating dust and dirt.

Security measures also play an important part in the care and control of cassettes since the contents of tapes often represent a truly valuable business asset that must be protected against theft, loss, or misuse. Cassettes and documents can be stored in standard lock-secured, fire-retardant, or desk-

Figure 19.19
Storing cassettes (Courtesy of National).

Figure 19.20
Cartridge safe (Courtesy of Ring King).

side files. Cassettes can also be stored in panels that can be inserted in standard three-ring binders.

FLOPPY DISKS

As one of the newest and fastest growing magnetic media now used for word processing, floppy disks present unique filing and retrieval problems

Figure 19.21
Storing floppy disks (Courtesy of National).

that call for special attention. Because a floppy disk is an expensive medium which frequently contains vital information, it is now considered good business practice to take the safest, most cost-effective filing and retrieval precautions.

When you consider that a single disk contains as many as 75 to 130 pages of information, including such vital data as accounts receivable and invoices, the importance of loss prevention and safe handling is obvious. Loose-leaf binders with heavy gauge vinyl pockets hold single floppy disks together with as many pages of related information as required.

By a simple adaptation of filing panels with file bars, you can make good use of any existing standard, lock-secured, or fire-retardant filing cabinets or desk-side file drawers. These versatile accessories provide a safe, simple solution to volume disk filing problems without the need for special file cabinets.

FILING IN AN OPEN PLAN OFFICE ENVIRONMENT

Many offices combine automated systems with an open plan environment. As will be discussed in a later chapter, open plan office environments are more space efficient, energy efficient, responsive to office workflow patterns, and cost efficient when office requirements change.

The characteristics of an open plan office filing system include the following:

☐ Individual work areas should provide drawers for personal items and a drawer extension for typing supplies and active files.

☐ Word processing filing supplies (card trays, carousels, and disk storage boxes) should be used.

☐ Files that travel or mobile file cabinets that bring shared files to the operator's fingertips should be used in an open office environment.

☐ Files should be adaptable to magnetic media and micrographics indexing and storage to minimize misfiling and to speed document retrieval.

☐ Lateral file cabinets should be used, preferably in a centralized location.

FUTURE OF RECORDS MANAGEMENT

Word and data processing, as well as reprographics, micrographics, and general records management, will be designed to increase the efficiency, accuracy, and economy of information handling. We are witnessing decreases in computer pricing, and filing will become more concerned with effective space utilization for hard copy. Active filing will most likely be done at the computer level; storage of things that cannot be computerized

Figure 19.22
Tempo 3 workstations: binder bins, lateral filing, file bins, and task and ambient lighting (Courtesy of Shaw/Walker).

Figure 19.23
Contemporary open plan office with mobile file (Courtesy of Esselte Pendaflex Corp.).

will have to be stored in a minimum of space because of soaring space costs.

Most analysts and office consultants predict that companies are going into integrated office systems, in which word processing equipment is supplemented by computers for extended storage and retrieval capability. The integration of word processing and records management appears inevitable. The capability of word processing equipment as an information storage and handling technology continues to increase far faster than does equipment costs because of continuing advances in technology.

Whether a company is large or small, management will have to take a good hard look at possible savings in its particular applications through the use of word processing and records management. Vendors are continuously engineering new products and systems to meet storage and retrieval requirements of the new media.

SUMMARY

The office that has a uniform and systematic plan for filing its documents operates more efficiently than the haphazard method of storing documents used by many businesses. A good filing system involves not only storing documents but also retrieving the documents when they are needed.

1. The following guidelines are useful in deciding about items that are no longer needed in your files:
   a. Refer to retention schedule first.
   b. If in doubt, ask your supervisor.
   c. Use your personal experiences.
   d. Dispose of useless paper.
   e. If the information is stored elsewhere, do not keep it.
2. Micrographics is the reduction and storage of information using the medium of microfilm.
3. Active files are those that must be constantly accessed by one or more people.
4. Suspended file folders are designed to be suspended from rails in the file drawer.
5. The answer to filing odd-size papers is to select folders and equipment that match the size of your documents.
6. Oversized documents, such as maps and newspapers, can be filed horizontally in a flat position.
7. Filing systems are grouped into three classifications: name (alphabetic) filing, numeric filing, and subject filing.
8. Name filing uses the principle of alphabetical filing.
9. Numeric filing uses the principle of assigning a number for each file.
10. Subject filing uses the principle of using the subject unit (not the name of the individual) as the point of reference.

11. A tickler file system is used as a reminder for following up on a particular file.
12. Files that travel on wheels are called roll-arounds.
13. Some general guidelines for manual filing systems are: keep papers moving, use charge-out forms which consist of a substitute card or paper that serves as a replacement for the missing file, limit borrowing time, file regularly, and develop a filing manual.
14. In an automated office, files can be accessed electronically by coding the index onto the visual display terminal. This automated process allows files to come to the work station rather than the operator going to the files.
15. Special packaging of mag cards, cassettes, and floppy disks provides a cost-effective and efficient filing system in an automated office.

CHAPTER RECALL EXERCISES

1. What prompted a change in filing systems in business offices?
2. List the advantages of using suspended file folders.
3. What can be used to file bulky items, such as catalogs and brochures?
4. How do the transparent plastic tabs indicate filing information?
5. Briefly describe name filing, numeric filing, and subject filing.
6. Describe a disadvantage in numeric filing.
7. What is a tickler file? Describe how an executive assistant should use this system.
8. What general guidelines would you use in setting up categories for a subject filing system?
9. Describe roll-around files. Why are they useful?
10. When should temporary file boxes be used?
11. Briefly describe a charge-out form and tell why it is important to an organized filing system.
12. Discuss the characteristics of an open plan office filing system.

PROBLEMS AND APPLICATIONS

1. You are executive assistant to three executives. One of the executives requests that you clear out the cluttered file cabinet that serves all three executives. You notice old catalogs, correspondence, and reports that are six to ten years old along with deeds and contracts pertaining to company business. Some of the documents belong to the other two executives. How would you go about straightening out and disposing of material considering the fact that some of the material belongs to more than one person?

2. Using the principles of name filing, arrange the following list into the correct order for filing.

Bruce Biel —
James Gilbert —
J. A. Gilbert —
Matthew Gilbert —
Daniel Bier —
Craig MacPherson —
Claude Mickler —
Fred Macron —
Frank Rao —
4 o'clock coffee —

E. Mickler —
Goldstein Laurence Advertising —
Good Technical Services —
The B.F. Goodrich Co. —
Impact Sign Systems —
Major's —
Leon Miller —
Miller Meeks and Lynch Realtors —
Leon Albert Miller —
Leon Bryan Miller —

3. If you were going to set up a filing system to file your class notes, class handouts, and other materials from this class, using subject filing, what would your headings be?

4. List some of the items you might keep in a desk file.

5. Make a tickler file of the projects you have to complete for all your classes for this session.

6. Develop a form that might be used as a charge-out form for files.

7. Make a list of the items you would include in a filing manual if you were developing one for a large department with a central filing system.

8. Using the latest office procedures periodicals, find photographs of open plan office filing systems. Make a file of these photographs.

9. Write a research report on the integration of records management with other office technologies.

LANGUAGE SKILLS DEVELOPMENT

1. Proofread the following pairs of names to determine if there are errors in any of the names. Put a check mark by any of the names that are not identical.

   a. Frank M. Freimann   Frank M. Freiman
   b. Isaac Hatgis   Isaac Hatgis
   c. Barry G. Hatfield   Barry G. Hatfeild
   d. Donna A. Kobialka   Donna F. Kobialka
   e. Mrs. Diana Kutina   Mrs. Diane Kutina
   f. Clifford A. McClory   Clifford A. MacClory
   g. Herbert T. Quandt   Herbert T. Quantd
   h. Ms. Elizabeth Quidort   Mrs. Elizabeth Quidort
   i. Abe P. Seifer,III   Abe P. Seifer, III
   j. Mr. Robert C. Seith   Mrs. Robert C. Seith

2. Fill in the blanks for each of the following statements:

   a. There is/are _____ space(s) after a period at the end of a sentence.
   b. There is/are _____ space(s) after a comma in a sentence.
   c. There is/are _____ space(s) after a period at the end of an abbreviation.
   d. There is/are _____ space(s) before a colon.
   e. There is/are _____ space(s) after a question mark.
   f. There is/are _____ space(s) after a semicolon.

g. There should be ____space(s) after a decimal point.

h. There is/are ____space(s) after a diagonal line.

i. There is/are ____space(s) after a period following a number used for an enumeration.

j. There should be ____space(s) following a quotation mark that ends a sentence.

3. Rewrite the following sentences, correcting any errors in parallelism:

a. For the first six months, she was punctual, creative, and enthusiastically did her job.

b. My duties in this job include scheduling projects and estimates on the turnaround time.

c. We are arranging an in-service course for all supervisors for the following reasons: to raise morale and train new employees.

d. As you know, our plan provides for the service to answer the telephone and greeting visitors.

e. To work for the company, each person must have a physical and required work experience.

HUMAN RELATIONS INCIDENTS

1. Ellie Lawson was recently promoted to supervisor of office services for the Larry David Manufacturing Company. As she inspected the work stations and the filing area, she was disturbed to see the file cabinets and documents in disarray. Active files with important papers were being stuffed into already overcrowded drawers often containing badly marked, dog-eared files. She discovered that this haphazard way of filing often leads to misfiled papers, irritated office personnel, angry clients, and lost business. When she approached the office employees requesting that they straighten up the file system and suggesting proper equipment, they indicated that setting up new files was not in their job descriptions and implied that this was a task to be assigned to maintenance people. What would your course of action be if confronted by this situation?

2. Mary Ann is executive assistant in an office where a general file is kept for reports which are used by several people in the department. Every time someone needs something from the file, they stop and ask Mary Ann what heading the report would be filed under. Since Mary Ann's work has been interrupted so often with these inquiries, she made a key to the file and posted it on the filing cabinet so everyone could find the information needed. However, most of the people still insist on asking Mary Ann for information rather than checking the posted key. Mary Ann would like to put a stop to this practice without offending anyone. How can she handle this situation?

MICROGRAPHICS EQUIPMENT

High rental costs are a fact of life for today's business people. Because office space is at such a premium, many firms are limiting the amount of space devoted to storage of company records.

Yet, because of its own and government regulations, a firm must keep many documents for a number of years. The question then becomes: How does a company keep all the documents it needs without devoting an inordinate amount of space for their storage? The answer for many firms is microfilm.

Today, microfilm is used for a number of purposes. Most birth certificates in this country are on microfilm. Many schools keep transcripts of students' grades on microfilm. Most libraries microfilm newspapers and magazines instead of keeping the original copies. Banks keep microfilmed copies of cancelled checks, and telephone operators refer to microfilmed lists of phone numbers. There are hundreds of uses of microfilm in daily life, in addition to business uses. Microfilm usage is expected to expand even further during the next decade, with business leading the way.

As more and more organizations convert their paper files to microforms to save space and facilitate retrieval, executive assistants will find themselves using this medium with increasing frequency. Even those executive assistants who are not directly involved in the microfilming process will probably have occasion to view microforms on a reader or reader/printer.

At the end of this chapter, you should be able to:

1. List the advantages of microforms. ☐ 2. Describe the types of microforms: roll film, jackets, aperture cards, microfiche, and ultrafiche. ☐ 3. Explain the microform process. ☐ 4. Define COM. ☐ 5. Describe microform reader/printers.

CHAPTER 20

ADVANTAGES OF MICROFORMS

Microfilm is one of the most popular ways to achieve space reductions since microfilmed documents require only about 2 percent of the space needed to file paper documents. Obviously, there is still a need for paper, but microfilming some of a firm's paper files will result in greater space savings.

Space savings result because a document is filmed at a size that is much smaller than the original piece of paper. This is known as the reduction ratio. When a document is filmed at a ratio that is 24 times smaller than the original document, that is called 24×. The most commonly used reduction ratios are 24×, 42×, and 48×; however, ratios of over 100× are possible. At one of the highest reduction ratios, 2500 pages can be stored on a piece of film that is smaller than an index card.

Since fewer file cabinets will be needed to store the microfilmed documents, another cost savings can be achieved. Industry estimates state that the cost of storing microfilmed documents is only 2 to 3 percent of the cost of storing paper files.

It is also less expensive to make copies of microfilmed documents than it is to make copies of paper documents. Duplicating microfilmed documents costs only about 15 percent as much as duplicating paper.

Mailing costs are also reduced since the cost of mailing microfilm is approximately 1 percent of the cost of mailing the same documents on paper. For these reasons, many firms find it economical to microfilm documents and file the film, rather than to store the original paper documents.

Figure 20.1
Fiche vault (Courtesy of Ring King).

TYPES OF MICROFORMS

The film or medium used to store the image of a document is called a microform. There are several different types of microforms in use today. They include roll film, jackets, aperture cards, microfiche, and ultrafiche.

ROLL FILM

Roll film is just what it sounds like—a roll of film containing micro-images of paper documents. The rolls of film may be wound on reels or stored in cartridges or cassettes, which protect the film from dirt and fingerprints.

Microfilm rolls may be either 16 mm or 35 mm. The 16 mm rolls are used for standard business documents such as letters and reports. The 35 mm format is generally used for filming graphic materials and large documents. These would include engineering drawings and blueprints, maps, and newspapers. With 16 mm film, the reduction ratio is generally about $24\times$; with 35 mm film, it is around $18\times$.

JACKETS

A microfilm jacket consists of two pieces of thin, clear plastic that are joined together at various points to form channels. Rolls of microfilm are cut into strips and inserted into these channels, either manually or by machine. These channels (or sleeves) come in two sizes to accommodate 16 mm and 35 mm strips of film.

A microfilm jacket is like a file folder. Instead of holding paper documents, a jacket holds strips of film. These strips can be removed and replaced with new strips if the information on the existing film becomes outdated.

Jackets are like file folders in another way, too. They can be used to store documents relating to a particular person or subject. For instance, an insurance company can have one jacket for each policyholder. All documents and correspondence relating to a policyholder are microfilmed, cut into strips, and inserted into the sleeves in the jacket.

APERTURE CARDS

An aperture card is a card, usually $3\frac{1}{4} \times 7\frac{3}{8}$ inches in size, that has a rectangular hole (aperture) for the insertion of a microfilm image. Most aperture cards contain one 35 mm frame, but some cards permit both 16 mm and 35 mm frames to be mounted in the opening.

The card may also be marked or punched with information relating to the microfilm image. For instance, the microfilm frame may contain an engineering drawing, and the rest of the card may contain typed or punched information identifying the drawing. Aperture cards can be color coded to facilitate filing and retrieval.

MICROFICHE

Microfiche are sheets of film, generally 4×6 inches in size, that contain rows of micro images arranged in a grid pattern. The images on a fiche are usually related. For instance, one fiche may contain a 100-page report, an insurance policy, or a book. There is usually an eye-readable title strip on the top or side of the fiche to identify its contents.

The number of images that can be housed on one fiche varies according to the reduction ratio used. The most common size microfiche (4 × 6 inches or 105 mm × 148 mm) can hold ninety-eight 8½ × 11-inch pages at a 24× reduction. At a 42× reduction, 325 letter-size pages can be housed on the fiche, and 420 pages can be accommodated at a 48× reduction.

Colored documents and graphic materials can be filmed on color microfiche.

ULTRAFICHE

The latest step in the miniaturization process is ultrafiche, which is basically a microfiche with a much higher reduction (over 90×). Ultrafiche vary in size, with two common sizes of 3 × 5 inches and 4 × 6 inches. At a reduction ratio of 150×, over 3000 standard-size pages can be stored on one ultrafiche.

MICROFORM PROCESS

At first glance, the microfilming process may seem very mysterious. Actually, it is no more mysterious than photography. In fact, the first person to use the microfilming process called it microphotography—a way to photograph documents on film in greatly reduced sizes. He was John B. Dancer, an English inventor, who, in 1839, reduced a 20-inch document to an image one-eighth of an inch long—a reduction ratio of 160:1.

Figure 20.2
Microfiche and Model 114 microfiche reader (Courtesy of 3M).

The first person to use microphotography for commercial reasons was a French portrait photographer named Rene Dagron. He manufactured jewelry containing minute photographs which could be viewed through a small lens. During the Prussian seige of Paris in 1870, Dagron devised a method of getting messages across enemy lines. The documents were microfilmed and attached to the legs of carrier pigeons.

CONVERTING TO MICROFILM

When a firm makes the decision to convert its paper documents to microfilm, there is generally a backlog of paper files that must be converted. Some firms decide to leave the existing paper files intact and microfilm only new documents as they are added to the files.

Other companies decide to tackle the enormous job of microfilming existing files. Generally, the records manager will go through the existing files and purge (eliminate) those documents that are no longer needed.

Next, a labor force must be assembled to microfilm the existing files. This can be done in a number of ways. The firm can send the files out to a microfilm service bureau to be filmed; it can train its own clerical and executive assistant personnel to use the microfilm equipment; or, it can hire temporary labor to handle this job.

Once the old files have been filmed, the company will have to train a number of employees to handle the ongoing operation of the micrographics center. These positions include the micrographics or records manager, camera people to film the original documents, and clerks to file and retrieve the microfilmed records. Often, a company looks among its own executive assistant and clerical personnel for the talent needed to perform the various tasks involved in running a micrographics system.

Even executive assistants who are not directly involved in running the microfilm operation may need to know something about the system since they may be microfilm users. For instance, they may be asked to do some research on a particular topic, and the documents they need exist only on microfilm. This is not an uncommon occurrence, particularly in large organizations. For these reasons, all executive assistants should have a basic understanding of what microfilm is and how it works.

PREPARING DOCUMENTS FOR FILING

The first step in the microfilming operation is the preparation of the documents for filming. Documents must be arranged in the correct sequence, and they should also be in the proper format and style. In most cases, the pages are coded for ease of retrieval.

Microforms are created from two sources: source documents and computer output microfilm (COM). Source documents are the original document pages, which are then filmed using a microfilm camera. COM documents consist of data that have been fed into a computer, which produces a magnetic tape containing the information. This tape is put into a COM recorder, which produces filmed images of the computerized information.

Source documents may be filmed on one of three types of microfilm cameras. With a planetary camera, a document is placed on the flat-bed table of the camera, and the film is exposed. Both the film and the source document are stationary during the filming process. This provides clear, precise film images, but the filming speed is slow compared to the speed of a rotary camera.

The rotary camera uses a moving belt mechanism that moves the document in precise synchronization with the film transport. This type of camera can film thousands of documents in an hour, but the quality is not as high as the quality of a planetary camera. A step-and-repeat camera exposes a series of separate images in rows and columns following a predetermined format or grid.

The COM recorder converts data generated by a computer into alphanumeric (letters, numbers, punctuation) and/or graphic images (maps, drawings) on 16 mm, 35 mm, or 105 mm film. No paper is used since the information contained in the computer's magnetic tape is transferred directly to roll film or fiche.

PROCESSING THE FILM

After the microfilm is exposed, it must be processed. Many firms send film outside to be processed, much as you would send out a roll of photographic film. However, some companies do the processing in-house, using their own employees. Some cameras and recorders contain internal processors and produce film that is ready to be used.

If only one copy of the microform is needed, the processing is the final step in the filming process. However, many firms need two or more copies of microfilmed documents. Sometimes, an extra set is filed as a back-up security measure in case the first set is lost or destroyed. In other cases, duplicate copies of the microform are sent to branch offices.

When more than one set of microforms is needed, the original set must be duplicated. A special microform duplicator must be used for this process. Any number of duplicate microforms can be made from the master set.

MICROFORM READERS

To view any micro-image, a reader must be used. A microform reader enlarges the image on the microfilm to a readable size and displays it on a screen. Some units magnify the image to three-quarters of its original size, while others produce an image that is the same size as the original paper

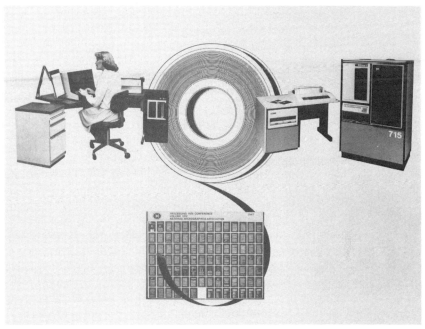

Figure 20.3
Linkup between a word processor and a COM system (Courtesy of 3M).

Figure 20.4
3M "571" Duplifiche system (Courtesy of 3M).

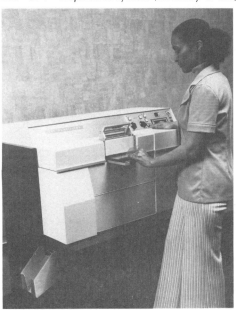

document. A few readers enlarge the micro-image to a size that is larger than the original paper document.

Microform readers come in various sizes, from hand-held units to desk-top and floor models. Most are designed to handle only one type of micro-form (roll film, fiche, aperture cards), but some machines will accept two or three different microforms.

Readers also vary in the method used to find a particular frame on the microform. With some roll-film readers, the user may have to go through the roll image by image until the proper frame is found. The frames may be numbered sequentially or coded in some way, or they may be titled according to name or subject matter. This is known as eyeball positioning.

Another method of indexing frames of microfilm is by using code lines or bars. These lines are used to separate individual frames of film. Some readers have an odometer, which counts the images until the correct frame is reached. The operator then stops film motion. The most sophisticated readers have automatic retrieval. With this feature, the user keys in the specific frame number desired, and the machine searches for that frame and displays it on the screen in seconds automatically. Some automated retrieval

Figure 20.5
3M ''800'' reader-printer (Courtesy of 3M).

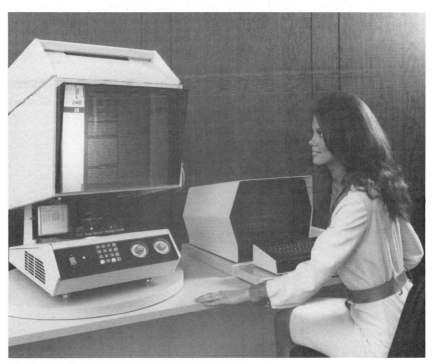

Figure 20.6
3M page search reader-printer (Courtesy of 3M).

systems are linked to computers and can search through thousands of frames of information in seconds.

Since most aperture cards contain only one image, an aperture card reader will usually display most or all of that card on the screen. When the operator needs to position the image on the screen, he or she manually moves the card or adjusts the machine's dial or lever.

To index a particular image on a fiche or jacket, the operator positions the microform on the glass plate in the front of the machine. A pointer is then moved along the plate, which contains a row and column grid showing the positions of all the frames. When the operator moves the pointer to a specific position on the grid, the frame located in that position is displayed on the screen. To find a particular frame, the operator moves the pointer to the position on the grid where that frame is located.

Automated fiche readers eliminate the need to manually find the correct fiche on the grid. With an automated system, the user keys in the fiche number on the keyboard, and the reader finds and displays the correct fiche automatically.

Microform readers only enlarge and display the image on the microform. To obtain a paper copy of that image, a reader/printer must be used. Reader/printers are similar to readers, but they have the additional capability of being able to produce a paper copy of a micro-image.

When an operator needs a hard copy of a particular image, the desired frame is located and displayed on the reader/printer's screen. The operator then pushes the print button. The image on the screen fades as an inside mirror projects the image onto a sensitized paper. After exposure, the paper is processed, producing a hard copy of the micro image in a few seconds.

Most reader/printers produce standard $8\frac{1}{2} \times 11$-inch copies. However, some machines produce different size copies; for example, $5\frac{1}{2} \times 8\frac{1}{2}$-inch prints or 24×39-inch ones.

Figure 20.7
When used independently of a computer, the terminal provides the features of Kodak's current image control reader-printer. (Courtesy of Eastman Kodak Co.).

SUMMARY

More and more executive assistants will find themselves using microforms. Some microformed documents might include company telephone directories, product catalogs, price lists, personnel information, bills, invoices, and other accounting documents. The executive assistant may also find that many periodicals stored in the company library are available only on microfilm or fiche.

Record-intensive businesses, such as banks and insurance companies, almost invariably use microfilm. An executive assistant working in these record-intensive industries will undoubtedly be a microfilm user, if not a microfilm producer.

1. High rental costs are making microfilm a fact of life for many firms.
2. Microfilm uses less space and is less expensive to copy and mail than the equivalent paper documents.
3. Microforms include roll film, jackets, aperture cards, microfiche, and ultrafiche.
4. Microforms are created in two ways: from source documents and from COM documents.
5. To view any micro image, a reader must be used.
6. Reader/printers are similar to readers but have the additional capability of being able to produce a paper copy of a microimage.
7. COM recorders convert data generated by a computer into alphanumeric and/or graphic images on microfilm or fiche.

CHAPTER RECALL EXERCISES

1. Why are companies converting their paper files to microfilm?
2. What are microforms? Explain their functions.
3. What types of cameras are used to file source documents?
4. What is computer output microfilm? How does it work?
5. Why would a company want more than one copy of microfilmed records?
6. How does a person view a microfilmed image?
7. How does a person obtain a paper copy of a microfilmed image?
8. What are some typical applications that an organization would put on microfilm?

PROBLEMS AND APPLICATIONS

1. Go to your school or neighborhood library and find out which, if any, periodicals are stored on microfilm. See if they use roll film or fiche. View

some of the periodicals on the library's reader and make a paper copy if a reader/printer is available.

2. Make a list of all the organizations, such as banks and insurance companies, which might use microfilm when dealing with the public.

3. Write to the National Micrographics Association and ask for copies of its pamphlets on micrographics.

4. Find a periodical article on the integration of word processing and micrographics. Write a summary of the article and be prepared to give an oral report to the class about your findings.

5. Make a list of as many applications as you can think of for a company to use micrographics.

6. Write a report on COM. Some of the items to include in the report are:

    a. definition
    b. applications
    c. costs
    d. categories of systems
    e. manufacturers
    f. components

LANGUAGE SKILLS DEVELOPMENT

1. Form the plurals and possessives for the following words:

	Plural	*Plural Possessive*
a. manuscript		
b. bush		
c. toy		
d. family		
e. sister-in-law		
f. executive		
g. boss		
h. editor-in-chief		
i. company		
j. child		

2. Indicate the preferred place to divide these words:
    a. self-assurance
    b. any
    c. $2000
    d. NSA
    e. Mr. Bill Preston
    f. 1,567,890
    g. family
    h. abound
    i. beginning
    j. manager's

k. appreciate

l. rhetorical

3. Punctuate these sentences:

a. Today most Americans have a healthier and longer life than ever before said Dr. Mary Kent a renowed gerontologist.

b. Dr. Kent also said that Americans are selecting a better quality of food than they did in past years.

c. The chapter Principles of Supervision is probably the most often read portion of the text.

d. The author of the book Increasing Sales will give a lecture at the university on Monday March 21.

e. Was he the student who asked Why can't I change the date of the final exam?

f. Elise and Allens new executive assistant is really doing the job right however Jans and Eds executive assistants are not quite up to par.

g. The up to date report should be in the mail no later than this afternoon unless of course we have some typing problems.

h. Theres always room for another chair in the room according to Ms. Nancy Drawn an interior decorator.

HUMAN RELATIONS INCIDENTS

1. The micrographics department at the National Corporation is very small, with four employees. Doug, one of the employees in the department, is very moody and difficult for the other employees to work with. Everyone else in the department has to "walk on eggs" around Doug to try not to offend him in any way in order to keep a good working relationship in the department. The other three employees are getting tired of making allowances for Doug and giving in to him just to keep peace in the department. What could be done about Doug's disposition and attitude? How can the other employees handle this situation?

2. Ruth Deam is the supervisor of the micrographics department. Most of the time Ms. Deam has been very fair, understanding, and pleasant to work with. However, during the past six months, Ms. Deam has been going through some marital problems at home, and she is letting these problems affect her work and her working relationship with the employees in the department. Ms. Deam often looks tired, worried, and depressed; and she snaps back at employees who ask questions or have problems with their work. What can the employees in the department do about this situation with Ms. Deam? What would you do?

EXECUTIVE ASSISTANT SKILLS AND RESPONSIBILITIES

The executive assistant is usually involved in assisting executives in such tasks as researching information, making travel arrangements, and setting up meetings. These tasks are a challenging part of the job that demands initiative and resourcefulness. The more skilled executive assistants become in these jobs, the more valuable they become to the organization.

Executive assistants in the electronic office are involved in a lot more tasks than the traditional jobs of answering the telephone, taking dictation, typing, and filing. They can use electronic technology and equipment to help them better perform the traditional as well as the new kinds of jobs. The electronic calculator is one piece of equipment that the executive assistant will find helpful. Knowledge of the electronic calculator is an asset that is certain to enhance the executive assistant's qualifications. ■ Chapter 21   Locating and Using Reference Tools □ Chapter 22   Making Travel Arrangements □ Chapter 23   Setting Up Meetings □ Chapter 24   Using the Calculator

SECTION VI

LOCATING AND USING REFERENCE TOOLS

One of the most important aspects of an executive assistant's responsibility is assisting corporate executives and professionals in gathering, analyzing, and verifying information for such diverse activities as:

- ☐ Preparing a special technical report.
- ☐ Preparing a special company publication.
- ☐ Preparing a sales presentation.
- ☐ Preparing a market survey.
- ☐ Preparing and updating a correspondence manual.

As an executive assistant in a corporation, your role will certainly involve researching information for your employer. It is an exciting and often challenging part of office work that calls for your initiative and resourcefulness.

At the end of this chapter, you should be able to:

1. List the steps in the information cycle. ☐ 2. Know how to use resources. ☐ 3. Know where to go for information. ☐ 4. Define information bank. ☐ 5. List the reference tools available for executive assistants.

CHAPTER 21

THE INFORMATION CYCLE

Your previous education has probably exposed you to assignments that required independent information and research gathering activities. Whether it was for a term paper, committee report, or advanced degree thesis, you embarked on a cycle of events that would ultimately lead to the end result—a well-prepared final document. Some of the steps in this information gathering process were to:

1. Use the library to collect data.
2. Organize the data into a first draft.
3. Revise and edit that draft.
4. Type the final copy and proofread for possible errors or revisions.
5. Deliver the final document.

Figure 21.1
Information-gathering process.

STEP 1

STEPS 2 & 3

STEP 4

STEP 5

The steps you took to produce your report in school are somewhat similar to the steps that occur in producing a document in an office.

KNOW WHAT YOU ARE LOOKING FOR

One of the first steps, of course, is to know exactly what you want to learn. Candidates for advanced degrees must state clearly in their theses the aim or purpose in writing. In researching business information, you must constantly be aware of the objectives (purpose) of the research and must stay within the bounds of these objectives.

KNOW WHAT RESOURCES ARE AVAILABLE

The next step is to explore the many outside resources that are available, such as company records, the library, personal interviews, observations, and surveys. Finally, you need to collect all the pertinent raw information (by using some of the sources mentioned above) and to transfer this information into an intelligent, readable document.

Use available sources wisely. If you were a reporter on your school paper or an executive assistant gathering information for an article for the company's newsletter or house organ, you might consider the question-and-answer interviewing technique as a primary information-gathering source. The advantages of using the interview technique are:

1. The interviewer is able to ask questions to clarify any unclear areas or ambiguous questions.
2. The interviewer can guide the interview by keeping the line of questions within the topic area. It allows the interview to deal with germane issues.

KNOW HOW TO USE RESOURCES

Once you have located the data, the next step is to transfer the data onto paper. This can be accomplished in the following ways:

Developing a Working Bibliography. When using library sources, make a list of the books, periodicals, reports, and other reference sources. This preliminary list of sources is called the working bibliography. Separate index cards can be used to make entries such as: (1) author, (2) title, (3) name and location of publisher, and (4) date of publication.

If your source is an article in a magazine, newspaper, or other periodical, you should record the full name of the author, the title of the article (in quotation marks), the name of the publication, the date, volume, and page number.

The following are examples of bibliography cards for a book and a magazine article.

```
                                    357.2
Randolph, Allen           05/WP
    Word Processing
Chicago: Book Publishers, 1980
```

```
Trackson, Ellen
   "Profile of an Executive"
   Corporations
May, 1980, pp 6-11
Vol. 3, no. 3
```

Taking Notes. The research person may take notes on cards or paper. Extracting summaries, phrases, or key words with page references is sufficient for recording most data. Cards are usually better for note taking since they can be sorted easily and a new card can be used for each book, source, or reference.

Using Copy Machines. Photocopy machines at libraries may be used to reproduce material that can be later incorporated into reports. Care must be taken to ensure that copyright laws are observed.

Making Tape Recordings. The executive assistant or investigator may use a tape recorder to record the information gathered in an interview. It is a courtesy to ask permission of the person being interviewed before using a tape recorder.

METHODS OF LOCATING INFORMATION

A rich source of information today which can be found in almost every city with manufacturing and commercial interests is the public library. It contains a well-rounded collection of books and reference tools that are most useful to the executive assistant or business person.

The emphasis of most libraries is on current information. To be current in a competitive business environment is vital. The increased complexities and frequent changes in federal and state laws impacting business make it imperative for the business person engaged in research to have efficient, up-to-date methods for keeping informed about all legal matters that affect daily operations and decisions.

Many library sources are in the form of journals, pamphlets, directories, and manuals sometimes known as loose-leaf services (a subscription service that provides complete and up-to-date information in loose-leaf page form, which the subscriber simply adds to a loose-leaf binder). Examples of loose-leaf services for business law and tax service publishers are Commerce Clearing House of Chicago and Prentice-Hall, Inc., in Englewood Cliffs, New Jersey. For the executive assistant or business person interested in keeping up to date with office and word processing equipment and systems, a loose-leaf subscription to *Reports on Word Processing* and *Office System* published by Datapro of Delran, New Jersey, is available.

It is always a good idea for the executive assistant to visit the local library, talk with the librarian, and generally become familiar with the systems and procedures used to locate titles, authors, and subjects. There is a gold mine of information that can be of tremendous value to the researcher. Once this contact with a business library is established, assistance in answering specific inquiries for data or statistics is often no farther away than the telephone, since public libraries also offer prompt and efficient telephone service.

COMPANY LIBRARIES

If your firm is large, it may have its own library to serve its employees. These specialized libraries are usually found in organizations dealing with market research, advertising, and insurance. Company libraries may also be found in investment management firms and other consulting-type businesses. The executive assistant assigned to collect data is fortunate if a company library is available. All informational needs are at your fingertips and can be handled quickly and thoroughly by staffs of well-trained information specialists who concentrate their efforts on this function.

You usually do not have to leave the building to use the company library. You can use the help of company librarians (information specialists who make it their business to know the information needs and interests of each

Figure 21.2
The library staff can assist in compiling information (Courtesy of Stanford University).

individual in the company). The specialists help you by knowing where to go or who to telephone for speedy answers to questions; and, if necessary, the specialists may take over the responsibility for research rather than expect you to do this. This occurs only in unusual or emergency circumstances, and the executive assistant or executive who delegates this responsibility should be discreet in this request.

Company libraries are seldom open to the general public. It is wise for the executive assistant to know of their existence as they may be the only library source needed to satisfy all informational needs.

COLLEGE OR UNIVERSITY LIBRARIES

Most large cities and towns that contain a college or university have an additional resource—a college library. Many of these libraries are located within the main complex of buildings, while others are in separate buildings or on satellite campuses. The facilities are usually available to the general public, but some of the smaller private universities have found it necessary to charge an annual fee for continuous use of their facilities.

Why would you seek out a college library when a public or company library is available? The scope of the assignment may be such that scholarly or education-related information is necessary. Business school libraries, for instance, tend to be more extensive than those in public libraries and usually maintain a good collection of current research publications in the form of doctoral studies on just the topic that you are looking for.

You should first try the company library, then the public library, and then turn to college and university facilities as the need arises. In addition to public, company, and university libraries, the federal government is also an excellent source of information and advice. Although many of the federal libraries are located in Washington, D.C., many federal branches and other facilities are located in principal cities.

Such federal agencies as the Bureau of Labor Statistics, the Department of Commerce, and its Bureau of the Census provide free publications to the general public. An executive assistant engaged in extensive research should obtain a list of government publications by writing to the U.S. Government Printing Office, Washington, D.C. 20401.

As libraries continue their efforts to acquire large quantities of new titles and publications, micrographic technology will enjoy widespread use. Micrographic technology permits the conservation of shelf space. The micro-publishing business has grown so dramatically in the past few years that there are now a number of catalogs listing the various publications available in the new formats. In the future, microfilm services will be widely available, not only in libraries, but in the office and home as well.

INFORMATION BANKS

A computerized information service for any executive assistant/researcher, which provides access to over 1.3 million on-line items, is a relatively new

Figure 21.3
Branner Earth Sciences Library, Stanford University (Courtesy of Stanford University).

phenomenon called the Information Bank. The Information Bank offers a wide variety of highly specialized services for business firms, industrial companies, the communications industry, government agencies, and academic and public libraries. Whichever service (or group of services) is selected—the end result is a structured information flow designed to meet current management needs.

It is an economical system to use; executive assistants or researchers in need of information can access the Information Bank with a local or short-distance call to a network of more than 70 dial-up points across the United States, Canada, Latin America, and Europe. The system's constantly expanding data base of over 1.3 million items is compiled from more than 70 worldwide publications, including the *New York Times, Wall Street Journal, BusinessWeek, Financial Times, Economist,* and *Harvard Business Review.*

The Information Bank is one of the most comprehensive current-affairs data resources in the world. It is a resource that is a must for executive assistants/researchers engaged in extensive information-collecting activities.

AUDIOCASSETTES

Another important resource media available is the audiocassette tape, a magnetic tape encased in a small plastic or metal cartridge containing recordings of speeches, articles, or summaries of current information in a particular subject area that can be played on any standard tape recorder for the listener. Libraries usually provide private listening stations for this.

REFERENCE TOOLS FOR EXECUTIVE ASSISTANTS

Besides the basic reference sources that usually appear on the top of the executive assistant's desk, the following sources describe the variety of reference tools at your disposal.

TELEPHONE DIRECTORIES

The telephone directory should be within easy reach of your desk at all times. It does not have answers, but it is loaded with the numbers of people who do—libraries, consultants, specialists, schools, industrial firms, trade associations, government agencies (domestic and foreign), and publishing houses. In addition to your local directory, it is a good idea to have out-of-town directories in which your branch offices or high-volume customers are located. For example, if you were looking for an office systems consultant, you would look under the special area "Communications Consultant," "Office Management Consultant," "Business Systems Consultant," or "Per-

Figure 21.4
Using the telephone directory (Courtesy of AT&T).

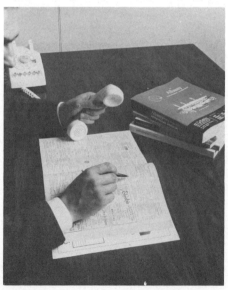

sonnel Consultants." Firms are listed under captions that indicate their particular specialities.

The telephone directory is useful not only for telephone numbers but also for correct spellings of company names and personal names and addresses.

ALMANACS

An almanac is a compendium of facts which contains the answers to many business questions. It includes a chronological record of recent events, statistics on government, labor, medicine, aviation, sports, education, literature, population patterns, science, religion, and geographic statistics.

YEARBOOKS

Yearbooks differ from almanacs in that they usually give more complete information on specific fields and concentrate on a broad subject area, a country, or current trends and events.

ENCYCLOPEDIAS

To explore an area in depth, an encyclopedia provides more factual data than yearbooks or almanacs. Here the executive assistant will find excellent articles on every imaginable subject and in-depth profiles of prominent and important personalities written in a concise but easy-to-understand style.

DICTIONARIES

The dictionary is the bible for the executive assistant or business person who is involved with words on a day-to-day basis. It is perhaps the most important tool of the executive assistant and is usually stored conveniently on the top of the desk. English-language dictionaries are useful for checking the meaning, spelling, or pronunciation of words, terms, or phrases. It is a good idea to replace dictionaries every five years, as new terms, spellings, and entries are added.

COMPREHENSIVE INDEXES AND BOOK LISTS

There are several sources that contain periodic lists of all in-print books published by commercial publishing firms and university presses. New books emerge on the market just as fast as food products appear on supermarket shelves. This ever-widening stream of publications published each year can be overwhelming if you do not know where to look. Every library and most bookstores will have at least one of these bibliographies. If it is not readily available, you should feel free to ask for it.

DIRECTORIES

Directories are other important reference tools. Directories are time-saving when you need brief data on companies, organizations, and individuals. They can be very helpful when researching manufacturers of a specific product, checking companies located in a particular area, or verifying company names, addresses, and telephone numbers.

SUMMARY

The more skilled a person becomes in collecting business information, the more valuable he or she is. The trick is to know where to look for information or who to ask for help in finding it. Time is a precious commodity in business and "spinning your wheels" in a fruitless effort to collect unrelated background or peripheral data is a waste of time.

1. The steps in gathering information are: (a) use the library, (b) organize the data collected, (c) revise and edit, (d) type the final copy, and (e) deliver the final copy.
2. To collect data, a researcher must know what to look for, what resources are available, and how to use the available resources.
3. Public, company, and college or university libraries are excellent sources available to the researcher.
4. Many libraries use micrographics, a form of publications transformed into miniature film and available for the reader to read on microform readers (which project an enlarged image of a page on a screen in front of a viewer).
5. Information banks provide the researcher with information stored in a computer which can be accessed immediately.
6. Information can also be recorded on audiocassette tapes and used by a researcher in a library.
7. The reference tools for researchers are: (a) the telephone directories, (b) almanacs, (c) yearbooks, (d) encyclopedias, (e) dictionaries, and (f) comprehensive indexes and book lists.

CHAPTER RECALL EXERCISES

1. Briefly describe a situation in which you were involved in collecting information. What reference tools, if any, did you use?
2. List some topics that an executive assistant might be assigned to research.
3. Why is it important to understand the problem before you begin to look for information?
4. Explain loose-leaf services.
5. What services does the public librarian render to the person seeking information?
6. Briefly describe the function of a company library.
7. Why would a researcher seek out a college library when a public library is available?
8. What informational sources are available from the federal government?
9. Although the telephone directory does not provide in-depth facts, what use can it be to the researcher?
10. Describe the several types of reference tools.

11. List the steps in the information cycle.

12. Define information bank.

PROBLEMS AND APPLICATIONS

1. Dorothy Foster is an executive assistant/researcher in a large consulting company. She has just been assigned the following preliminary investigation: There is an ongoing conflict over the relationship of nutrition and such diseases as cancer, strokes, heart attacks, and arthritis. The American Medical Association (AMA) believes that there is no relationship between nutrition and such diseases. A group of preventive medical scientists strongly believe that there is a correlation between good nutrition and disease. A local community college is planning to start a course in nutrition and health. They have contracted your consulting firm to collect data and summarize the two points of view in a brief report. Outline the steps you would take in this assignment.

2. Indicate which reference tools and sources of information you would use to gather information for the research project in the case above. List the step-by-step approach used.

3. a. Using 3 × 5-inch cards, go to the library and do a working bibliography on one of the following topics:

Home Computers

Electronic Mail

Training Office Employees

Writing Job Descriptions

b. Make an outline of what you would include in an eight-page report on the topic you have chosen.

c. Write your objectives or the statement (purpose) of your topic.

4. Use the reference sources discussed in this chapter to complete the following items:

a. Name of an office systems consultant in your area.

b. Name of the CEO of General Motors; biographical information about the CEO at GM.

c. Habits of the hummingbird.

d. Population of Denver, Colorado.

e. Manufacturing plants in Knoxville, Tennessee.

f. Meanings and pronunciation of these words: cadmium and ukase.

5. Find a library in your area (school library, company library, or public library) which subscribes to *Datapro Reports*. Spend some time reviewing the types of articles found in this publication.

6. Write to the U.S. Government Printing Office and ask for a list of government publications.

LANGUAGE SKILLS DEVELOPMENT

1. Use the correct capitalization and punctuation in these sentences:
   a. The class taught by professor greene meets on monday evenings at 6 pm
   b. The town council is planning to vote on issue 10 according to mayor richland
   c. My favorite relative aunt marge will be visiting during the summer.
   d. Do you know who the secretary of the debate association will be when the meetings resume during the fall quarter
   e. The secretary read the minutes of the last meeting before a packed house
   f. The minutes said that the treasurers report was not accurate
   g. The book learning to read will be used by all the seniors enrolled in education 451
   h. The house is planning to vote on the bill before this session is over
2. Following are some words that are frequently misused. Use each of the words correctly in a sentence.
   a. adept, adopt
   b. awhile, a while
   c. access, excess
3. Choose the correct number usage for these sentences:
   a. Dave rode his bicycle over (100, one hundred) miles in (1, one) day.
   b. To build the model, we need to buy (2, two) bottles of glue and (15, fifteen) brackets.
   c. During the past (4, four) years, sales have risen to nearly (4, four) million units.
   d. (15, Fifteen) students did not turn in their reports on time, and the instructor penalized each of the reports (10, ten) percent.
   e. Please turn to page (6, six) in your textbook to find the answer to question (20, twenty).
   f. Volume (8, eight) is missing from the new group of books we purchased for the library.
   g. The (fifteen-, 15-) page report is due by the (10, 10th, tenth) of October.
   h. The company is located on (5th, fifth, 5) Avenue in New York.

HUMAN RELATIONS INCIDENTS

1. Helen, Eleanor, and Alice are executive assistants in a small office. Alice has a tendency to wear too much makeup and inappropriate (frilly) clothes to the office. The problem, though, is

that Alice also wears too much perfume. Since the office is a small place, the perfume saturates everything and everyone in the area, making it difficult for Helen and Eleanor to enjoy the work atmosphere.

Helen and Eleanor have spoken to the supervisor, Mr. Harris, on several occasions; and he made it a point to discuss how to dress for the office in a recent staff meeting when all three of the department members were present. Alice apparently did not realize the remarks were directed specifically to her. Is there a way these personal matters can be discussed tactfully? What should be the next step for Helen and Eleanor?

2. Jack is an executive assistant in a public relations company. Since Jack's supervisor, Ms. Jamison, is away from the office for several days a month, Jack does much of the research for reports that Ms. Jamison writes. On several occasions during the past six months, Jack has even written a rough draft of the entire report, at Ms. Jamison's request. Jack thinks he is doing too much of Ms. Jamison's job and is not being paid to write these reports. Is this part of Jack's job? Should he refuse to do this job? How would you handle this situation?

MAKING TRAVEL ARRANGEMENTS

Most businesses that have attained a world prominence in multinational trade have found it necessary to send executives to domestic and international markets to protect, maintain, and expand markets for their products and services. The traveling executive is an emissary for the company. It is, therefore, essential that the executive keep up to date on national and international economic and monetary trends, on U.S. foreign policy as it affects commerce, and on general corporate and technological developments throughout the world.

The competitiveness of today's business makes it imperative that traveling executives be able to react fast, decide fast, and move fast in order to maintain their positions in the world market.

The executive assistant for the traveling executive must possess the skill and know-how to support and handle these specialized travel arrangements. To handle travel arrangements efficiently, it is necessary to keep up with the changes in the transportation field, as well as hotels, restaurants, and other related services.

At the end of this chapter, you should be able to:

1. Discuss the methods available for handling travel arrangements. ☐ 2. Explain how travel funds are handled in most companies. ☐ 3. Compare the modes of travel available. ☐ 4. Describe the purpose of an itinerary. ☐ 5. Know the rules and etiquette for overseas travel.

CHAPTER 22

METHODS OF HANDLING TRAVEL ARRANGEMENTS

A company may have several options regarding arrangements for traveling executives: (1) use of an in-house travel department, (2) use of travel agents, (3) use of the executive assistant, and (4) a combination of each.

IN-HOUSE TRAVEL DEPARTMENT

Large corporations find it convenient to handle travel arrangements in house. These departments are specialists when it comes to setting up trips and working very closely with carriers (companies engaged in public transportation). In-house travel departments have "in-ticketing" for most domestic and international carriers. The executive assistant for the traveling executive is then relieved of most of the decision-making and intricate details.

As soon as the executive informs you of the trip, you telephone the travel department, and the travel department obtains the necessary trip ticket, secures hotel reservations, issues a company credit card for expenses, and prepares the typed itinerary (a plan of travel, a proposed route).

You must work closely with the personnel of the in-house travel department. As soon as the employer knows he or she is going on a trip, you must find out the following information:

- [ ] Where is he or she going?
- [ ] On what date is he or she leaving?
- [ ] On what date is he or she returning?
- [ ] What time of day would he or she like to leave? Return?
- [ ] Is any particular airline preferred?
- [ ] Is any particular hotel or location preferred?

With this information in mind, you would then follow these steps to make travel reservations, using the services of the in-house travel department:

1. Call the travel department and give them the needed information. They will give you a choice of flights and possible hotels.
2. Find out which flights (and hotels) your employer prefers.
3. Type out a travel reservation request. If your employer does not know of a hotel (or if the travel department has not recommended one), just fill in the approximate location, such as "near the airport" or "downtown" and your in-house travel department will usually take care of it. You might keep a list of favorite hotels, changing the list when there is an objection or a problem with one of the hotels.
   a. Have your employer's immediate supervisor sign the travel reservation request.
   b. Hand-deliver both copies of the travel reservation form to the in-house travel department. It is best not to send it through interoffice mail.

c. The in-house travel department will send the second copy back to you with confirmed flights and reservations.

d. On the day before the trip, go to the in-house travel department and pick up the tickets. They should not be sent through the mails.

e. Check over the itinerary to make sure it is complete. (Preparation of an itinerary is discussed later in the chapter.)

TRAVEL AGENTS

An executive assistant who uses an in-house travel department or arranges the trip himself or herself realizes these can be quite complicated steps. As indicated earlier, some large corporations use in-house travel departments with "in-ticketing" service. This usually requires having a fully knowledgeable travel department on the premises—an added company expense only justified if the department is kept busy on a full-time basis. Because they are not actually involved in the travel industry, it is difficult for personnel in a travel department of a company or an executive assistant to remain aware of the changing fare bases and excursions. In the long run, this might mean added expense for the company in salaries and increased costs in travel. Very often the company may ultimately have to turn to a good travel agent.

A travel agent is an experienced professional travel counselor who provides the public with a variety of services ranging from planning and coordinating travel arrangements to providing simple travel advice—all within the budget limitations established by a client (company or individual).

Businesses cannot afford shoddy service, missed connections, or executives housed in third-rate hotels. Business appointments that are not kept result in lost business and generate poor relations for the company. A company or executive assistant who has the responsibility of selecting a travel agent should look for an agent with professional association membership in the American Society of Travel Agents (ASTA). ASTA members are consumer minded. The society requires at least three years of experience in business and appointment by at least two major transportation conferences, one of which must be either the Air Traffic Conference (ATC) or the International Air Transport Association (IATA) for full membership.

Selecting an ASTA travel agent, or one that belongs to another professional association, usually assures against unscrupulous operations. Also, travel agents who have the letters CTC after their names have received advanced travel and tourism training from the Institute of Certified Travel Agents.

The executive assistant who calls a travel agent should be prepared with all the basic information:

☐ When the employer wants to travel.
☐ Which airport or railroad station is most convenient.
☐ Seating preference—smoking, nonsmoking, class of travel.
☐ Auto rental or other transportation arrangements.
☐ Hotel accommodations.

In addition, the executive assistant should know what part of a given city is important to the executive—the center of town or the airport area. It is important for an agent to know how long the trip will be because one additional day can mean a substantially lower fare which would more than offset one additional night in a hotel.

Having supplied the agent with all basic information, you should write on the calendar all pertinent dates for follow-up. Travel agencies have no service charge and work on a very nominal commission basis. Travel agents derive their income from commissions paid by the airlines, hotels, and tour operators with whom they book reservations. In some instances, when the agent receives no commission, a small charge may be required. You should ask the travel agent in advance for the amount of any service charges or cancellation fees.

In searching for a good agent, there are various considerations. If time is of the essence, a convenient location, near the office, is important, since you might have to pick up the tickets. Select an agency that handles travel arrangements for commercial travel, rather than individual recreational tours.

It may seem unfair, but sometimes the size of the staff of an agency and the volume of business the agency produces tend to be important factors. Because of a large agency's needs, the airlines, for instance, frequently provide their bigger customers with special agency executive desks, which are staffed by employees of the airline. This helps the client in the long run with added efficiency and availability.

Having found an agency, you should develop a rapport with some of the staff. Courtesy goes far, and a smile works in any language. It can come through the telephone. A good executive assistant knows how to ask questions involving travel arrangements briefly, so as not to waste the time of a busy executive.

EXECUTIVE ASSISTANT AS TRAVEL ARRANGER

If you do have the training and knowledge of travel, it may be convenient to arrange the travel plans without the aid of a travel agent or in-house travel department. Basically, the same ground rules apply in knowing the executive's preferences as to hotel chains, airlines, and seating arrangements. You then simply communicate these preferences directly to the carrier or hotel.

Some firms subscribe to domestic and international official airline guides (OAG). If the company does not have these in the office, a travel agent might save a copy for you since these are published monthly for international travel and every two weeks for domestic travel. A novice should not select flights without doublechecking schedules since timetables constantly change. However, these publications will help determine suggested connections and time allowed for travel in your employer's schedule.

TRAVEL FUNDS

Company policy varies as to the amount and type of currency carried by the traveling executive. Most companies provide multipurpose credit cards, such as American Express and Mastercharge to meet most travel needs. The use of credit cards facilitates preparing expense reports and enables executives to verify expenditures. In addition to carrying credit cards, it is best to carry some form of emergency currency.

When going on a trip, especially if it is out of the country, you should make preliminary arrangements to have traveler's checks available for the traveling executive. Usually traveler's checks can be obtained by:

1. Typing a cash advance form and two copies.
2. Taking the original and one copy to the accounts payable department.
3. Having the supervisor sign the form and taking it back to the accounts payable department. There, you would be able to get the traveler's checks.

Expense reports are filled out in order to reimburse a traveling executive for money spent in the course of business activities. If the executive wishes to draw money on an advance basis, you would fill out a special form, such as "request for advance expense money."

You complete the form after checking with the executive to find out: (a) the total amount of money needed, (b) whether it should be in cash or traveler's checks, and (c) if cash is needed, the denomination preferred.

Expense reports should always be filled out promptly. You should confer with the executive to complete the report as soon as the executive returns from a trip. Remember, the executive will not be reimbursed until the expense report is processed.

Filling out an expense report can be done quickly if you follow some universal guidelines:

1. Put all expenses related to one trip on the same expense report.
2. Itemize expenses on a daily basis.
3. Describe each expense.
4. Determine whether the company owes your boss money of if your boss owes the company money. (If the total advance is larger than the total expense, your employer owes money to the company. If the total expense is larger than the total advance, the company owes your employer money.)

Each company has its own unique policy of reimbursing for expenses. The forms may vary also, but generally they should reflect an itemized accounting of expenses, justified by receipts. It is a good idea to remind your executive not to throw away any receipts. You may even wish to set up some organized procedure that your executive may use in keeping track of expenses.

	PLEASE TYPE OR PRINT
REQUEST FOR ADVANCE EXPENSE MONEY	☐ PERMANENT ADVANCE REQUEST ☐ CREDIT CARD REQUEST Date _____

EMPLOYEE'S NAME	EMPLOYEE NUMBER	POSITION
ORGANIZATION NAME	ORGANIZATION NO.	LOCATION

PERMANENT ADVANCE ☐ NEW ADVANCE OF $_____ ☐ CHANGE AMOUNT	FROM $_____ TO $_____	CREDIT CARD ☐ AIR TRAVEL ☐ AUTO RENTAL

REASON FOR REQUEST (MUST BE FILLED IN)

EMPLOYEE'S SIGNATURE DATE	DIVISION CONTROLLER DATE
DEPT. MGR.'S SIGNATURE DATE	GROUP CONTROLLER DATE
	CORPORATE CONTROLLER DATE

Figure 22.1
Request for advance expense money.

TRAVEL INSURANCE

Travel insurance covers the traveling executive while on company business. The company may provide blanket coverage, or the executive may elect to take out personal coverage. In planning the trip, you should remind the executive about company policy and follow through to see that coverage is applied for.

MODES OF TRAVEL

In a typical year scheduled airlines in the United States carry 240 million passengers, move 6.4 million ton miles of freight and mail, including nine

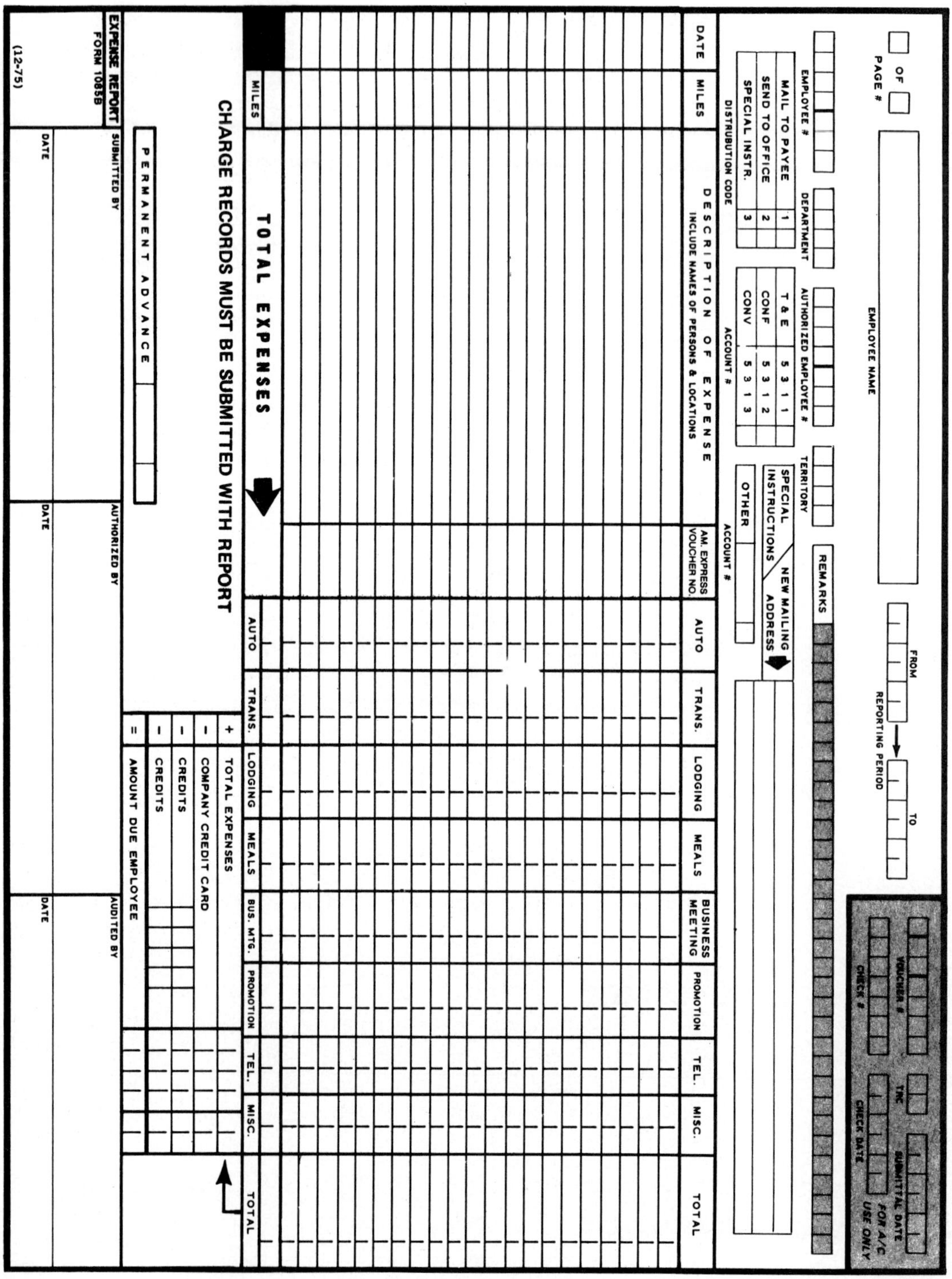

Figure 22.2
Expense report.

out of every ten first-class letters between cities.

A majority of passengers that fly the nation's airlines are traveling executives. They select air travel because of the time-saving factor. A tight schedule of meetings, luncheons, and conventions necessitates jet travel. Most commercial carriers serve cities throughout the United States and Canada. Regional airlines fly to cities too small for jet runways.

CORPORATE JETS

The trend toward corporations owning their own jets has been on the increase. Top executives engaged in multimillion dollar negotiations where timing is critical rely on corporate jets to whisk them across the continent on a moment's notice.

Your responsibilities may be somewhat different when the corporation jet is used. For instance, you may have to request meals or office supplies.

Air taxi and special charter flights are other alternative means to avoid the fixed carrier schedules and may prove more convenient than scheduled airlines.

TRAIN TRAVEL

The Amtrak system, through its public relations efforts, is trying to promote rail travel for tourists, as well as business people. In addition, the energy crisis of the past few years has increased the passenger load as more and more executives are leaving their cars at home and taking the train.

It may very well be more convenient to take a train from Boston to New York or from New York to Washington, D.C., for instance. The high-speed metroliners serving these routes provide central city-to-city service.

Business travel by plane is fast and comfortable, but a major drawback to going by plane is getting to the plane and getting back. Airports in most cities are far from downtown areas. So, business travelers are often forced to take long cab rides in order to take the plane. Tens of thousands of hours and dollars are wasted annually because highly paid executives get bogged down in traffic between the office and the airport. By taking the train more, especially on business trips under 500 miles, the executive will be in a better frame of mind and may save the company some money. Train travel also provides the executive an opportunity to work while traveling.

Amtrak has hundreds of new, luxurious cars in service in the Northeast corridor between Boston and Washington, D.C., and in other business corridors in the Midwest and on the West Coast. The French designed Rohr Turbotrains recently went into regular service between New York City and Buffalo.

Since many travel agencies shun handling rail service, you should become familiar with the rail services by consulting the *Official Guide to the Railways*, which contains schedules of all railway and steamship lines in the United States, Canada, Mexico, and Puerto Rico.

AUTO RENTALS

If the executive has business appointments within a major city, local taxi or public transportation will probably be adequate. However, if the itinerary includes extensive travel outside the city limits, car rental service may be necessary. There is a wide selection of companies to choose from in this highly competitive field.

Car rental arrangements can be made through the travel agent, airline, in-house travel department, or directly with the car rental agency. Rental companies make it very easy for the traveler to obtain a car. A simple toll-free number often will confirm a reservation. The executive can pick up a rental car within a few steps of the airport terminal. Some rental companies now provide door-to-door service from the airport to the car and back again.

You should specify the type of car preferred by the executive (size, power options, color, rates, and dates needed). The cost of rental cars varies, depending on the make and size of car, the year, and optional features. In addition, the cost of car rental usually includes the length of time the car will be used, plus a mileage charge for each mile traveled during the rental period. There are economy plans that offer no mileage charge and no drop charge. A drop charge is an extra fee for returning the car at a different location from that of the point of origin.

For the executive who must call on business associates, a well-polished, late model auto is part of the overall positive, first impression that has become a part of the business and social world of the traveling executive. However, some employers may encourage their traveling executives to economize on traveling expenses by shunning the "blue chip" auto rental companies. You must be aware of company policies and the executive's preference in travel mode and make the necessary arrangements.

ROOM ARRANGEMENTS

If you handle the travel details for the executive, you are usually asked to make the hotel arrangements. Usually the executive has a preference and may select a quality chain hotel either in a midcity location or near the airport if he or she wants to rent an auto. For many hotels and motels there are toll-free numbers to call for reservations. You should take the following points into consideration when making hotel reservations:

1. Type of room desired (floor, proximity to lobby, elevator, and view). Most motels use the term "down and out" which means a room on the first floor facing the outside. This is convenient for parking next to the room and facilitates loading and unloading baggage.
2. Kind of accommodations (twin beds, kitchen facilities, tub or shower, conference desk, suite, and bar facilities).
3. Rates.
4. Number of persons in party.

5. Date and approximate time of arrival. Usually, hotels will hold your reservation until 6 p.m. If you wish a guaranteed reservation after 6 p.m., the guest is responsible for paying for the room even if it is not used.
6. Date of departure.
7. The need for a written confirmation.

If you or your executive does not know of a hotel in the destination city, various directories can be consulted, such as: *Hotel and Motel Red Book, Leahy's Hotel-Motel Guide and Travel Atlas, Mobil Travel Guide,* and *The Travel Agent* (published by Travel Agent Magazine).

In addition, most major hotel and motel chains have their own directories which you should use for planning and making travel arrangements for the executive. Toll-free numbers should be used whenever possible for making reservations.

PREPARATION OF THE ITINERARY

After you finalize the details for the trip, a comprehensive itinerary is developed. An itinerary is basically a step-by-step plan that includes a schedule of appointments and activities. It serves as a helpful reminder for the executive and includes when, where, and how the traveler will go. Knowledge of the purpose of the trip and the time frame is essential if you are to create an intelligent and workable itinerary.

Planning an itinerary involves more than setting time schedules to match travel plans and activities. It goes far beyond that; an intelligent executive assistant considers such things as the uncertainties of carrier schedules, company policy, and the executive's personality and makes them a part of the travel plan.

The executive assistant planning an itinerary might be responsible for deciding how much time should be devoted to each activity on the itinerary. In other words, should the employer spend another night in City A or fly on to City B for the night?

Jet lag results when the executive flies long distances, and experiences a time change, which may cause physical and mental disorientation. The knowledgeable executive assistant should allow a period of recuperation after long-distance flights and not schedule any meetings or activities during that period.

All materials, correspondence, appointments, and confirmations pertaining to the trip should be assembled, analyzed, and finally, outlined in the form of a concise and easy-to-read itinerary.

The executive assistant should prepare several copies of the itinerary, and should distribute it to several key people. The executive assistant should also keep a copy handy for reference. Possibly, a copy should be sent to the executive's spouse. A thumbnail itinerary, in addition to the formalized itinerary, should be prepared for the executive to carry for easy referral.

There is no set format for typing an itinerary, and you should select a style that is easy to read and consistent. Columns of information and appropriate headings should be set up containing such data as date, time, and activity; it should also include the city, hotel, type of carrier, flight number, and other related information.

ORGANIZING FOR TRAVEL

Obviously, the executive will pack personal items at home. You may help pack the materials relating to business activities that are necessary to make the trip successful. You should organize the executive's attache case or briefcase. Depending upon the length of the trip and the business to be conducted, you should pack the following items in a special attache case with compartments:

- ☐ Papers, files, reports.
- ☐ Calculator, appointment book or schedule, address book.
- ☐ Ruler, pen, pencils.
- ☐ Tickets.
- ☐ Office supplies—memo pads, scissors, small stapler.
- ☐ Portable dictating machine, blank cassettes.
- ☐ Business cards.
- ☐ Letterhead stationery, envelopes, stamps, clips.
- ☐ Information on companies to be visited and related correspondence.
- ☐ Background information on people to be seen.

OVERSEAS TRAVEL

Global travel, once very limited, is now almost commonplace. All countries are actively seeking new industry and investment from the United States and are working to increase their exports to this country.

The executive assistant to an executive of a multinational corporation has an added responsibility when assisting with the planning of international travel since doing business successfully in foreign countries may often hinge on social graces, amenities, and cultures that are vastly different.

An executive who takes the time to learn the history and culture of the countries being visited will find a warm welcome. The ability to talk knowledgeably about a host country can be very helpful in creating an atmosphere of mutual respect and understanding.

As a business traveler, the executive would most likely travel to and from Europe or Asia by air. You should secure a return reservation before the executive leaves the United States. Then, if business requires that the return plan be altered, the return reservation puts the traveler in a better position to secure later or different flights. If an executive has return reservations, it puts her or him in an advantageous position over others, including tourists, who may be trying to book passage on the same flight.

The better prepared the business traveler is before arrival in a foreign country, the better the chances of success. An overseas traveling executive will never be far from a U.S. Embassy or Consular Office where expert help in working with local business interests can be obtained. Any reasonable requests will be handled quickly and efficiently by the embassies.

Information and guidance on business problems can be obtained from the Economic Commercial Attache at any U.S. Embassy or Consulate or from American Chambers of Commerce assigned to overseas countries.

Most experienced business travelers carry as little cash as possible and rely upon the use of traveler's checks which can be cashed, as needed, with little or no difficulty. You can find out about current exchange rates and can obtain foreign currency by consulting special banks.

It is helpful, however, for the executive to have a small amount of foreign currency on hand before arriving in a foreign country. This will make it possible to take care of small incidentals like cab fares and tips without having to negotiate a traveler's check.

A list of the serial numbers of the traveler's checks should be kept separately from the checks themselves. If the checks are lost, the list of serial numbers will make their replacement easier.

GUIDELINES FOR BEHAVIOR FOR THE INTERNATIONAL TRAVELER

The experienced American traveler in foreign countries should keep in mind that his foreign counterparts are much more formal and conventional in their behavior and language. Europeans, for instance, tend to practice the kind of polite behavior that our parents and grandparents used to exhibit before it gave way to the casualness and familiarity that characterizes social and business behavior in American society today.

Most foreigners are aware that Americans are friendly and informal, but it is wise to moderate these qualities when overseas. Too much friendliness and familiarity may be misinterpreted as a lack of respect.

The following information is specifically for the foreign traveler or traveling executive. It is appropriate in an office procedures book insofar as the information is useful to you in your role in helping the executive prepare for foreign travel. There are occasions when you might accompany the executive during trips to provide office services and support, and, therefore, these guidelines would apply to the traveling executive assistant as well.

1. Dress for all business meetings should be formal business attire. All appointments should be made in advance.

2. Foreign business associates should be greeted with the correct title. Avoid addressing foreigners with a first name, unless you have established very close relationships—certainly not at the first meeting.
3. Know and practice foreign greetings at the beginning of a meeting by shaking hands with Europeans and gracefully bowing when meeting Orientals.

If you are not sure about social behavior, ask your host; or if you have the time, call the commercial attache at the nearest U.S. Consulate or Embassy. Showing your host that you want to do the right thing can compensate for any mistakes or omissions you may make.

You can assist your boss in planning the trips by conferring with the area trade specialist at one of the district offices of the U.S. Department of Commerce. The largest office is at 26 Federal Plaza in New York City, and there are 42 other offices in major cities across the country.

Information from foreign tourist agencies and from foreign travel airlines includes simple foreign phrase books, descriptions of customs and social amenities, maps, and places to visit.

DOCUMENTS

A valid U.S. passport is a must. A traveler should carry the passport at all times and avoid packing it with luggage. A passport takes several weeks to obtain and requires proof of citizenship by means of a document from the state of birth. Photographs are also necessary. Do not surrender the passport except to authorized immigration authorities and, when required to do so, to hotel receptionists.

Many foreign countries also require your passport to carry a visa stamp before you may enter. Visa stamps are issued for a small fee by the embassies and consulates of the host countries. You should check with the consulate, embassy, airline, or travel agent before the departure date to find out which visas are required.

Vaccinations against smallpox, cholera, and yellow fever are required prior to entry into some foreign countries. These vaccinations have been established under regulations by the World Health Organization (WHO). If you are in doubt about any vaccination procedures, this information is available from the consulate or embassy of the country concerned. Your airline or travel agent will gladly assist you also. Make sure your employer has all the necessary documentation before the departure date. It is also important that these documents be kept up to date and renewed so the executive is ready to travel at a moment's notice.

FOLLOW-UP ON TRAVEL

While the traveling executive is on the road, you must carry out the tasks necessary to maintain a smooth and continuous workflow. Answering correspondence and telephone and reception tasks are the normal day-to-day activities that consume a large portion of your time. Time spent in productive activity, such as transferring files, restocking supplies, updating company manuals, and researching data for reports makes the day go faster. It is just as important to perform conscientiously in the employer's absence as it is in the employer's presence.

It is a wonderful feeling of confidence for a returning executive to find the office in order. After your employer has settled down and has taken care of important priority items, you should prepare the expense report to be submitted for reimbursed funds. Helping the executive unpack the attache case and returning materials to the files are other important tasks.

You might also ask your employer if he or she liked the hotel accommodations and/or the airline carrier so you will know whether to use similar accommodations for future trips. Give this feedback to travel agents after the trip.

SUMMARY

The executive assistant for the traveling executive must possess the skill and know-how to support and handle travel arrangements.

1. A company can have the following arrangements for travel: (a) in-house travel department, (b) travel agents, (c) travel arrangements handled by the executive assistant, and (d) a combination of the above.
2. Small companies rely on the service of travel agencies as experts in planning and coordinating travel arrangements.
3. Reliability of travel agents can be assured if they are members of the American Society of Travel Agents (ASTA).
4. Travel agents have no service charge and work on a nominal commission basis.
5. Executive assistants should know their employer's preferences in regard to travel, hotels, and carriers prior to making travel plans.
6. Expense reports are filled out in order to reimburse a traveling executive for money spent in the course of business activities.
7. Corporate jets are used as a convenience when timing is important to bypass the red tape of airports.
8. The energy crisis has increased rail travel.
9. Most major hotel chains have their own directories, and the executive assistant can simply use a special toll-free number for reservations.
10. An itinerary is a step-by-step schedule of appointments and activities.
11. The executive assistant should allow for a rest period so the traveling executive can recover from jet lag.
12. The format of itineraries varies from company to company.
13. The overseas traveler should understand the culture and customs of the country visited.
14. There are occasions when the executive assistant accompanies the executive during trips.
15. Productive activities such as updating files, restocking supplies, and

answering routine correspondence should be performed by the executive assistant when the executive is out of the office.

CHAPTER RECALL EXERCISES

1. List some of the advantages of using a travel agent for arranging trips.
2. How would an executive select a reputable travel agent?
3. What information should an executive assistant give a travel agent in preparing a trip for an executive?
4. Briefly describe an expense report.
5. What is the chief advantage of selecting air travel? What are some of the disadvantages of air travel?
6. What criteria will determine whether an executive selects train travel?
7. List some of the sources an executive assistant can use to secure hotel and motel reservations.
8. What is an itinerary? How can it help the executive?
9. What agencies can an executive use for guidance and counsel on overseas problems?
10. What documents must a traveler carry? Which vaccinations are required for some overseas travel?

PROBLEMS AND APPLICATIONS

1. You are executive assistant to Mr. Art Ashford, executive vice-president at Steelmate Products, Inc. He has telephoned you from a hotel and said that, in spite of a confirmed written reservation, there are no hotel rooms available in Cincinnati for the next two days because of a large national convention being held there. Since you are the executive assistant responsible for his travel arrangements, what can you do to help Mr. Ashford?

2. Mr. David Poindexter is expected to return from a business trip in New Orleans. He has a full schedule of meetings and appointments. He telephones you at 4:30 p.m. the day before he is scheduled to return, informing you that all flights are canceled due to a heavy fog and that he will be arriving the following evening. What should you do regarding his appointments and meetings?

3. Geraldine Fox has just returned from a business trip to New York City. Her luggage was lost on the plane. She has her important papers and receipts in her luggage. Since you are her executive assistant, how will you be able to prepare her expense report without the necessary information?

4. Visit your library to determine if there are books or pamphlets available to help travelers become aware of weather conditions, customs, and other important facts about locations in the United States and abroad.

5. Assume that the executive for whom you work is going to Korea for

the first time for an important business meeting. The executive wants you to find out as much information as you can to help this trip be a success. Where would you go for information? What types of information would you be looking for? What would you include in your report to your boss?

6. You are executive assistant to Ms. Jennifer Brinks in a new company that has been in existence for just a few months. Ms. Brinks has just returned from her first business trip and needs to submit her expenses for reimbursement. Since there are no expense reports available, Ms. Brinks has asked you to develop an expense report to be used throughout the company by traveling executives. Develop and type an expense account form for Ms. Brinks' approval.

7. Type up an itinerary for Bruce Johnson who will be going to Pennsylvania on a business trip from September 24 to 27. Mr. Johnson will be staying at the Pocono Hershey Lodge on September 24 and 25. The lodge is located on Route 22 West in Pocono. Mr. Johnson is attending a meeting of the ASTM scheduled for September 25 and 26. He is flying to Scranton on September 24, leaving your city at 5:06 p.m. on United flight 451 and arriving in Scranton at 8:30 p.m. He will then drive a rented car, which you have already reserved, from Scranton to the lodge.

On September 26, Mr. Johnson is leaving Scranton to travel to Burlington, Vermont, where he will be speaking to the SAS on September 27. He is flying out of Scranton at 9:30 p.m. on September 26 and will arrive in Burlington at 10:15 p.m. He will be spending the night at a Quality Inn on Route 24 East. The SAS meeting starts at 9 a.m. on September 27. Mr. Johnson plans to fly out of Burlington on September 27 at 1:20 p.m. and arrive back in your city at 3:05 p.m. on United 344. You can supply any additional information that is not given in this problem.

LANGUAGE SKILLS DEVELOPMENT

1. Rewrite the following sentences, eliminating any errors.
   a. Speaking in a loud voice the meeting was called to order by Sam.
   b. The employers were more frightened by the rumour then they cared to say.
   c. All the children which are in first grade should not be at school untill 10:00 a m.
   d. It is generally understood, of course that the floor does not need to be waxed.
   e. Obviously, moved by the size of the crowd the speaker gave an excellent presentation.
   f. On her 1st day on the job Joyce, was fifteen minutes later.
   g. The following people should be prepared to give there reports tomorrow; Hal, Edith and Joanne.
   h. Arranging the papers on the desk, the vase fell off and broke before Adam could catch it.

2. Form the plurals of the following words:
   a. court martial
   b. bill of lading
   c. cupful
   d. IOU
   e. deer
   f. memorandum
   g. baby
   h. bird dog
   i. comedy
   j. copy
3. Put hyphens in any of the following words which need them:
   a. black and white television set
   b. highly paid worker
   c. Cuyahoga County taxes
   d. Minneapolis St. Paul road
   e. quiet mannered man
   f. up to date book
   g. old fashioned dress
   h. forty six year old woman
   i. self contained person
   j. vice president Morris

HUMAN RELATIONS INCIDENTS

1. Bob is executive assistant to Mr. Coach, who is a representative in the marketing department. Recently, Bob discovered that Mr. Coach has been padding his travel expense form. The amount of money usually is not a large sum ($25 or less). Bob is not sure what his obligation is in this situation. Should he confront Mr. Coach with his finding? Should he just keep quiet? What would you recommend that Bob do?

2. Rita is an executive assistant to Mr. Reynolds, who is vice-president of international sales. Three gentlemen from another country will be visiting the company next week. Mr. Reynolds told Rita confidentially that it is important that these gentlemen have a good time while they are visiting. Mr. Reynolds asked Rita if she would help entertain the guests one evening for dinner and dancing at a nice restaurant on the outskirts of town. Mr. Reynolds asked Rita to bring a couple of her girlfriends also to the dinner to help with the entertaining. Rita is confused about Mr. Reynold's invitation and is reluctant to attend the dinner. Is this part of her job? What would you suggest for Rita?

SETTING UP MEETINGS

Meetings are a necessary and often very productive way of conducting business. True, many business people complain about the frequency and obligation of attending meetings. Poorly planned meetings can be devastating to individuals, as well as time and money wasting to organizations. Most organizations spend between 7 percent and 15 percent of their personnel budgets directly on meetings. Some meetings are poorly prepared, the speakers are incompetent, or the meeting is not necessary.

However, it is a fact of business life that people must communicate in groups to get things accomplished, and a large majority of businesses, organizations, and associations could not function without meetings. A well-run meeting can be a stimulating, dynamic, face-to-face means of communicating. If they are well prepared and adhere to formalized proceedings, meetings can develop solutions collectively; and problems can be solved in the best possible manner.

The executive assistant should possess an awareness of the policy of conducting meetings. Usually, business meetings are conducted according to procedures outlined in the universally accepted *Robert's Rules of Order*.

The executive assistant should work very closely with the executive responsible for organizing and implementing the meeting, conference, or convention. The degree of support varies from executive to executive and the size and complexity of each meeting. Some principal areas of executive assistant involvement include room and site selection, correspondence with speakers, participants, and panelists, invitations, audio/visual materials scheduling, conference materials, agendas, recording and transcribing minutes, and miscellaneous follow-up.

The purpose of meetings and conferences is to bring people together, to explore issues and problems, to make new decisions, to exchange views, to solve problems, to make recommendations, to educate, to inform, to demonstrate, and in some cases, to entertain.

The executive assistant to a busy executive will be involved with the task of helping to prepare for meetings, reporting meetings, and assisting in follow-ups afterward. At the end of this chapter you should be able to:

1. Describe the executive assistant's responsibilities in helping to set up meetings. ☐ 2. Explain the criteria used for site selection for informal meetings. ☐ 3. Explain how to set up and type an agenda. ☐ 4. Know how to take and type minutes for meetings.

CHAPTER 23

INFORMAL MEETINGS

Informal meetings are usually held on the company premises and usually relate to normal business activity. As soon as your employer informs you that a meeting will be planned, it is your responsibility to begin some of the preplanning groundwork. Informal meetings may not be complicated, but they must be carefully planned. The following steps should be taken in planning an informal meeting:

☐ *Select a time and date that are convenient for all participants.* This task might involve communicating with the executive assistants of other executives. They will know if the executive is available and may give you a confirmation on the spot. After a date and time has been selected, a notation on your executive appointment calendar should be made.

☐ *Send a written reminder of the meeting after the phone communication has been established.* The form should be very simple and should be timed to arrive the day before the meeting. In addition, an agenda of topics should be distributed so that members can prepare appropriate responses and contributions.

MEMORANDUM

TO: Robert Strumphler, Admissions Department
FROM: Joseph Reihing, Marketing Department
DATE: April 17, 19—

SUBJECT: ADMISSIONS CRITERIA FOR NEW
             HOTEL/RESTAURANT PROGRAM

This is just a reminder that our meeting to discuss admissions criteria for the Hotel/Restaurant Program will be held on Monday, April 24, at 9 a.m. in the Conference Room of Building A.

☐ *Prepare the room.* If the meeting is scheduled to take place in a company conference room, you may provide refreshments. Materials, reports, and correspondence for each participant can be distributed before the meeting. If the meeting is to be in the executive's personal office, make sure that the room is in good order with enough chairs available for all members and that all the materials needed are assembled.

☐ *If requested, you may need to sit in on the meeting to distribute materials, take notes, and generally assist the executive in a variety of supportive services.* Informal meetings may lack established protocol, procedures, or rules of order characteristic of larger meetings. The advantages of an informal meeting usually relate to the small number of participants. It is easy to call people together quickly, and the meeting can progress on an informal and flexible basis.

☐ *At the end of the meeting, make sure that the room is in good order and that materials are collected and returned to the proper individuals.* If you recorded the minutes, they should be typed, reviewed by the chairperson, and distributed to the parties involved.

SITE SELECTION AND MEETING ROOMS

The physical surroundings of a meeting location site or room can affect the meeting's outcome. That is not to say that a comfortable and physically attractive meeting room will guarantee a good meeting, but an inappropriate meeting room may contribute to a poor and unproductive meeting.

The executive assistant may not make the final decision as to where to hold the next meeting of the board of directors, but some assistants often have input concerning the site selection; and their responsibilities include arranging the meeting room.

Consider a change of environment for your next meeting. Instead of the usual staff meeting in the company meeting room, arrange your meeting in a downtown hotel. A hotel atmosphere can be a change of pace from an

Figure 23.1
An executive assistant placing material on conference table prior to meeting (Courtesy of G.F. Business Equipment Co.).

Figure 23.2
Meeting room (Courtesy of Herman Miller, Inc.).

office meeting room; in fact, many hotel staffs are experts in planning and arranging business meetings for 10 to 1000 participants. You simply arrange with the hotel staff for the executive's needs, and everything is settled. Using the services of professional hotel meeting planners is comparable to using the services of a travel agent when planning a trip.

The executive assistant and executive in charge of meeting planning may decide to select a hotel meeting site that is in a central city. This may facilitate easy accessibility for participants arriving from various parts of the city. For a meeting where most of the participants are arriving from other cities, an airport hotel facility may be the best solution.

The number of people attending a meeting determines the size of the meeting space. Not only the correct shape of the meeting room should be chosen but also the correct size. Too large a room for a small group of people will result in an uncomfortable feeling. The participants may feel intimidated by the huge surrounding empty space. Sounds will echo; people will not be able to hear because there is nothing to contain and reflect voices.

Conversely, in a too small room, people will feel crowded and uncomfortable. Overcrowded conditions will produce a hot, stuffy room. These negative environmental factors will lead to disinterest, fatigue, and lack of concentration.

Executive assistants and meeting planners must make an estimate of the number of people expected and then choose a room that fits the group. Hotel staffs offer business firms various brochures and/or meeting planner's guides which include room layouts and other services essential for successful meetings.

LUNCHEON AND DINNER BUSINESS MEETINGS

The luncheon and dinner business meeting can provide an excellent atmosphere for top executive sessions, directors meetings, and award presentations. Whether a luncheon meeting is planned in a local restaurant or a restaurant within a hotel, care must be taken to ensure that the facilities are adequate and private, and the food, service, and ambience are first rate.

If you use a hotel, you should rely heavily on the expertise of the hotel and convention bureau staff. By explaining the goal of each food or beverage function succinctly, you can receive valuable assistance in planning everything from the seating arrangements to the menu.

Consider these points when planning luncheon or dinner meetings:

- [ ] Type of food or beverage function, such as dinner, dance, business, or cocktails.
- [ ] Time of day.
- [ ] Expected attendance.
- [ ] Type and size of rooms needed, seating capacity, and decor.
- [ ] Lighting and ventilation control.
- [ ] Restrictive policies or practices which may affect your function.
- [ ] Who will arrange room set-up; who will clean.
- [ ] Table identification, place cards, or programs.
- [ ] Decorations, flowers, and props.
- [ ] Menus.
- [ ] Entertainment.
- [ ] Audio/visual equipment.
- [ ] Cost factors.

If a meeting is held in a hotel room, the group may prefer to work right through lunch. If time is of the essence, you can have room service, and meetings may progress right up to the time the food is served.

CONVENTIONS

Large-scale conventions and conferences require intricate planning since they entail a variety of special services. The executive assistant usually works with the hotel or convention staff in planning these events. The greater the amount of lead time, the better planned a convention will be. Some hotels require several years of notice to book their facilities.

As an executive assistant, you may be involved in the early planning stages of a convention. Site selection should be consistent with the size of the group. Although some convention planners book resort facilities and combine their meetings with pleasurable surroundings, others confine their meetings strictly to inner-city locations.

If the schedule is crammed with meetings during the course of the day, resort locations have little attraction for attendees because they cannot take advantage of the external facilities. In planning meeting schedules, therefore, it would be better to schedule enough time before, after, or between meetings to enable the convention participants to tour the surroundings and use the facilities. Often the participants bring their families to conventions; therefore, a resort is a good place to keep them entertained.

When will you want to hold your meeting? Determine the weather at various potential meeting sites during that period. Don't dismiss a particular site because you believe you might be going there in the off-season. You might actually be choosing one of the most attractive times of the year, and rates may be lower, facilities less crowded, and services more available.

Most meeting sites operate convention bureaus. Write and request information on meeting facilities, accommodations, transportation, sightseeing, and recreation. The promptness and quality of their responses should give you an idea of the appropriateness of their meeting sites.

The convention bureau should be able to provide a complete list of hotels and their facilities. Additional information can be gathered from the individual hotels. Your hotel selection process should include an analysis of the quality of the hotel, accommodations, services, meeting rooms, convenience and accessibility, food services, general attitude of personnel, transportation, and costs.

You may find that a particular hotel satisfies all of your criteria except size. Before eliminating the hotel from your consideration, determine whether there are nearby hotels which could accommodate part of your group.

You should visit the hotel prior to the convention date and confer with the hotel staff or convention coordinator to make sure that the facilities are adequate and that plans are moving along as scheduled. Having selected your hotel(s), you will want to review the following requirements with the hotel convention director:

1. Expected attendance and type of meeting.
2. Dates you prefer; what convention rates apply.
3. The group's arrival and departure times.
4. Sleeping accommodations needed; number, type of rooms needed (single or double), rates for each.
5. Number of hospitality suites needed, dates, types, and rates.

6. Who will supply, mail, and type reservation forms; where they will be returned; who will handle confirmation and room assignments.
7. Release date for unassigned accommodations.
8. Rules, regulations, licenses needed, and hotel policies and laws applicable to your meetings.
9. Who will sign the letter of agreement; when it will be signed.

SPEAKERS FOR CONVENTIONS

The executive assistant may first contact the potential guest speaker by phone or letter. You may be asked to compose a letter to ask a guest speaker to participate in the convention. It is important to include all essential information, such as dates, topics, locations, and reimbursement policies. A sample letter requesting a speaker for an educational convention is shown below.

Dear Professor Gilmore:

Each year the State Department of Education is host for a two-day convention for teachers of business and distributive education. This year's convention is scheduled for Thursday and Friday, March 17 and 18, at the Holiday Inn in Los Altos Hills.

We would very much like to have you speak as the representative of the two-year colleges. The topic of your speech would be "Articulation."

The stipend is $150 plus expenses. You should be able to fly in about noon of March 17 and be gone by 7:30 p.m.

I would appreciate hearing from you by January 15 because the program needs to go to the printer soon after that date. Because of your unique position in the two-year college, the message that you could bring to the teacher educators would be a major contribution to this convention.

     Sincerely,

If time is of the essence and you need a speedy commitment because of printing schedules, a telephone call to a prospective speaker may be more appropriate than a letter.

After the speaker has accepted the invitation to participate, a follow-up letter is necessary to confirm the details and supply additional information. The following letter is an example of a follow-up letter.

Dear Dr. Levy:

I am delighted that you have agreed to participate in our Annual Chiropractic Convention. The convention will be held in Los Angeles, July 13–17, 19—, at the Bonadventure Hotel.

This year's theme "Chiropractic Goal Rush!" should give an indication of the vast array of topics the program presents. There is a tremendous amount of excitement regarding this convention. I'm certain the registrants who attend your session will profit from your extensive experience.

We are trying to get the conference organized and would appreciate an outline of your topic as soon as possible. Also, please send a picture (black-and-white glossy) and biography.

The association will, of course, pay for your travel expenses, hotel accommodations, and meals.

Again, thank you for your support, and I will be in touch with you in the next two or three weeks to provide you with additional information.
　　　　Sincerely,

AUDIO/VISUAL EQUIPMENT AND REQUIREMENTS

To determine the need for audio/visual or equipment requirements, ask the speakers what their needs are. The speakers may request such items as an easel, a chalkboard, a movie projector, or wooden pointer. If a speaker wants to show a film, offer to secure the equipment and a projectionist. If the request is for large or heavy equipment, get enough porters from the hotel to help your speaker. Use a checklist to help plot meeting rooms and audio/visual requirements.

Arrangements must be made with the hotel security staff to make sure that equipment and vendor displays are protected against theft and vandalism. The security staff will also monitor hotel rooms and patrol general hotel areas where people gather to assure personal safety and security.

The executive assistant's role in assisting the executive in convention planning may require the task of assembling all the printed information, typing the final copy, and forwarding it to a printer according to schedule. Examples of printed convention materials are announcements, program booklets, special hotel rate cards, name tags, luncheon tickets, rosters, and special convention folders.

After the information is completed and returned from the printer, the executive assistant may coordinate the efforts of assembling this in a special folder or packet. This folder may include a convention booklet describing the schedule of events, location of meetings, list of vendors, hours of exhibits, and speakers' backgrounds.

The packet may also include luncheon tickets, roster of attendees, name tags, association literature (application blanks, publication orders, sample publications), writing paper, and various maps and tourist attractions for the convention city.

REGISTRATION DESK

A registration desk should be set up in the hotel lobby. The registration desk should be staffed by people who will be responsible for registering the attendees, collecting money (if necessary), and distributing the convention packets. To facilitate distribution, conference name tags or badges can be prepared in advance and arranged in alphabetical order.

Decisions must be made about the organization and placement of the registration desk. The executive assistant should make sure that the signs are placed in strategic locations to alert incoming guests where to register for the meetings.

MISCELLANEOUS RESPONSIBILITIES

Responsibility for coordinating a large-scale convention is a time-consuming and demanding task. Every meeting or convention is unique, often requiring

Figure 23.3
Planning a conference (Courtesy of American Seating).

one or more services not previously mentioned. Below is a listing of miscellaneous items of importance which may apply to convention responsibilities of the executive assistant:

1. Telephone equipment in meeting rooms and hospitality suites; telephone message service.
2. Rest room locations.
3. Parking and garage facilities.
4. Photographer.
5. Coffee service.
6. Entertainment and decorations.
7. Publicity: preparing news releases and announcements to be sent to magazines, journals, and newspapers.
8. Programs for spouses and families, such as tours, luncheons, and recreational facilities.

DUTIES DURING THE CONVENTION

On the day of the convention, the executive assistant and other staff members should arrive early to check on last-minute preparations. A quick visual inspection of the meeting rooms is needed to ensure that chairs have been properly arranged, ventilation and lighting is adequate, and all visual and audio equipment is in place. Nothing frustrates a speaker more than to find the equipment in the room not set up. It is devastating to speakers to "fuss" with setting up screens, inserting slides into trays, or threading films into projectors.

Coordination with the hotel staff regarding meal arrangements should be next on the list. Provision should be made for some degree of flexibility in this area. Extra place settings should be prepared for unexpected guests.

After all the rooms and equipment have been checked, the executive assistant should be available at the reception desk to greet conference members with a pleasant welcome. It is important to coordinate the efforts of assistants who help greet conventioneers and direct them to coat-check rooms, registration areas, and convention meetings.

Once the convention has begun, the executive assistant should move away from the registration area (good assistants should be able to handle this operation) and circulate to troubleshoot any problem, direct speakers to rooms, and generally work with the hotel staff in offering any assistance.

THE AGENDA

An agenda is a list of topics to be discussed at a meeting or conference. The agenda is mailed to participants prior to the meeting in order to allow them time to review the proposed topics. This advance notice is prepared by a chairperson or recording secretary and is usually typed by the executive assistant. Even though items may be unarranged when they are handed to the executive assistant, it is the responsibility of the executive assistant to type the agenda in good order.

The format for an agenda will vary, but these items are usually included:[1]

1. Call to order.
2. Announcements and introductions of new members and guests.
3. Reports of standing committees.
4. Old business.
5. New business.
6. Adjournment.

An announcement of an agenda follows:

PARENT-TEACHER ASSOCIATION
John F. Kennedy High School
Springfield, Missouri
Saturday, March 8, 19—

AGENDA

1. Call to order, Leonard Spector, President
2. Review and Approval of Minutes of February Meeting
3. President's Report
4. Treasurer's Report—Edward Casio
5. Fund Raising Committee Report—Joan Viscosi
6. List of School Problems—Marge Landers
7. New Business—Plan to increase parent participation—Barbara Halpern
8. Adjournment

MINUTES

Minutes are a record, usually in summary form, of the proceedings of a meeting. It is the responsibility of a recording secretary of an organization to take minutes. However, in small, informal groups the task of taking minutes usually rests with the executive assistant. The person assigned to take minutes should arrive early to make any preparations necessary. Minutes can be recorded using shorthand or a recording machine. Whatever the method, the executive assistant should plan for adequate supplies—enough pencils and papers or a dictation machine in good working order with an adequate supply of audio cassettes.

If you are required to take shorthand, you serve as a neutral observer, capturing the ideas and thoughts and recording key words or phrases. If you

---

[1]Arnold Rosen, *AVT Machine Transcription* (New York: Media Systems Corporation. A subsidiary of Harcourt Brace Jovanovich, Inc., 1975), p. 171.

try to record too much, you will probably fall behind. If you record too little, your minutes will appear overly abbreviated, and you may often miss some important points. The trick is to listen for key words and phrases. Try to capture basic ideas and the essence of what the speaker is saying.

The executive assistant's role also may be supportive to the chairperson who conducts the meeting. If the chairperson forgets something during a meeting, the executive assistant may, at the discretion of the chairperson, politely interrupt the meeting to offer the correction or significant information that has bearing on the discussion.

You need stamina to take good minutes; you must write fast. You have a great deal of information in your head and must continue to digest it. Here are some suggestions to help you take minutes at a meeting:

- ☐ Listen for key words or phrases.
- ☐ Try to capture basic ideas, the essence of the thought.
- ☐ Don't write down every word.
- ☐ Underline or use asterisks or circle key motions or suggestions for highlighting during transcription.

Whether the minutes are transcribed from shorthand notes or machine recording, they must be correct, complete, and consistent with company policy. The format for the minutes of a meeting will vary, but these items will usually be included:[2]

1. Time, date, and place of the meeting.
2. Names of members present and members absent.
3. Name of presiding officer.
4. Approval, disapproval, or approval with amendments of the minutes of the previous meeting.
5. All important topics discussed, in the order of presentation, including motions and resolutions, usually including the names of the persons making the motions or resolutions and the seconds.
6. Items tabled for future action.
7. Time of adjournment.
8. Signature of the secretary who prepared the minutes.

Following is an example of correctly transcribed minutes.

FIVE TOWNS RESTAURANT ASSOCIATION
Executive Board Meeting
Charley's Steak Pub
Route 37
Hamilton, Ohio
January 31, 19—

Attendance: Kay Thompson, Lionel Birdsong, Donna Chester,

---

[2]Ibid., pp. 172–173.

	Nicholas Mosely, Donald Hall, Erv Stedberg, Leslie Petro
Staff:	Lorraine Lomax

1. OPENING REMARKS

The meeting was called to order at 2:05 p.m. by President Kay Thompson.

2. APPROVAL OF MINUTES

The minutes of the December meeting were approved.

3. CONVENTION UPDATE

Lorraine Lomax explained that plans for the June Convention scheduled for Columbus, June 21–23, 19—, were progressing well. Don Hall presented convention promotional material prepared by Adam Walters.

4. CHAPTER EXHIBITS AND CONFERENCES

The following motion was made after a lengthy debate.

Motion: To draft a statement for board approval asking chapters not to conduct equipment shows.

Petro, Chester   Carried

5. OPEN MEMBERSHIP TO CHEFS

Donald Hall presented a proposal to change the by-laws to accept chefs as members of the Five Town Restaurant Association.

Motion: Not to change Association by-laws.

Petro, Chester   Carried

6. TRUTH IN MENUS

The problem of false claims on menus was introduced by Kay Thompson. This is a problem that downgrades the restaurant business. A subcommittee will look into the problem and report recommendations at the next meeting. The subcommittee will be composed of Kay Thompson, Lionel Birdsong, and Nicholas Mosely.

7. ADJOURNMENT

There being no further business, Kay Thompson adjourned the meeting.

SUMMARY

The range and complexity of meetings vary from an informal conference in an executive's office to an elaborate board of director's meeting held in an oak-paneled, plushly carpeted conference room, to a national convention attracting hundreds of participants.

Whatever type of meeting the executive might be involved in, the executive assistant will usually be the one who will spend time and energy planning and arranging the details that are necessary for any successful meeting.

1. Arranging meetings and helping the executive are additional duties for the administrative assistant.
2. Professional hotel and conference staffs work very closely with executive assistants to ensure that meetings and conferences run smoothly.
3. Most executive assistants are involved in informal meetings; that is, meetings held within the office premises.
4. Some administrative assistants have input concerning site selection and the arrangement of meeting rooms for conferences.
5. Luncheon meetings provide a good atmosphere to conduct business activities.
6. An agenda is a list of topics to be discussed at a meeting or conference.
7. Minutes are a record, usually in summary form, of the proceedings of a meeting.
8. The role of the executive assistant at a meeting is to record the proceedings, act as a neutral observer, and sometimes support the chairperson with facts and significant information.
9. Formats of agendas and minutes may vary, but they should be accurate and consistent.

CHAPTER RECALL
EXERCISES

1. Compare the difference between a meeting and a convention.
2. Describe some preparations an executive assistant must make for informal meetings.
3. What criteria is used in selecting meeting rooms?
4. What are some of the advantages of selecting an off-premises meeting site?

5. The number of people attending a meeting determines the size of the meeting space. Explain this statement.
6. What precautions should an executive assistant take to ensure a successful luncheon meeting?
7. What are some of the advantages in holding a convention during the off-season?
8. Briefly describe how a hotel convention director can help the executive assistant to plan the convention.
9. What is the purpose of setting up a convention registration desk?
10. List the items to be included in an agenda.
11. What are some guidelines for the executive assistant to follow to take minutes?

PROBLEMS AND APPLICATIONS

1. Your employer has asked you to plan a luncheon meeting for six clients who will be arriving from out of town. You have made arrangements with an ethnic restaurant specializing in meat dishes. One hour prior to the luncheon you discover that one of the clients is a vegetarian. What can you do?

2. You have sent a letter to a prominent person inviting her to speak at a conference sponsored by your employer. She writes back to you indicating that she would be very happy to speak at your conference, but she has had a bad experience at the conference hotel. If you would consider changing the hotel, she would be glad to participate. How would you reply to this person?

3. You have worked hard preparing a special conference for your employer. As you listen to the keynote speaker in the dining room, you are embarrassed for the speaker because the noise of the waiters clearing dishes is drowning out the speaker. A similar format is scheduled for a luncheon tomorrow. What can you do to ensure a quieter setting for the speaker?

4. You have taken minutes during an informal conference hosted by your employer. A rough draft of the minutes is submitted for your employer's approval. You get the minutes returned with these notes:

"These minutes are too long. You are to summarize only the highlights. Certain directions, policies, and statements made at our meeting are not to be recorded formally; they are just mentioned orally and should not be made part of the minutes."

After your employer's recommendations, you are still not clear on exactly what is meant. What should you do?

5. Write a letter to a local radio or television personality and invite her or him to be the keynote speaker at the Founder's Day banquet of an organization in which you are supposedly a member. Be sure to include all the facts and information the speaker needs in order to make a decision.

6. Attend a meeting of an organization of which you are a member and keep the minutes of the meeting. Type a copy of the minutes. If you are not a member of an organization, attend a local Board of Education or council meeting and take minutes.

7. Assume you are attempting to organize a new professional organization for students who are majoring in office systems. Type up an agenda of the first organizational meeting.

8. Visit your local visitor's bureau, convention center, or chamber of commerce to see what materials are available for groups that are interested in holding meetings or conventions in your town or city.

LANGUAGE SKILLS DEVELOPMENT

1. Choose the correct word in each sentence:
   a. This letter is (in direct, indirect) conflict with what the training department instructed us to do.
   b. (In direct, Indirect) lighting may be the most economical way to light this room.
   c. (Thats, That's) exactly what I was referring to yesterday.
   d. (None, No one) of the reports meet our high standards.
   e. (None, No one) in the group could make it to the organizational meeting scheduled on Sunday.
   f. The cat turned over and started to lick (it's, its) leg.
   g. (Their, There) are days when I wish I had stayed in bed.
   h. (Already, All ready) the days are getting shorter and the leaves on the trees are starting to change colors.
   i. When you are (already, all ready) to go, let me know; and I'll get the car.
   j. There is going to be a lively debate (among, between) the contestants.
2. See how many errors you can find in this letter. Rewrite the letter, making any needed corrections and changes.

Dec. 2, 19—

Dear Sirs;

Please be advised that on August 14th I ordered a glass door for my screened in patio. It arived yesterday but it did not fit anywhere near properly.

I do realize now that I might have made a gloss error when measuring the door but I know that you must realize that errors do happen, don't they. I am writing you now to ask if there is something that can be done?

Please realise that I would be very appreciateve of any suggesions you can make that will save me the additional expence of buying a new glass door for my patio.

Respectively Yours,

HUMAN RELATIONS INCIDENTS

1. Your boss, Ms. Jenkins, is the president of a professional organization for this year. This is a very prestigious position, and she wants to do a good job for the organization. Ms. Jenkins is in charge of making most of the planning decisions regarding the annual convention to be held in a neighboring state. However, she does not seem willing to delegate any of the responsibilities of the convention either to you or to anyone else in the organization. You feel your past experience with conventions could help Ms. Jenkins. She is getting behind in her regular work responsibilities, in addition to working evenings and weekends for the professional organization. How can you convince Ms. Jenkins to let you help her with these arrangements?

2. Abbie is executive assistant to Mr. Heckler. Mr. Heckler is in the process of arranging for a large meeting to be held in a state which is located about 800 miles from the company. Since there are a lot of things to be done at the meeting, Mr. Heckler asked Abbie to accompany him to this meeting. Abbie is excited about going to the meeting and would like to attend, but the problem is that she is deathly afraid of flying in an airplane. She has never flown before and does not want to try it. What can Abbie do? Should she tell Mr. Heckler?

USING THE CALCULATOR

Today, executive assistants in the electronic office do a good deal more than answer the telephone, transcribe dictation, and file. They are surrounded by electronic technology and equipment that relieve them of some of the repetitive work characteristic of past generations.

The electronic calculator is usually a small but powerful and sophisticated instrument. Inside, a tiny *microcircuit*, smaller than a postage stamp, replaces thousands of transistors in earlier devices. This miniaturization is a product of space-age technology.

For the executive assistant, the electronic calculator can be a useful tool in assisting the executive with calculating commissions or costs, maintaining petty cash funds, postal costs, expense reports, bank and security transactions, purchase orders, invoices, and doing other transactions that can be adapted to the calculator.

An executive assistant in a small office might use the calculator for figuring the weekly or monthly payroll, assisting with royalty or commission rates, and very often, assisting the executive with handling certain private financial transactions, such as assembling records in preparing income tax returns.

In a business world that is more competitive than ever, knowledge of the electronic calculator is another asset that is certain to enhance your qualifications. It gives you an added edge to be able to figure quickly and accurately any type of application. You need not be a mathematics whiz to master the numbers around you. Just a little imagination, and you will be able to calculate practically any business or personal application.

At the end of this chapter, you should be able to:

1. Name the applications for the use of electronic calculators. ☐ 2. Name the criteria used for selecting a calculator. ☐ 3. Distinguish between display, printing, and programmable models of calculators.

CHAPTER 24

APPLICATIONS FOR THE CALCULATOR

Large firms usually have separate accounting or payroll departments to handle the firms' financial transactions. In a small firm or decentralized department, the executive assistant may be asked to maintain or assist with financial records.

PETTY CASH FUND

When cash is needed to make payment or reimburse employees quickly and conveniently, a petty cash fund is established. The fund may range from $10 to $100 and should be kept in a locked cash box and stored in the office safe or locked desk drawer overnight. As an executive assistant, you will be responsible for controlling the records of the petty cash fund. The electronic calculator will help you keep a running total of petty cash expenditures and check on the individuals who are spending excessively from the fund. As the cash is depleted, a check is issued, periodically, to replenish the fund.

In replenishing the petty cash fund, you should prepare a summary report of all payments made. A voucher should accompany each cash expenditure. It should show the amount paid, the date, to whom the payment was made, the purpose of the payment, and the signature or initials of the person authorizing payment.

POSTAL RECORDS

Another financial task for the executive assistant is maintaining postal records. The executive assistant in the electronic office may use a postage meter to record postage. If no postage meter is available, it is important to know the number of first-class letters you have mailed, the number that are domestic versus international, and the number of packages mailed, by weight and type of handling. This information will permit you to reconcile all the postage expenditures. From your records you can quickly calculate that 376 letters at 20 cents postage amounts to $75.20, without resorting to pencil and paper calculations.

NUMBERS IN CORRESPONDENCE

A calculator can be very handy to check outgoing letters, memos, or reports that contain arithmetic calculations. Not only must you be an excellent proofreader, but you must also doublecheck any mathematical calculations in the body of letters. You can do this easily by using your calculator. For example, 13 boxes of magnetic cards at $28.76 a box should equal $373.88. Or, if your employer is quoting a price, minus a discount of 6 percent, you would multiply the price, $373.88, by the discount ($373.88 × .06 = $22.43) and then subtract this from the undiscounted price ($373.88 − $22.43 = $351.45).

BANK RECONCILIATIONS

In a small office, it may be your responsibility to reconcile a bank statement, usually at the end of the month. The calculator makes this task easy, especially if you follow the directions listed on the reverse side of many bank statements.

PAYROLL RECORDS

Separate payroll departments are responsible for completing payroll records for employees in large organizations. There are numerous occasions, however, when the executive assistant is expected to prepare the payroll. Computing a payroll is very detailed and demands a great deal of mathematical accuracy. Federal and state laws require that payroll data cover how much each employee earned and how much has been withheld from wages for various deductions.

Payroll information must be recorded on special forms which are consistent with state and federal regulations. These forms are completed each pay period, and the data is then transferred to the employees' forms so that they may have a record of their earnings.

Following is an example of how you might calculate a weekly payroll report:

Total Earnings.   Total earnings consist of pay for regular hours worked plus pay for overtime hours worked. Regular earnings can be found by multiplying total hours by the hourly rate. Overtime pay is usually 1.5 times the hourly rate.

Deductions.   FICA (Social Security) tax is deducted from the employee's wage each pay period. The exact amount of this deduction can be found by knowing the present FICA tax rate and the wage rate for each employee. This rate is subject to change by Congress.

A withholding tax deduction is determined by the employee's earnings and the number of personal exemptions to which the employee is entitled. You should refer to a special withholding tax table provided by the Internal Revenue Service for the amount of this deduction.

Some cities, counties, and states require a tax on personal income to be deducted from the employee's earnings. You should be familiar with such deductions by consulting the local state or municipal tax office.

Additional payroll deductions, such as health and hospital group premiums, payroll deductions for government bonds, and employee dues may be made on a voluntary basis.

In order to calculate the net pay for each employee, you would calculate the total deductions for each employee and subtract this figure from total earnings or gross pay to determine the net pay earned by each employee.

INVOICES

Another very common business application used by the executive assistant in which an electronic calculator would be suitable is extending invoices.

You might be involved in preparing such financial statements as purchase requisitions, purchase orders, and sales invoices. You might be required to complete the following calculations:

1. *Extending an invoice to find the individual amount for each item and the total amount.*
   a. Set the decimal control at 2. The decimal control permits you to set any number of decimal points desired which will appear in each calculation and the total.
   b. Multiply the unit price of each item by the quantity to find the individual amount.
   c. Accumulation register is a built-in memory which may be entered directly and accumulated with either the subtotal or total key.
   d. Add the accumulation register or the add register. The add register holds (stores) an accumulated negative or positive balance to find the total amount.
2. *Extending invoices with quantity pricing.* This application allows you to extend invoices which include items priced by the item, by the dozen, by the case, by the carton, by the box, by the hundred (C), or by the thousand (M).
   a. Set the decimal control at 2.
   b. Convert the number of items within the quantity category; for example, when the number of items are priced by the dozen, divide by 12 and then multiply by the unit price. When the number of items are priced by the gross, divide by 144 and then multiply by the unit price. When the number of items are priced by the hundred, divide by 100 and then multiply by the unit price. When the number of items are priced by the thousand, divide by 1000 and then multiply by the unit price.
   c. Accumulate the individual products and total to find the total of the invoice.
3. *Extending invoices with cash discounts.* This application requires you to extend invoices and to find the net amounts after deducting a cash discount. Cash discounts are discounts awarded to the purchaser if the bill is paid by a certain time period. For example, 2/10, n/30 means that a purchaser who pays the bill within ten days is entitled to a 2 percent discount.
   a. Set the decimal control at 2.
   b. Find the individual amounts by converting the number of items within each category.
   c. Subtotal the accumulation register or the add register to find the gross amount.
   d. Multiply the gross amount by the percentage rate of discount.
   e. Subtract the discount into the accumulation register.
   f. Find the net amount by totaling the accumulation or add register.
4. *Extending invoices with cash discounts and sales tax.* This application

involves all of the preceding steps with the addition of a sales tax computed on the net amount.

a. Set the decimal control at 2.
b. Find the individual amounts by converting the number of items within each category and adding these items to find the gross amount.
c. Multiply the gross amount by the percentage rate of discount.
d. Subtract the discount from the gross amount to find the net amount.
e. Multiply the sales tax rate by the net amount and add this amount to the new total. This will give you the total of the invoice.

SALES COMMISSIONS

You can find the amount of commission earned by each salesperson by simply multiplying the total sales of each salesperson by the rate of commission. Not all salespersons' commissions are the same, and the rates vary depending upon the compensation plan of the individual.

SELECTION OF A CALCULATOR

Calculators have come a long way in a short time. They have gotten smaller; they are more sophisticated; and they are more economical. Because of minute chips built into computers, small calculators have astonishing powers to help executive assistants, accountants, students, housewives, and executives tackle a huge range of tasks. The electronic calculator can compute large numbers of statistics, thus freeing the human brain for more productive office tasks. The electronic calculator can compute with amazing feats of memory and execution. Those people once fearful of math can now compute statistics and business applications with ease and speed.

Knowing your own applications within the office can help determine the correct electronic calculator to fit your needs. There may be occasions when you are asked to help with this selection process. Understanding the various calculators and their features can be a bonus in your list of credentials.

The types of electronic calculators available include display, printing, combination printing and display, and programmable models. All calculators have the capacity to perform many business calculations quickly, accurately, and easily.

ELECTRONIC DISPLAY CALCULATORS

Display units are designed to be used when a printed record is not required. They range from tiny, pocket-size models to desktop units. They have a great variety of features, functions, and power sources. Following are some of the basic characteristics of the electronic display calculator:

Figure 24.1
Hewlett Packard 38 E display calculator (Courtesy of Hewlett Packard).

Display Screen. Calculations and results appear on a display screen with either light-emitting diode (LED), liquid crystal, fluorescent, or digitron.

Standard Keyboard. It features the standard ten-key keyboard which includes digits 1 through 9, as well as 0 and a decimal point.

Internal Memory. There is an internal memory system which allows numbers to flow from one register (add, subtract, multiply, and divide) to another, thus eliminating the need to reenter amounts for further calculations.

Floating Decimal Point. This feature means that the decimal automatically appears when you use the calculator.

Automatic Features. These features, such as the retention of constant multipliers or divisors, facilitate repetitive operations.

PRINTING CALCULATORS

Printing calculators include many of the features of display calculators, but they provide printed tape records for all calculations instead of displaying them. The tapes may be used to check work and can then be filed for future reference. Some units feature two-color printouts, using red to indicate negative entries.

Figure 24.2
Monroe Model 1830 programmable calculator (Courtesy of Litton Industries).

Figure 24.3
Burroughs C-7400 programmable calculator (Courtesy of Burroughs Corp.).

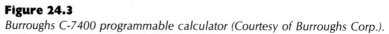

COMBINATION DISPLAY AND PRINTING CALCULATORS

This type of calculator provides all the advantages of display plus a hard copy for calculations. In most combination units, the depression of any numeric entry key will result in the appearance of the corresponding number on the display. The number displayed will not be printed until a function key is depressed. Calculated results will be printed and automatically displayed. In some models the display will show immediate results that are not printed on the tapes.

PROGRAMMABLE CALCULATORS

Programmable calculators provide the executive assistant with computer-like programmability. The user can program the machine or can purchase preprogrammed models. (See Figure 24.4.)

Programs can be stored on various media, such as magnetic cards, cassettes, or cartridges, which are read into the calculator. Preprogrammed media can be designed for a wide range of applications and enable executives and executive assistants to customize calculators for their particular needs.

SUMMARY

From tiny pocket calculators to fully programmable models, today's electronic calculators accommodate an almost unlimited range of user's needs.

For the executive assistant, this microelectronic revolution promises to ease, enhance, and simplify routine arithmetic tasks. Math functions can be performed at your desk with astonishing efficiency and speed. Mass production of the miracle chip has already made possible home computer systems that sell at a price that most people can afford, and prices will continue to fall. For most offices, the electronic calculator is as much a part of the executive assistant's equipment as a typewriter.

1. The key component of electronic calculators is the tiny microcircuits which replaces thousands of transistors used in earlier calculators.
2. Calculators are not needed for computing mailing costs if the office uses postage meters to calculate postage expenditures.
3. In a small office, the executive assistant might be asked to compute weekly payroll records.
4. Cash discounts are deducted from invoices, and sales taxes are added to invoices.
5. Calculators for office applications come in all sizes and shapes and four main categories: (1) display, (2) printing, (3) combination printing and display, and (4) programmable.
6. Typical financial applications that are suitable for electronic calculators for the executive assistant are:
   a. Petty cash disbursements.

Figure 24.4
HP-37E and HP-38E provide business management functions such as amortization scheduling, five-variable financial problem solving, and a full array of statistical and mathematical capabilities (Courtesy of Hewlett-Packard).

    b. Calculation of postal costs.
    c. Checking numbers within correspondence.
    d. Preparation of bank reconciliations.
    e. Maintenance of payroll records.
    f. Calculation of weekly payrolls.
    g. Computation of invoices.
    h. Preparation of sales invoices.
7. Programmable calculators enable the executive assistant to build in programs.

CHAPTER RECALL EXERCISES

1. How can the executive assistant effectively use an electronic calculator in her or his work?
2. How does knowledge of the electronic calculator enhance the executive assistant's qualifications?
3. Explain how a calculator can be useful in checking numbers within the body of correspondence.
4. Briefly describe how you would compute cash discounts and sales tax in an invoice.
5. List the basic characteristics of a display calculator.
6. What is the main advantage of a printing calculator?
7. Briefly describe a programmable calculator.

PROBLEMS AND APPLICATIONS

1. Part of Lucy Moldonado's responsibilities is the preparation of her employer's tax return. Four weeks after the tax form was submitted, Mr. Logan, Lucy's employer, stormed into her office shouting, "Look at this letter from the Internal Revenue Service! There is a $1500 error in the itemized expenses. They want to schedule an audit. Didn't you proofread before you sent it out? Don't you know that you should check the totals?" What can be done? Whose fault was the error?

2. Use a calculator to solve the following problems:

ADDITION

a. 42,031; 1,001; 589; 428
b. 281; 598; 337; 678; 442
c. 28.04; 691.01; 38.89; 432.45
d. 2,413.90; 2,996.43; 607.43; 24.43

SUBTRACTION

a. $488 - 21$
b. $5,003 - 346$
c. $3.456 - 2.996$
d. $561.32 - 149.99$

MULTIPLICATION

a. 341×43
b. $1,669 \times 2,436$
c. 7.642×26.43
d. $.00125 \times 21$

DIVISION

    a. 888 ÷ 91
    b. 1,221 ÷ 43
    c. 24.42 ÷ 20
    d. 4,006.91 ÷ 62.84

3. Make the extensions for the figures from the following invoices:

  a.

Quantity	Style	Description	Unit Price	Total
30	A-2	bracelets	$4.50	$
241	P-41	costume pins	2.69	
28	C-10	earrings	4.11	
			Total	$
			Shipping	$10.54
			Total	$

  b.

Quantity	Description	Unit Price	Amount
2 dozen	drills	$13.41/each	$
4 gross	garden nozzles	8.33/dozen	
200	hammers	9.25/each	
3500	bolts	21.32/thousand	
3 dozen	fly swatters	6.21/dozen	
		Total	$
		Add 6% sales tax	
		Total	$

4. Compute the net invoice cost of each of these problems.

List Price		Discount
a. $4,431	less	10 percent
b. $589.43	less	30 percent
c. $84,567.06	less	20 percent
d. $4.56	less	2 percent

5. Calculate the amount of the discount and the amount due after the discount is taken.

    a. $421.13   2/10, n/30
    b. $8,453.34   1/10, n/60
    c. $679.57   2/10, n/30

LANGUAGE SKILLS DEVELOPMENT

1. *Proofreading Exercise.* Two of the three listed numbers are identical; one is different. Identify the different number.

   a. 687-3301   687-3301   678-3301
   b. 241-38-1227   241-38-2227   241-38-2227
   c. (208) 385-2031   (208) 385-2031   (208) 385-0231
   d. (403) 258-2332   (304) 258-2332   (403) 258-2332
   e. $51,004.56 $51,004.65 $51,004.65
   f. 449-72-4825   449-72-4825   494-72-4825
   g. 665-43-673   665-43-673   665-43-763
   h. $29,078,4312 $29,078,4132 $29,078,4132

2. Choose which of the sentences below are spaced correctly.

   a. The clock was not correct;it was five minutes fast.
   b. There are 17, 573 students enrolled at the university this year.
   c. Bring the following items to typing class tomorrow: eraser, eraser shield, and correction paper.
   d. "Don't be late,"was the only thing the mother said to her son.
   e. Of course,I'll be happy to watch your house while you are away.
   f. You left the lights on again! Please be more careful in the future!

3. Correct any of the following words which are not spelled correctly.

   a. believe   f. omited
   b. accomodations   g. personnel
   c. situated   h. apologys
   d. financail   i. recieve
   e. buisness   j. reccomended

HUMAN RELATIONS INCIDENTS

1. In correspondence which you type for Ms. Rugiana, she insists that you type the % sign rather than typing the word "percent." For example, Ms. Rugiana requests that you type, "The discount is 6%." You know from reference manuals and your office procedures courses that the sentence should be typed, "The discount is 6 percent." Ms. Rugiana says that the percent sign would not be on the typewriter if it was not correct to use it; furthermore, it is faster to type %, and it certainly takes less space on the paper.

Should you type the correspondence the way Ms. Rugiana prefers or insist on typing it the correct way? Should you try to convince Ms. Rugiana to change? What would you do?

2. One day just before closing the office, you were hurriedly getting some invoices ready to be mailed. Since it was already past

5 o'clock, you quickly put the invoices in the envelopes without proofreading the figures very carefully. The next morning as you were looking at the carbon copies of the invoices, you noticed that two of the five invoices mailed have errors in the figures. The errors are not significant, less than a dollar in both cases.

Since the number of errors are so small, should you just forget about them and hope no one discovers the errors? What should you do?

A Professional Placement
Service Dedicated To The
Placement of Secretaries

TOP RATE
Pay + Cash

SPECIAL INTERESTS AND
ACTIVITIES

THE BUSINESS WORLD

Increased productivity has been achieved through the use of automated equipment. Many firms are finding that the office environment also has an impact on the productivity and morale of workers.

Employment opportunities for office work are increasing faster than the average for all other occupations. Executive assistants should be cognizant of job hunting strategies so they can choose the jobs they really want. The executive assistant has job possibilities not only in traditional executive assistant areas but also in a number of other areas. Executive assistants are moving into all areas of jobs, and many firms are actively seeking them to fill positions. ■ Chapter 25   The Office Environment □ Chapter 26   Job Hunting, Résumés, and Interviews □ Chapter 27   Career Options

SECTION VII

THE OFFICE ENVIRONMENT

Today, more than half of the labor force in the United States is employed in offices; all indications are that this trend will continue. This means that more companies will be hiring more people to work in their offices. The investment in labor is a substantial part of a company's operating budget—approximately 90 percent. For this reason, companies are becoming increasingly concerned about worker productivity.

A recent study conducted by Louis Harris and Associates for Steelcase, Inc., a leading manufacturer of office furniture, confirmed the tremendous changes taking place in offices today. The study revealed that 73 percent of office workers have learned new skills in the past five years; 72 percent have had task modifications; 45 percent have begun using computers and other types of automated office equipment; and the majority of those interviewed changed locations within an office or were working in redesigned offices.

One of the most interesting facts uncovered by the study is that 92 percent of the office workers interviewed see a direct relationship between the office environment and their job performances. An overwhelming 74 percent said they could accomplish more work in a day if their working conditions improved. These people said there were a number of obstacles in the office environment that prevented them from working as effectively as they could. Some obstacles included inadequate access to tools, materials, and equipment; noise and distractions; poor workflow; and work overload.

As more companies realize the validity of these statements, they are attempting to improve the office environment in order to increase worker productivity and improve morale.

At the end of this chapter, you should be able to:

1. Discuss the types of office environments. ☐ 2. Define the open office environment. ☐ 3. Describe what is meant by the human element in office environments. ☐ 4. Define what is needed for effective office lighting and office furniture.

CHAPTER 25

TYPES OF OFFICE ENVIRONMENTS

The executive assistant works in one of four basic types of office environments. Senior executive assistants may have private offices. Middle-level executive assistants may share offices with their executives, or they may be located just outside the offices of their executives. The fourth type of arrangement is one in which a number of executive assistants are grouped together.

CONVENTIONAL OFFICE

In the first three types of arrangements, conventional office furniture, such as desks, work tables, and file cabinets, is used. In the grouped bull-pen arrangement, either conventional or open-plan furniture can be utilized.

The conventional executive assistant office includes a desk, chair, and one or more file cabinets. Desks come in many styles, from basic steel models to elaborate wood desks. They are available with single or double pedestals in two- or three-drawer heights. An executive assistant desk usually has a typing return, giving the desk an L-shaped appearance.

OPEN OFFICE

While conventional furniture is still the most widely used furniture in offices today, experts expect that situation to change during the next decade. As the office population increases, space will become a major problem for many firms, particularly those in high-rent districts in metropolitan areas. One solution to this space crunch is the open office.

The open office concept gained in popularity during the 1970s. Today, approximately 30 percent of office workers in the United States work in some type of landscaped or open-plan office. Basically, the open office consists of movable panels that hook together to form working spaces or stations. Furniture components such as desks, files, typing returns, and shelves are hung on these panels or screens, creating modular work stations.

The open-plan concept was born in the late 1950s in Germany and Sweden. In order to increase efficiency and improve communications between office workers, designers in these two countries eliminated floor-to-ceiling walls and replaced them with free-standing panels (also called landscape screens).

Office landscaping was introduced into the United States in 1964, but the idea did not become popular until the early 1970s.

The rising cost of office space is one factor that influences many firms to try the open office approach. Open planning makes use of vertical air space since shelves, bins, and files are hung on panels instead of being placed on the floor.

The lower cost of changing space in the office is another factor. Studies show that the cost of moving traditional office walls ranges from $7 to $25 per square foot, while the cost of changing open landscaped offices is less than $1 per square foot.

Figure 25.1
Open office system (Courtesy of Vogel Peterson).

Lower cost of maintenance is another plus for the open office. With a completely open area (no floor-to-ceiling walls), there is only one heating, air-conditioning, and lighting system for the entire office area. For walled offices, each office has to have its own heating, air-conditioning, and lighting system.

Increased productivity of office workers is said to result from the better communications flow, less distracting environment, and more attractive working conditions provided by the open office.

The open office is a particular blessing to executive assistants because it provides them with more privacy than any other type of arrangement except a private office, which only top executive assistants usually have. Each executive assistant's work area is enclosed by landscape screens/panels that come in various heights to provide privacy while a person is seated (five feet high or less) or standing (six feet high or more).

These panels are movable and can be arranged in many different ways to form work areas or work stations of various shapes. The most commonly used shapes include squares, rectangles, curves, hexagons, T-shapes, Y-shapes, and cross-shapes.

Figure 25.2
Hexagonal-shaped work station (Courtesy of Westinghouse Electric Corp.).

There are two basic types of screens used to form work stations: acoustic and nonacoustic. Acoustic screens are fabric covered and absorb sound instead of bouncing it back the way a metal or wood surface does. Nonacoustic screens have no sound-absorbing qualities.

The use of acoustic screens in a work station makes the area a more pleasant place to work since the screens muffle the noise made by typewriters, telephones, and people. The executive assistant can work undisturbed by distracting noises.

In the open-plan arrangement, work stations are laid out so that employees who work together are grouped together, thereby improving the communications and workflow. For instance, an executive assistant who works for three people would be located in an area close by or adjacent to these three people. A clerk who performs a particular function—handling insurance claims, for example—would be located in an area with all the other clerks performing that function. There might even be an opening at desk height in the panels to make it easy for the clerks to pass material back and forth.

The open office is an attractive place to work. Screens and work station components come in a variety of styles, fabrics, and colors. In many companies, the old gray steel desks are being replaced by a rainbow assortment of colors and textures designed to lift the executive assistant's spirit and improve work output. Frequently, graphics are hung on the walls; carpets are laid on the floors; and plants and trees are placed in strategic positions to enliven the office environment still further.

Another advantage of the open office from the executive assistant's point of view is that open office furniture is extremely flexible. It can be put together in varying sizes and shapes and can include components or accessories designed to help the individual do a better job. These components are assigned according to job function and title because work stations are tailored to the needs of the individual worker.

For example, a clerk-typist might have a 4 × 6-foot rectangular work station with a small work surface, supply drawer, shelf, and typing stand. An administrative assistant, on the other hand, might have a work station that is 8 × 10-feet in size, with two work surfaces, a machine stand, a whole wall of files, and a small conference table.

Standard components or hang-ons (so called because they hang on screens instead of standing by themselves on the floor) include the following: work surfaces, pencil drawers, shelves, typing stands, file cabinets, tub files, machine stands, book storage units, tack and chalkboards, wardrobe units

Figure 25.3
Cluster 120 work stations (Courtesy of Esselte Pendaflex Corp.).

Figure 25.4
Right-angled word processing work station (Courtesy of Westinghouse Electric Corp.).

for storage of clothing, and trays to hold business forms, paper supplies, and file folders.

In addition to these standard components, which can be mixed and matched to fit a number of varying job functions, there are also specialized components designed for specific job tasks. A good example of this type of specialized work station is the word processing work station.

A word processing assistant must use special equipment, such as transcription equipment and text-editing typewriters. The word processing work station must be able to accommodate this equipment on machine height stands and must also have components to house the supplies needed to run these machines (tapes, magnetic cards, paper, envelopes, and typewriter ribbons). These work stations should also include acoustic screens to eliminate some of the noise made by word processing machines.

Some firms use a combination of open planning and traditional furniture. Executive assistants may find that their work stations are composed of free-standing panels and traditional desks, typing stands, and file cabinets. This is often the case when a company does not want to replace its entire furniture system, so the company uses existing desks and files with new panels.

THE HUMAN ELEMENT IN THE OFFICE ENVIRONMENT

Today's furniture systems are designed with the human element in mind. They are designed to increase worker comfort, thereby improving worker productivity. This is accomplished in a number of ways. First, noise and visual distractions are reduced through the use of acoustic panels. Second, the executive assistant's tools—typewriter, phone, files, paper—are within easy reach. In addition, work surfaces can be easily raised and lowered to allow for varying height differences, making each employee as comfortable as possible.

A variety of components can be plugged into the system as needed to accommodate each person. For instance, if a new executive assistant finds he or she does not need the former executive assistant's lateral file but does need more shelf space, the file can be easily removed and a shelf hung-on in its place. This type of flexibility makes the executive assistant's life easier since he or she does not work in an office that was designed around another person's size, needs, and work habits. Each work station is individualized to the present occupant's particular requirements.

Even though the floor space taken up by the work station may not be any larger than the area the executive assistant had before, there is more working room since shelves, files, and other components can be hung on the screen over the work surface, making use of air space rather than floor space. This also makes management happy since floor space is now quite expensive.

Another change in office furniture that is a real boon to executive assistants and typists is the introduction of posture seating. Investigations have shown that humans were not designed to sit. Squatting is actually a much more natural position. Because of the human's upright position, the back is a weak link in human anatomy. So, when a person is sitting, reading, writing, or typing, it places a strain on the back.

Chairs should be designed to support the back, and this is especially true of office chairs because office workers spend so much time sitting. However, designing back-support chairs is not as easy as it sounds because of the great variation in height, weight, size, and muscular coordination of people. Also, people working in an office just do not sit in one position. They lean over to write or type and lean back to talk or read.

In the past, an office chair was just a chair; it did nothing to improve the posture or comfort of the office worker. Recently, that situation has changed—much to the relief of executive assistants, typists, and other sedentary workers who spend so much time sitting. Posture support chairs are one of the latest, and most practical, aspects of modern office design.

A posture chair has a backrest that supports the natural (S-shape) curvature of the spine, providing both sacrum and lumbar support whether the person is sitting erect or leaning forward or backward. The seat cushion is firm enough to prevent the person from sinking too far into the cushion when sitting down, and the front edge of the seat is padded to reduce tissue pressure in the thighs.

In addition, the top edge of the backrest is contoured and is high enough to provide good support, even when the chair is tilted backward. In a chair with arms, the armrests are long enough to support the full arm and base of the hand. Armpads are firm and flat.

A good office chair will also have a height adjustment feature that allows the person sitting in it to adjust the chair for height. Chair height should be adjusted so that the feet rest on the floor without pressure on the thighs.

Since a person usually sits in an erect position when typing, the chair should provide firm support to the lower and middle back. The chair should also be without sharp edges to protect the typist from banging ankles or legs.

A good chair can mean the difference between feeling good after a long day of typing or feeling like you never want to see a typewriter again.

SYSTEMS FURNITURE

The latest advances in office furniture have resulted in systems furniture that is designed to meet the needs of the electronic office. The main requirements for this furniture are that it deal with the heat and noise produced by electronic office equipment, that it provide sufficient work space and lighting, and that it accommodate the electrical requirements of the automated office.

Electronic furniture, such as text-editing typewriters, computer terminals, and micrographics readers, produce a lot of heat and noise. Noise can be lessened by acoustic screens and acoustic machine enclosures. To cope with the heat produced by these machines, some furniture manufacturers have created vents.

Automated equipment is, for the most part, large and bulky. Therefore, furniture designed to meet the needs of people who operate the equipment must allow sufficient space for this equipment and the machine supplies. Also, machine tables must be at the proper height if the operator is to be comfortable when using them. For optimum operator comfort, there must also be sufficient lighting over the machine so eyestrain is minimized.

The main problem created by electronic office equipment is one of wire management. Every machine has an electrical wire; and if there is no place to put these wires, there can be an unsightly and unsafe tangle of wires on the floor.

Systems furniture manufacturers deal with this problem by running wires through a raceway (an open space) at the bottom of the landscape screens. The wires run through the raceway to a power pole or tube that carries the wires to electrical outlets, which may be located in the wall, ceiling, or floor, depending on the system. This keeps the wires off the floor and eliminates a potential safety hazard.

OFFICE LIGHTING

Another significant change that is taking place in today's offices is in the area of lighting. Most businesses today are still using fluorescent ceiling lights. As a result, many areas of the office have too much light because ceiling lights must provide uniform light over the entire room. So, in order to provide enough light for work areas, other parts of the room—such as aisles and walkways—have more light than is needed. This is not only expensive, but it also causes employee discomfort since the light bounces off surfaces, such as desks, files, and screens, and causes glare, which can result in eyestrain and headaches.

A new type of lighting system that provides light only where it is needed

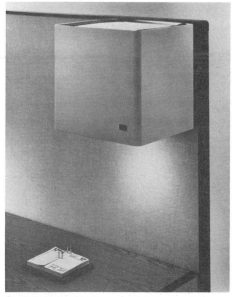

Figure 25.5

Steelcase H.I.D. lighting (Courtesy of Steelcase).

has recently been introduced and is gaining acceptance in many companies. This system is called **task and ambient lighting.**

Task (direct) lighting fixtures are placed directly above the work surface

Figure 25.6

Task lighting (Courtesy of Shaw/Walker).

to provide enough light for specific tasks such as writing, reading, and typing. It is similar to a desk lamp in concept; however, there are some important differences. The light rays are filtered through a lens that diffuses the light so that the work surface is evenly illuminated. With regular desk lamps, there is usually a band of light across the desk, while the remaining area of the desk is in shadow. With task lighting, both glare and shadow are eliminated, allowing you to see what you are reading or typing clearly without eyestrain.

Ambient (indirect) lighting fixtures replace regular ceiling lights. The ceiling has no lights or light fixtures. Instead, ambient lighting fixtures stand on the floor or attach to a landscape screen and direct light rays up to the ceiling where they are reflected back down to the floor.

Fixtures are strategically located in a room so that light is distributed to areas where it is most needed, areas where people work. Aisles and hallways would not be as brilliantly illuminated as work areas. A word processing center, for example, would be given much more light than a hallway.

You will find task and ambient lighting a pleasant surprise. You will have plenty of light in the work station, but the light will not be as harsh as regular office lighting. It will be closer to the kind of lighting you are used to at home. Glare and distracting reflections will be minimized, thus reducing eyestrain and headaches.

SUMMARY

The combination of individually tailored work stations, posture support seating, task and ambient lighting, and furniture for the electronic office is a powerful one that should make the executive assistant's life more comfortable. Executive assistants who work in an open office environment will find it functional, quiet, private, and attractive.

1. System furniture is designed around people's needs. In other words, the furniture adapts to the people instead of the other way around.
2. The open office is designed to save space, lower the cost of making changes, increase productivity, improve communications between co-workers, give needed privacy, and provide an attractive working environment.
3. There are two basic types of screens used to form work stations: acoustic and non-acoustic.
4. Posture seating makes sitting more of a pleasure.
5. Ambient lighting reduces glare and eyestrain.

CHAPTER RECALL EXERCISES

1. How does the open office differ from traditional office layouts?
2. What advantages does the open office offer the executive assistant?

3. Describe three types of traditional office layouts for the executive assistant.
4. What is the difference between acoustic and non-acoustic screens?
5. What kinds of hang-on components are needed in an executive assistant work station?
6. How does posture seating improve executive assistant comfort and productivity?
7. What is task and ambient lighting, and how does it differ from conventional lighting?
8. Why does the use of electronic furniture require a different working environment?
9. Explain how landscape screens provide both privacy and better communications between office workers.
10. What requirements are met by furniture designed for the electronic office?

PROBLEMS AND APPLICATIONS

1. You learn that your company is going to redesign the executive assistant work area. At present, all the executive assistants sit at desks in a bull-pen type of arrangement in the center of the room, while executives have private offices around the perimeter.

You have been asked by your supervisor to define your major job functions and to list the office furniture and components you think you need to accomplish those tasks most efficiently. List the functions you think should be included on this list. What components would you ask for in order to perform your duties as an executive assistant?

2. As the supervisor of a word processing center, you are responsible for the working environment in the center, as well as the personnel and equipment. After looking at various open office furniture systems, you decide that this approach would work well in your center. Now, you have to convince top management of its suitability.

Put together a report on the advantages of modular work stations, posture seating, and task and ambient lighting. Also include catalogs and photographs from manufacturers of this equipment, as well as magazine articles on the subject.

Put together a packet of materials to include in your report.

3. Visit three work areas where the open office plan is used. Make a list of the following facts:
   a. type of company.
   b. components used by the executive assistants.
   c. color of the walls in the rooms; color of the components.
   d. use of plants or other decorating devices.
   e. type of lighting used.
   f. number of people working in one work area.
   g. type of chairs used by the employees.

LANGUAGE SKILLS DEVELOPMENT

1. Look up the meanings for the following words. If you are not sure of the spellings of these words, learn to spell them. Use each word correctly in a sentence.

   alacrity   gregarious
   cognizance   inadvertent
   congruity   reciprocal

2. Choose the correct word in each sentence:
   a. If the package doesn't arrive this afternoon, (maybe, may be) we should call UPS.
   b. It (maybe, may be) that the package was lost in transit.
   c. The other dancers appeared to be (indifferent, in different) to the new steps being performed on the dance floor.
   d. Jason said the same thing but (indifferent, in different) words.
   e. I will call you (sometime, some time) next week and arrange a meeting.
   f. Even though the cake took (sometime, some time) to bake, the end result was worth the effort.
   g. (Whoever, Who ever) parked in front of that house should move his or her car immediately.
   h. (Whoever, Who ever) would write such a letter to me?

3. Put in hyphens wherever they are needed in these words:
   a. 5 inch card
   b. blunt tipped scissors
   c. low intensity lighting
   d. two thirds majority
   e. long time ago
   f. foreign markets department
   g. world trade center
   h. five year period
   i. six cylinder motor
   j. foreign made trucks
   k. thoroughly confused manager
   l. snow covered streets

HUMAN RELATIONS INCIDENTS

1. Marian worked in an office with two other executive assistants. One of the other workers insisted on keeping the temperature in the room too cool for the other workers. The others tried wearing sweaters and making comments about the cold room.

How could this situation be solved? How can everyone in the room be happy with the temperature? Should the other workers confront the one worker who insists on the cool room?

2. Dan had worked for several years as the only executive assistant in a small, conventionally arranged office. When he changed jobs, Dan was looking forward to having a job where he would have an opportunity to have more interaction with people. Dan now works at Cooper Industrials and is an executive assistant in a large room that is arranged in the open office style. After two weeks on the new job, Dan is now ready to turn in his resignation. He is distracted by the other people in the area and misses the peace and quiet of his former job. Also, periodically throughout the day, the company plays music that is "driving Dan up a wall." Dan also misses being "in charge" of an office, and he feels like he is only one small person in such a large company.

Dan asked for a transfer to a conventionally arranged office but found there are no offices like that at Coopers. What should Dan do? Is there a solution to this problem without his resigning his job?

JOB HUNTING, RÉSUMÉS, AND INTERVIEWS

Although many other areas of employment have experienced ups and downs during the past decade, the employment opportunities for office work have been and continue to be healthy. Office administration graduates of schools throughout the country are blessed with plenty of jobs—three job offers for every applicant.

Employment of executive assistants is expected to increase faster than the average for all occupations through the 1980s as the continued expansion of business and government creates a growing volume of paper work. The U.S. Bureau of Labor predicts that several hundred thousand jobs will become available each year due to growth, expansion of electronic technology,[1] and that 38 million of the 50 million white-collar jobs in the U.S. will eventually be automated.

With all of these factors favorable to the executive assistant trainee, why then is job hunting necessary? If graduates can look forward to several job offers, why hunt? Won't the jobs come to the graduates? The reason the wise executive assistant applicant develops a job hunting strategy is because he or she is discriminating, and the effort spent on job hunting depends upon the nature of office work desired. An intelligent choice means not settling for any job but seeking a job you really want. Knowing how to get a job is an acquired skill, like skiing or playing the piano. It takes practice and know-how, but it can be learned.

The prospect of looking for a job may seem overwhelming, but it need not be. Job hunting can be a traumatic experience for those who are fresh out of school or in a strange city. This chapter should provide you with a rapid rundown of the basic tools and techniques needed for job hunting.

At the end of this chapter, you should be able to:

1. Describe a job-hunting strategy. ☐ 2. List the sources of employment. ☐ 3. Give the principles for writing an effective résumé and application letter. ☐ 4. Know how to prepare for a job interview.

---

[1]New job titles, requirements, and career paths will open as the electronic office continues to make inroads into business organizations.

CHAPTER 26

JOB-HUNTING STRATEGY

The best job-hunting strategy is a well-thought-out plan that provides ample time. Do not wait until the last week before graduation to begin your job-hunting efforts.

Start a job-hunting file or folder and list the names of potential employers and personnel agencies. Include everything that pertains to that company or agency: conversations, miscellaneous information, and names of people. Be especially aware of guest speakers (office equipment salespeople, executive assistants, consultants, and government employees) who may be future employment contacts. Ask them for their business cards. Speak to representatives of companies during business and equipment shows and field trips or when they come to your school. Add their brochures and cards to your file.

In order to decide about a specific career, you must assess your own traits. Job hunting is a means to an end. Selecting the right job means determining how you are going to spend a major portion of your working time; and an intelligent selection can make those hours happy and productive rather than devastating. You are on the threshold of a critical period in your life because career decisions may be life decisions. Therefore, the better suited you are to your job, the greater your chances for success.

There is often a big difference between who you are and who others want you to be. List your assets and your liabilities. Some people are born knowing what they want to do; others discover along the way. If you have a flair for electronic equipment, start there. There are many opportunities in this area as more and more companies are converting to electronic offices.

Another key question to ask yourself is what do you like to do. This is different from "What do you do well?" because many people are good at things they do not particularly like. You need to ask yourself the reverse also: "What do you dislike?" Here again, list items in every area of your life, such as:

Do you like working with statistics?

Do you feel uncomfortable about unstructured work?

Do you like to travel?

Do you enjoy being a leader?

Do you dislike machines?

Do you yearn for big city life?

Do you enjoy working with people?

Do you prefer a private office?

How do you feel about sports? Opera? Museums? Restaurants?

What have you done in the past that you are proud of?

When you answer these questions, you are establishing guidelines for yourself. Before you begin to look for a job, you should have a fairly good idea of where you want that job to lead. Before you come to that decision, though, you have to ask yourself what your own personal priorities are and how you see your career fitting into your everyday life. It might be helpful if you were to divide your life into areas: job, family, social life, leisure, and special interests.

Assessing yourself honestly can be a helpful preliminary step to job hunting. You have to decide what kind of a job you want for yourself, not what others want for you. You might have excellent shorthand skills but find shorthand tedious. In that case, you should avoid a position that requires heavy shorthand. It is you who will be going to work every day, not your parents, your guidance counselor, or your teacher.

Be honest with your self-appraisal and bold with your ambitions. If your job-hunting strategy is well planned and your assessment is accurate, your ambitions and abilities will adjust to each other as you go along in your career.

SOURCES OF EMPLOYMENT

A well-planned job-hunting strategy includes back-up or contingency plans. Do not rely on one source. For example, the college placement office may be convenient and familiar, but do not rely on it solely. Use several sources to locate job leads. The following are sources of employment to consider in your job hunting campaign:

COLLEGE PLACEMENT OFFICE

An excellent source of job prospects is your own college placement office. It is right in your own backyard and usually attracts top companies. Your own department may have its own placement service, or a central office may integrate its efforts with all departments and provide career placement service to students. The placement office usually arranges for company representatives to conduct interviews on campus. Notices are sent out, and interested candidates may sign up for the date and company of their choice.

Career day is another source for employment leads. Schools devote an entire day to host company representatives that visit campus, set up booths, and counsel students on career choices and employment opportunities.

EMPLOYMENT AGENCIES

Many executive assistant openings are listed with employment agencies, both public and private. The employment agencies are in a position to put an employer in contact with a selected number of prospective employees.

Public Employment Agencies. There are state, county, and federal agencies located throughout the country. There is no charge for services provided by these agencies. The public agencies provide a diverse range of services for the applicant, such as:

- ☐ Testing and counseling.
- ☐ Providing information on labor supply and demand.
- ☐ Initiating training courses to help in alleviating existing shortages of qualified workers.
- ☐ Relating veteran's service training to civilian occupations.
- ☐ Developing special programs for recruiting older workers, the handicapped, and members of minority groups.

Private Employment Agencies. With the proliferation of executive assistant jobs and the need for highly skilled people to operate electronic technology, the private employment agencies are beginning to specialize in openings for executive assistants with special skills and training. Special departments and agencies are emerging to handle word processing operators, marketing support representatives, business equipment sales representatives, and other related electronic office workers.

In addition to placing executive assistants and operators, other private employment agencies specializing in placing word processing specialists for higher-level management and consulting and marketing support have a ready market for the electronic office of the future.

Private employment agencies usually charge a fee for their services; but because they specialize, it is often worth the money. In some cases, the fee for a private employment agency is the first week's salary or a percentage of the first month's salary. The fee depends largely on the nature of the open position (higher fees are usually charged for higher-level positions), the location of the agency, and the reputation of the agency.

For executive assistant and word processing positions, the trend is for the employer to pay the fee. When you register with a private employment agency, you are usually asked to sign a contract. Be sure you understand the extent of your financial obligations. Also, be sure the agency is professionally qualified to do its job. It is a good idea to check if the agency has a good reputation and has membership in a professional national employment agency association.

Temporary-Help Agencies. There are many circumstances where the job seeker is not ready to settle into a permanent job. A temporary-help agency's main function is not to place people in permanent jobs but to rent out office workers for varying periods of time, such as a day, a week, or several months.

The use of part-time or temporary-help agencies is particularly helpful to students who wish to gain valuable office experience on a part-time or temporary basis during semester breaks or during summer sessions. It can be the best of all possible worlds for the job seeker because it enables you to try out a job before making any sort of permanent commitment. It is like getting the chance to "test drive" a company to see if the ride is to your liking. In addition, a temporary-help agency provides the applicant with the opportunity to be tested and classified on the basis of present skills.

There are many agencies that specialize in executive assistant and information processing temporary jobs. When you find an office that seems right for you, you are probably in a good position to ask to stay. Often, a part-time or temporary job may lead into a permanent job.

Advertisements. Classified newspaper advertisements and magazine and journal ads are full of excellent possibilities for the diligent executive assistant. Executive assistant jobs may cover several pages in a large city newspaper. Usually, the job is for an immediate opening; and, since time is of the essence, you should look at this source when you are ready and willing to enter the job market. Besides looking under the alphabetical listing of "S" for secretary, you should search for other headings, such as:

Administrative assistant	Legal secretary
College grad	Magnetic media operator
Executive assistant	MT-MC/ST operator
Information processing	Typist
Gal/man Friday	Word processor

The titles indicate the specialized nature of each position. Frequently, the word "secretary" or "executive assistant" is omitted as more companies advertise under the brand name of their electronic equipment, such as:

Vydec operator	Amtext
Mag card	Wang
Xerox	Lanier

You should also look under a specific industry for a job, such as advertising, public relations, broadcasting, marketing, and fashion design. Reading the fine print often reveals that office skills are required.

Reading help wanted ads gives you a valuable source of information concerning the trend in employment opportunities, salary ranges, and qualifications, including skills needed. It is a good idea to read the want ads thoroughly on Sundays because that is the day that carries the most employment advertisements.

As you read the ads, if something interests you, circle it. Some of the ads include a box number; others have a phone number. Whichever ad you decide to act on, be prompt; reply the same day if possible. Study the ad carefully to determine if your qualifications match their requirements. Your follow-up will consist of an application letter and your résumé.

FRIENDS AND OTHER CONTACTS

Thousands of available jobs are filled, not by advertisements, but by word-of-mouth. A friend tells a friend of an opening in the firm. Companies are delighted to obtain employees by referrals through present employees, company officers, and even customers. It benefits the company by saving the agency fee, and the company is able to find someone quickly at the same time. Let everyone know that you are seeking a job and the type of position you desire.

Recommending friends, however, sometimes does not work. It may cause embarrassment for your friend if you do not live up to expectations.

Do not be shy or backward about having relatives help. If your uncle has customers that are in need of executive assistant help, use his contacts. In the job-hunting arena, every bit of influence counts; it is perfectly ethical and proper. Influence can only get you the interview, not the job. You get yourself the job. A contact is a valuable door-opener; that is all.

Think back to the people who crossed your path. Remember your job-hunting file. Refer to your collection of business cards, the names of business equipment salespeople, marketing support representatives, and guest speakers; call them. They may not remember you, but they may turn you over to someone else to talk with. It is a start.

PROFESSIONAL AND INSTITUTIONAL ASSOCIATIONS

Another good source for office-related positions includes professional associations, nonprofit institutional organizations, including churches, charitable organizations, and fraternal or community groups. The Future Secretaries Association (FSA), the Professional Secretaries International (PSI), and the International Information/Word Processing Association (IWP) hold conventions and distribute publications that may be helpful in learning about job openings. Local chapters of these professional associations often offer employment advertisements in their local newsletters.

You may not use all of the employment sources described, but it is important that you know what is available and select those sources that might lead to good job prospects. The important thing is not to be lazy; you cannot sit home waiting for job offers to come knocking at your door. Job hunting is an effort. It is almost full-time work without pay, but there is a payoff—a good job, first of all, and you will have been "seasoned." As you go through the process of using some of the sources of employment, going from office to office, writing letters, preparing your objectives, talking to new people, and articulating your goals, you will find that these activities will build up your confidence, establish your communication skills, and help ease the transition from being a student to being a mature person ready to enter the working world.

RÉSUMÉ WRITING

How skillful you are at writing will give the prospective employer a good opportunity to evaluate your potential. Writing to get the job involves a letter of application and a *résumé*, which is a summary of your qualifications for the job sought.

The word résumé is a French word meaning "summary." It is another important job-hunting tool that provides the prospective employer with a catalog of what you have to offer in terms of qualifications, experience, educational background, and skills. In other words, it should contain brief but sufficient information to tell a prospective employer:

- [ ] What you can do.
- [ ] What you have done.
- [ ] What you know.
- [ ] What kind of job you would like.

Your résumé should accomplish several objectives: it should serve as an introduction; it will save time for both employer and applicant; and it will help you obtain an interview.

Refer to your self-appraisal or self-assessment list; it is an excellent step in preparing a detailed inventory of your educational background, work, and personal qualities and interests so that you will know exactly what assets you have to offer an employer.

This self-appraisal will help you evaluate more objectively your skills, abilities, and interests in relation to the kind of job you are seeking. Try to put yourself in the place of an employer and include everything you think the employer would be interested in knowing about you as a prospective employee. Even recent graduates with little or no work history should prepare the asset list. You may not use all the information on your personal inventory form, but it is best to list all you can.

There is no one best organizing principle for a résumé. Nevertheless, all good ones will highlight the important points around a specific job objective.

Here are some guidelines for preparing an effective résumé:

1. *Keep it brief.* A one- or two-page résumé should cover your background. Ideally, a one-page résumé is preferable, especially if you are a recent graduate. The trick is to extract the main points from your self-appraisal list in brief, concise form. Remember to think of the person who will be reading your résumé. Tell your story briefly and avoid an undesirable, overcrowded appearance.
2. *Determine your priorities.* Put your best foot forward. Determine what is more important in your arsenal of job experience—working at a fast foods restaurant or as a typesetter for an insurance company. They are both important, but you should emphasize the one more relevant to your career goals. Summer and part-time work experiences are important. They demonstrate to an employer that you displayed a sense of ambition and responsibility during your school years. Your current or most recent job should appear first, and it merits the most information.
3. *List your education.* Since your work experience might be limited, your educational background may take precedence in your résumé. As you gain experience and begin revising your résumé for career changes, you may want to place the education category after work history. In addition to colleges, list any degrees or diplomas you have obtained. List the schools that you have attended, the most recent one first. List specialized courses that might be unique in terms of training for the electronic office and which would indicate to a personnel manager that you have an understanding of the techniques, skills, and terminology of the office: word processing concepts, reprographics, micrographics, photocomposition equipment, and, of course, skill in a variety of electronic text-editing and dictation/transcription equipment.
4. *Furnish references upon request.* There are two schools of thought regarding references as a basis for employment. Some employers feel that character references are more accurate if they are obtained from a professional person in a responsible position. On the other hand, many employers and personnel managers do not place too much confidence in references because the people named as references will generally not write anything unfavorable about the job applicant. A good rule would be not to include references on your résumé. You may indicate that you will be happy to furnish references upon request.

   Eventually, when a company has made a positive decision about your employment, the personnel manager will check your present or previous employers and may contact your college regarding your degrees.
5. *Don't exaggerate.* It is sometimes tempting to exaggerate your ability, education, skills, and interests or to take credit for accomplishments that are questionable. Be honest, even if your credentials are modest. Professional personnel people can detect exaggerations because you may look "too good." False documentation can haunt you for years, and outright distortions or lies can cripple your career permanently.
6. *Be consistent in your choice of format, words, and phrases.* Use brief phrasing rather than complete sentences. For example, say "Served as

president of FSA'' rather than ''I served as president of our chapter of FSA.'' Use the third person and the past tense.

7. *Be careful about physical appearance.* Nothing turns a manager off more than when the appearance of your résumé is unattractive, messy (from poor erasures), or incorrect (contains misspelled words). Résumés should be individually typed. You could record your résumé on magnetic media and play back (print) the quantity desired automatically. This will give the appearance of individually typed résumés which create the impression that you are being selective in applying for a job.

Adjust your margins to give your résumé a well-balanced look. Use ample white space before and after headings. There are no rules about style, headings, and enumerations. Whatever you do, be consistent throughout. You are competing with other job applicants, and your résumé will be compared with others. Make it stand out for attractiveness and ease of reading, as well as content.

LETTER OF APPLICATION

The letter of application (also known as a cover letter) should be prepared after your résumé is complete. The same meticulous care needed for résumé preparation is needed for the application letter. It is your sales message, and it should serve to move the reader to act. It should not repeat the experience of the résumé but should highlight some of the reasons why an employer should hire you instead of someone else. The first step is to get the employer to read your résumé, so keep these facts in mind:

☐ Address your letter to a specific person by name, when possible.
☐ Since the first paragraph is so important, make sure that it attracts the reader's attention.
☐ Tell your story in terms of why you should be considered. What can you contribute to the company?
☐ Be sure to refer to your résumé. It gives the details of your experience and background.
☐ Use simple, direct language and correct grammar.
☐ Type your letter neatly in a personal business letter style, using standard-size white paper (8½ × 11 inches).
☐ Use businesslike writing style. Avoid appearing aggressive, overbearing, familiar, or overly humorous. You are writing to a stranger about a subject that is serious to both of you.
☐ Use a closing that suggests action. With local firms, take the initiative in suggesting that you telephone for an interview.

THE JOB INTERVIEW

Your résumé and application letter did the trick; they have secured you an interview. This is the last step, but it is an extremely critical step in your job-hunting campaign.

Before the interview, you expressed yourself in written communication, and now the interview will give you the opportunity to use oral communication to your advantage.

A job interview is your showcase for merchandising your talents. An interview is an opportunity to practice your ability to express yourself under pressure or reply aptly to unexpected questions. Each interview introduces you to one more person. It gives you a chance to appraise the job and the employer. It enables you to decide if the job meets your career needs and interests and whether the employer is of the type and caliber you want to work for. Don't be cavalier in your attitude; prepare. Spend time thinking about the company and its business before you have the interview.

BEFORE THE INTERVIEW

Even if it is a job that does not sound promising, learn all you can about the company, its products or services, its standing in the industry, and the number and types of jobs available. You can do this by requesting company brochures, annual reports, and other material from your library or directly from the company.

You have to think or "psyche yourself up" that they need you! You should convince yourself that they will be lucky if they hire you. You know what you have to offer—a good education, solid skills, high personal standards, and an eagerness to work.

Anticipate possible questions. If you do not have a résumé that includes references, be prepared to furnish the names, addresses, telephone numbers, and business affiliations of responsible people for references.

Learn the salary scale for the type of position you are seeking. The placement counselor at your school can provide some information on salary levels. You can also check the classified newspaper ads to give you an idea of salary range. Every year the International Information/Word Processing Association (IWP) publishes a salary survey for executive assistants and correspondence and administrative assistants. This gives comprehensive salary information for word processing and related occupations by geographic region. You can obtain a copy by writing to IWP, Willow Grove, PA 19090. You cannot expect to start at the same salary that an experienced executive assistant can demand.

Dress for the interview as you would for the job you are seeking. Be on the conservative side if you are in doubt. Always look professional; don't show up for an interview sloppily dressed, casually dressed, or lugging a shopping bag.

DURING THE INTERVIEW

The interviewer is responsible for helping to select the best applicant and much of his behavior is oriented toward that goal. Most interviewers are polite and helpful; they genuinely want the applicant to be successful. If you visualize the interviewer in these terms, the chances are that you will be more at ease and receptive. Here are some suggestions to help you have a favorable interview:

☐ *Be courteous.* Courtesy is always in style, and it makes a positive first impression. Approach the interviewer with a smile; greet the interviewer by name and introduce yourself. Be friendly but businesslike.

☐ *Show poise.* Do not appear nervous. Let the interviewer control the interview. Your answers should be brief but complete, without rambling.

☐ *Be frank and honest.* Do not be afraid to ask questions. If you do not know or understand aspects of the job, ask the interviewer.

☐ *Do not smoke.* Even if you are a smoker, do not smoke during the interview. If you are offered a cigarette, refuse it politely saying, "No thanks, not just now." If you are a nonsmoker, you merely decline by saying, "No, thank you."

☐ *Answer questions wisely.* Answer only what is asked (no more, no less) unless the interviewer asks you to comment on or discuss a subject. Make sure you understand the question.

☐ *Know how to handle controversial questions.* An interviewer may ask some tough questions that border on controversial or personal issues. You do not have to answer these questions, and you should know the difference between tough questions and ones that are simply illegal. Political, sexual, and racial topics are examples of controversial issues.

Use common sense in handling questions that might be controversial or discriminatory. Be noncommittal about controversial matters. If the interviewer asks you about your previous employer or work situation, avoid criticism or negatives. Simply say, "My work at ABC Company gave me some valuable experience, and I enjoyed much of it."

☐ *Know how to handle discriminatory questions.* Title VII of the Federal Civil Rights Acts of 1964 specifically prohibits discrimination based on sex, as well as race, religion, and national origin. It is rare that you will encounter an interviewer that asks questions of a discriminatory nature, such as requests for information about marital status, number of dependents, religion, and age; but if you do, handle the questions in a manner that is comfortable to you and yet does not compromise your principles.

Some interviewers may ask for illegal information. If you prefer not to answer, make your refusal polite but firm. You might say something like, "I don't think that has any bearing on my qualifications to do the job." Or, you might be impelled to point out to an offending interviewer that the questions are out of line and you are going to report the incident to your state's Human Rights Commission, the Department of Labor, or the National Employment Association. Of course, you have probably hurt any chance you had of getting hired by this organization, but you probably would not want to work for this company anyway.

☐ *Be aware of chauvinism.* This is another form of discrimination that may surface during an interview. The chauvinist is a different problem. He or she practices a form of discrimination that is sometimes more insidious and harder to handle. It perpetuates the mythology of a male's or female's distaste for men or women in business. It is particularly unfortunate when such philosophies and beliefs are felt by personnel managers and job interviewers.

☐ Be prepared to take some employment tests, such as typewriting, shorthand, and language skills.

AFTER THE INTERVIEW

The interviewer usually lets you know when the interview has ended. If he or she does not, watch for the cues to indicate that the interview is over. As soon as this happens, you should rise and give the interviewer a firm handshake, not a limp, lifeless one.

Try to remember the name of everyone you meet, including executive assistants and receptionists. They can be most helpful when you place follow-up telephone calls and want to be sure you are not disturbing the person you are calling.

Leave as quickly as possible and thank the executive assistant and the receptionist as you leave.

Job hunting is a slow and, for some people, a devastating experience. Do not expect instant results after your first interview. Sometimes, you will have several interviews with the same company, weeks apart. The first interview may be just a screening procedure to discover if you have the general qualifications required. It may be brief with very little interaction between you and the interviewer. A follow-up interview may mean more questions and answers.

If you are really interested in the job and have not received an answer within a reasonable time, say ten days, you might want to contact the company directly and ask if they have reached a decision yet.

While you are waiting, do not depend upon one job lead. Continue your job hunting in other places. A delay in one job may open the door to an unexpected opportunity somewhere else.

SUMMARY

In spite of the plentiful supply of executive assistant jobs, wise applicants develop a job-hunting strategy because they are selective in the type of jobs they want.

1. A job-hunting file should contain names of potential employers, executive assistants, consultants, and office systems salespeople.
2. Your plan should include self-analysis. Decide what kind of work you want and which job will give you the best chance to use your talents and training.
3. Use as many resources as possible: college placement office, newspaper help wanted ads, employment agencies, and friends and relatives.

4. A résumé is a summary of your qualifications, experience, and educational background and skills.

5. Guidelines for an effective résumé are: keep it brief, list your priorities, list your education and work experience, don't exaggerate, use a consistent format, and strive for neatness and accuracy.

6. A good résumé may be the edge that opens the door to an interview. The letter of application should accompany your résumé and should highlight some of your attributes as outlined in your résumé.

7. Plan for the interview; learn in advance all you can about the job and the company; anticipate questions you might be asked so that you will respond quickly and well.

8. First impressions are important; how you look, what you say, how you say it, and how you conduct yourself—all add up to that vital first impression.

9. Courtesy, poise, self-confidence, honesty, clear speech, and good credentials are important in getting the job.

CHAPTER RECALL EXERCISES

1. Cite reasons why the future employment outlook for executive assistants will be favorable.
2. Why should executive assistants engage in job-hunting techniques if jobs are readily available?
3. What should a job-hunting file contain?
4. What kinds of questions should be considered in a self-analysis?
5. Describe how career days can help in your job search.
6. Compare the main difference between the job applicant in public and private employment agencies.
7. Why are temporary-help firms particularly helpful to students.
8. Briefly discuss the ethics of using relatives as a source of employment.
9. What is a résumé? How does it differ from a cover letter?
10. Describe the correct physical appearance of a résumé.
11. Why is it important to learn about the company before going on an interview?
12. What is the best way to handle controversial questions.

PROBLEMS AND APPLICATIONS

1. Marlene Stillman went on several interviews during the last weeks prior to graduating from the Office Administration Program at Drake Community College. A week after one of the interviews, she received a letter from Sperix Computer Corporation that indicated she had been accepted for an executive assistant position at her desired salary. Since no other job offers were forthcoming, Marlene wrote to Sperix accepting the job. A few days after Marlene accepted the job from Sperix, the First National Bank

called to tell Marlene that the Personnel Department had reviewed her résumé, application letter, and interview and found her highly desirable for the position of executive assistant with the bank.

This job is close to Marlene's home; the pay is higher; and the career opportunities are more promising than the job at Sperix. Marlene really wanted to work for the First National Bank originally. Since she has accepted a previous job offer, what can she do?

2. Lillian Stinson, a mature woman, completed the office systems program at Mason College. She graduated at the top of her class and was anxious to resume her career as an executive assistant after an interruption of 15 years to raise a family. During one of her interviews, the interviewer mentioned that the company was revamping the entire document processing department and was looking for younger employees. The interviewer went on to say that Lillian, as a mature woman, would probably not fit in with the company's expansion plans. What would you do in Lillian's place if you were confronted with this situation?

3. Find a copy of the current *College Placement Annual* in your library or college placement center. Make a list of companies listed in the Annual for which you would like to work. Using the alphabetical listing of the companies, read what the annual has to say about each of the companies you have chosen.

4. Make a list of your strong points, your weak points, your likes, your dislikes, your education, work experience, and activities. Spend some time thinking about your goals and objectives. Then, develop a résumé which stresses your strong points and your goals. Type an error-free copy of your résumé, using a high-quality grade of bond paper, proper headings, and effective use of margins and white space.

5. Using one of the companies you chose from the *College Placement Annual* in problem 3, do a thorough search on the company. Consult such sources as the business reference books, the company's annual report and other promotional literature, and the *Wall Street Journal*. Write a short report on the company.

6. Write an unsolicited letter of application to the company that you have researched (problem 5). Assume that you are applying for an executive assistant position with the company.

7. Thoroughly search the Sunday want ads for executive assistant positions. Circle at least three of the ads that advertise jobs that appeal to you. Write a letter of application to one of the companies. Refer to the want ad in your letter.

8. Start a job-hunting file or folder. Include names and addresses of companies that you might like to work for.

9. Make a list of ten questions that you think you might be asked on a job interview. Compose answers to those ten questions. Using role playing, ask those questions of someone in your class.

10. Describe how you think a student should dress for a job interview on campus at the college placement center for a job as executive assistant.

LANGUAGE SKILLS DEVELOPMENT

1. Choose the correct word in each sentence:
   a. (Its, It's), of course, your decision about which date to leave.
   b. (Whose, Who's) products are guaranteed to last for more than a year?
   c. Do (your, you're) children understand the dangers of playing with fireworks?
   d. The community clubs have handled (their, there, they're) obligations so thoroughly during the past three months.
   e. The dog kept wagging (its, it's) tail at the stranger.
   f. (Your, You're) quite sure that you locked the keys in the car?
   g. (To, Too, Two) be quite honest, I don't think she is going to make a good mayor for this town.
   h. (Whose, Who's) planning to clean the kitchen tonight?

2. Choose the correct usage of numbers in these sentences:
   a. The rate on (26, twenty-six)-week Treasury bills averaged (10, ten) percent down from August (29, 29th).
   b. The interest rate on (6, six)-month, money-market certificates is established by federal law.
   c. The sticker price on the subcompacts will average ($5500, $5500.00).
   d. So many of the (13,000,000, 13 million) members are out of work directly or indirectly because of foreign imports.
   e. The sausage is sold in (6, six) states and (53, fifty-three) restaurants.
   f. The steel company produced about (700,000, 700 thousand) tons of steel last year.
   g. This is my (3rd, third) visit to your office.
   h. (600, Six hundred) people attended the annual banquet last night.

3. Put in hyphens and apostrophes where they are needed.
   a. money market certificates
   b. 30 month certificate
   c. the firms national division
   d. best training program in town
   e. front wheel drive subcompact
   f. four door liftgate version
   g. brokers second encounter
   h. 14 member committee
   i. Strogiers plan
   j. business research organization
   k. nations economic future
   l. American workers productivity
   m. sweaty palmed buyer
   n. major machine tool firm

HUMAN RELATIONS INCIDENTS

1. Karen Stinberg is an executive assistant in a large accounting firm. Last year the workload increased to the point where she told her employer that she simply had to have an assistant. Mr. Marks, Karen's employer, agreed and suggested that Karen start interviewing applicants for the position.

Karen was about to call the personnel department to set things in motion when she had a sudden inspiration. She knew a recently divorced friend, who was job hunting and having a hard time because she had very little work experience. Karen thought the assistant's job would be perfect for her—a good way to break into the business world.

Karen's friend agreed; Mr. Marks approved; and everything started off very well. Alice Steele, Karen's friend, seemed enthusiastic, cooperative, and eager to learn. Then little by little, the situation changed. Alice began to disregard instructions and, on several occasions, refused to help Karen with rush assignments. Late arrivals became more frequent, and Alice seemed to spend more and more time conversing with coworkers. Those conversations, Karen eventually learned, often included references to how hard she was trying, how too much was expected of her, and so on. The enemy, it seemed, was Karen. Karen finally decided to speak to Mr. Marks. His reaction: "You hired her—you deal with it!" What should Karen do?

2. Fred had been an office manager of a large company for about 15 years when he decided to take an early retirement to "enjoy life." After several months of leisure time, Fred decided to enter the work force again as a part-time administration assistant, working approximately 20 hours a week.

The other administrative assistants are having a difficult time working with Fred. He constantly leaves little notes for the other assistants, making suggestions on how they can improve productivity and do a better job.

Even though all the administrative assistants have the same job classification, Fred assumes a manager's role with other assistants. They resent his pushiness but are reluctant to hurt Fred's feelings. Is there some way Fred could be informed that he is not the office manager but a part-time executive assistant, just like the other employees?

CAREER OPTIONS

If there is one unifying theme throughout this book, it is that the executive assistant career is not disappearing; rather, it is changing and evolving as the office itself evolves. One of the most significant changes taking place is the number of career options available. The door has opened onto a myriad of choices not previously available.

Of course, executive assistants have always had some choices: they could choose the type of firms to work for, such as manufacturing, government, and service organizations; they could determine which areas within these organizations they were most interested in, such as sales, marketing, production, and personnel. These choices are still available and present the executive assistant with a satisfying array of options.

What about the person, though, who wants to branch out from traditional executive assistant jobs? What kinds of opportunities are available? In the past these opportunities were limited, and executive assistants who moved into other areas of the organization were more the exception than the rule. This is no longer the case; executive assistants are moving into all areas of business, and many firms are actively seeking them to fill these positions. It is important for you to be aware of these career options, as well as the traditional executive assistant positions.

At the end of this chapter, you should be able to:

1. Name the career options available for the executive assistant. ☐ 2. List some characteristics and skills needed to excel in these career alternatives. ☐ 3. List some problems associated with various career options.

CHAPTER 27

ALTERNATIVE JOB CHOICES

You need to ask yourself if you want a job or a career. A career provides enjoyment and job satisfaction, while a job is mainly a way to earn a living. A person plans for a career, choosing jobs and training carefully in order to make choices that will advance that career. A person looking for a job will often take the position that offers the most immediate satisfaction. It may pay the most or offer the most vacation, but it may not necessarily advance the person's career. If you want a career, then the time to start planning is now. Investigate the various types of opportunities available to people with your education, training, and skills.

Keep an open mind. Otherwise, you may dismiss possible opportunities because they do not immediately appeal to you or because you do not know enough about them. For instance, you may refuse to consider a job in the data processing field because the idea of working with computers frightens you. Yet, by doing this, you may be passing up a career that could be very rewarding—both mentally and financially.

CAREERS IN MANAGEMENT

If you think that you could never be a manager, think again, because managers are made, not born. All it takes is the right training, skills, and attitudes—and a lot of determination.

Many firms are looking among their own employees for people who have management potential, and these firms then either train these people in their own programs or finance their further education. Many firms find some executive assistants make excellent management material. In their jobs as executive assistants, these people have developed a number of skills that are essential to good managers.

Executive assistants may know more of the actual internal workings of the company than their bosses. They have learned to handle a number of jobs by determining the priority of each and have learned to meet self-imposed deadlines. They have learned to work harmoniously with other executive assistants, other departments, managers, suppliers, and customers, and these human relations skills are invaluable in any type of management position.

Executive assistants must have excellent communication skills, both verbal and written, another prerequisite of a good manager. In carrying out their jobs, executive assistants must become intimately involved in the workings of their departments. This helps them to understand how to get jobs done quickly and efficiently. This kind of knowledge is at least as important as formal training.

One of the most important advantages executive assistants have over new business school graduates is actual work experience. They have learned how and why an organization survives and flourishes. They understand how interdependent the various departments are within a firm. They have discovered the value of teamwork and shared objectives. These are very im-

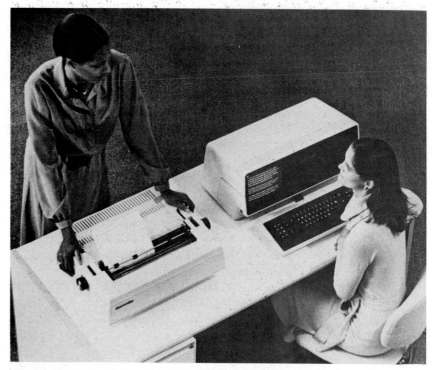

Figure 27.1
Manager of a word processing center (Courtesy of Burroughs Corp.).

portant assets that should give executive assistants a good foundation upon which to build other management skills.

Of course, there are a number of problems you will run into if you decide to climb the management ladder. A major problem involves interpersonal relationships with both executive assistants and other managers. You may find that you are no longer considered "one of the gang" by the executive assistants. Some may even feel that you have "gone over to the other side," and, of course, they are right. You are now a manager; but, initially at least, you may find yourself with a foot in each camp, not quite sure where you belong.

It is very important at this point that you think of yourself as a manager. If you do not think and act as a manager, other people within the organization will not treat you as a manager; and that will hamper your effectiveness considerably.

If you continue to socialize exclusively with executive assistants, you will have a hard time getting other managers to accept you as anything more than a high-level executive assistant. Like it or not, there is an office hierarchy; and if you are to take your proper place in it, you must think, act, and dress as a manager.

There are some purely functional reasons why you should begin to socialize with other managers. First, you can learn a lot from them, even in informal sessions. Second, it will help you to gain acceptance into the management "club." Third, it is extremely difficult to establish authority over people who consider you "one of them."

When you become a manager, you may find yourself in the position of supervising the people who were formerly in the same position you were in. If you do not establish your new position as an authority figure early on, you may never be able to do so. On the other hand, the new manager does not want to alienate former coworkers.

The best way to handle this situation is to encourage some of the other executive assistants to try for management slots. Of course, not everyone wants or is qualified for a mangement position, but there are generally one or two people with the desire and potential for a career in management. Sometimes, all they need is the encouragement and example of a former executive assistant who made it. In this way, you can become a role model for other executive assistants and can encourage and help to train them without jeopardizing your own career.

The term manager is a broad one that covers a number of job functions. For the executive assistant, there are some management positions that are more readily obtained than others.

Word Processing Manager.   One of the most common management positions for executive assistants today is the manager of the word processing operation. Because word processing is still a relatively new phenomenon in the business world, most firms do not have people with a formal education in word processing ready to jump in and fill the gap.

It is usually a case of on-the-job training, and the person who almost always has the most actual work experience in this area is the executive assistant. Since the manager of a word processing operation must understand all phases of the operation—including running the equipment—you may find yourself in the enviable position of being the only person in the company who is really qualified to run the operation. You can use this advantage to further your career, while at the same time providing a needed service to your company.

Manager of Another Department.   Of course, even though word processing is one of the most logical management positions for the executive assistant, it is not the only option available to you. You could become the manager of one of a firm's departments, such as sales, records management, personnel, or data entry.

In these situations, your office training would not be quite as appropriate as it is in word processing. However, the broad-based management skills that you have acquired (communications and interpersonal relationships, for example) would still be valuable.

You should try to discover where your interests and talents lie. If you are interested in people and have a knack for selecting the right person for a particular job, you might want to concentrate on the personnel area. If you like numbers and forms, you might zero in on data entry. If there is a hidden librarian lurking beneath the surface, you might do well in the records management department.

Aptitude and desire are the key words. Management positions are available, and executive assistants are in a good position to try for them.

CAREERS IN SALES

Many of the skills learned as an executive assistant can be successfully transferred to a sales career. For instance, executive assistants are used to dealing with a large number of people in various positions, from mail clerks to presidents. They have learned to follow through and follow up on jobs, an important asset for any salesperson. They are also quite capable of dealing with the ton of paperwork that accompanies any major sale, and paperwork is the typical salesperson's Waterloo.

So, if you want to get out from behind your desk and tackle the outside world, a job in sales may be just the thing—provided, of course, that you are willing to accept the challenge of meeting quotas and the risk of working on commission, and are also willing to travel. An increasing number of people have accepted this challenge and have found themselves on their firms' list of top salespeople.

MARKETING SERVICES REPRESENTATIVE

Today, the marketing services area, particularly in firms selling office products, is actively recruiting sales representatives. A marketing services rep (sometimes called a marketing support rep) demonstrates equipment to potential customers. These demonstrations occur in the firm's sales office, on the customer's premises, or at trade shows, which may be held in a number of different cities.

After a sale has been made and the equipment delivered, the marketing services rep goes to the customer installation to train the firm's employees to operate the machines. The rep is responsible for servicing the account and supporting the sales effort.

Right now, sales of office equipment are increasing at a rapid rate—faster than most manufacturers can train marketing service representatives. Many firms have turned to colleges to find students who are trained in operating their equipment. Other firms are "raiding" their customers to find executive assistants who can proficiently operate their equipment.

Executive assistants who can operate word processing or other types of office equipment should investigate the possibility of a career as a marketing services representative.

PHOTOTYPESETTING JOBS

The expanding field of phototypesetting provides another career opportunity for the executive assistant. As more firms abandon hot type machines in favor of phototypesetting equipment, more people who can operate this equipment will be needed.

The executive assistant profession provides an obvious source of people power for this field. One of the prime requirements for this job is the ability to type rapidly and accurately. The executive assistant obviously meets that requirement.

From there, it is just a matter of learning the operation of the particular phototypesetting machine used and the codes that tell that machine what to do. This is a relatively easy learning process that takes about a week.

DATA PROCESSING CAREERS

Another area where typing skills are valuable is in data processing, particularly in data entry. Data entry involves inputting raw data (information) into the computer system. This information is generally input through some type of keyboard device such as a terminal. (Figure 27.2.)

The executive assistant would have to learn the operation of the particular machine being used and the codes that tell the machine what to do; but after that, it is mainly a matter of fast, accurate typing.

LEGAL ASSISTANTS AND PARALEGALS

Executive assistants who are interested in law might consider a career as a legal executive assistant or a paralegal. Legal assistants work for lawyers and perform standard office functions, while paralegals get involved in legal research instead of, or in addition to, their office duties. Paralegals actually help lawyers work on cases.

Both of these professions require additional training and education. Legal administrative assistants must be familiar with legal terms in order to take dictation or transcribe recorded dictation. Paralegals require education or on-the-job training in the basics of legal work, such as doing research, writing briefs, and preparing for cases.

The National Association of Legal Secretaries provides free training programs for legal secretaries. It also has an employment service and a professional examination and certification program for legal executive assistants.

MEDICAL ASSISTANTS

Medical executive assistants can work in a hospital, a health care organization, a doctor's office, or dentist's office. The main requirement, in addition to traditional office functions, is the ability to understand and spell medical terms.

Some doctors will allow you to obtain this knowledge on the job, but others require some prior knowledge of medical terminology. Some science background and a familiarity with Latin will help you understand many medical terms.

Some schools offer specialized courses for the medical executive assistant. These will include courses in science, as well as medical terminology.

Figure 27.2
Careers in data processing are opening up for executive assistants (Courtesy of Burroughs Corp.).

The American Association of Medical Assistants (an organization for medical technicians, nurses, and office personnel) offers a certification program for Certified Medical Assistants, Administrative.

GOVERNMENT CAREERS

You may also want to consider a career with a government agency or organization. These include jobs for local, state, and federal legislatures, as well as government and civic organizations such as human rights, police and fire departments, and state employment services.

For many of these jobs, a civil service examination must be taken. Government offices post listings of future civil service exams. Executive assistants interested in applying for civil service jobs should check these listings periodically to see if any of the open positions are of interest. They will then have to sign up to take the civil service exam and wait until they are called. This may take some time, depending on the number of openings for a particular job and the score obtained by the applicant.

JOBS IN THE ARMED FORCES

The U.S. Armed Forces offer additional career opportunities for interested executive assistants. These positions include openings in all areas, as well as traditional executive assistant and administrative positions.

Of course, you will have to make a commitment of several years, but you will have a chance to get additional education and training at government expense. This will, of course, increase your job marketability when you leave the service.

COURT STENOGRAPHERS

Court stenographers use a stenographic machine to take down verbatim the proceedings of a court case. This is very demanding work that calls for tremendous concentration, speed, and accuracy. But, it is exciting to be a part of the judicial system, and it pays very well. It should be noted, however, that some courts are switching from court stenographers to special recording machines that have four tracks to record the remarks of the judge, the witness, the prosecuting attorney, and the defense attorney.

SUMMARY

An executive assistant career, while a rewarding one, need not be an end in itself. It can be used as a springboard to other positions. The important thing to remember is that there are options available.

1. Today's executive assistant has a number of career opportunities, in addition to the traditional choices available.
2. Some positions available to executive assistants include management positions, word processing supervisors, careers in sales, marketing services representatives, phototypesetting positions, data processing careers, careers with the government, and careers as court stenographers.

CHAPTER RECALL EXERCISES

1. What office skills help prepare a person for a career in management?
2. What problems does the new manager, who was a former executive assistant, have?
3. How can the executive assistant handle the problems of being a new manager?
4. Why does word processing offer the most management openings to executive assistants?
5. How has the government helped to increase career opportunities for women?
6. What benefits does a sales career offer the executive assistant?
7. What does a marketing services representative do?
8. Why are executive assistants especially well suited for the position of marketing services representatives?

9. What skills would an executive assistant need to get a job as a photo-typesetter? A data processing operator?
10. What is the difference between a legal executive assistant and a paralegal?
11. What courses will help the medical executive assistant do the job better?
12. How does an executive assistant go about getting a civil service position?
13. Why is a job as a court stenographer so demanding?
14. Describe the new recorders now being used in courtrooms.

PROBLEMS AND APPLICATIONS

1. Go through the classified want ads in Sunday's paper and cut out all the jobs that could be handled by someone with an executive assistant background. List the skills requested in these ads. Determine if the skills are acquired through education or on-the-job training. Determine if job experience is necessary for the jobs.

2. Five students should enact a role-playing session. They should portray five executive assistants who work in the same firm and have been friends. One of them is promoted to be the manager of the group, and the other four resent it. How does the new manager establish authority without alienating the group?

3. Check the listings of job openings at your nearest government office and write down the jobs that could be filled by someone with your training. Also, note the education and work experience required for each job.

4. Interview two people who are employed in the types of jobs described in this chapter. Ask what education and training are needed to effectively perform their jobs. Ask for job descriptions, if they are available.

5. Read a recent article that talks about developing supervisory or managerial skills. Write a summary of that article. Be prepared to report on the article to the class.

LANGUAGE SKILLS DEVELOPMENT

1. It is sometimes confusing trying to determine whether a word is written as one word, with a hyphen, or as two words. Write each of the following words correctly.
    a. part time
    b. worth while
    c. co operate
    d. over look
    e. editor in chief
    f. under take
    g. over draw
    h. text book

    i. through out
    j. news stand

2. Divide these words in the preferred place.

    a. rainy   g. remarked
    b. air-conditioned   h. rolling
    c. Margaret   i. equipped
    d. couldn't   j. knowledge
    e. $1478.54   k. Ed.D.
    f. around   l. January

3. Use the correct punctuation and capitalization for these sentences.

    a. Thank you mr conrad for making my trip so enjoyable this spring.

    b. Mr chairman I failed to notice who seconded that motion.

    c. Our neighbors all of whom have been most kind to us are planning a barbeque on the fourth of july.

    d. Anyone who can swim is certainly welcome to visit the village pool this summer.

    e. No I don't like the way the secretary has been taking the minutes of the Society for the Advancement of Management meetings.

    f. Well you are probably correct that we should change the treasurer before another week goes by but I do regret having made this decision.

    g. As soon as we hear from you we will begin to make plans to visit lake placid.

    h. In our previous telephone conversation you said that june is a perfect time to make a visit to the mountains.

HUMAN RELATIONS INCIDENTS

1. Jennifer is an executive assistant in the claims department. She is very ambitious and has learned to do all the office jobs better than anyone else. She is constantly learning new tasks and is actively seeking advancement. The problem is she wants to keep all her skills and knowledge to herself. Sometimes the supervisor asks Jennifer to help someone who is having a problem, and Jennifer will reluctantly show the person as little as she can to get by. What do you think is expected of Jennifer? Is there some way she could become more of an asset to the company? Is Jennifer likely to advance on the job?

2. Monroe was hired in the word processing center with the understanding that he would be the next supervisor of the center. Monroe had several years of operator experience at a previous

company. When Mr. Ellis, the supervisor of the word processing center, announced his retirement, the company started a job search for the opening.

Monroe heard about the retirement and the job opening when he saw the notice on the bulletin board. He immediately complained about this oversight and told the personnel department that he was supposed to have that job. They suggested that he apply for the job, and he would certainly have as much consideration as anyone else. What should Monroe do? Who is at fault here?

REFERENCE GUIDES

Abbreviations ☐ Additional Sources of Information ☐ Addressing Envelopes ☐ Capitalization Rules ☐ Compound Words ☐ Easily Confused Words ☐ Footnotes and Bibliographies ☐ Forms of Address ☐ Manufacturers of Text-Editing and Word Processing Systems ☐ Metric Equivalents ☐ Number Rules ☐ Proofreader's Marks ☐ Punctuation Rules ☐ Punctuation Styles for Letters ☐ Spelling Rules ☐ Word Division Rules

APPENDIX

ABBREVIATIONS

1. Write out words except where abbreviations are always used (Mr., Mrs., etc.).
2. Do not abbreviate firm names unless correspondence from the respective firms shows the names abbreviated.
3. Use capital letters and no periods for familiar abbreviations (IRS, FBI).
4. May abbreviate the United States when it comes before a noun but not when it follows a noun (U.S. Postal Service, Supreme Court of the United States).
5. May abbreviate the titles Reverend and Honorable if the full names follow the titles (Rev. Eugene Lasley).
6. Abbreviate academic degrees if they follow full names (Betty Moore, Ph.D.).
7. Spell out names of countries and their states, territories, and possessions.
8. In text, spell out names of months and days of the week.
9. Abbreviate time periods of the day (a.m., p.m.); time zones may be abbreviated (EST, CST).
10. Do not abbreviate the given names of individuals (William not Wm.).
11. Spell out a company or organization name when it is first used, and then you may abbreviate it in the remainder of the writing if the abbreviation is well known.
12. Do not abbreviate civil, military, or religious titles preceding last names.
13. Abbreviate social titles (Mme., Mrs.).
14. Abbreviate seniority titles that follow full names (N.E. Moore, Jr.).
15. Spell out common units of measure (miles, feet).
16. When the word number is not followed by a numeral, spell it out. The abbreviation No. should be used when a numeral directly follows the term (No. J-142).
17. Type in lowercase letters with periods at the end of each abbreviated word commonly abbreviated terms which are derived from foreign expressions (etc., et al.).
18. Spell out terms indicating direction within an address (125 West 150 Street).
19. Use only one period if an abbreviation containing a period falls at the end of a sentence. The class begins at 8 a.m. In sentences ending with question marks or exclamation marks, place the mark directly after the period. Does the class begin at 8 a.m.?
20. In lowercase abbreviations, place a period after each letter or group of letters representing a word (f.o.b. delivery).

Alabama	AL	Montana	MT
Alaska	AK	Nebraska	NB
Arizona	AZ	Nevada	NV
Arkansas	AR	New Hampshire	NH
California	CA	New Jersey	NJ
Canada	CN	New Mexico	NM
Colorado	CO	New York	NY
Connecticut	CT	North Carolina	NC
Delaware	DE	North Dakota	ND
District of Columbia	DC	Ohio	OH
Florida	FL	Oklahoma	OK
Georgia	GA	Oregon	OR
Hawaii	HI	Pennsylvania	PA
Idaho	ID	Puerto Rico	PR
Illinois	IL	Rhode Island	RI
Indiana	IN	South Carolina	SC
Iowa	IA	South Dakota	SD
Kansas	KS	Tennessee	TN
Kentucky	KY	Texas	TX
Louisiana	LA	Utah	UT
Maine	ME	Vermont	VT
Maryland	MD	Virginia	VA
Massachusetts	MA	Washington	WA
Michigan	MI	West Virginia	WV
Minnesota	MN	Wisconsin	WI
Mississippi	MS	Wyoming	WY
Missouri	MO		

ADDITIONAL SOURCES OF INFORMATION

Anderson, Ruth I., Dorothy E. Lee, Allien R. Russon, and Jacquelyn Wentzell Crane, *The Administrative Secretary*, 2nd ed. (New York: McGraw-Hill Book Co., 1976).

Casady, Mona, *Word Processing Concepts* (Cincinnati: South-Western Publishing Co., 1980).

Cecil, Paula, *Management of Word Processing Operations* (Menlo Park, CA: Benjamin/Cummings Publishing Co., 1980).

Church, Olive D., and Anne E. Schatz, *Office Systems and Careers: A Resource for Administrative Assistants* (Boston: Allyn and Bacon, 1981).

Clark, James L. and Lyn Clark, *How: A Handbook for Office Workers* (Belmont, CA: Wadsworth Publishing Company, 1975).

Curchack, Norma and Patricia A. Parzych, *Secretarial Training for the Changing Office* (New York: Harcourt Brace Jovanovich, 1977).

Dallas, Richard J. and James M. Thompson, *Clerical and Secretarial Systems for the Office* (Englewood Cliffs, NJ: Prentice-Hall, 1975).

Fulton, Patsy J., Theodore Woodward, and Howard L. Newhouse, *General Office Procedures* 7th ed. (Cincinnati: South-Western Publishing Co., 1977).

Hanna, J Marshall, Estelle L. Popham, and Rita Sloan Tilton, *Secretarial Procedures and Administration* 7th ed. (Cincinnati: South-Western Publishing Co., 1978).

Jennings, Lucy Mae, *Secretarial and Administrative Procedures* (Englewood Cliffs, NJ: Prentice-Hall, 1978).

Kleinschrod, Walter, Leonard Kruk, and Hilda Turner, *Word Processing: Operations, Applications, and Administration* (Indianapolis: Bobbs-Merrill Co., 1980).

Littlefield, C. L., Frank M. Rachel, Donald L. Caruth, and Robert E. Holmes, *Management of Office Operations* (Englewood Cliffs, NJ: Prentice-Hall, 1978).

Moon, Harry R., *Office Procedures,* 2nd ed. (Bronx: Milady Publishing Corp., 1977).

Place, Irene, Edward E. Byers, and Elaine F. Uthe, *Executive Secretarial Procedures,* 5th ed. (New York: McGraw-Hill Book Co. 1980).

Quible, Zane K., *Introduction to Administrative Office Management,* 2nd ed. (Cambridge: Winthrop Publishers, 1980).

Rosen, Arnold and Rosemary Fielden, *Word Processing* (Englewood Cliffs, NJ: Prentice-Hall, 1977).

Terry, George R. and John J. Stallard, *Office Management and Control,* 8th ed. (Homewood, IL: Richard D. Irwin, 1980).

Westgate, Douglas G., *Office Procedures 2000* (Toronto: Gage Publishing Ltd., 1977).

ADDRESSING ENVELOPES

```
State Offices
112 Fairmont Drive
Kingsport, TN 37664  ②
                                              ④  REGISTERED MAIL

HOLD FOR ARRIVAL  ③

              ①  MS JAN LAURITSEN
                 CENTRAL BANK
                 4435 SLOAN AVENUE
                 DAYTON OH 45220
```

No. 6¾ *Envelope measures 6½ × 3⅝-IN.*
No. 10 *Envelope measures 9½ × 4⅛-IN.*

1. The name and address should be typed in all caps, single spaced and with no punctuation.

   On a small envelope, start on line 12, 2 inches from the left edge.
   On a large envelope, start on line 14, 4 inches from the left edge.

   The name and title should be on the first line.
   The street or box number should be on the second line.
   The city, state, and ZIP code should be on the bottom line.

2. A typed return address begins on the third line, three to four spaces from the left margin.
3. Special notations to the addressee are typed in all caps about three lines below the return address.
4. Special mailing notations are typed below the stamp (about line nine) to end five to six spaces from the right edge of the envelope; these notations are typed in all caps.

CAPITALIZATION RULES

THE FOLLOWING SHOULD BE CAPITALIZED:

1. The first word of a sentence.

   Consult the dictionary for the correct spelling of words.
   This project should be completed by May 23.

2. The first word of the salutation and of the complimentary close of a letter.

Dear Ms. Moore   Sincerely yours
My dear Paige   Very cordially

3. All words except articles, prepositions, and conjunctions in the titles of books, articles, poems, and plays.

Reference Manual for Executive Assistants
How to Successfully Start a Business

4. Proper nouns and adjectives.

Albert Einstein   England, English
Japan, Japanese   Ronald Reagan

Do not capitalize words derived from proper nouns and adjectives and having distinct special meanings.

french fries   china plates

5. The standard names of geographic divisions, districts, regions, and localities.

Continental Divide   the South
New World   the Midwest

Do not capitalize words designating points of the compass unless they refer to specific regions.

We live on the north side of the street on the east side of town.

6. The popular names of districts, regions, and localities.

the Bible Belt   the Flats
the Windy City   the City of Brotherly Love

7. The names of rivers, lakes, mountains, and oceans.

Tennessee River   Smoky Mountains
Pacific Ocean   Boone Lake

8. Names for the Deity, for a supreme being, and for the Bible and other sacred books.

God   the Virgin Mary
Jehovah   the Koran

9. The names of religious denominations.

Southern Baptists   Judaism
Presbyterians   Catholics

10. The names of historical periods, events, and documents.

   the Reformation   the Declaration of Independence

11. The names of political entities, divisions, parties, and legislative and judicial bodies.

   Congress   the Democratic party
   Parliament   the Supreme Court

12. The names of departments and bureaus of the federal government.

   Department of Commerce   Tennessee Valley Authority

13. Titles when they precede a name.

   Mayor Bohinc   Professor Deal

14. The names of constellations, planets, and stars.

   Venus   Polaris

15. The names of holidays, holy days, months of the year, and days of the month.

   Christmas   Passover
   January   Friday

16. Trademarks

   Kleenex   Xerox

17. The names of buildings, streets, parks, and organizations.

   Red Cross   Severance Hall
   Cairn Lane   University Center

COMPOUND WORDS

1. When two or more words act as a single adjective and are placed *before* a noun, they are hyphenated.

   The telephone book provides an up-to-date directory for us.
   Please send a follow-up letter in two weeks.

2. In some cases a compound adjective is so well known that the hyphen is not needed to indicate a single thought unit.

   word processing equipment   income tax form

3. When two proper nouns are used as a single adjective before another noun, the proper nouns are hyphenated.

Ohio-Pennsylvania turnpike

4. When the elements of a single proper noun are used as an adjective, they are not hyphenated.

Cleveland State University orchestra

5. Adverbs ending in -ly that are combined with adjectives are not hyphenated.

lightly salted potatoes

6. When the first word of a compound is a comparative or a superlative ending in *er* or *est,* the compound is not hyphenated.

lowest ranking officer

7. When a series of hyphenated adjectives have a common ending, use suspending hyphens.

long- and short-term plans

8. Words beginning with *ex* and *self* are usually hyphenated.

self-defense   self-control

9. When a prefix is added to a proper noun, place a hyphen between the prefix and the proper noun.

pre-summer sale   post-World War I

10. Compound numbers from 21 to 99 are hyphenated when they appear in written form.

sixty-four people   twenty-two cars

EASILY CONFUSED WORDS

A While/Awhile

A while—noun meaning a short time. (We plan to pave the driveway in a while.)

Awhile—adverb meaning a short time. (Doug wrote that play awhile ago.)

Accept/Except

Accept—to take or receive. (Please accept this gift from me.)

Except—to leave out or exclude. (I received letters from everyone except Brannon.)

Addition/Edition

Addition—process of uniting or joining. (They plan to put up a new addition to their house.)

Edition—particular version of printed material. (Will there be a third edition of your book?)

Advice/Advise

Advice—suggestion or recommendation (noun). (Children sometimes find it difficult to follow the advice of their parents.)

Advise—counsel or recommend (verb). (I would advise you to get your registration materials in early.)

Affect/Effect

Affect—to influence or change (verb). (The snow will affect the skiing conditions at the resort.)

Effect—a result or consequence (noun). (The new absentee policy had no effect on the employees.)

Effect—to bring about or accomplish (verb). (The police plan to effect a change in the curfew.)

All ready/Already

All ready—all are prepared. (The contestants were all ready to receive the prizes.)

Already—by or before this time. (It is already past two o'clock.)

All Together/Altogether

All together—everyone in a group. (We must work all together to accomplish this goal.)

Altogether—wholly; entirely. (The weather is altogether too bad to attend the game.)

All Ways/Always

All ways—by all methods. (Have you tried all ways to be on time?)
Always—at all times. (I am always on time.)

Any One/Anyone

Any one—any one person or thing in a group. (Any one of the problems can be solved for extra credit.)

Anyone—any person. (Anyone who rides the bus to school is eligible.)

Biannual/Biennial

Biannual—occurring twice a year. (The biannual meeting of the club will be in March.)

Biennial—occurring once every two years. (The biennial report should be published in December.)

Capital/Capitol

Capital—a city in which the official seat of government is located. (The capital of Tennessee is Nashville.)

Capitol—building used by the U.S. Congress or in which a state legislature convenes. (Would you like a tour of the U.S. Capitol?)

Cite/Sight/Site

Cite—to quote or mention (verb). (Can you cite the source for that statement?)

Sight—to see or take aim; a view (noun). (The sight of the old farmhouse stirred many memories.)

Site—a location (noun). (This is the ideal site for our new home.)

Complement/Compliment

Complement—that which completes or makes perfect (noun). (Bacon always is a good complement with eggs.)

Compliment—to praise or flatter (verb). (Did you compliment the hostess on the delicious meal?)

Council/Counsel

Council—a governing body (noun). (The council will meet every third Wednesday.)

Counsel—to give advice (verb). (Listen to the faculty who are there to counsel you.)

Envelop/Envelope

Envelop—to wrap, surround, or conceal (verb). (Please envelop the dish before you put it in the refrigerator.)

Envelope—a container for a letter (noun). (Don't forget to put the postage on the envelope before you mail the letter.)

Farther/Further

Farther—a greater distance. (I just cannot walk any farther.)

Further—additional; to help forward. (Can I give you any further help?)

Formally/Formerly

Formally—in a formal manner. (Please dress formally for the dinner.)

Formerly—in the past. (He was formerly with the HB Company.)

Its/It's

Its—possessive form of it. (The family had its reunion last year.)

It's—contraction of it is. (It's my opinion that the problem should be solved again.)

Loose/Lose

Loose—not fastened (adj.). (The dog was running loose in the neighborhood.)

Lose—to fail to keep (verb). (Please don't lose this check.)

Miner/Minor

Miner—a person who works in a mine. (He worked as a miner for many years.)

Minor—a lesser thing; a person under legal age. (This problem is of minor significance.)

Passed/Past

Passed—past tense or past participle of pass. (The hostess passed around refreshments at the party.)

Past—gone by or ended. (Raking leaves is now in the past.)

Principal/Principle

Principal—highest in importance; a capital sum; a school official. (She is the new principal at the elementary school.)

Principle—an accepted rule of action; a general truth. (You need to apply the principles you learned to solve this problem.)

Stationary/Stationery

Stationary—not moving. (Please keep the ladder stationary while I paint the wall.)

Stationery—writing material. (Please order two new boxes of stationery for me.)

FOOTNOTES AND BIBLIOGRAPHIES

FOOTNOTES

1. Indent and single space footnotes; double space between them.
2. Position footnotes at the bottom of the page or all together on one page at the end of the report.
3. Separate footnotes from the body of the report with a 1½-inch long line.
4. Indicate footnotes in the body of the paper with superior numbers to the right of the portion needing documenting.

Here is the information needed to footnote books and periodicals.

Books

[1]Author (first name, last name), *Book Title* (City of Publication: Publishing Company, Date of Publication), page numbers.

Periodicals

[1]Author, "Title of Article," *Name of Journal,* date, page numbers.

If a footnote has been given previously in the paper, you can use a shortened version of the footnote for subsequent uses. A shortened footnote contains author's last name and the page number (Smith, p. 7).

BIBLIOGRAPHIES

1. List the entries alphabetically.
2. Single space each entry; but double space between them.
3. The first line of each entry is at the left margin and subsequent lines are indented.
4. The surname of the author appears first.
5. Type the title, "Bibliography" 1½ to 2 inches from the top of the paper.
6. Items in a bibliography may be separated into groups, such as books, government publications, and interviews.

BIBLIOGRAPHY

_____

_____
_____
_____

_____
_____
_____

_____
_____
_____

FORMS OF ADDRESS

Title	Address
President of the United States	Mr./Madam President
Wife of the president	Mrs. (full name)
Vice-president	Ms./Madam Vice President
Chief Justice of the Supreme Court	Mr./Ms. Chief Justice
U.S. Senator	Senator (surname)
U.S. Representative	Mr./Ms. (surname)
Cabinet member	Mr./Ms. Secretary
American ambassador	Mr./Ms. Ambassador
Governor of state	Governor
Mayor	Mr./Ms. (surname)

Protestant clergy	Right Reverend Sir
	Bishop (surname)
	Very Reverend Sir
	Reverend (surname)
Catholic clergy	Your Eminence
	Cardinal (surname)
	Your Excellency
	Archbishop (surname)
	Right Reverend Monsignor
	Monsignor (surname)
	Father (surname)
	Mother (name)
	Sister (name)
	Brother (name)
Jewish clergy	Rabbi (surname)
President of a college or university	Dr. (surname)
Dean of a school	Dean (surname)
Professor	Professor (surname)
Physician	Dr. (surname)
Lawyer	Mr./Ms. (surname)
Two or more men	Mr. (surname) and Mr. (surname)
	Messrs.
	Gentlemen
Two or more women	Ms./Mrs./Miss (surname) and Ms./Mrs./Ms. (surname)
	Mesdames
Married couple	Mr. and Mrs. (name)
Service personnel	(Grade) surname

MANUFACTURERS OF TEXT-EDITING AND WORD PROCESSING SYSTEMS

AM JACQUARD
3340 Ocean Park Blvd.
Santa Monica, CA 90405

ADLER-ROYAL TEXT EDITING
DIVISION
1285 Central Avenue
Hillside, NJ 07205

ADVANCED COMPUTER
TECHNIQUES
437 Madison Avenue
New York, NY 10022

APPLE COMPUTER, INC.
10260 Bandley Drive
Cupertino, CA 95014

APPLIED COMPUTER SYSTEMS
615 N. Mary Avenue
Sunnyvale, CA 94303

ARTELONICS
2952 Bunker Hill Lane
Santa Clara, CA 94560

BASIC FOUR
14101 Myford Road
Tustin, CA 92680

BURROUGHS CORPORATION
Office Systems Group
30 Main Street
Danbury, CT 06810

CADO SYSTEMS CORP.
2771 Toledo Street
Torrence, CA 90503

COMPTEK RESEARCH, INC.
One Technology Center
45 Oak Street
Buffalo, NY 14203

COMMODORE BUSINESS
MACHINES
300 Valley Forge Square
King of Prussia, PA 19406

COMPUCORP
1901 South Bundy Drive
Los Angeles, CA 90025

CPT CORP.
8100 Mitchell Road
Minneapolis, MN 55440

DATAMARC
1251 Columbia
Richardson, TX 75081

DATAPOINT CORP.
9725 Datapoint Drive
San Antonio, TX 78284

A.B. DICK CO.
5700 W. Toughy Avenue
Chicago, IL 60648

DICTAPHONE CORP.
120 Old Post Road
Rye, NY 10580

DIGITAL EQUIPMENT CORP.
Word Processing Division
Continental Blvd.
MK 1-1/J14
Merrimack, NH 03054

EXXON OFFICE SYSTEMS CO.
777 Long Ridge Road
Stamford, CT 06923

FOUR-PHASE CORP.
10700 N. Deanza Blvd.
Cupertino, CA 95014

HAZELTINE CORPORATION
Word Processing Division
Commack Road
Commack, NY 11725

HONEYWELL INFORMATION
SYSTEMS
200 Smith Street
Waltham, MA 02154

IBM
Office Products Division
Parsons Pond Drive
Franklin Lakes, NJ 07417

LANIER BUSINESS PRODUCTS
1700 Chantilly Drive, N.E.
Atlanta, GA 30324

LEXITRON CORP.
1840 Dehavilland Drive
Thousand Oaks, CA 91359

LEXOR CORPORATION
7100 Hayvenhurst Ave.
Van Nuys, CA 91406

MICOM/PHILLIPS
4040 McEwin
Dallas, TX 75234

MOHAWK DATA SCIENCES
1599 Littleton Road
Parsippany, NJ 07054

NBI INC.
1695 38th Street
Boulder, CO 80301

NIXDORF COMPUTER INC.
168 Middlesex Turnpike
Burlington, MA 01803

NORELCO-PHILIPS BUSINESS
SYSTEMS
175 Froelich Farm Blvd.
Woodbury, NY 11797

OLIVETTI CORPORATION OF
AMERICA
155 White Plains Road
Tarrytown, NY 10591

OLYMPIA USA, INC.
Box 22, Route 22
Somerville, NJ 08876

PHILIPS INFORMATION SYSTEMS
4040 McEwen
Dallas, TX 75234

PRIME COMPUTER, INC.
Prime Park
Natick, MA 01760

PROPRIETARY COMPUTER
SYSTEMS
16625 Saticoy Street
Van Nuys, CA 91406

Q1
125 Ricefield Lane
Hauppauge, NY 11787

RADIO SHACK CORP.
A Division of Tandy Corporation
1300 One Tandy Center
Fort Worth, TX 76102

ROYAL BUSINESS MACHINES,
INC.
150 New Park Avenue
Hartford, CT 06106

SAVIN BUSINESS MACHINES,
INC.
Columbus Avenue
Valhalla, NY 10595

SHASTA GENERAL SYSTEMS
1329 Moffett Park Drive
Sunnyvale, CA 94086

SONY CORP. OF AMERICA
9 West 57 Street
New York, NY 10019

SYNTREX, INC.
246 Industrial Way West
Eatontown, NJ 07724

WANG LABORATORIES, INC.
One Industrial Avenue
Lowell, MA 01851

WORDPLEX CORPORATION
141 Triunfor Canyon Road
Westlake Village, CA 91361

XEROX CORPORATION
Office Products Division
1341 West Mockingbird Lane
Dallas, TX 75247

XMARK CORPORATION
3176 Pullman Street
Costa Mesa, CA 92626

ZENITH DATA SYSTEMS
1000 Milwaukee Avenue
Glenview, IL 60025

METRIC EQUIVALENTS

Unit	Approximate Equivalent	
millimeter (mm)	0.04 inch	
centimeter (cm)	0.39 inch	
decimeter (dm)	3.94 inches	
meter (m)	39.37 inches	
dekameter (dkm)	32.81 feet	
hectometer (hm)	109.36 yards	
kilometer (km)	0.62 miles	
square centimeter (cm^2)	0.155 square inch	
hectare (h)	2.47 acres	
square kilometer (km^2)	0.386 square mile	
cubic centimeter (cm^3)	0.061 cu inch	
dekastere (dka)	13.100 cu yards	
milliliter (ml)	0.0018 pint	0.27 fluidram
centiliter (cl)	0.018 pint	0.338 fluidounce
deciliter (dl)	0.18 pint dry	0.21 pint liquid
liter (l)	0.908 quart dry	1.057 quarts liquid
dekaliter (dkl)	1.14 pecks	2.64 gallons
hectoliter (hl)	2.84 bushels	26.4 gallons
kiloliter (kl)	28.4 bushels	264. gallons
milligram (mg)	0.015 grain	
centigram (cg)	0.154 grain	
decigram (dg)	1.543 grains	
gram (g)	0.035 ounce	
dekagram (dgk)	0.353 ounce	
hectogram (hg)	3.527 ounces	
kilogram (kg)	2.2046 pounds	

NUMBER RULES

Rule 1. Numbers from one to ten generally should be spelled out.

Spring arrives in three days.

Rule 2. Use numerals for numbers above ten.

The keyboarding class has 15 males enrolled.

EXCEPTIONS TO THE RULES

1. In the same reference, related numbers should be used in the same form.

At the garage sale we sold 5 tables, 12 chairs, and 15 benches.

2. Numbers above thousands can be expressed in a combination of figures and words for clarity.

   Sales are expected to reach $3 million this year.

3. A number that comes at the beginning of a sentence should be spelled out. It is better not to begin a sentence with a number, however.

   Sixteen people in the village pick up their mail at the local post office.

4. A number used directly with a word is placed in figures.

   Turn to page 6 of your textbook and read paragraph 2.

5. Percentages are expressed in figures, and the word "percent" is spelled out.

   The bank offers 15 percent interest on their savings accounts.

6. Amounts of money are expressed in figures. Omit the decimal and zeros in even amounts of money.

   The order amounted to $125.

7. Dates are expressed in figures. Use cardinal figures when dates are written after the month; use ordinal figures for expressing figures before the month.

   Please submit all reports by March 4.
   The 4th of May is a little late to begin a new project.

8. Time is expressed in figures (often with a.m. or p.m.). Figures or words can be used to express time when o'clock is used.

   Class begins at 10 a.m.
   The Open House begins at 2 o'clock.
   The Open House begins at two o'clock.

9. House numbers, except for the house number "one," should be expressed in figures.

   1370 Sloan Avenue
   One Cairn Lane

PROOFREADER'S MARKS

Add space	#
	themanuscript pages
	^
New paragraph	¶All copy should be . . . .

Transpose letters	*At* time of the meeting
Use italics	<u>Now</u> is the time
Close up word	to pro⌢duce
Lower case	the ∕spring of the year
Use capital letters	<u>d</u>r. Smith
Reverse	after the manuscript (been∕has)
delete	cla⸍rify
Add	markings on ∧*the* manuscript
Move down	⎵certain material
Move up	⎴clean the typefaces
Move to left	⊏ now is a good time
Move to right	⊐ now is a good time
No new paragraph	*no-¶* All copy should be
Use single spacing	**ss** ⊏
Use double spacing	**ds** ⊏
Move as shown	(Where the material . . .).

PUNCTUATION RULES

USE AN APOSTROPHE

1. To form the possessive of nouns.
   a. add 's to singular nouns. (Betty's)
   b. add 's to singular nouns ending in s unless the addition of an s makes the word difficult to pronounce. (boss's)
   c. add ' to plural nouns ending with s. (girls')
   d. add 's to plural nouns that do not end in s. (children's)
2. When letters are omitted to form contractions.

   aren't for are not
   shouldn't for should not

3. To indicate the omission of figures in dates.

   the '80s

4. To form the plural of most letters, numbers, and words used as words.

A's   6's

5. To indicate a quotation within a quotation.

USE AN ASTERISK

1. To indicate a footnote (when only one appears in the entire document) and its related reference or explanation.
2. To indicate an omission of an entire paragraph.

USE BRACKETS

1. To make a correction or to insert a comment within quoted material. The brackets separate the information from the rest of the quoted material.
2. To indicate a parenthetical expression within parentheses.

PLACE A COMMA

1. Between words, phrases, or short clauses in a series.
2. Around parenthetical words or expressions. Parenthetical words are considered unnecessary for the completeness of a sentence. Some parenthetical expressions are the following: however, of course, in addition, also, too, for example, furthermore, as a matter of fact, consequently, hence, therefore, and nevertheless.
3. Around nouns of direct address.
4. Around appositives (words that rename or explain previously mentioned nouns).
5. To separate two independent clauses that are joined by a conjunction. Place the comma before the conjunction.
6. To separate two or more independent adjectives that modify a noun.
7. After an introductory dependent clause.
8. After an introductory infinitive phrase, introductory participial phrase, or a long (five or more words) prepositional phrase.
9. Around nonrestrictive clauses or phrases. Nonrestrictive means the clauses or phrases are not essential for the sentence.
10. Around a short quotation.

USE A COLON

1. Before a formal listing or enumeration of items.
2. To introduce long one-sentence quotations and quotations of two or more sentences.
3. After salutations in a business letter when mixed punctuation format is used.

USE A DASH

1. In place of commas to set off a parenthetical expression more clearly.
2. In place of a semicolon for emphasis before the second independent clause.

3. In place of a comma for emphasis in a compound sentence before the conjunction.
4. In place of parentheses for emphasis or clarity.
5. Before or after a single word used for emphasis.
6. To repeat, emphasize, or summarize a statement.

USE A DIAGONAL

1. When fractions are typed (1/2; 2/3).
2. To type or write the expression *and/or*.
3. When certain business terms are indicated (n/30).
4. With certain abbreviations (c/o).

USE AN EXCLAMATION POINT

1. To indicate a strong emotion such as anger or fear.
2. To punctuate a one-word expression or a short exclamatory statement.

USE ELLIPSIS POINTS

1. To indicate the omission of one or more words in quoted material.

USE A HYPHEN

1. To divide a word at the end of a line.
2. Between a compound adjective that functions as a single unit to modify a noun.
3. To write out numbers consisting of two or more words read as a single unit.

USE PARENTHESES

1. To set off parenthetical expressions when commas would be confusing.
2. To set off special references, instructions, or other explanatory statements.
3. To include expressions that help clarify the meaning of a sentence.
4. To enumerate items in a sentence.

USE A PERIOD

1. After a declarative and imperative sentence.
2. After abbreviations such as titles, degrees, calendar months, and geographic names. (Only one space follows the period at the end of the abbreviation.)
3. After initials, except for radio and television broadcasting call letters.
4. After a sentence containing a request that is phrased in the form of a question.
5. As a decimal point in amounts or percentages.
6. In outlines and lists, after all complete sentences.

USE A QUESTION MARK

1. At the end of a sentence that asks a question.

2. To express doubt. The question mark is written in parentheses.
3. To raise several questions within one sentence.

USE QUOTATION MARKS
1. To enclose a direct quotation.
2. To emphasize a word or phrase.
3. To indicate titles of magazine articles, chapters of books, and speeches.

USE A SEMICOLON
1. Between two or more closely related independent clauses that are not connected with coordinating conjunctions.
2. Between two independent clauses separated by a transitional expression. Some transitional expressions are the following: accordingly; nevertheless, in fact, furthermore, however, and consequently.
3. To separate a series which contains commas or complete thoughts.

USE THE UNDERSCORE
1. To indicate the titles of books, magazines, and newspapers.
2. To identify distinctive names of ships, trains, and planes.
3. To place emphasis on a task or command.
4. To emphasize a word or expression being defined.

PUNCTUATION STYLES FOR LETTERS

STANDARD (MIXED) PUNCTUATION
1. Insert colon after salutation.
2. Insert comma after closing.

_____

_____
_____
_____

Dear Ms. Deal:

_____
_____
_____

_____
_____

Sincerely yours,

_____

—————————

————
————

OPEN PUNCTUATION

1. Omit colon after salutation.
2. Omit comma after complimentary closing.

—————————

—————————
—————————
—————————
—————————

Dear Ms. Deal

————————————————————————
————————————————————————
————————————————————————

————————————————————————
————————————————————————

Sincerely yours

—————————
—————————

SPELLING RULES

Remember that there are exceptions to most spelling rules. If you are in doubt about the correct spelling of a word, check the dictionary.

1. Write the *i* before *e* except after *c* and when the sound is pronounced like *a*.

receive	believe
beige	lien
eight	weigh

2. When a prefix or suffix is added to a word or when words are combined that create a double letter, retain both letters.

bookkeeper   misspelled

3. Change the final *y* to *i* when preceded by a consonant before adding a suffix (except for one beginning with *i*).

beauty	beautiful	beautifying
carry	carrier	carrying

4. Retain the *y* before *-ly* and *-ness* suffixes for one-syllable words. (There are some exceptions)

dry	dryly
day	daily

5. Double the final consonant after a word that ends in a consonant preceded by a vowel, when the suffix begins with a vowel or y.

bag	baggage
swim	swimming

6. Double the final consonant after a word that ends in a consonant preceded by a vowel with the accent on the last syllable when the suffix begins with a vowel.

begin	beginning
confer	conferring

7. Do not double the final consonant:
   a. After a word that ends in a consonant preceded by a vowel, when the accent is not on the last syllable.

benefit	benefited	benefitting

   b. When a suffix beginning with a consonant is added to a word that ends in a consonant preceded by a single vowel.

shipment	section

   c. When a suffix is added to a word that ends in a consonant preceded by more than one vowel.

brief	briefly	briefing

   d. When a word ends in more than one consonant before the suffix.

   attachment

8. Drop the silent e when a word ends in silent e followed by a suffix that begins with a vowel.

type	typing
hope	hoping

9. Do not drop the silent e when a word ending in silent e is followed by a suffix beginning with a consonant.

time	timeless
hope	hopeful

10. Do not drop the silent e when a word could be mispronounced or

confused if the silent e were dropped.

| die | died | dying |
| hoe | hoeing | |

11. Do not drop the silent *e* when a word ends in *-ce* or *-ge* and is followed by a suffix beginning with a vowel.

| courage | courageous |
| notice | noticeable |

12. Do not change *y* to *i* before adding a prefix when a final *y* is preceded by a vowel.

| convey | conveyed | conveyance |

WORD DIVISION RULES

If possible, avoid dividing words at the end of a line. Do not divide:

1. Words of one syllable.
2. Words with five or fewer letters.
3. Words when only one or two letters of a word are separated from the rest of the word.
4. Proper nouns, dates, titles, numbers, abbreviations, or contractions.
5. More than two consecutive lines.
6. The last word on a page.

If you must divide a word, divide:

1. Between syllables (check the dictionary if you are in doubt about where the syllables are found).
2. Hyphenated words at the hyphen.
3. After a prefix or before a suffix.
4. Between two vowels that are pronounced separately.
5. After a one-syllable vowel that comes in the middle of a word.

SUBJECT INDEX

Access code, 248
Acoustical screens, 87, 450
Adhesive binding, 309
Administrative assistant:
  advancement, 84–85
  functions, 84–85
Air Traffic Conference (ATC), 398
Ambient lighting in office environment, 456
American Simplified Keyboard, 58
American Society of Travel Agents (ASTA), 398
AMS simplified letter form, 126, 132
Amtrak, 403
Annoyance Call Bureau, 269
Aperture cards, 369
Audio cassettes, 389–390
Automated approach, 9
Automated filing systems, categories, 327–328
Automated typing, and error correction:
  editing authors' changes, 106–107
  typographical errors, 106

BASIC, 189
Batch mode, 190
Bell System, 268
Better Business Bureau, 231
Bibliography, working, 385–386
Binding, 309–310
Booz, Allen & Hamilton, 9
Box files, 323
Burt, William Austin, 54
Business research:
  audio cassettes and, 390
  bibliography, 385–386
  company libraries, 387–388
  information bank, 389
  information gathering, 384–385
  public libraries, 386–387
  references, 390–391

Cablegrams, 254
Calculators, see Electronic calculators

Calendar, maintenance of, 38, 39, 40
Call forwarding, 245
Call pickup, 245
Call timing, 245
Carbon copies, 98–99
Career:
  advancement to manager, 478–479
  court stenographer, 483
  in data processing, 481
  in government, 482
  in law, 481
  in management, 477–479
    advantages of executive assistant, 478
    in broad spectrum of departments, 479
    as word processing manager, 479–480
  in marketing, 480
  in medicine, 481–482
  in phototypesetting, 480–481
  in sales, 480
Carousel files, 324–325
Carterphone Decision, 241
Cathode ray tube (CRT), 62
Central dictation units, types, 166
Centralized files, 318
Centralized high-speed copiers:
  advantages, 296
  company policy, 297–298
  cost, 292–296
  features, 298–299
  speeds, 296
Central processing unit (CPU), 186–187
Centrex series, 243
  see also Telephone systems
Certified mail, 228
Certified Professional Secretary, 28
Chairs, 90
Chamber of Commerce, 231
Charge-out forms, 356
Chauvinism, and job interviews, 470–471
Coated paper copiers, 294
COBOL, 189

C.O.D. (mail), 228–229
Cold type machines, 283
Collating with centralized high speed copier, 299
Collators, 204–205
   types, 308
College libraries, business research, 388
College placement office, job hunting, 462
Color copier, 300
Colored stationery, correction fluid for, 105
Communication, listening and, 25
Communications Satellite Corporation, 234
Company libraries, research, 387–388
Computerized filing, 328–329
Computer output microfilm (COM), 188, 371
Computers:
   data processing, 12
   input:
      keypunch machines, 186
      key-to-disk, 186
      key-to-tape, 186
      magnetic input device, 186
      MICR, 186
      OCR, 186
      peripherals, 183–184
      terminals, 184–186
   mode of operation, 190–191
   output:
      computer output microfilm, 188
      on CRT screen, 188
      disk drive, 188
   processing, 186–187
   programming languages:
      BASIC, 189
      COBOL, 189
      FORTRAN, 189
   software, 189
   terminals, 12, 13
   types:
      mainframes, 182
      microcomputers, 180
      midicomputers, 182
      minicomputers, 182
Conference or consulting call, 245
Console addressing machines, 204
Convenience copiers:
   speeds, 293–294
   types:
      coated paper, 294
      desk top, 293
      plain paper, 294

      roll and sheet-fed, 294–295
      table top, 293
Conventions:
   agenda, 422–423
   equipment requirements, 420–421
   inviting speakers, 419–420
   minutes, 423–426
   miscellaneous responsibilities, 422
   planning, 417–419
   registration desk staff, 421
Copier abuse, prevention , 303–304
Copiers, adding paper, 302
Corrections, implements for:
   correctable ribbons, 102—103
   correction fluid, 103–105
   correction paper, 103
   correction tape, 106
   erasers, 100
Correspondence assistant:
   advancement, 84
   function, 83
Court stenographer, career, 483
Cover letter, 468
Creativity, 22
CRT, 90, 185–186, 188
Cursor, 62
Customs, U.S., 229

Dagron, Rene, 371
Dancer, John B., 370
Data communication:
   data processing distribution, 256
   description, 255–256
Datapost®, 255
Data processing careers, 481
Desk:
   drawers, 36–37
   organization, 35
Desk drawer files, 352-354
Dictation:
   administrative, 169–170
   equipment:
      central systems, 165–166
      desk-top units, 161–165
      portable machines, 159–161
   indexing and:
      electronic cueing, 160–161
      paper strip, 160–161
   medium of, 160
   and productivity, 166–169

techniques, 171–174
Direct distance dialing (DDD), 245
Direct inward dialing (DID), 243
Direct outward dialing (DOD), 243
Direct voice path, 246–247
Disk drive, 188
Display text processing system, 63
   components, 63–64
Distributed data processing (DDP), 191–192
Duplicators, types:
   offset, 305–307
   spirit, 304–305
   stencil, 305

800 toll-free number, 255
Electromatic Typewriters, Inc., 55–56
Electronic approach, 9
Electronic calculator:
   balancing bank statements, 432
   controlling petty cash, 431
   invoice preparation, 432–434
   payroll record, 433
   proofreading arithmetic, 431
   sales commissions, 434
   totalling postage expenditure, 431
   types:
      display and printing, 437
      electronic display, 434–435, 437
      printing, 435–436
      programmable, 437
Electronic cueing, 160–161
Electronic mail, 13, 234–235
   facsimile machine, 13–14
   facsimile systems:
      analog unit, 250
      compatibility, 253
      function, 250–253
      hybrid terminals, 258
      polling procedure, 253
   future:
      intra-industrial compatibility, 257
      and U.S. Postal Service, 256
      intracompany mail, 14
      teletypewriters, 254
Electronic office:
   and efficiency, 90–91
   word processing, 90
Electronic Office Project, 90
Electronic typewriters, 58, 59
Employment agencies, job hunting, 463–465

Ethics, 24
Executive assistant:
   advancement, 8
   as CRT operator, 13
   description, 4
   flexibility, 25–27
      with technology, 25
   functions, 83
   human relations, 19–20
   as information expeditor, 5–6
   as public relations representative, 6–7
   standard office equipment, 8
   technical skills, 20–22
   traditional approach and disadvantages, 8
      as generalist, 8
   in word processing center, 19
   in work groups, 11

Facsimile unit, *see* Electronic mail
Federal Communications Commission, 241
Fiber optics copier, 300–301
FICA, and payroll records, 432
Files, portable, 354
Filing:
   charge-out forms, 356
   expediting, 355
   magnetic media:
      cassettes, 358–359
      floppy disks, 360–361
      mag cards, 357–358
   manual, 356
   materials, 343
   open plan office environments and, 361
   procedures:
      material selection, 341–342
      record retention, 339–340
Filing equipment, types:
   box files, 323
   carousel files, 324–325
   centralized, 318
   decentralized, 318
   horizontal files, 328
   lateral files, 320–322
   lateral mobile files, 327
   microform files, 331
   movable files, 326
   oval track files, 327
   rotary files, 324–325
   shelf files, 325
   tub files, 324

vertical files, 318
visible files, 323
word/data processing files, 330
Filing systems:
  automated, 357
  confidentiality, 357
  classification, 345
  definition, 318
Floppy disk, 67, 108, 360–361
"Flush left," 280
"Flush right," 280
FORTRAN, 189
Future Secretary Association, job hunting, 465

Glidden, Carlos, 54

Hang-on screens in open office, 451
High-speed ink jet printing, 204
Horizontal files, 322
Hot type machines, 283

Information bank, 388–389
Intelligent printer, 301
Intelligent typewriter, capabilities, 58–59
Interactive, 191
  see also Computers
Interface device, use with phototypesetter and word
  processor, 289
Internal memory, typesetters and, 284
International Air Transport Association, 398
International Business Machines (IBM), 55, 80
International Data Corporation, 180
International Information/Word Processing Associa-
  tion, 93
  and job hunting, 465
Invoice preparation with electronic calculators,
  432–434

Job hunting:
  college placement office, 462
  cover letters, 468
  employment agencies, 463–464
  through friends and contacts, 465
  newspapers, 464–465
  professional affiliations, 465–466
  self-review, 461–462
Job interview:
  chauvinism, 470–471
  discriminatory questions, 470
  ending, 471

nature of, 468–469
  preparation, 469
Jogger/stacker, 205

Key operators, duties, 301–303
Keypunch machines, 186
Key systems, 242–243
  see also Telephone systems
Key-to-disk, 186
Key-to-tape, 186

Landscape screens in open office, 448
Lateral files, 320–322
Lateral mobile files, 327
LED, 149
Letterhead, 120
Letter telegram, 254
Letter writing:
  letter parts:
    attention line, 124–125
    body, 127
    complimentary close, 127
    copy notation, 130
    dateline, 123–124
    enclosure notation, 129
    reference line, 126
    salutation, 125–126
    second page heading, 130–131
    signature line, 127–129
    subject line, 126
  placement on paper, 122–123
  styles:
    block, 131
    modified block, 131
    simplified, 132–133
  supplies, 119–122
Library, and business research, 386–387
Linotype, 283
Longhand, 144–145
Loyalty, 23

Machine dictation, techniques:
  adjusting machine, 150
  LED, 149
  preparation, 148
  proofreading, 150–151
Mag cards, 357–358
Magnetic card machine, 61
  communications capabilities, 61–62
  display screens, 62

Magnetic ink character recognition (MICR), 186
Magnetic input devices, 186
Magnetic media filing techniques, 357–361
Magnetic Tape Selectric Typewriter (MT/ST), 60
Mail:
　addressing, 216
　area mail processing, 231
　certified, 228
　classes, 225–226
　dating and time stamping, 211
　electronic, 234–235
　envelope selection, 214
　express, 226
　first class, 225
　forwarding, 233
　fourth class, 225
　future, 233–234
　handling during employer's absence, 212
　incoming:
　　distribution, 202
　　opening, 200–201
　　sorting, 200
　insurance, 228–229
　inter-office routing, 212
　logging, 212
　mailing schedule, 215
　outgoing:
　　addressing, 204
　　collating, 204–205
　　folding and inserting, 205
　　sorting, 205–206
　　weighing and stamping, 205
　parcel and package preparation, 218
　presorting by ZIP code, 215
　priority, 225
　problems, 231–232
　registered, 229
　second class, 225
　self-service postal centers, 230
　special delivery, 226
　sorting, 211
　third class, 225
　Vertical Improved Mail (VIM), 232–233
Mailgram®, 226–228, 254
Mailmobile, Bell and Howell's, 202
Mail opening equipment, 210
Mainframes, 182
Maturity, 27
Meetings:
　dining and, 417

　informal:
　　location selection, 415–416
　　preparation, 414–415
Memorandums:
　carbons, 135–136
　closings, 154
　placement and margins, 135
　plain paper, 135
　second page, 134–135
　spacing, 134
　typist's initials, 134
Message communication, 250
MICR, 186
Microcomputers, 180
Microfiche, 369–370
Microforms, 331
　advantages, 368
　and mailing costs, 368
　process:
　　computer output microfilm, 371–372
　　duplication, 372
　　microphotography, 370
　　records conversion, 371
　　rotary cameras, 372
　types, 369–370
Microform readers, 372–376
　reader/printer, 375
Micrographic technology, library and, 388
Midicomputers, 182
Minicomputers, 182
Modular work stations, 87
　attributes, 89–90
Motivation, 23
Movable carriage, 54
Movable files, 326
MT/ST, 80
Multiprocessing, 190

Name filing, 347–349
National Secretary Association, see Professional Secretaries International
Networking mode, 191
Noise level, 87
Numeric filing, 349–350

Office environment:
　conventional office, 448
　distractions, 452
　landscape screens, 448
　lighting, 454–456

ambient, 456
open office:
  acoustic screens, 450
  attractiveness, 451
  efficiency, 449
  hang-on screens, 451
  privacy, 449
  work stations, 452
Office equipment:
  furniture for automated equipment, 464
  posture chairs, 453
Office worker, productivity, 9
Official Guide to the Railways, 403
Offset duplicators, 305
On-line operating mode, 190
On-line terminals, 184
Optical character recognition (OCR), 28, 72, 186, 285–286
Organization, 23
Oval track files, 327

Padding, 309
Paper jams in copiers, 303
Parcel Airlift Mail (PAL), 229
Passport, U.S., 230
Person-to-person, 26–27
Photocomposers, difference from phototypesetters, 288
Phototypesetters:
  components:
    light source, 284
    master character image, 284
    photosensitive material, 284
  hyphenation, 288
  input, 285–286
  line justification, 287–288
  storage, 284
Phototypesetting:
  advantages:
    justified margins, 280
    proportional spacing, 280
  word processing, 288–289
Pica, 281
Plain paper copiers, 294
Plastic comb binding, 309
Portable files, 354
Postage meters, 230–231
Postal Service Consumer Advocate, 232
Post Office Box, 230
Posture chairs, 453

Printer, 75
Printing calculators, 435–436
Print shop, advantages of in-house, 307
Printwheel, 75
Procedures manuals, 86
Professionalism, 27, 28, 29
  certification, 28
Professional Secretaries International (National Secretary Association), 4, 28
  job hunting, 465
Programmable calculators, 427
Proofreaders, 83

Records management, 14
  filing systems, 14
  future, 361, 363
Reduction, centralized high speed copier, 299
Registered mail, 229
Remington, E. & Sons, 54
Remington Model 1, 54
Remote job entry (RJE), 90
Reprographics equipment, 304
Research, see Business research
Resume:
  appearance, 468
  guidelines to writing, 467–468
  objectives, 466
Roll- and sheet-fed copiers, 294–295
Roll film, microfilm and, 369
Rotary files, 324–325

Self-correcting machines, 57
Self-starter, 23
Secretary, definition, 4
Shared logic systems, 64–66
Shared resource system, 66
Shelf files, 325
Sholes, Christopher, 54
Shorthand:
  dictation supplies, 145–146
  dictation techninques, 146
Single-element machines, 57
  type styles, 57
Soule, Samuel, 54
Southern Pacific Communication, Datapost® and, 255
Space Available Mail (SAM), 229
Speaker phone, 245
Spiral binding, 309
Spirit duplicators, 304–305
Standalone system, 63–64

Stapling, centralized high speed copier, 299
Station-to-station, 267–268
Stencil duplicators, 305
Storage, phototypesetters and, 284
Stored mailgram, 254
Strike-on typesetter, 282–284
Subject filing, 346, 350–352
Supply cabinet, arrangement, 37–38

Tabletop addressing machines, 204
Telegram, 254
Telephone:
    accessories, 247–249
    economical use, 269–270
    emergency calls, 269
    future, and microprocessors, 249–250
    long distance calls, 267, 268
    techniques, 263–265, 267
Telephone directory, 390
Telephone systems:
    Centrex series, 243
        direct inward dialing (DID), 243
    features, 245–247
    key systems, 242–243
    private, 241
    private automatic branch exchange (PABX), 243
    private branch exchange (PBX), 243
        direct outward dialing, (DOD), 243
Teleprocessing mode, 191
Telex, types, 254
Temporary agency, 42
Text-editing typewriters:
    compatibility, 72
        see also Word processing
    display screen features, 69, 70
    editing and operating features, 70–72
    functions:
        editing, 67
        input, 66
        output, 66
        revision, 66–67
        storage, 67–68
    magnetic tape, 60
    maintenance, 74–75
    punched paper tape, 59–60
    supplies, 72–73
    training, 75
Text-editing units, 58
Thurber, Charles, 54
Tickler file, 36, 39, 352–353

Time management, 41
Time schedule, preparation, 42
Time sharing mode, 191
Toner in copy machines, 302–303
Touch regulator dial, 100
Transcription, 147–151
Travel, work in employer's absence and, 408–409
Travel arrangements:
    air travel, 401, 403
    auto rental, 404
    behavioral guidelines, 407–408
    economic and commercial attache, 407
    expenses, 400–401
    hotel directories, 405
    hotels, 404–405
    in-house travel department, 397–398
    itinerary preparation, 405–406
    jet lag, 405
    Official Airlines Guide, 399
    overseas culture, 406–407
    packing business material, 406
    passports, 408
    train travel, 403
    travel agents, 398–399
Travel insurance, 401
Tub files, 324
Twain, Mark, 55
Typebar machine, 56
Typebars, 54
Type font, 281–282
Typesetters:
    categories, 282
    internal memory, 284
    leading, 284
    points, 281
    script, 280
    standard, 280
    style manual, 281
    type size and picas, 281
    type styles and fonts, 281–282
Typewriter, history, 54–55
Typewriter alignment scale, 101
Typing:
    professional techniques, 97–98
    specialized techniques, 109
Typing balls, typesetter and, 284
Typographer, 54

Ultrafiche, 370
United Parcel Service (UPS), 205

U.S. Customs, 229
U.S. embassy, foreign travel and, 407
U.S. Postal Service (USPS), 205

Vertical Improved Mail (VIM), 232–233
Video display terminals, 62
Visible files, 323

WATS lines, 246
Western Union, 226–228
  Mailgram®, 254
  stored mailgram, 254
  telex directory, 254
Weyerhaeuser Company, 214
"White noise," 88
Women's Liberation Movement, and executive assis-
    tant, 4, 125
Word/data processing files, 330–331
Word processing:
  components:

    equipment, see Chapter 4
    people, 81
    procedures, 85–87
    work environment, 87–90
  definition, 80
  goal, 11
  intercommunication, 255
  phototypesetters and, 288
Work area, disorganization, 34
Work groups, 11
World Almanac, 391
World Health Organization (WHO), vaccinations, 408
Writing:
  principles, 117–119
  reports, 136

YWCA typing courses, pioneering of, 55

ZIP code, 204–205, 215